IDENTITY AND BELONGING

IDENTITY AND BELONGING
RETHINKING RACE AND ETHNICITY IN CANADIAN SOCIETY

EDITED BY
SEAN P. HIER AND
B. SINGH BOLARIA

Canadian Scholars' Press Inc.
Toronto

Identity and Belonging: Rethinking Race and Ethnicity in Canadian Society
Edited by Sean P. Hier and B. Singh Bolaria

First published in 2006 by
Canadian Scholars' Press Inc.
180 Bloor Street West, Suite 801
Toronto, Ontario
M5S 2V6

www.cspi.org

Canadian Scholars' Press gratefully acknowledges financial support for our publishing activities from the Government of Canada through the Book Publishing Industry Development Program (BPIDP).

Library and Archives Canada Cataloguing in Publication

Identity and belonging : rethinking race and ethnicity in Canadian society / edited by Sean P. Hier and B. Singh Bolaria.

Includes bibliographical references.

ISBN 1-55130-312-4

1. Canada--Ethnic relations--Textbooks. 2. Canada--Race relations--Textbooks. 3. Ethnicity--Canada--Textbooks. I. Hier, Sean P. (Sean Patrick), 1971-II. Bolaria, B. Singh, 1936-

HN105.5.I44 2006   305.8'00971   C2006-904248-9

Cover design: Aldo Fierro
Cover photo: "Micko in Merida Mirror" by Robert Shirley/stockXchng. Copyright © Robert Shirley. Reprinted by permission of Robert Shirley.
Text design and layout: Brad Horning

06   07   08   09   10   5   4   3   2   1

Printed and bound in Canada by Marquis Book Printing Inc.

Canadä

We dedicate this book to Marco, Jacob, and Emanuel,

whose infinitely more complex worlds will, in all likelihood,

seem far less complicated.

TABLE OF CONTENTS

PART THREE
THE NEGOTIATION OF DIFFERENCE

PART FOUR
MULTICULTURALISM, POLITICS, AND BELONGING

PREFACE

The creation of this text is, all things considered, a notable achievement—politically and culturally, in a generational sense, and, last but not least, sociologically. Sean Hier is a Euro-Canadian of Irish-German background, who was born in Canada in the early 1970s and who is at the beginning of his professional career. Singh Bolaria, by contrast, is an Indo-Canadian, born in India in the 1930s and retired from (or, at least, claims to be retired from) a professional career that spanned more than 40 years. We consider the creation of this text to be a notable achievement because it is highly unlikely that we would have even met on Canadian soil, and in the professional context that we did, had Singh been born in 1900 and Sean in 1940. But the point is that we did meet on Canadian soil, and the point is that we came together to produce this text for a complex set of political, cultural, generational, and, last but not least, sociological reasons. Telling our readers how the text actually came to fruition—that we ran into one another in the mail room one day, Sean asked Singh why he never updated *Racial Oppression in Canada*, and the rest is history—seems to fully capture neither the complex material and historical forces that continue to structure our relationship nor the reasons why we continue to write on race and identity in Canadian society.

In what follows, we present students with a few basic guidelines and theories about processes of identity formation that are often overlooked or ignored in the literature today. There is far greater ethno-racial and cultural complexity to the everyday world than sociologists of late seem willing to acknowledge, and that complexity is only going to intensify in the future. But increases in cultural complexity do not equate *a priori* to greater conflict and division. It is necessary to reflect on what identity is, where our identities come from, and how they are shaped, maintained, and reproduced. It is also important to reflect on the place of identity and difference in contemporary politics, and to understand the sociological implications of identification. The four sections of the reader present a number of reading passages that address several important themes in the sociologies of race, ethnicity, and identity. The reading selections also offer a critical engagement with questions of race and ethnicity in Canadian society.

A NOTE FROM THE PUBLISHER

Thank you for selecting *Identity and Belonging: Rethinking Race and Ethnicity in Canadian Society,* edited by Sean P. Hier and B. Singh Bolaria. The editors and publisher have devoted considerable time and careful development (including meticulous peer reviews) to this book. We appreciate your recognition of this effort and accomplishment.

TEACHING FEATURES

This volume distinguishes itself on the market in many ways. One key feature is the book's well-written and comprehensive part openers, which help to make the readings all the more accessible to undergraduate students. The part openers add cohesion to the section and to the whole book. The themes of the book are very clearly presented in these section openers.

The general editors, Sean P. Hier and B. Singh Bolaria, have also greatly enhanced the book by adding pedagogy to close and complete each section. Each part ends with critical thinking questions pertaining to each reading, annotated further readings, and many references. Annotated relevant websites are set at the back of the book as an appendix.

Introduction:
Identities without Guarantees

… social scientists have prolonged the life of an idea [race] that should be explicitly and consistently consigned to the dustbin of analytically useless terms. (Miles and Brown 2003, 90)

Race is fundamental in modern politics. Race is situated at the crossroads of identity and social structure, where difference frames inequality, and where political processes operate with a comprehensiveness that ranges from the historical to the intrapsychic. (Winant 2004, xi)

These opening passages are borrowed from two influential sociological studies of race and racism. As the passages suggest, sociologists neither agree on the analytical usefulness of the concept of race nor do they agree on the ways that the race concept operates in social life. Given the very obviousness of race and difference in everyday life, it may surprise students to learn that an ongoing sociological debate about the analytical significance of race has persisted for over two decades. Yet it is precisely the obviousness of race, the taken-for-granted quality about the fact of race and human group difference, that we critically assess in the sections to follow. We encourage students to keep an open mind about what is often assumed to be the facts of human diversity. The four sections of the reader have been designed to critically assess the complexity of race and identity in Canadian society. By way of an introduction to race and identity, we examine recent popular developments in the sociology of identities to establish a critical-analytical framework to make sense of how Canadians explain their identities through the racial idiom.

TOWARD A DISCURSIVE UNDERSTANDING OF IDENTITY

In a provocative passage of the introduction to *The Archeology of Knowledge*, Michel Foucault (1972) quips: "Do not ask me who I am and do not ask me to remain the same: leave it to the bureaucrats and our police to see that our papers are in order" (p. 17). Taken out of the broader context of his many influential writings, this statement may seem whimsical and aberrant, even arrogant. But Foucault was developing a body of work that challenged commonly held assumptions about truth, power, and identity. He was teaching his audiences to reject universal, objective truth claims and to understand that knowledge about identity, society, and social life is part of a continual process of *becoming*. For Foucault, to offer an answer to the question "Who am I?" is to locate an identity that is specific to a certain time and place, and that is always only ever partial, temporary, and fleeting. There is, in other words, no authentic "I" to which Foucault can refer, and there is no one fundamental identity that constitutes his experience as a human being. For Foucault, there are only complex sets of social relations that configure to naturalize and normalize what are always temporary historical forms of knowledge about who we *think* we really are.

These opening comments might strike students who are just beginning their studies of race, identity, and belonging as a little odd and, perhaps, a little crazy. Few students will have read Foucault's work, and those who have read Foucault probably found his arguments very challenging to comprehend. Nevertheless, the point that he makes is an important one, and it speaks to something that sociologists had demonstrated long before the world was introduced to Michel Foucault; namely, that our identities (e.g., racial, ethnic, sexual, national, and so on), however intimate and cherished they may be, do not exist independently of the times, the places, and the circumstances in which we live.

Foucault's work has significantly influenced sociological writings concerned with race, identity, and belonging over the past decade, and it will be helpful to summarize a few of his basic lessons. The central thrust of Foucault's work was to "create a history of the different modes by which, in our culture, human beings are made into subjects" (Foucault 1982, 208). What this means is that Foucault was interested in *explaining* how human subjectivity — that is, the multi-faceted ways in which we come to see, know, and define ourselves — is formed socially and historically, and in understanding the lifelong processes involved in "becoming" ourselves. Social scientific explanations for processes of becoming, argued Foucault, cannot begin from the point of individual consciousness or personal experience — not from the voices of individuals who lay claim to particular identities (e.g., gay, woman, African-American). Rather, Foucault was interested in understanding how individuals make sense of and define their existence through historically constituted "subject positions" such as "heterosexual," "parent," and "Canadian." As historical configurations or "regimes of truth" that come about through, and are constitutive of, certain kinds of cultural and historical knowledge (e.g., knowledge of what it means to be masculine, sane, healthy, responsible, and so on), subject positions reflect historical power relations that, first, produce particular types of subjects at particular moments in time and, second, are sustained by a sequence of practices and techniques that individuals engage in to justify, rationalize, and reproduce their identities (e.g., rituals, dress, vernacular speech patterns). Rather than representing expressions or manifestations of a natural, inner essence, then, our identities, for Foucault, are always illusive socio-historical constructions that never remain the same.

The arguments that Foucault makes about the ways we come to see, know, and talk about ourselves and others led him to emphasize the importance of "discourse" and "discursive formations" as the primary means through which knowledge is formed and transmitted. Discourse refers to "sets of ready-made and pre-constituted 'experiencings' displayed and arranged [primarily] through language" (Hall 1977, 322) or "a group of statements which provide a language for talking about—a way of representing—the knowledge about a particular topic at a particular moment (Hall 1992, 291). What this means is that discourses are the ways language and other systems of communication are used to transmit cultural and historical meanings. They are the predominant linguistic and semiotic systems that people use to experience, make sense of, and act in the world. When a number of discourses come together to comprise a complex assemblage of cultural meanings (e.g., as laws, moral codes, origin stories), they constitute discursive formations. Discursive formations convey knowledge about people, places, and events, and they often comprise those aspects of social life to which we rarely give serious thought (i.e., common-sense, taken-for-granted assumptions about how the world is). But communication systems such as language, speech, and writing—in short, discourses—are never fully referential; they are always open to contestation, struggle, redefinition, and subversion. For this reason, it is best to think of discursive formations as more or less dominant but flexible systems of meaning that do not causally determine what we think, but rather frame the context in which we think about and make sense of ourselves, others, and the world around us.

To summarize, Foucault offers a set of arguments to conceptualize identities and subjectivities in terms of discourse. A discursive understanding of identity is, first, anti-essentialist: it rejects claims to a natural, trans-historical, essential identity—a real "me." This point is very important; by maintaining an emphasis on the power that inheres in, and that is constituted through, historically specific discourses, sociological explanations for identity formation are not reduced to the unique experiences of, and personal claims made by, individuals who "hold" or embody an identity. It follows, second, that because discourses are bound to history, they contain spatial and temporal dimensions that cannot be understood and explained independent of the social and historical context in which they appear. Third, the regimes of truth that are constituted through subject positions structure the ways we make sense of the world, but they are not absolute. Discourses and subject positions can, and regularly do, change (consider, for example, the changing expectations associated with the subject positions of "mother" and "father" over the last 40 years), and it is in and through discourse that we realize our subjectivities—the many ways we understand, explain, reflect on, and present ourselves. For this reason, Foucault argued that discourses both enable and constrain individual actions, and that discourses both constitute subject positions and produce new ones. Finally, because discourses are social constructions based on human activity, we can study the history of specific discursive identity formations. That is, we can study and lay bare the social, cultural, political, and economic conditions under which certain identities emerge, and we can expose those identities as partial, temporary, fragile, and susceptible to change. The latter point is particularly important because it suggests that normative identities and regimes of truth (e.g., heterosexuality, femininity, racial inferiority/superiority) can be resisted, reconfigured, or rejected. Indeed, Foucault maintained an analytical focus not simply on discursive identities, but also on subjectivities that reflect and reinforce historical relations of power and privilege.

RACE AS DISCOURSE

What, then, is implied by a discursive understanding of race? A discursive understanding of race involves conceptualizing race as a social construction (as opposed to a biological reality) located in time and space. As a social construction with spatial and temporal dimensions, the discourse of race is susceptible to change. While race discourses are caught up in changing forms of knowledge and power, explanations for their emergence and reproduction cannot be based exclusively or even primarily on specific historical manifestations or on the particular ways identities are individually experienced. The study of race and identity is significantly limited when it only seeks to gauge the experiential dimensions of racial identities (e.g., what it means to be black, Caucasian, Chinese, and so forth). This does not mean that sociologists should ignore personal experiences and individual accounts. From a sociological point of view, there is considerable value in understanding the situated or experiential dimensions of identities at certain moments in time (i.e., how identities are lived and experienced by people in particular social locations). What a discursive understanding of race foremost necessitates, however, is a comprehension of the complex and multi-faceted ways in which the idiom of race changes through history, the regimes of truth that give it credence, and the forms of power-knowledge that sustain (and that are sustained by) race discourses.

Students may be surprised to learn that the concept of race is not very old. The discourse of race first appeared in Western European writings in the early 16th century (Banton 1987), and its popular usage as a way to classify and identify groups of human beings dates only to the 19th century. Through much of the 16th to 18th centuries, the race concept was not commonly used to classify and order human beings. Based largely on colonial and imperial interactions, Western European writings were more likely to classify the peoples of Africa, Asia, and the Americas using concepts such as pagans, heathens, uncivilized, barbarians, and, particularly, non-Christians. While many of these representations were negative, some involved positive attributions based on the characteristics of strength, agility, and courage (Miles and Brown 2003). Although used infrequently at this moment in history, the discourse of race denoted the common history or shared lineage of a group of people. Certainly, skin pigmentation and other physical features (e.g., hair type) were used throughout history to signify difference and to classify groups of human beings living in geographically dispersed areas of the world. Long before northwestern European expansion in the 15th century, for example, the ancient Mediterranean cultures of Greece and Rome were attuned to colour differences; they readily distinguished between Ethiopians, Egyptians, and certain Asian populations. But the Greeks and Romans also held Ethiopians (and Egyptians), with whom they enjoyed frequent contact, in high regard (Snowdon 1983), and representations found in Greek and Roman poems, writings, philosophy, and art did not approximate modern understandings of race and natural difference. In fact, so fluid were race discourses leading up to the 18th century that the

French aristocracy used the race concept prior to the revolution of 1789 to denote their common if not exclusive ancestry in France (Guillaumin 1995).

Throughout the 16th and 17th centuries, discourses of race were heavily influenced by Western European interpretations of the Bible—one major variant of which was the theory of creationism. During this first phase of the racial idiom, it was widely accepted that God had created a single original pair, Adam and Eve, and that all human beings were descendants of the original pair (a theory known as monogenesis). Variations in custom and culture were attributed to God's overall plan for humanity (understood as fixed and unchanging), and climate (environment) was accepted as the predominant explanation for differences in skin colour.

Given that human existence was traced to Adam and Eve, it was possible to calculate the number of human generations that had inhabited Earth. In the mid-17th century, for example, James Ussher published *Annales veteris testamenti,* where he used the "begats" (generational links) in the Bible to identify the eve of creation as 23 October 4004 B.C. Ussher's date, which was printed in some English translations of the Bible, was widely accepted, and this date meant that Earth was no more than 6 000 years old. Because the Earth and, by association, humanity was believed to be no greater than 6 000 years old, and because creationism was widely accepted as fact, theories for the origin of existence that involved human evolution were encumbered by the time frame of existence offered by the creationists. Combined with the fact that Western Europeans were in possession of drawings that dated back thousands of years and that depicted human beings who looked the same as modern-day humans, a strong cultural foundation to support critical and sustained dialogue on the natural evolution of the human form was absent.

As Western Europe entered the 18th century, the theory of a single human origin (Adam and Eve) was amended in a number of important ways. In this second phase of the racial idiom, information about other peoples and places continued to circulate in Europe. Up to this point, human beings were most commonly classified along geographic lines. But as the 18th century set in, writings increasingly appeared that not only classified human beings on the basis of body type and facial appearance, but also started to use the discourse of race more frequently. Theories began to emerge suggesting that, although human beings descended from Adam and Eve, somewhere along the way the human family had divided into separate types (a theory known as polygenesis). Certain observers argued that Africans had been in Europe and the Americas for generations, and that Europeans had been in Africa for generations, but that their skin colour had not lightened or darkened, respectively. Not only did they call into question the validity of environmentalism as an explanation for skin tone, but other writers also queried how environment could be used to explain phenotypic (physical) variation in body type, eye shape, height, and other observable features.

Theories emphasizing multiple lines of descent gained momentum from advances in natural history in the late 18th and 19th centuries. At this time, natural historians were increasingly finding transitional fossils buried deep in the earth. These fossils showed changes in human and animal forms, and rudimentary theories of transmutation (the gradual change from one species to another) were appearing with greater frequency (and in more diverse forms). Naturalists collected, described, and classified human and animal fossils, and the physical evidence they garnered began to conflict with the arguments made by the creationists—particularly the belief in a relatively young Earth. Classificatory systems offering racial types appeared in the work of men such as Linnaeus, Buffon, and Blumenbach, and racial typologies, while by no means developed in opposition to creationism, nevertheless called into question many of the tenets of monogenesis. Still, polygenism was entirely oppositional neither to creationism nor monogenism: the polygenists supported the theory of a single original pair, but they also argued that somewhere along the human line the species had broken into different types.

One of the most important contributions to settling the struggle between monogenists and polygenists was Charles Lyell's (1830) *Principles of Geology*, where he expanded the theory of uniformitiarianism. Originally introduced by James Hutton, the theory of uniformitiarianism held that the processes shaping Earth today are the same, uniform processes that have always shaped Earth (e.g., wind, rain, soil erosion, and glacial movements). Lyell reasoned that because natural processes shaping the physical features of Earth are the same uniform processes that have always shaped Earth, and because physical changes on Earth require very long periods of time, the Earth must be greater than 6 000 years old. For all its influence, the scientific theory of uniformitiarianism continued to conflict with biblical accounts of the origin of Earth, but it also enabled scientists and naturalists to think about the mechanisms of natural evolution and human change over long periods of time.

One of these naturalists was Charles Darwin. In 1859, Darwin published *The Origin of the Species by Means of Natural Selection or the Preservation of Favoured Races in the Struggle for Life*. It was here that Darwin introduced the theory of natural selection. Based on his observations of a variety of species inhabiting the Galapagos Islands, Darwin argued that certain members of the same species who possess slightly different physical characteristics are favoured to survive in particular environments. He explained that when certain physical characteristics that are advantageous to particular environmental conditions appear in a few members of a species, those members of the species enjoy an increased likelihood for survival. An increased likelihood of survival, in turn, increases the likelihood for reproductive successes and the transmission of the favoured characteristics to offspring. Over long periods of time, Darwin maintained, new species emerge and old ones die off on the basis of selective natural advantages.

The publication of *Origin* had at least four discernable influences on Victorian England. First, it contradicted the belief in a constant, fixed world. Darwin was able to demonstrate how plant and animal species develop and change in an uneven way, as well as how new species develop over long stretches of time. Second, his theory of natural selection offered considerable support to Lyell's contention that Earth is older than 6 000 years. Concomitantly, it also called into question the belief in divine creation. Darwin presented sound evidence for processes of natural selection that take place over millions of years— certainly far more than 6 000 years. Third, he settled the monogenist–polygenist debate, making it irrelevant in a certain sense by establishing clearly how Europeans were related to Africans (and to apes). Darwin had offered no insight into comparative human racial advancement, save for characteristics that enable the survival of certain members of species. These arguments, however, were simplified, recontextualized, and applied to human civilizations, and they became important influences in debates taking place in the context of colonialism and imperialism. And finally, the publication of *Origin* facilitated the development of a third phase of the racial idiom: race as subspecies. Increasingly, the tensions between race as lineage and race as type gave way to new configurations of knowledge and power that posed the argument that the world's human population could be divided by inheritance or, eventually, genetic structure. Still, despite its significance, the belief in white racial superiority achieved its height in Western Europe in the 1920s and 1930s (Banton 1987). Lucid conceptions of race in the 19th century were not pervasive, and conceptions of race as "type" and as "subspecies" coexisted for some time.

Therefore, the concept of race has been in use for a relatively short period of human existence. Although it first appeared in the English language in the 16th century, it was not put into common use until the 19th century. The racial idiom has endured a number of discernable phases over the last 300 years, and it is most certainly incorrect to conceptualize race as a natural, inevitable way of classifying oneself and others. Race was, for some time, predominantly caught up in religious interpretations of existence. In the 17th and 18th centuries, religious explanations combined with an anthropological frame of reference, and in the 19th century there was a notable shift toward a predominantly scientific and, eventually, genetic framework. The cultural history of race, in short, is fluid or flexible. Race has always been bound by time and space, and the cultural meanings associated with it continue to be influenced by shifting social, political, and economic factors.

SIGNIFICATION, IDENTITY, AND THE GUARANTEE OF RACE

Despite the persistence of a small group of contemporary researchers who strive to establish what they believe to be (or at least claim to be) the natural foundations of race and human group difference, biologists and physical anthropologists generally agree that there is little to be gained scientifically from using the concept of race to infer intellectual, social, and/or cultural characteristics from biological groupings of human beings. In natural- and social-scientific circles, it is widely accepted that the notion of biological race as a reliable indicator of group temperament, mental aptitude, or social habit is based on the falsification of science. For this reason, and given the historically changing ways that race has been conceptualized and understood, social and cultural theorists have started to explain race not as a biological fact but as a cultural system of interconnected meanings. One of the more popular versions of this argument is that, although there is no scientific utility to be gained from the biological conception of race, because people in everyday life continue to use physical features, usually skin colour, to signify natural or innate human socio-cultural characteristics, the race concept has a social and/or cultural utility.

While there is much to be learned from studies of identity, discourse, and the experiential dimensions of perceived racial difference (social race), the trend toward conceptualizing race as a social reality has not gone without criticism. One of the most influential critics has been the world-renowned cultural theorist Stuart Hall.[1] For Hall (1996), the question of racial identity is not a question of who "we" are or where "we" came from. The question of political and historical urgency, rather, is what human beings might *become*. Far from emphasizing an essential, fixed quality of human beings, Hall maintains that racial identities are the subjects of the continuous play of history, culture, knowledge, and power (Hall 1990). What this means is that racial identity formations have histories, and like any history their character is subject to change. By emphasizing the analytical notion of becoming rather than being—that is, by looking forward to what could be rather than backwards to what was or what may have been—Hall resists the urge to reduce racial identities to a single, homogeneous experience.

Although Hall emphatically insists on conceptualizing race as a discursive system of meaning that avoids essentialism and the temptation to reduce racial identities to a single experience, he denies neither the existence of physical differences between and among groups of human beings nor the significance that is attached to these differences. There are physical differences between people—some groups of people are lighter than others, some are taller than others—but it is only through language and cultural systems of meaning that these grosser physical differences become significant and assume meaning. What matters, in other words, are not the bare facts of physical difference (e.g., skin tone), but rather the meaning and significance we attribute to physical differences at particular moments in time. This is as true for 17th-century creationism as it is for 21st-century genetics. Hall argues that there is a cultural function to 21st-century science, just as there was a cultural function to 17th-century monogenesis. That function is to fix human group difference and to establish a system of meaning whereby one group of people is understood to be different from another group of people based on a range of cultural characteristics. What is so different about science, however, is that it offers a *guarantee of difference* that neither religious nor anthropological systems of meaning could offer. Under the guise of science, culture and biology become metonymical: the genetic code stands in for cultural variation, to the extent that we signify the natural physical features of the body to make sense of and explain socio-cultural characteristics, aptitudes, and abilities as never before in the history of race designations. This is a clear example of what Michel Foucault termed bio-power: the administration of human beings through the production of "docile bodies." Again, it is not that Hall is denying the physical diversity among human beings. The point is, rather, that once we accept a conception of human physical diversity based on the cultural construct of science and forged on the basis of otherwise meaningless physical variations, we quickly begin to use the "natural" text of the body (skin color, cranial shape, body type) to infer cultural characteristics such as trustworthiness, intelligence, sexuality, and aesthetic preference. What Hall is saying, then, is that it is not the truth of the genetic code and what it tells us about human social and cultural diversity that matters to sociological understanding of race and identity. What matters is the faith people instill in scientific knowledge itself and how scientific truth-claims—which are discursive systems—intersect with other systems of cultural production to construct and reproduce systems of human classification and diversity.

The analytical and, indeed, political importance of Hall's insights becomes clear in the context of anti-racist politics and the politics of identity. As previously noted, there is a ubiquitous tendency in sociological analyses of race and identity to acknowledge that there is no biological reality to race. Sociologists commonly argue that biological race is a false, pernicious, deterministic notion, and they frequently brand those who try to establish the link between biology and culture as "racists." However, these same people persist in using the concept of race as though it can tell us something about the socio-cultural characteristics of different biological or natural "races." They speak from particular social positions and lay claim to the rightness of their argument on the basis of race and natural difference (e.g., as a black man or a South-Asian woman). In conducting their politics or affirming their identities, they fall back on *the guarantee of biological race* through the signification of physical difference while simultaneously pronouncing its death. In this sense, two diametrically opposed political positions (racism and anti-racism) can be understood to derive their comprehension of human biological and cultural variation from the same cultural knowledge system (i.e., science). Both racists and anti-racists rely on the guarantee of race, on the biological naturalness of cultural identities, to establish the "rightness" of their respective socially, culturally, historically, and politically situated arguments.

For Stuart Hall, then, we should neither deny physical differences between groups of people nor try to reduce or minimize their cultural and social significance. Rather, we should abandon the guarantee of race that functions to fix identity, that naturalizes cultural diversity, and that is predicated on the presumption that the substance of one's politics derives from the makeup of one's biology or genetic code. What this means is that a person's or a group's arguments and politics are not necessarily or even regularly correct simply because they racially identify as, for example, white, black, South Asian, Chinese, Japanese, Korean, Latin American, or Mexican. The challenge that lies before us at the beginning of the 21st century—a century of unprecedented diversity in Canada—is to develop an ethically responsible politics of inclusion and acceptance that can negotiate diversity and difference without falling back on the guarantee of race—that is, without falling back on the biological trace and the fixity of difference to guarantee the rightness of a particular political position. One way to begin is to look beyond (or away from) the institution of science, and one strategy is to substitute a politics of authenticity (being) with a politics of creativity (becoming). The ethical imperative of our time, in other words, is to have the courage and the integrity to develop identities without guarantees by virtue of membership in a particular *social or cultural* group.

RETHINKING RACE AND ETHNICITY IN CANADIAN SOCIETY

Recent demographic projections based on Statistics Canada data indicate that persons belonging to a visible minority group will comprise 20 percent of the Canadian population by 2017. In Canada's major cities, the proportion of persons classified as visible minority is expected to exceed 50 percent. In the city of Toronto, for example, more than 100 visible and non-visible ethno-racial groups speak over 100 languages. While Canada has always been ethno-racially diverse, demographic changes over the past 35 years have exercised a profound influence on Canadian culture, as well as on Canadian political and social institutions. As the ethno-racial composition and complexity of the country continue to diversify, critical understandings of race, ethnicity, identity, and belonging become increasingly important goals for social justice, fairness, and inclusion in Canada.

To this end, we present 16 reading passages in four sections to rethink race and ethnicity in Canadian society. The first section, "Situating Race, Ethnicity, and Belonging," offers four papers that conceptualize race, ethnicity, and identity. The papers in this section critically analyze race or ethnicity as a primordial human characteristic. They demonstrate how ethno-racial identities are social constructions, and how processes of identity formation generally, and contemporary identities specifically, are part of a wider human process of signifying self and Other. The section closes with a highly influential paper on essentialism, establishing a link between race and/or ethnicity and gender.

The second section addresses processes of collective identity formation in the context of nationalism, advanced communication, and differential power relations. The papers elaborate the themes established in the first section, and they show how ethno-racial and nationalistic identities are fluid, contextual, and "imagined" through processes of mediation and/or communication.

While maintaining a strong focus on the flexibility of ethno-racial identities, the third section shifts the focus from the structure of identity formation to the processes involved in negotiating sameness and difference. Four papers are presented that address identity formation in the context of power and oppression, diversity, complexity, and ambivalence. The final section shifts the focus to politics, multiculturalism, and belonging. The papers in the final section discuss some of the contradictions at the nexus of identity, culture, and politics. They also complement sociological understandings of processes of identity formation with identity ascription or self-identification.

NOTE

1   For an excellent statement on identities and the guarantee of race, see Stuart Hall, *Race, the Floating Signifier* (Northampton: The Media Education Foundation, 2002).

REFERENCES

Banton, Michael. 1987. *Racial Theories.* Cambridge: Cambridge University Press.

Foucault, Michel. 1972. *The Archeology of Knowledge.* New York: Pantheon.

———. 1982. "Afterward: The Subject and Power." In *Michel Foucault: Beyond Structuralism and Hermeneutics,* ed. H.L. Dreyfus and P. Rabinow, 208–264. London: Harvester Wheatsheaf.

Guillaumin, C. 1995. *Racism, Sexism, Power, and Ideology,* 208–226. London: Routledge.

Hall, Stuart. 1977. "Racism and Reaction." In *Five Views of Multi-Racial Britain.* London: Commission for Racial Equality.

———. 1990. "Cultural Identity and Diaspora." In *Identity: Community, Culture, Difference,* ed. Jonathan Rutherford, 222–237. London: Lawrence & Wishart.

———. 1992. "New Ethnicities." In *"Race", Culture, and Difference,* ed. A. Rattansi and J. Donald, 252–260. London: Sage/Open University Press.

———. 1996. "When Was the Post-Colonial." In *The Post Colonial Question,* ed. L. Curti and I. Chambers, 51–71. New York: Routledge.

Lyell, Charles. 1830. *Principles of Geology; Being an Attempt to Explain the Former Changes of the Earth's Surface, By Reference to Causes Now in Operation.* Philadelphia: J. Kay, jun. & brother; Pittsburgh: J.I. Kay & Co.

Miles, Robert, and Malcolm Brown. 2003. *Racism.* New York: Routledge.

Snowdon, Frank. 1983. *Before Color Prejudice: The Ancient View of Blacks.* Boston: Harvard University Press.

Winant, Howard. 2004. *The New Politics of Race: Globalism, Difference, Justice.* Minnesota: University of Minnesota Press.

ONE

SITUATING RACE, ETHNICITY, AND IDENTITY

The question is not whether men-in-general make perceptual distinctions between groups with different racial or ethnic characteristics, but rather, what are the specific conditions which make this form of distinction socially pertinent, historically active. (Hall 1980, 338)

In the final sentence of the introduction to their highly influential *Racial Formation in the United States*, Michael Omi and Howard Winant (1994) argue, "Race will *always* be at the centre of the American experience" (p. 5, original emphasis). For many readers, this statement will seem reasonable and logical, even obvious. When Canadians, particularly, reflect on the significance of race in America, images of slavery, of civil rights struggles, and of Rodney (Glen) King[1] arise. While race is widely accepted as a central, palpable characteristic of human beings, the validity—and the generalizability—of Omi and Winant's claim requires suspending the fact that, first, the classificatory designation of "race" has a relatively recent advent in human history, and that, second, the period of time in which the geo-spatial territory of "America" has existed constitutes considerably less than 1 percent of human existence.[2] As we noted in the introduction, the earliest recorded use of the term "race" in the English language only traces to 1508, and that prior to the 19th century (only about 200 years ago) the concept of race was not commonly used as a means to classify and categorize human beings. From a contemporary vantage point, it may seem reasonable to argue that race will always be at the centre of the American experience, as Omi and Winant surmise. We should not, however, lose sight of the fact that race and the American experience have neither always been, nor, judging from recorded human history, always be at the centre of the human experience.

The point we wish to emphasize is that societies, cultures, civilizations, and so forth are constantly changing. Although people tend to assume uncritically that their current social circumstances and ways of living are natural, normal, and inevitable, how they understand and explain the world, and the significance they attach to social relations and relationships, is historically specific. For instance, approximately 6 000 years before the death of Jesus Christ (B.C.), or before the current era (B.C.E.), highly developed civilizations, with elaborate customs and norms, stratified social hierarchies, and forced labour systems existed in the Tigris-Euphrates valley (Egypt) and in Sumer (southern Iraq), the latter numbering 500 000 people. By at least 200 B.C., a sophisticated Mayan civilization supported 5 to 7 million people. And when Julius Caesar was murdered in 44 B.C., the Roman Empire supported a population of 50 million people, spanning all of the Mediterranean and major portions of current-day Western Europe. It is reasonable to speculate that the people who inhabited these once-flourishing civilizations would not have imagined that their complex societies would one day be reduced to an obscure passing reference in a 21st-century textbook on identity and belonging. And it is reasonable to speculate that the people who inhabited these civilizations would not have imagined that certain of their customs, traditions, and ways of life would one day be deemed antiquated, immoral, primitive, or barbaric by 21st-century audiences. Given the last few hundred years of racial oppression, subjugation, and genocide, the latter assessment, in one sense, is indeed curious. The multi-ethnic, multilingual, cosmopolitan society that was 2nd-century (A.D.) Rome, for example, was not fixated on race and skin colour; instead, wealth and literacy opened the doors of social privilege for citizens in the Empire (Cantor 2003).

The contingent, historical specificity of societal arrangements was not lost on Karl Marx and Friedrick Engels. The famous opening lines of the *Manifesto of the Communist Party* cite historical moments involving temporal relations between freeman and slave, patrician and plebian, lord and serf, and guild-master and journeyman. But the introduction to the *Manifesto* also addresses "the history of all hitherto existing society" (p. 473). As Marx ([1843] 1978) explained elsewhere in his theory of human nature, while the content or manifest form of socio-historical patterns of human designation and classification—the social organization of society—change on the basis of particular struggles over resources and production, the fact that human beings create systems of classification does not. In other words, human beings demonstrate tendencies toward classifying and ordering the social world (a human group constant), but the actual ways in which they classify and order, and the patterns of social stratification that are reinforced by those designations, take place in the context of specific historical systems of material production and exchange.

In the study of identity and race, few, if any, contemporary social scientists would argue that race is a natural, bio-genetic feature of human beings that determines culture, intelligence, sexuality, trustworthiness, and so on. It is widely accepted that race as a human designation traces to a specific moment in history, and that the racial idiom developed in the material context of colonialism, colonization, and conquest. But this is where agreement ends. On the one hand, there is a group of social scientists who analytically reject the concept of race as scientific myth, and they argue that race is an ideological construct whose origin can be traced to a particular moment in time and which took root in the context of specific political and economic relations. They conceptualize race as a temporal historical construct caught up in historical-material forces of production, and they offer explanations for why, and under what conditions, racial identities become salient. This group of social scientists maintains that race is a false human designation, and that there is no analytical value to be gained from continuing to reinforce and, by implication of its use in social scientific research, justify the false claim that the human population can be classified discretely by race.

On the other hand, a second group of social scientists is concerned to explain the ways racial identities are experienced by different, and, often, disadvantaged groups. Rejecting arguments that race is an historical myth that offers no analytical value to contemporary researchers, they invoke Thomas and Thomas's (1928) dictum that if men [sic] define social situations as real, then these situations are real in their consequences. For this second group of social scientists, it does not matter if race is "real" in a biological sense because millions of people believe that it is real and use it as an organizing dimension of social life. Race, in this latter regard, is understood as "socially real" even if there is no biological justification to divide the world's population into discrete racial groups. Judging from the plethora of scholarly research and writing, clearly, in the words of Cornell West (1993), "race matters." But when we address *matters of race* in the social sciences, it is important to understand why, how, and under what circumstances race matters. The readings in this section are concerned with these ongoing social-scientific dilemmas and debates.

SECTION THEMES: REPRESENTATION, PRIMORDIALISM, EXPERIENCE, AND ESSENTIALISM

The section opens with a reading passage drawn from Robert Miles and Malcolm Brown's excellent book, *Racism*, examining "representations of the other" generated in the Western world from the 8th through the 19th centuries. Miles and Brown argue that the category of race does not signify a natural, intrinsic feature of human beings; that popular use of the race concept traces to 18th-century developments in science and naturalism; and that historical applications of race as a primary mode of human classification are caught up in, but not reducible to, representations of African, Asian/Oriental, and Middle Eastern others long before the period of "European" expansion. At least since the consolidation of cultural and economic power by Greco-Roman city-states from the 8th to 12th centuries A.D., Western representations of others have taken place in the context of particular economic, political, religious, geographical, and cultural configurations.

Miles and Brown begin by arguing that the interrelated forces of trade, production, and warfare, combined with exploration and adventure seeking, have brought human beings into contact for thousands of years—long before European colonial expansion in the 15th century. They explain that when groups of people speaking different languages and possessing different customs, habits, appearances, and patterns of self-presentation come into contact, they re-present one another through conversation, art, writing, myth, and the production of cultural objects. Representational images of "others" derive from the direct experiences of traders, travellers, and explorers, for example, but many representations are also "experienced" indirectly through images appearing in books, journals, paintings, and other forms of storytelling. Representations of others—and, necessarily, of self—take place in the context of particular political and economic circumstances, no matter how rudimentary these representations may appear to contemporary observers; they are always influenced by the historical, spatial, and temporal characteristics of those who are represented; and they always involve a dialectic of self and other: to represent "others" necessarily implies an image of "self" as somehow different.

Yet, significantly, and somewhat paradoxically, Miles and Brown examine representations of the "European other" before European expansion. Prior to the 15th century, there was no collective understanding of a geo-spatial territory known as "Europe." Long before the consolidation of capitalist interests in northwestern Europe in the "long 16th century" (1450–1640), regions centred around the Mediterranean had spread across the old world. Medieval city-states in Greece and Rome — Venice and Genoa, for example — were able to attain economic and political dominance in these networks of human interactivity. Due to elaborate systems of travel, trade, and military activity, information about the peoples of Africa was brought back to the Greco-Roman world. Shifting moral, social, and religious significance was attached to dark skin and other phenotypical features in Greco-Roman thought, but there also existed the view that skin colour was influenced by environmental factors such as geographical proximity to the equator. As feudal Europe was emerging throughout the 12th and 13th centuries, shifting representations of the other were applied to the peoples of North Africa, of India, and of the Middle East.

However significant representations of pre-15th century others were to the political, social, cultural, and economic affairs of the Greco-Roman Empire, it is important to realize that they were not *racial* representations. Miles and Brown explain that even as the European merchant classes began to colonize the Americas in the 15th and 16th centuries, representations of others were heavily influenced by religion, politics, economics, and cultural conceptions of civilization. During the 18th century, developments in the natural sciences led to a flurry of writings about biological types of human beings (taxonomies). These biological classification systems did not replace older, pre-European representations of others, but rather combined certain elements of older representations with new, scientific developments. These systems also came into conflict with environment and religion as the predominant explanations for phenotypical, cultural, and material differences between geographically dispersed groups of people.

In the next reading passage, Anton Allahar offers one explanation for why race and ethnic identities become important to people at certain moments in history, and he examines the political dimensions of race and ethnic classifications, designations, and appropriations. Allahar begins with an observation alluded to in the previous reading: that there is a pan-human propensity to covet the familiar, to define what is "ours," to construct a sense of "home," sometimes in ethnic or racial terms. But Allahar probes the reasons why certain racialized or ethnicized understandings of territory, nation, region, or country — in short, of "home" — are constructed. Are these constructions simply projections of more fundamental material/economic or class interests? Are ethnic and racial identity constructions based on fundamental, natural, primordial connections between people sharing similar ancestry? Or is it that one of these social dimensions for human meaning making — class versus ethnicity/race — is epiphenomenal (secondary) to the other?

Allahar argues that explanations for why and how groups of people construct ethnic and racial identities have tended to take one of two forms, primordialism or structuralism, although he encourages readers to construe the distinction as analytical rather than empirical. What this means is that these terms should be thought of as ways that social scientists attempt to explain why people embrace ethnic and racial identities, not necessarily the actual ways that people explain their identities in everyday life. He contends that, as human beings, we cling to identities, connections, loyalties, nationalisms, and so forth, but rarely do we consider where our identities actually come from. Ethnic and racial identities appear to us as natural, normal, ascribed, and inevitable, as though our current identities would take root under any circumstances. But ethnic and racial identities are not "real," argues Allahar, in the sense that they are not natural or inevitable. Rather, identities are the result of social, historical, political, cultural interactions. For this reason, Allahar urges us to think about identities in terms of "soft primordialism"; although people come to think about their identities as natural and normal—in short, primordial—the notion of a natural identity is in fact a social construction. As the social construction of the "naturalness" of ethnic and racial identity, we can ask hard analytical questions about what economic, political, cultural, and social forces make these identities salient and affable. While seemingly contradictory notions, the social construction of primordial identities, Allahar concludes, is more than an oxymoron: it draws analytical attention to the significance of material or social relations and their role in the social construction of particular identities.

In the third reading passage, Carl James addresses the social construction of race and ethnicity from a different analytical perspective, prioritizing the experience of ethnic and racial identities more than the complicated process(es) of identity formation (although he does not entirely neglect the latter). James begins with the observation that, although race is part of everyone's daily experience and identity, it is more significant for some groups of people. Using classroom discussions at Ontario college and universities to try to better understand how race is lived and experienced, interpreted and reproduced, he first addresses how whiteness is perceived—or, rather, ignored—by a few white students. James contrasts these perceptions with an essay excerpt by one of his students of Trinidadian origin, and he reflects on the fluidity of ethnic identities.

James proceeds to link the different ways in which race and ethnicity are experienced to wider patterns of social stratification. He explains that societies are organized on the basis of historical relations of power, to the extent that dominant institutions—church, media, workplace—are designed to meet the needs and desires of dominant group members. Thus, the socializing experiences that people have in various social institutions influence their identities, their experiences of inclusion/exclusion, and their feelings of belonging (see also Omi and Winant's reading passage in Part Two).

In the final reading passage, Radha Jhappan assesses some of the contemporary political uses, and abuses, of gender and racial identities within and outside feminism(s). Jhappan begins by critically analyzing the role that feminism has played in debunking many, predominantly Western, male-centred, assumptions embedded in mainstream socio-political scholarship. She also, importantly, critically analyzes the reductionism of the feminist critiques of patriarchy *and* the primordialism that has engendered feminist critiques of other feminist critiques of patriarchy.

Jhappan points out that feminism has successfully revealed the debilitating reductionism, the narrow androcentrism, and the dubious universalism embedded in mainstream political discourse. The problem, she explains, is that the feminist assault on "malestream" knowledge production has largely been staged by Western women of European ancestry ("white" women) — women, moreover, from middle-class backgrounds, who are heterosexual and able-bodied. In other words, while mainstream, ancestrally Euro-, hetero-, able-ist, middle-class feminists went to great lengths to demonstrate how patriarchal, "Cartesian" assumptions in socio-political thought depreciated the unique experiences and social positions of women, they fail(ed) to understand (or appreciate) the importance of uniqueness within the feminist movement. Jhappan explains that black feminists and feminists of colour have questioned the utility of placing the social category of gender before, or over and above, race as a primary source of social oppression. The difficulty to emerge from the latter assault on the mainstream feminist assault on patriarchy, with its attendant gender essentialism through the prism of mainstream feminism, however, is that the critique of male essentialism that gave way to gender essentialism has been replaced with race essentialism. Put simply, feminists debunked the essentializing patriarchal assumptions of Western scholarship only to reproduce similar, essentializing patterns; and women of colour and black women debunked the ethnocentrism of (white) Western feminist scholarship only to reproduce similar, essentializing patterns of the authentic "minority voice."

Jhappan uses the term essentialism in a manner similar to the way Allahar conceptualizes soft primordialism; although most academics of colour accept the argument that race and, by corollary, racial identities do not exist as immutable, "natural" phenomena, these concepts are used analytically to prioritize race over all other social and cultural markers of identity. She proceeds to identify and explore eight interrelated "traps" of race essentialism. Her main point is that many of the problems identified as existing between white people and people of colour also exist within communities of colour, and that progressive social justice movements cannot reproduce the same essentializing patterns they seek to problematize and traverse. It was precisely this latter point, the guarantee of race, that Stuart Hall warned against (see introduction).

NOTES

1. Glen King was an African-American motorist in Los Angeles who was beaten by four Euro-America (white) police officers on 3 March 1991. Unknown to the police officers, the beating was caught on videotape by a third party, George Holliday. When the four police officers were acquitted of using excessive force to subdue King, what came to be known as the "LA Riots" broke out on 29 April 1992. Throughout the news coverage, Glen King was mistakenly referred to as "Rodney" King based on a police-report error. The name remains with him to this day.

2. Consider, for example, that the Old Stone Age, or paleolithic era, ranged from almost 3 million years ago to 12 000 years ago, and Columbus arrived on the shores of the Americas less than 600 years ago.

REFERENCES

Banton, Michael. 1998. *Racial Theories*. Cambridge: Cambridge University Press.

Canton, Norman. 2003. *Antiquity: From the Birth of Sumerian Civilization to the Fall of the Roman Empire*. New York: Perennial.

Hall, Stuart. 1980. "Race, Articulation, and Societies Structured in Domination." In UNESCO *Sociological Theories: Race and Colonialism*. Paris: UNESCO.

Marx, Karl. [1843] 1978. "Economic and Philosophic Manuscripts of 1844." In *The Marx-Engels Reader*. 2nd ed., ed. J. Tucker. New York: W.W. Norton and Company.

Omi, Michael, and Howard Winant. 1994. *Racial Formation in the United States*. New York Routledge.

Thomas, W.I., and D. Thomas. 1928. *The Child in America: Behavior Problems and Programs*. New York: Knopf.

West, Cornel. 1993. *Race Matters*. New York: Vintage.

REPRESENTATIONS OF THE OTHER

ROBERT MILES
AND MALCOLM BROWN

INTRODUCTION

Migration, determined by the interrelation of production, trade, and warfare, has been a precondition for the meeting of human individuals and groups over thousands of years. In the course of this interaction, imagery, beliefs, and evaluations about the Other have been generated and reproduced in order to explain the appearance and behaviour of those with whom contact has been established, and to formulate a strategy for interaction and reaction. The consequence has been the production of "representations" (cf. Moscovici 1981, 1982, 1984) of the Other, images and beliefs that categorize people in terms of real or attributed differences when compared with Self ("Us"). There is, therefore, a dialectic of Self and Other in which the attributed characteristics of Other refract contrasting characteristics of Self, and vice versa.

BEFORE EUROPEAN EXPANSION

European explorers and traders of the 16th and 17th centuries did not set out without expectations of the characteristics of the peoples they would meet. They occupied class positions in feudal societies that had a long tradition of imagining the Other, partly as a consequence of the experience of direct contact. Thus, for example, the African was represented in European thought long before European involvement in the slave trade (Jordan 1968, 6; Walvin 1973, 2–7; 1986, 69–72). These earlier representations were created and reproduced in a politico-spatial context in which Europe was not imagined, and, therefore, to all intents and purposes, did not exist. The economic and political domination of northwestern Europe is historically specific and, prior to the 15th century, the geographical region that is now Europe had been subject to invasions from Asia, and the "old continuous nations" of Europe were haltingly emergent rather than extant (Seton-Watson 1977, 21–87).

The European regions that achieved economic and politico-military significance prior to the 15th century were around the Mediterranean. Before then, the regions that are now Italy and Greece established and maintained a dominant economic and cultural position, sustained partly militarily. These societies were built largely upon the use of slave labour, and the imperialistic activities of their ruling classes brought them into contact with other populations in Europe and northern Africa. Contact and interaction occurred in different arenas. The most important were travel, trade, and military activity. Travellers' accounts supplied information about populations that were identified as culturally and physically different, while trade and military activity ensured more extensive and direct forms of contact.

In the context of a growing knowledge of the geographical extent of human existence, there developed in Greco-Roman thought an idea of the unity of the human species. A conception of human diversity, spatially dispersed, but bound together by characteristics that distinguished human beings from both gods and animals, existed and was transformed in various ways over five centuries, although it did not seriously challenge the continuity of class and sexual divisions within Greco-Roman society (Baldry 1965, 24–25, 122, 198–203). Moreover, it did not eliminate the perception of "barbarians" beyond the borders of Greco-Roman society. The barbarian as Other was seen to lack the capacities of intelligible speech and reason, capacities that were considered to be the quintessence of Greco-Roman culture, even though they were recognized as human beings (Baldry 1965, 21–22, 143).

With the military expansion of the Greco-Roman empire into Africa, captured Africans were enslaved like other prisoners of war, while others became, in effect, mercenaries. Additionally, Africans travelled to and were resident in the Greco-Roman world for educational, diplomatic, and commercial purposes (Snowden 1970, 121–122, 186; 1983, 33). How were Africans represented in light of this interaction?

First, Africans were identified using certain physical features, notably skin colour but also hair type and nose shape (Snowden 1970, 2–5; 1983, 7). There was a definitive colour symbolism within Greco-Roman culture by which whiteness was positively evaluated and blackness negatively evaluated, associated with death, and a conception of an underworld (Snowden 1983, 82–83). However, the characterization of Africans as black-skinned did not sustain a negative stereotype or constitute a legitimation of slavery (Davis 1984, 33). Rather, and second, Africans were identified as human beings with the capacity for freedom and justice, piety and wisdom (although some conceptions included elements of idealization and unreality). They were respected as warriors and soldiers (Snowden 1970, 181; 1983, 55–59, 68), and, although some writers associated beauty with whiteness, there was a widely held assumption that the criteria of beauty were subjective. Indeed, other writers extolled blackness as beautiful (Snowden 1983, 63, 76).

Third, there was speculation about the origin of phenotypical and cultural differences. The dominant explanation in the Greco-Roman world was environmental in nature, the argument being that human physical appearance and cultural variation were determined by climate, topography, and hydrography (Baldry 1965, 50). This argument was used to explain the full range of phenotypical diversity that was known at that time. For example, concerning Africans, it was suggested that skin colour and hair type were the product of constant exposure to the hot sun, while the opposite was believed of northern peoples (e.g., Snowden 1970, 172–173; 1983, 85–87).

In addition to the representations of the African as an *experienced* Other (in the sense that there was direct contact and interaction with certain African populations) there were also representations of an *imagined* Other (in the sense that the representations had no empirical reality, although that was not how they were experienced at the time). That the boundary between the experienced and the imagined Other is an artificial one in the Greco-Roman frame of reference is made evident in the *Natural History* of Pliny the Elder; this text included a primarily (though not exclusively) phenotypical typology of populations, many of which were given a particular spatial location in the world, mainly in Africa, India, and the Caucasus. This typology included Ethiopians, although their spatial location was imprecise, and also *Cynocephali, Blemmyae, Anthropophagi,* and *Sciopods.* These populations were attributed with various physiological and cultural characteristics: the *Cynocephali* were dog-headed humans, and the *Sciopods* had a single, very large foot, while the *Anthropophagi* were represented as eaters of human flesh (Friedman 1981, 8–21).

This typology, and associated representations and explanations, was expanded and modified by other writers and passed into medieval European literary tradition. Within this tradition, a causal relationship between physical appearance, moral character, and spatial location was asserted, and, as in Greco-Roman thought, climate was considered to be a major determinant, but the threefold climatic division of Greek thought was expanded (Friedman 1981, 52). Additional transformations occurred, the most significant being the popular religious meanings attributed to these representations. Within the Greco-Roman world, natural events considered to be indicators of God's intentions toward human beings were defined as *portenta* or *monstra.* Initially, *monstra* defined unusual individual or anomalous births, but its meaning was extended through the Middle Ages to include whole populations of people supposedly characterized by anomalous phenotypical characteristics, although the sense of divine warning remained (Friedman 1981, 108–116).

This premonitory meaning was subsequently transformed into one of punishment as Christianity became the prism through which knowledge about the world was refracted, as a result of which a biblically inspired explanation for the material world predominated. Consequently, the nature and origin of these *monstra* had to be explained consistently with the biblical representation of history as interpreted by the Church. Concerning their nature, the issue was whether or not they were human, a crucial matter that determined whether or not they could be the object of missionary activity and conversion (Friedman 1981, 178–180). It was also necessary to explain the origin of these *monstra.* One explanation advanced by medieval European writers was that they were part of God's creation plan, the purpose of which had yet to be revealed. Others argued that one or a group of Adam's descendants had induced God's wrath; as a result, their descendants had been physically disfigured and exiled to the periphery of the world. This explanation accepted a single origin of humanity as set out in the Bible but accounted for the subsequent diversity in human form. While the latter remained a subordinate explanation for a long period, it received increasing expression and support during the medieval period (pp. 88–103) and came to play a major ideological role in European expansion. The consequence was an association between the Other qua *monstrum* and sin. Before the interests of the feudal monarchies and merchant capital of Western Europe combined in order to colonize the Americas, the main focus of external interest (and concern) was the Middle East, North Africa, and India, collectively known as the Orient. Daniel has observed that "Europe's idea of the 'foreigner' was based for many formative centuries exclusively on the Arab world" (1975, 322). Thus, not only did Europeans create a discourse of an imagined Other at the edge of European civilization, but they created a discourse of a real Other represented as a result of conflicting material and political interests with a population that came to mark the boundary of Europe, spatially and in consciousness.

The European image of Islam and Muslims achieved a significant degree of coherence in the 12th and 13th centuries, although a number of key themes that recur through the centuries were evident much earlier (Daniel 1960, 275, 1975, 31–39). The Muslim Other was portrayed as barbaric, degenerate, and tyrannical, characteristics that were thought to be rooted in the character of Islam as a supposedly false and heretical theology. The object of much of the attack was the Prophet of Islam, Muhammad, who was represented as an impostor; his life as exemplifying violence and sexuality (Daniel 1960, 78, 107; Ruthven 1997, 101). These were not portrayed as purely personal failings. It was argued that the theology Muhammad created for his own ends embodied violence and sexuality, with the consequence that Muslims inevitably behaved in similar ways. Thus Islam was portrayed as founded on aggression and war, as spreading itself by the same means, and as permitting and encouraging polygamy, sodomy, and general sexual laxity. It was argued that Islam reproduced the idea of the "holy war" against all non-Muslims, in the course of which the latter would be either brutally murdered or enslaved, and a notion of Paradise as a garden of sexual delights and passions (e.g., Daniel 1960, 123–125,136–154; 1966, 5; 1975, 234, 243).

The equation of Islam with violence was sustained by a clerical agitation that culminated in the Crusades. Muslim occupation of the Holy Land was considered illegitimate, and, therefore, as evidence of aggression (Lewis 1982, 22). War against the Saracen to regain the Holy Land was justified theologically in the name of God, and as a means to recover the unity of Christendom. Muslim resistance to the European armies was interpreted as further evidence of an inherent tendency toward violence and cruelty, while identical acts of war by Christians were seen as entirely legitimate, even as means to glorify God (e.g., Daniel 1960, 109–113;1975, 111–139). It was not until the late 17th century that the Muslim world ceased to be perceived within Europe as an external threat (Harbsmeier 1985, 73), after which the stereotype of unrestrained Muslim sexuality—symbolized by belly dancers, harems, snake charmers, and degenerate sultans—predominated (Turner 1994, 98; Said 1995, 40, 182, 188 *et passim*). The perception of Islam as violent and threatening was revived toward the end of the 20th century (Halliday 1996; Said 1997; Commission on British Muslims and Islamophobia 1997; Brown 2000), particularly after four aircraft were hijacked and crashed in the USA on 11 September 2001.

EUROPEAN EXPANSION AND COLONIZATION

Once emergent European city- and nation-states began to expand their material and political boundaries to incorporate other parts of the world within a system of international trade (Braudel 1984, 89–174), subsequently linked with colonial settlement, the populations they confronted were within the arena of Europe in an economic and political sense, though not spatially. When colonization became an objective, a class of Europeans initiated direct relationships with indigenous populations, a contact increasingly structured by competition for land, the introduction of private property rights, the demand for a labour force, and the perceived obligation of conversion to Christianity. Collectively, these were embodied in the discourse of "civilization."

Europeans who travelled in pursuit of trade, military advantage, religious mission, or curiosity carried expectations derived from extant verbal and written accounts of the Other (e.g., Dickason 1984, 18, 80). They came therefore with intentions and objectives that influenced their perceptions of those populations with whom they came into contact, perceptions that were sustained and discursively reworked. Thus, Columbus reported finding "savage" but not "monstrous" people (Friedman 1981, 198). Representations based on the empiricism of direct experience permitted a transformation in the content of representations of the Other, but the existence of the Other as a mirror of what the European was not remained largely unquestioned. Travellers' accounts were published, for profit, education, and entertainment, with the result that representations of the Other circulated throughout Europe(e.g., Dickason 1984, 67). Significantly, travellers' sense of the normal served to identify the abnormal characteristics of people with whom contact was established and of their mode of life. Hence, with regard to Africa, Curtin has observed that "the reporting often stressed precisely those aspects of African life that were most repellent to the West and tended to submerge the indications of a common humanity" (Curtin 1965, 23). A negative representation of the Other therefore defined and legitimated the "positive" qualities of author and reader (cf. Febvre and Martin 1976, 281; Hakluyt 1972, 33).

After initial contact, more complex representations were constructed, including positive elements. For example, a respect developed for aspects of the life of Native North Americans, including their perceived strength and agility, and their hunting and fishing skills (Nash 1972, 68). The Caribs were represented as depraved by virtue of their supposed cannibalism, but were also attributed with courage and strength (Robe 1972, 45). For some observers, certain Indian populations were represented as living in a condition of original harmony and egalitarianism (Baudet 1976, 26–28, 35–36). Thus the existence of non-Europeans was interpreted as a measure of the loss within Europe of an earlier "golden age" or "paradise" (cf. Popkin 1974, 129; Baudet 1976, 10–11). This discourse served to identify the observers as living in an unnatural, depraved condition, desirous of rediscovering their ideal prelapsarian conditions. This supports the argument that the conception of the "noble savage" existed long before Rousseau (Symcox 1972, 227–228; Baudet 1976, 11; Friedman 1981, 163–177; Dickason 1984, 59, 81).

Nevertheless, the majority of descriptions in Hakluyt's collection of accounts of non-European peoples are pejorative. South American Indians were described as "a warlike kind of people" and "very ugly and terrible to behold" (Hakluyt 1972, 139), Indian Brahmins as "a kind of crafty people, worse than the Jews" (p. 259), the Javanese as "heathen" (p. 293), and the population of an island off the African coast as "treacherous" (p. 362). Hence, if there was no single representation, neither was there an equality of negative and positive meanings. European representations were hierarchically ordered around the view that Europeans were superior by virtue of their "civilization" and achievements (including world travel and trade): the condition of the Other was represented as proof of that interpretation.

These representations were instrumental. For example, Columbus initiated the idea that those Indians who were named Caribs were, by custom, eaters of human flesh and, by a process of linguistic transformation, this name gave rise to the label "cannibal." Spanish explorers and colonizers in the Caribbean and Mexico increasingly applied the term to peoples with whom they established contact, although in the written records of the period there is no firsthand witness account of human flesh being eaten. The increasing use of the term correlates with indigenous resistance to the Spanish presence, attempted military subjugation of indigenous peoples, and their induction into unfree labour (Sanders 1978, 101; Arens 1979, 44–77).

Thus, these representations refracted a purpose, as discovery was followed by settlement, and settlement by the introduction of systems of unfree labour (Miles 1987) to exploit the natural resources for the benefit of the European ruling classes. Contact and interaction did not occur in a neutral context, but in a context of conflicting interests and unequal military resources, usually effected by force. The European classes involved in this process (reconstructed representations of these indigenous populations, both to legitimate their actions and in response to their experience of those populations. Consequently, there was a complex interaction between class interests and empirical observation. The representations of the Other that resulted from this were neither absolutely homogeneous, nor static (see, for example, George 1958; Walvin 1986, 77), because colonization had neither a singular character nor a universal course, and because it had political and ideological repercussions in Europe.

For most of the 17th and 18th centuries, the alleged difference was explained in environmentalist terms (Barker 1978, 79). The physical appearance of the African, and specifically the colour of the African's skin, increased in significance as a sign of differentiation (Jordan 1968, 216–217, 512). By the late 18th century the claim that blackness was the result of God's curse was no longer considered satisfactory, and the argument that climate was the key determinant increased in significance (p. 525). Specifically it was proposed that the heat of the sun in tropical regions either burnt the skin, or caused it to change colour as protection against the heat. Additionally, some argued that once this transformation had occurred, blackness became an inherited characteristic (Curtin 1965, 40–41; Jordan 1968, 11; Barker 1978, 85). Climate was also believed to determine cultural characteristics. For example, the attributed quality of laziness was also explained by reference to the heat of the sun.

However, climate was not considered to be the sole environmental determinant. Samuel Stanhope Smith argued in 1787 that the human species had originated in Asia in a "civilized" form and that subsequent migrations were followed by "degeneration" into savagery and gradual alterations in physical appearance. The causes of these transformations were identified as climate, the state of society, and habits of living. Smith placed considerable emphasis upon the latter two factors and this environmentalist argument continued to predominate in American and European discourse in the late 18th century (Jordan 1968, 487, 513–515; also Popkin 1974, 139; Barker 1978, 52, 79).

Environmentalist arguments implied that the characteristics attributed to the African were, in principle, subject to modification. If the African was a savage, this was a human condition that could be improved (Barker 1978, 99; also Curtin 1965, 66). Hence Stanhope Smith, for example, claimed that Africans in America were becoming more capable of instruction and that their physical appearance was undergoing modification (Jordan 1968, 515–516). Environmentalism therefore sustained strategies for "civilizing" the African: heathenness and savagery could be changed through missionary work and plantation production (e.g., Curtin 1965, 123–139, 259–286). The idea of the "civilizing mission'" was particularly significant during the 19th century (Kiernan 1972, 24).

This discourse had implications for the economic role that many Africans were forced to perform in the Americas. African slavery in the Americas was justified, first, by the claim that Africans (unlike Europeans) were specifically suited to work under tropical conditions (Curtin 1961, 104; 1965, 116; Barker 1978, 61). The logic of environmentalism implied that this suitability could be acquired, although this seemed to be less readily accepted by Europeans concerning themselves, implying inconsistency in environmentalism as an explanation for the hypothesized differences between Europeans and Africans. This ambiguity was partially removed in the 19th century with the emergence of the discourse of "race." Second, it was justified by the argument that it enabled Africans to escape from savagery. Entry into slave relations of production permitted Africans to step along the road of "progress" toward "civilization," placing them initially in an economic position similar to the European poor (Kiernan 1972, 242; Barker 1978, 68, 151–152, 160, 198, also chap. 4).

THE SIGNIFICANCE OF SCIENCE

The idea of "race" took on a new meaning in Europe with the Enlightenment and the development of science from the late 18th century (Banton 1987, 28–64; see also Eze 1997). From this time, "race" increasingly came to refer to a biological type of human being, and science purported to demonstrate the number and characteristics of each "race," and a hierarchical relationship between them. Thus it was claimed that every human being either belonged to a "race" or was a product of several "races," and therefore exhibited the characteristics of that "race" or those "races," and that the biological characteristics of each "race" determined a range of psychological and social capacities by which they could be ranked.

Stated in its most extreme form, "race" was believed to determine economic and cultural characteristics and development (cf. Barzun 1938, 19–21; Banton 1977, 47). This was a discourse of "race" that may be described as biological determinism (cf. Gould 1984, 20; Rose et al. 1984, 3–15). Thereby, the Other was represented as biologically distinct, a "race" apart, with fixed capacities. There is now a considerable literature on the ideological career of the idea of "race" (e.g., Gossett 1965; Banton 1977, 1987; Stepan 1982; Augstein 1996), some aspects of which are particularly relevant to this study.

First, the scientific assertion of the existence of different biologically constituted "races" led to a clash with religious ideas about the nature and development of the human species. Biblical interpretation suggested that the human species was divinely created, and that all human beings, past and present, were descended from Adam and Eve. This implied some ultimate homogeneity of the human species. One way of harmonizing these assertions was to claim that God had responded to human sin by damnation: those damned, and their descendants, were marked by distinctive features (such as black skin). Another, with an equally long pedigree, placed less emphasis on divine intervention. This argument maintained that environmental factors (such as the influence of the sun) had modified the original and single biological form represented by Adam and Eve, creating a number of different types that were subsequently reproduced by hereditary means. Using this latter argument, many "race" scientists of the 18th and 19th centuries claimed that their explanation for "race" differentiation was consistent with Christian theology.

In the late 18th century, scientific analysis revived an objection that had been articulated in the 16th century by Hakluyt (see Sanders 1978, 223–224): that phenotypical features did not change when members of "races" moved to different geographical locations and were subjected to different environmental conditions. The example of Africans enslaved in the Americas was often cited to support this view, as was that of Europeans in the tropical colonies. The conclusion was that environmental factors, including climate, were incapable of altering the physical features of "race." The implication was that distinct "races" of human beings had always existed, and that "racial" hierarchy was therefore natural, inevitable, and unalterable. This assault on environmentalism led to a fundamental conflict with Christian theology (Stanton 1960, 69, 169; Haller 1971, 69–79; Stepan 1982, 36–46). The conclusions to which it gave rise were accorded even greater legitimacy as science occupied an increasingly ascendant position over theology. By the mid-19th century this theory of polygenism was dominant, and many of its key assumptions survived into the post-Darwinian era (Stocking 1968, 39, 45–46, 55).

Second, the scientific discourse of "race" did not replace earlier conceptions of the Other. Ideas of savagery, barbarism, and civilization predetermined the space that the idea of "race" occupied, but were themselves reconstituted by it. Thus, extant imagery was refracted through the representational prism of "race," and environmentalism declined in importance (Miles 1982, 111–112). For example, "civilization' was initially considered attainable by all human beings, including the most "savage," given sufficient time and assistance, but this was challenged in the late 19th century by the scientific idea that the human species was divided into permanent and discrete biological groups. As a result, savagery became a fixed condition of the "Negro" or African "race," a product of a small brain, and civilization became an attribute of large-brained "white" people (Stocking 1968, 35–37,121–122).

Third, in generating and reproducing the idea of "race," many scientific writers drew upon and criticized each other's work, seeking new methods of measurement and solutions to emergent anomalies. The science of phrenology originated in the work of Gall and Spurzheim in Germany and was developed by George Combe in Scotland (Gossett 1965, 71–72), a friend of Samuel Morton, an American, who published *Crania Americana* in 1839 and *Crania Aegyptiaca* in 1844 (Gould 1984, 50–69). The cephalic index (a measurement of skulls that divided the length of the skull by the breadth) was invented by Anders Retzius in Sweden (Gossett 1965, 76). F. Tiedeman, a German anatomist, measured brains in order to establish differences between "races," with his results stimulating a critical reply from Josiah Nott in the United States (p. 77). With George Gliddon, Nott had a major impact on "race" theory with *Types of Mankind,* first published in 1854, which appeared in at least nine editions before the end of the century (Gossett 1965, 65; Banton 1977, 50–52). Thus the increasingly international character of the scientific enterprise facilitated the formulation of the discourse of "race." Consequently, the scientific idea of "race" had a widespread circulation, and its proponents represented *various* Others (Africans, North American Indians, Indians) as "racially" different and inferior to "Caucasians."

Fourth, although the *ideas* of biological type and hierarchy remained constant, the *forms* of classification and the *content* of attribution changed over time. For most of the late 18th and early 19th centuries, "race" classifications were based on skin colour, hair type, and nose shape, but there was increasing emphasis on the dimensions of the skull (Benedict 1983, 22). This became prominent during the early 19th century (Curtin 1965, 366), and considerable effort was expended in assessing, for example, cranial capacity, facial angle, and cranial index. Indeed, there was much debate about the relative validity of these different measures. The science of "race" therefore underwent a complex evolution. In part, this complexity was due to its essential error: as each attempt at classification broke down under the weight of logical inconsistency and empirical evidence, a new classification was formulated. It was also due to increasing sophistication of measurement (Stocking 1968, 57).

Fifth, those who formulated the idea considered themselves to be members of a "race," but they also identified a hierarchy of "races" within Europe. Efforts were made in the late 19th century, for example, to identify the different "races" of which the British population was composed, using hair and eye colour and skull measurements (Beddoe 1885). Concerning Europe as a whole, various classifications were devised, the most common being a distinction between Teutonic (or Nordic), Mediterranean, and Alpine "races" (Ripley 1900, 103–130). In the USA, this classification was combined with an argument that human intelligence was fixed and hereditary in order to produce a hierarchy of acceptable and unacceptable immigrants (Kamin 1977, 30–51; Gould 1984, 146–233).

Within Europe, representations of the Other as an inferior "race" focused *inter alia* on the Irish (Curtis 1968, 1971) and Jews (Mosse 1978). This was sustained partly by claiming biological superiority for the Nordic "race." In Germany, Giinther (1970) interpreted European history in a book titled *The Racial Elements of European History* (first published in 1927) using the scientific idea of "race" to refer to human groups with distinct and measurable physical and mental characteristics. He identified the Nordic "race" as especially creative, with a need for conquest, a special aptitude for military science, and a low crime rate, and he feared social decay in Europe as a result of "the running dry of the blood of the ... Nordic race" (1970, 198). Portentously, he stated that "the question put to us is whether we have courage enough to make ready for future generations a world cleansing itself racially and eugenically" (p. 267). Giinther was only one of a large number of scholars (and activists) who used a scientific discourse of "race" to assert a superiority of the Nordic "race" and inferiority of Jews (Mosse 1978, 77–93, 113–127).

Sixth, the scientific conception of "race" has been shown to be mistaken, although a number of scientists continue to assert its key ideas in various forms. The exposure of the error had a long genesis that began with the work of Charles Darwin and finished with the emergence of population genetics. The first step was the formulation of a theory of evolution that questioned the validity of the idea of fixed and permanent biological species. However, when the human species was located in evolutionary theory in Europe in the latter half of the 19th century, the idea of "race" was retained, the argument being that each "race" could be ranked on an evolutionary scale. Thus, what came to be known as Social Darwinism (Jones 1980; Clark 1984, 1988) asserted that there was a struggle for survival among different human "races," in the course of which those with lesser intelligence or capacity for "civilization" would disappear. "Disappearance" was evidence of a "natural" inability to evolve. Thus, evolutionary theory was developed initially in a way that endorsed the idea of discrete biological "races," and the classifiers of the human species continued to produce their typologies (Haller 1971, 121–152; Banton 1977, 89–100; Stepan 1982, 47–110).

A further decisive development was the identification of the statistical limitations of phenotypical measurement by those who continued to defend the utility of such measurement. The work of Boas in the early 20th century is particularly important because he also demonstrated the influence of the social environment on physiological features by use of the cephalic index (e.g., Boas 1940, 60–75). Boas believed in the existence of biological "races," but rejected the argument that they were fixed because of evidence that phenotypical features such as head form responded to environmental influences (Stocking 1968, 170–180). He also argued that, although the world's population could be divided into "races" using phenotypical criteria, each such category contained within it a range of variation that overlapped with the variation of any other category: "With regard to many characteristics of this kind, we find that the difference between the averages of different races is insignificant as compared to the range of variability that occurs within each race" (Boas 1940, 42). So, although two populations may have a different average height, it does not follow that any two individuals selected from these populations will demonstrate the same difference. In other words, group differences do not correspond to individual differences (cf. Stocking 1968, 192–193).

The full implications of Darwin's evolutionary theory could only be explored with the emergence of a science of genetics that identified the biological basis of evolutionary processes. Genetics shifted attention partly away from phenotypical differences such as skin colour and analyzed biological features that were not evident to the naked eye and that, in a complex interaction with the environment, determined biological changes in the human species. It was generally concluded after the Second World War that the scientific conception of "race," grounded in the idea of fixed typologies and based upon phenotypical features, did not have any scientific utility. Moreover, the evidence showed no causal relationship between physical or genetic characteristics and cultural characteristics. Genetics demonstrated that "race," as defined by scientists from the late 18th century, had no scientifically verifiable referent (Boyd 1950; Montagu 1964, 1972).

REFERENCES

Arens, W. 1979. *The Man-Eating Myth: Anthropology and Anthropophagy.* New York: Oxford University Press.

Augstein, H.F., ed. 1996. *Race: the Origins of an Idea.* Bristol: Thoemmes Press.

Baldry, H.C. 1965. *The Unity of Mankind in Greek Thought.* Cambridge: Cambridge University Press.

————. 1977. *The Idea of Race*. London: Tavistock.

————. 1987. *Racial Theories*. Cambridge: Cambridge University Press.

Barker, A.J. 1978. *The African Link: British Attitudes to the Negro in the Era of the Atlantic Slave Trade, 1550–1807*. London: Frank Cass.

Barzun, J. 1938. *Race: A Study in Modern Superstition*. London: Methuen.

————. 1965. *Race: A Study in Superstition*. New York: Harper and Row.

Baudet, H. 1976 *Paradise on Earth: Some Thoughts on European Images of Non-European Man*. Westport: Greenwood Press.

Beddoe, J. 1885. *The Races of Britain: A Contribution to the Anthropology of Western Europe*. Bristol: J.W. Arrowsmith.

Benedict, R. 1983. *Race and Racism*. London: Routledge and Kegan Paul.

Boas, F. 1940. *Race, Culture and Language*. New York: Free Press.

Boyd, W.C. 1950. *Genetics and the Races of Man: An Introduction to Modern Physical Anthropology*. Oxford: Basil Blackwell.

Braudel, F. 1984. *Civilisation and Capitalism: 15th to 18th Century*. Vol. 3, *The Perspective of the World*. London: Collins.

Brown, C. 1984. *Black and White Britain: The Third PSI Study*. London: Heinemann.

Clark, L.L. 1984. *Social Darwinism in France*. Birmingham: University of Alabama Press.

————. 1988. "Le Darwinisme Social en France." *La Recherche* 19:192–200. Commission on British Muslims and Islamophobia.

————. 1997. *Islamophobia: A Challenge For Us All*. London: Runnymede Trust.

Curtin, P.D. 1965. *The Image of Africa: British Ideas and Action, 1780–1850*. London: Macmillan.

Daniel, N. 1960. *Islam and the West: The Making of an Image*. Edinburgh: Edinburgh University Press.

————. 1966. *Islam, Europe and Empire*. Edinburgh: Edinburgh University Press.

————. 1975. *The Arabs and Medieval Europe*. London: Longman.

Davis, D.B. 1984. *Slavery and Human Progress*. New York: Oxford University Press.

Dickason, O.P. 1984. *The Myth of the Savage and the Beginnings of French Colonialism in the Americas*. Edmonton: University of Alberta Press.

Eze, E.C., ed. 1997. *Race and the Enlightenment: A Reader*. Oxford: Blackwell.

Febvre, L., and H.-J. Martin. 1976. *The Coming of the Book: The Impact of Printing, 1450–1800*. London: New Left Books.

Friedman, J.B. 1981. *The Monstrous Races in Medieval Art and Thought*. Cambridge, Mass.: Harvard University Press.

George, K. 1958. "The Civilised West Looks at Primitive Africa: 1400–1800." *Isis* 49:62–72.

Gossett, T.F. 1965. *Race: The History of an Idea in America*. New York: Schocken Books.

Gould, S.J. 1984. *The Mismeasure of Man*. Harmondsworth: Penguin.

Gunther, H.F.K. 1970. *The Racial Elements of European History*. New York: Kennikat Press.

Hakluyt, R. 1972. *Voyages and Discoveries*. Harmondsworth: Penguin.

Haller, J.S. 1971. *Outcasts from Evolution: Scientific Attitudes of Racial Inferiority, 1859–1900*. Urbana: University of Illinois Press.

Halliday, F. 1996. *Islam and the Myth of Confrontation*. London: I.B. Tauris.

Harbsmeier, M. 1985. "Early Travels to Europe: Some Remarks on the Magic of Writing." In *Europe and its Others*. Vol. l, ed. F. Baker, 72–88. Colchester: Essex University Press.

Jones, G. 1980. *Social Darwinism in English Thought: The Interaction between Biological and Social Theory*. Brighton: Harvester Press.

Jordan, W. 1968. *White over Black: American Attitudes toward the Negro, 1550–1812*. Chapel Hill: University of North Carolina Press.

Kamin, L.J. 1977. *The Science and Politics of I.Q.* Harmondsworth: Penguin.

Kiernan, V. 1972. *The Lords of Human Kind: European Attitudes to the Outside World in the Imperial Age.* Harmondsworth: Penguin.

Lewis, B. 1982. *The Muslim Discovery of Europe.* London: Weidenfeld and Nicolson.

Miles, R. 1982. *Racism and Migrant Labour: A Critical Text.* London: Routledge and Kegan Paul.

———. 1987. *Capitalism and Unfree Labour: Anomaly or Necessity?* London: Tavistock.

Montagu, A. 1972. *Statement on Race.* London: Oxford University Press.

———. ed. 1964. *The Concept of Race.* New York: Free Press.

Moscovici, S. 1982. "The Coming Era of Representations." In *Cognitive Analysis of Social Behavior,* ed. J.-P. Codol and J.-P. Leyens, 115–150. The Hague: Martinus Nijhoff.

———. 1984. "The Phenomenon of Social Representations." In *Social Representations,* ed. R.M. Farr and S. Moscovici, 3–69. Cambridge: Cambridge University Press.

Mosse, C.L. 1978. *Toward the Final Solution: A History of European Racism.* London: Dent and Sons.

Nash, G.B. 1972. "The Image of the Indian in the Southern Colonial Mind." In *The Wild Man within: An Image in Western Thought from the Renaissance to Romanticism,* ed. E. Dudley and M.E. Novak, 55–86. Pittsburgh: University of Pittsburgh Press.

Popkin, R.H. 1974. "The Philosophical Basis of Modern Racism." In *Philosophy and the Civilizing Arts,* ed. C. Walton and J.P. Anton, 126–165. Athens: Ohio University Press.

Ripley, W.Z. 1900. *The Races of Europe: A Sociological Study.* London: Kegan Paul, Trench, Trubner and Co.

Robe, S.L. 1972. "Wild Men and Spain's Brave New World." In *The Wild Man Within: An Image in Western Thought from the Renaissance to Romanticism,* ed. E. Dudley and M.E. Novak. Pittsburgh: University of Pittsburgh Press. 39-54

Rose, S., L.J. Kamin, and R.C. Lewontin. 1984. *Not in Our Genes: Biology,Ideology and Human Nature.* Harmondsworth: Penguin.

Ruthven, M. 1997. *Islam: A Very Short Introduction.* Oxford: Oxford University Press.

Said, E.W. 1995. *Orientalism: Western Conceptions of the Orient.* London: Penguin.

———. 1997. *Covering Islam.* London: Vintage.

Sanders, R. 1978. *Lost Tribes and Promised Lands: The Origins of American Racism.* Boston: Little, Brown and Co.

Seton-Watson, H. 1977. *Nations and States: An Enquiry into the Origins of Nations and the Politics of Nationalism.* London: Methuen.

Snowden, F.M. 1970. *Blacks in Antiquity: Ethiopians in the Creco-Roman Experience.* Cambridge, Mass.: Harvard University Press.

———. 1983. *Before Colour Prejudice: The Ancient View of Blacks.* Cambridge, Mass.: Harvard University Press.

Stanton, W. 1960. *The Leopard's Spots: Scientific Attitudes toward Race in America, 1815–59.* Chicago: University of Chicago Press.

Stepan, N. 1982. *The Idea of Race in Science: Great Britain, 1900–1960.* London: Macmillan.

Stocking, C.W. 1968. *Race, Culture and Evolution.* New York: Free Press.

Symcox, C. 1972. "The Wild Man's Return: The Enclosed Vision of Rousseau's Discourses." In *The Wild Man within: An Image in Western Thought from the Renaissance to Romanticism,* ed. E. Dudley and M.E. Novak, 223–248. Pittsburgh: University of Pittsburgh Press.

Turner, B.S. 1994. *Orientalism, Postmodernism and Globalism.* London: Routledge.

———. 1995. *Historical Capitalism with Capitalist Civilisation.* London: Verso.

Walvin, J. 1973. *Black and White: The Negro and English Society 1555–1945.* London: Allen Lane.

———. 1986. *England, Slaves and Freedom, 1776–1838.* London: Macmillan.

CHAPTER 2

THE SOCIAL CONSTRUCTION OF PRIMORDIAL IDENTITIES

ANTON ALLAHAR

INTRODUCTION

There is a curious tension that may be observed in the makeup of the human being. It is a tension between a restless curiosity and desire to explore the unfamiliar, on the one hand, and a conservatism born of insecurity, on the other. While humans are easily bored with the routine and repetitive aspects of daily living, and are often moved to seek out that which is new or different, they also seem to cherish the personal and psychological comforts that come from being rooted in the familiar and the predictable (whether emotional, physical, or social) terrain of "home." This is the principal source of their identity, which Anthony Smith describes as "a matter of social and spiritual location. For in that location lies a sense of security" (1984, 97).

For many those roots are merely a belief, a dream, a fiction, an invention, as captured in the very titles of such books as Benedict Anderson's *Imagined Communities* (1983) and Eric Hobsbawm and Terence Ranger's *The Invention of Tradition* (1983). But perhaps none captures the sentiments and yearning for "home roots" better than Alex Haley's (1976) enormously popular work of fiction, *Roots*. This book and the films it inspired gave to young black Americans a sense of pride and belonging (born of anger) to an imagined community where myths and traditions of an idyllic past in a racially homogeneous and peaceful Africa were invented. It served literally to manufacture an idea of "home" as a place of spiritual escape or refuge, all with a view to combatting the alienation, poverty, and disenfranchisement that had become the condition of so many black Americans in the aftermath of slavery.

In a period that is witnessing the dissolution of old political blocs, the economic decline of the West, ethnic cleansing, the redrawing of national boundaries, and the emergence of new ethnic states globally, political theorists have not yet come up with a coherent explanation of the forces at play. Is it indeed the vindication of Marx? Are the class contradictions engendered by capital now too deep to be contained? Are these the last days of capitalism as we know it? Or, given the spectacular failure of socialism in the USSR and Eastern Europe, have we moved beyond Marx and class to a situation in which class consciousness and class identity have given way to supposedly more natural and long-standing bases of identity and political behaviour: ethno-racial, national, religious, tribal?

The challenge to social theory and praxis, then, is one that pits class consciousness against ethno-racial consciousness to determine which is more fundamental and consequential for analyzing and explaining social and political action. Stated differently, is class consciousness "true consciousness" and ethno-racial consciousness false or epiphenomenal? Or is it the other way around? In answering these questions the present chapter will address the presumed naturalness of human roots (primordialism) versus their social constructedness (structuralism), and it will confine the debate between primordial and structural identities to one between race and ethnicity, on the one hand, and class, on the other, with a view to reconciling them theoretically.

PRIMORDIALISM AND "NATURAL" COMMUNITY

The term "primordialism" or "primordial attachment" will be understood in two senses: the hard and the soft. The hard version of the term holds that human beings are attached to one another (and their communities of origin) virtually by mutual ties of blood that somehow condition reciprocal feelings of trust and acceptance. It is the type of attachment that siblings or parents and their offspring are said to experience, and implies an unquestioned loyalty or devotion purely on the basis of the intimacy of the tie. In this sense primordial attachment is natural, automatic, and supposedly prior to explicitly social interaction.

The soft meaning of the term stresses the social, non-biological bases of attachment and draws attention to the importance of interpretation and symbolic meaning in the individual's social organization of his or her life. In other words, feelings of intense intimacy and belonging do not have to be mediated by blood. They can be socially constructed as in the case of fictive kinship or love for one's country, and excite in adherents the same passion and devotion found among blood relatives.[1] Understood in the soft sense, then, primordial attachment depends on the circumstances at hand and understands that socio-political identities are situational, not biological; flexible, not fixed. All such identities, however, speak to the gregariousness of human beings and their decided preference for group membership as opposed to social rejection or isolation.

It is not accidental, therefore, that human beings should feel ties to their parents, siblings, relatives, community, place of birth, or even country of birth. Such ties are a complex mix of myth, belief, emotion, and the realities of physical existence. As Steven Grosby argues,

> we attribute the properties which we see as constitutive of the family to the larger collectivity ... use of terms like home in 'homeland', father in 'fatherland', or mother in 'motherland'[2]. Primordial properties are seen as fundamental in the larger collectivity as well as in the family. (Grosby 1994, 165)

Known generally as primordial ties, such attachments are the stuff of life as humans go about their daily affairs and seek to impart meaning to what they do. Such largely symbolic meaning is seldom explicitly articulated, but is nonetheless shared by all members of a given community. So at a certain level those people, places, and things that are closest, that sustain physical and emotional life, come to acquire a power and control over humans that they elevate to the level of the sacred, in much the same way as they develop and maintain their beliefs about God and religion.

The often unquestioning devotion that follows is to be seen as an acknowledgement of the vulnerability of the individual human being, and the fact that his or her survival is dependent on forces larger than him or her: "One's parents give one life. The locality in which one is born and in which one lives nurtures one; it provides the food necessary for one's life" (Grosby 1994, 169). Thus, Edward Shils wrote earlier of the prominence and ubiquity of self-identification "by kinship connection and territorial location"; but, he charges, such self-identification must be related to "man's need to be in contact with the point and moment of his origin and to experience a sense of affinity with those who share that origin" (1968, 4).

CLASSICAL VIEWS ON COMMUNITY AND BELONGING

One of the clearest descriptions and analyses of the origins of social attachment or belonging is presented by Emile Durkheim in *The Division of Labour in Society*. In his treatment of simple or "mechanical solidarity," Durkheim emphasizes the primacy of group or community sentiments over the individual, and introduces the notion of "collective consciousness" as the primary source of identity. He talks of a social solidarity through similarity or sameness and writes that "we all know that a social cohesion exists where cause can be traced to a certain conformity of each individual consciousness to the common type." Further, we are told, the similarity that is rooted in the collective consciousness automatically leads members to "love their country ... to like one another, seeking one another out *in preference to foreigners*" (1984, 60; emphasis added).

In this context, "foreigners" are best understood as belonging to the realm of "the other," real or imagined, as discussed by Robert Miles (1989, 11–30); fear or intolerance of "foreigners as others," who are seen as different or strange, is also at the base of xenophobic feelings that result in their automatic exclusion from one's community. On the basis of Gergen's review of the psychological literature on perception and aversion, Kenneth Gergen tells us, "The other appears strange, alien, and unknown.... The common reaction to the unknown, the unpredictable, or the strange is aversion" (1968, 116). Following Durkheim, then, a total identification with the whole, born perhaps of xenophobia and individual insecurity, leads to the suppression of egoism or individualism, and binds the individual directly to his or her community or society. As a consequence, members are moved to react passionately against anything that threatens its solidarity or cohesiveness:

The solidarity that derives from similarities is at its maximum when the collective consciousness completely envelops our total consciousness, coinciding with it at every point. At that moment our individuality is zero (Durkheim 1984, 84).

PRIMORDIALISM: BEYOND BLOOD

The suggestion here is that the primordial tie of blood is not the only type of primordial tie that exists. Ethnic, religious, national, political, and other forms of identity or attachment not necessarily based on blood have been known to elicit high levels of uncritical devotion and commitment among adherents. This is why some say primordial attachments are blind and even irrational (Bonacich 1980, 10), or, according to Orlando Patterson, purely emotional and belonging "centrally to that area of experience which Weber designated as non-rational" (1983, 26).

But to argue that some aspect of behaviour is irrational is not to say that it does not exist or is not real, since the consequences are quite real for those whom they touch, whether or not the latter accept the definition of the situation adopted by those who initiate the behaviour in question. Thus, whether or not a blood tie actually exists between a given person and his or her community is less important than the fact that he or she believes it does and acts in accordance with such a belief (Allahar 1993, 46–47; 52). Grosby says it well when he observes that primordiality only asserts that human beings classify themselves and others in accordance with primordial criteria. It does not say that the referents of the criteria necessarily exist in the form in which those who refer to them believe (Grosby 1994, 168).

Following Shils, Clifford Geertz attempts to systematize the treatment of the concept primordialism and to elaborate its meaning. He speaks of "a corporate sentiment of oneness" and "a consciousness of kind" (1973, 260, 307), which can be seen to stem from the sharing of a common geographical space, common ancestors, common culture, and common language and religion, and which in turn produce "congruities of blood, speech and custom." Such congruities, Geertz argues,

> are seen to have an *ineffable*, and at times overpowering, coerciveness in and of themselves. One is bound to one's kinsman, one's neighbour, one's fellow believer, ipso facto; as a result not merely of personal affection, practical necessity, common interest, or incurred obligation, but at least *in general part* by virtue of some *unaccountable* absolute import attributed to the tie itself. (1973, 259; emphasis added)

This is a crucial and powerful summary statement that has been the target of much criticism recently (Bonacich 1980; Mason 1986; Hoben and Hefner 1990; Eller and Coughlan 1993). The critics, however, while pointing out some important flaws in the details of the primordialist argument, are unable to dismiss its general claim. Bonacich, for example, identifies the creation of a new (ethnic) group such as Asian-Americans, the combination of two previously warring and hostile nations, and underscores the social as opposed to the primordial identity held by Asian-Americans (1980, 11). Similarly, Hoben and Hefner challenge the notion of primordial identities as fixed or given, since at the very least they are "renewed, modified and remade in each generation. Far from being self-perpetuating, they require creative effort and investment" (1990, 18). Eller and Coughlan attack (a) the a priori "givenness" of primordial identity, (b) its ineffability or inexplicability, and (c) its emotional or affective content (1993, 187–192).

The first of these criticisms dealing with the "a priority" of primordial sentiments may be responded to along with those of Bonacich and Hoben and Hefner, by pointing out the essential correctness of the criticism if "primordial" is interpreted according to what I call the hard sense or meaning of the term: original, pre-existing, prior, first. It is possible, however, to apply a softer understanding of the term, which stresses its symbolic nature as opposed to its absolute, inflexible, scientifically proven existence or origins. This is what Weber alludes to when he speaks of ideas becoming effective forces in history, and it matters little, Miles points out, if those ideas are proven false:

> Scientifically discredited notions can have a life of their own, a relative autonomy. But ... it is not being suggested that their continued existence is not without explanation. (1982, 19)

Hence, the soft approach to primordial identity and attachment as socially constructed reality ought not to be difficult to grasp. As far as Bonacich goes, surely the newness of the Asian-American ethnic group will mean literally that its origins as a distinct group with a *sui generis* identity are also quite recent, and that the attachments of its members may indeed not be as deep as those of older, more established ethnic or other groups. Nor is there a rule that states that all ethnic groups, old and new, must have primordial links with the same degree of intensity among their members; or that symbolic identity is equally useful to all groups and individuals at all times. And certainly the soft approach to defining primordialism can accommodate the objections of Hoben and Hefner, as well as the "a priority" concern raised by Eller and Coughlan; for in this rendering social reality is seen as an entirely socially negotiated matter.

On the question of the ineffability of primordial ties, the latter authors seem to answer their own criticism by acknowledging the fact that "social actors are often unable to explain their feelings and behaviours, at least not in a sociologically interesting and useful way; there is nothing surprising in that" (1993, 190). Since not everyone is a sociologist, however, or agrees on what is sociologically interesting, and since large numbers of people behave as if their links to their kin and other primary groups were ineffable, the ineffability of those ties are real for them; and this is what informs the social meanings that underpin their social actions in their worlds: "Blood is thicker than water" seems to be sufficient justification for most people to rally to the side of their kin, whether real or imagined, whenever the latter is threatened.

So inability to explain some emotional attraction or attachment does not mean that that attraction or attachment does not exist. Related to this, Eller and Coughlan voice an objection to using the term "primordial," which they describe as "unanalytical and vacuous ... unsociological and thoroughly unscientific" and advocate "dropping it from the sociological lexicon" (1993, 183–184) because it has come to be equated with the emotional and because to discuss emotions as having primordial bases smacks of socio-biology and genetic programming:

> If bonds simply are, and if they are to have any source at all, then they must have a genetic source. Sociobiological explanations thus become, curiously, the last bastion of any kind of analytic enterprise.... (1993, 192)

The response to this criticism is quite straightforward. Human beings are emotional beings and they do have genetic makeups. Unlike lower forms of animals, however, they are often able to control their emotions and impulses, and transcend or even alter aspects of their genetic makeup. And in the same way that the feminists have successfully argued that biology is not destiny, that culture and social learning can overlay biological and natural urges, so, too, primordially based emotions and sentiments need not be seen as absolute, rigid, and inflexible—hence the above call for the softer use of the term. For situationally created identities can and do include primordial ones whenever social actors claim long-standing attachments to groups and communities of feeling and meaning, which in their estimation require no elaborate explanation or justification, and when those claims serve to inform their social actions.

This is what Geertz seemed to imply, for in his own elaboration of the concept he is clear to point out that the strength of primordial attachments or bonds is subjective and varies with person, time, and place. Also, following Shils, he invests those bonds with religious contents that *"seem* to flow more from a sense of natural—some would say spiritual—affinity than from social interaction" (1973, 260; emphasis added). The insistence on the naturalness of primordial ties as opposed to their generation in the process of social interaction is unfortunate, confusing, and somewhat contradictory. And this is precisely what opens up the argument to so much criticism on the grounds that primordial attachments are absolute, underived, and given, so to speak, from time immemorial. On the other hand, use of the word "seem" suggests a less-than-inflexible stand on Geertz's part, an attempt to introduce the element of unpredictability and inconsistency that may stem from human choice and human error:

> The power of the "givens" of place, tongue, blood, looks, and way-of-life to shape an individual's notion of who, at bottom, he is and with whom, indissolubly, he belongs is rooted in the non-rational foundations of personality. (1973, 277)

Indeed, and this is a point too often missed in critiques of Shils and Geertz, their comments were directed at those who lived in the colonies and other less developed countries and regions of the world. This is particularly true in the case of Geertz, who was clearly making recommendations to the leaders in those countries and offering advice on what needed to be done as their countries achieved modern statehood and began to experiment with national and civil politics. Plainly eschewing any notion of the primordial as genetically or biologically fixed, then, Shils writes that "in nationality the primordial element begins to recede" (1968, 4), and Geertz cautions that

> what the new states—or their leaders—must somehow contrive to do as far as primordial attachments are concerned is not, as they have so often tried to do, wish them out of existence by belittling them or even denying their reality.... They must reconcile them with the emerging civil order by divesting them of their legitimizing force ... by neutralizing the apparatus of the state in relationship to them, and by channeling discontent arising out of their dislocation into properly political rather than parapolitical forms of expression. (1973, 277)

If nothing else, this acknowledges and speaks directly to the social and political construction of primordial sentiments (Horowitz 1975, 133). They do exist, particularly in the colonial and newly independent countries, but they are not insurmountable. And the power differentials between the leaders and the masses in those countries must take account of the old primordial bases on which the new political realities will be constructed. They must begin from the subjective and irrational meanings that individuals use to make sense of their worlds; and if they happen to be fictitious, mythical, and primordial, then so be it.

THE CHALLENGES TO PRIMORDIALISM: CLASS AND MODERNITY

While primordial sentiments of village, clan, tribe, and kin formed the basis of much social action in mechanical and gemeinschaft-type communities, most commentators, even those who do not like the term or incorporate it into their analyses, seem to agree that the exigencies of modern living would eliminate the need for, and the utility of, any such sentiments. The idea is that the generalized adoption of the nuclear-family type, the growth of individualism, bureaucratic rationalism, increases in geographical and social mobility, the appearance of cosmopolises and exposure to culturally plural encounters, and the advent of modernity and post-industrialism generally (Bell 1975, 167) would militate against the persistence of primordial identities. Indeed, as survival in modern society increasingly demands rational and calculated behaviour, new forms of identity could be expected to supersede primordial ones: class, political (ideological), occupational, religious, national, and even gender.

Of interest here is the fact that these new identities are virtually all achieved and socially constructed, as opposed to the primordial ones, which were seen largely to be ascribed. The point is, though, that whether achieved or ascribed, human beings are gregarious and choose to belong to groups, collectivities, and bodies through which they derive security and from which they develop an identity. Thus, in societies where the division of labour is minute, where organic solidarity prevails, where social mobility is widespread, and individualism is the norm, it is expected that achieved identities will be most salient. This is what Milton Gordon referred to in the context of the U.S. as the "liberal expectancy thesis," whereby race relations in that country would become normalized as part of "a call to the conscience of America" (1975, 88). As social institutions acknowledged and responded to the dictates of modern living, human beings were expected to opt for rational forms of attachment such as class, as opposed to some other irrational primordial identity (e.g., race), since class affiliation would be more likely to offer the opportunities and protections that village and tribe offered in pre-modem societies.

The proletarianization of the bulk of the population in modern, capitalist societies means that wages and secure employment will be the principal determiners of one's life chances and lifestyle. In the contest between capital and labour, for example, the unprotected, non-unionized worker has a great deal more to worry about than his or her membership in an extended family, neighbourhood association, or racially constituted group.[3] Therefore, given the social and political climate of modern societies, where ascribed characteristics such as race and national origin are not seen as acceptable, or even legal, bases for stratification, the more rational embrace of a situational identity such as class can be understood; class position is said to be achieved. In such a context, where one supposedly chooses one's position in the social hierarchy, class inequality is viewed as more just than racial or other forms of inequality. Further, ideologically speaking, in a society that embraces the puritanical ideals of hard work and sacrifice, even a humble or lower-class position could be made to appear virtuous; it is not difficult, Smith tells us, to "find an affirmation of lowly origins as a legitimation of status," nor is it considered embarrassing "to trace one's ancestry to the peasantry, the working class or kidnapped slaves" (1984, 97). In a contemporary industrial setting, then, class emerges as a rallying point for identity.

Certainly it was felt by Marxists that in the struggle to overthrow capitalism, (proletarian) class identity or consciousness would prevail over other types of (primordial) identities (Glazer and Moynihan 1975, 7, 15). The homogenizing impact of the factory experience and wage slavery were supposed to provide the means by which workers everywhere would be made to recognize their class interests vis-à-vis capital and unite against its exploitive and alienating forces. Forms of identity and consciousness that were not based on class were dismissed as divisive of workers; as false consciousness (Parkin 1979a and 1979b; Hall 1980; Solomos 1986).

If one looks at the political history of the 20th century it becomes clear that the Marxist expectations around class were vindicated. In several countries, segments of the working class and the peasantry came together to advance class claims and successfully brought about revolutionary changes aimed at bettering the conditions under which they lived and worked. As a matter of fact, appeals to class solidarity under the rubric of socialism have proved more successful in this century than any other appeals and attempts to mobilize human populations anywhere. The success of socialism, as measured by the social benefits that have accrued to workers as a class (health care, education, employment, housing), has not been equalled by any other social movement based on sentimental appeals to race, tribe, nation, or religion. Class identity, then, as it has become crystallized and sharpened under capitalism, seems able to transcend other forms of political identities as a meaningful basis for social action.

AFTER CLASS

But now that class, in the analytical sense, occupies less prominence in the public mind, and given what has been described as the gregariousness of humans and their clear preference for social acceptance over rejection, around what new bases of identity can people be expected to rally? The ubiquity of political chaos and bloody struggles for self-determination around the globe today are increasingly finding their attendant class and economic dimensions overshadowed by the more popularized and visible primordial concerns of race, ethnicity, tribe, and nation. Contemporary manifestations include: ethnic cleansing in Bosnia, Rwanda, and Burundi; neo-Nazi movements in Europe and the United States; racial and tribal warfare in South Africa and Yugoslavia; vicious ethno-religious warfare in the Middle East, Northern Ireland, and India; ethno-national threats to divide Canada, among many others. And while all of these many have fundamental economic and class explanations at their base, the fact remains that at the surface they are popularly portrayed as ethno-racial and are accepted as such both by direct participants and by the public at large. In other words, as long as such conflicts and the sentiments underlying them are defined and accepted as primordial in nature they become real to their participants and very real in their consequences.

This reassertion of persistent, primordial identities forms part of what Dahrendorf describes as a process of "refeudalization" (in Glazer and Moynihan 1975, 16), and what Harold Isaacs calls "a massive retribalization running sharply counter to all the globalizing effects of modern technology and communications" (1975, 30). Ethnicity is a case in point, and as ethnic groups begin to become significant transnational actors, whether legitimately or through acts of terrorism, the hope of modern society's doing away with primordial identities is fading away fast. John Stack Jr. writes that ethnicity today, in both developed and developing societies, provides a "sense of belonging and/or peoplehood ... reinforced by racial, religious, linguistic and cultural differences" (1981, 18). In addition, because modem societies are so large, and because they foster social relations that are increasingly impersonal and superficial, ethnicity fulfills "the need to escape the alienation and rootlessness of modern life ... [f]ulfills fundamental needs for a communal identity and serves as ... a means of gaining place or advantage in advanced industrial societies" (pp. 26–27).

Or as Patterson argues, the loss of community, coupled with the entrenchment of individualism and materialism today, has produced in the average person "an acute sense of loss, a feeling of being cut off from all roots, and of powerlessness, as a result of the atomization and apparent heartlessness of modern mass society" (1983, 33).

It is to developments such as these that one might trace the return in some areas to embracing community-type activities and all the apparently anachronistic primordial attachments that they suggest. For example, current attempts at re-establishing and even reinventing racial, ethnic, national, cultural, religious, and other socio-political identities have produced the highly charged climate of political correctness and all the divisive consequences that have accompanied it. For what is being sought is the imposition of forms of legality, of thought, behaviour, and expectations, on a societal base that was geared to modernity, and which just cannot accommodate all these seemingly atavistic and contradictory demands in a smooth manner.

But there are those who will find this too strong a characterization. Commenting on the English-speaking Caribbean, for example, Lloyd Best argues that class has always been wholly inappropriate for analyzing inter-group relations in such an ethnically diverse region (in Oxaal 1975, 45), and he speaks of race and nationality as "transcendental bases of solidarity" (1992, 8). While the picture of social and ethnic stratification painted by Best is the old, familiar one associated with colonial and post-colonial societies, Glazer and Moynihan's portrait looks at the situation of endemic ethno-racial struggle in the Soviet Union, Yugoslavia, and Israel in the 1970s and describes a "new stratification" in which ethnicity plays a key role, reasoning that it was probably always that way, but that in the past "the preoccupation with property relations [class] obscured ethnic ones." On this basis these commentators criticize the primacy of class, arguing instead that "it is property that begins to seem derivative and ethnicity seems to become a more fundamental source of stratification" (1975, 16–17). Finally, Stuart Hall et al. think that class identity is but a special instance of a larger ethno-racial identity: "Race is the modality in which class is lived. It is also the medium in which class relations are experienced" (1978, 394).

The intellectual standoff is best resolved by a more flexible approach that conceives of identity, in this case situationally created ethnic identity, as a resource that can serve to buttress class claims, or that can cut across such claims at a given moment. Stated differently, while racism is strong within the white working class, for example, members of that class do not automatically share the same economic and political interests as the elite members of their own ethnic and racial community (Bonacich 1980). Thus, a situationally created identity (class, racial, or otherwise) is a matter of rational human choice and calculation, which "can be used to summon up a social organization for the attainment of ends when it is needed, but it can also be latent and ignored" (Rex 1986, 27).

Rationality is the key here mainly because class affiliation, which is tied to occupation, income, and economic position, clearly addresses more compelling and immediate requirements of survival than does ethnic or racial affiliation. But to the extent that ethnicity and race can influence class position and the structure of opportunity in society, individuals can be expected, to the extent it is possible, to emphasize or de-emphasize their ethno-racial attributes.[4] However, if there is no direct correspondence between class membership and racial attributes, class identity can be expected to play a more significant part than ethnicity in the behaviour of individuals living in modern society. As Orlando Patterson writes:

> Where a plurality of allegiances involves a conflict between class interests and other interests, individuals in the long run will choose class allegiance over all other allegiances, including ethnic allegiance. (1975, 312–313)

But what this author needs to acknowledge is that social living is seldom so black and white; there are often several hues of grey and the strength of ethnicity cannot be denied. It is thus clear that in today's society "[e]thnicity has become more salient because it can combine an interest with an affective tie" (Bell 1975, 169). Added to this, the current climate in which "political correctness" and related concerns are having a decisive impact on economic choices and arrangements means that it is short-sighted to assume the unencumbered operation or carrying out of the market principle.

NOTES

1   This of course is not to deny that blood relatives sometimes turn their passions against one another in acts of violence. But by and large families are about blind faith, love, and caring.

2   The idea of home as a place of refuge is well captured by the poet Robert Frost, who describes it as the place where, when you've got to go there, they've got to take you in (Isaacs 1975, 35).

3   This is not to say, however, that family ties and racial characteristics do not impact on employment opportunities; but rather, given the limitations of space and scope in the present paper, in societies that officially and constitutionally endorse a meritocratic ideal, these shall just have to be taken as given. In the context of the present point, to mount a critique of the ideology of merit and equal opportunity will just take us too far afield.

4   This relates to the sociological phenomenon of "passing," according to which some members of ethnic minorities are not visible to the majority and can gain social acceptance in the circles

of the latter so long as they de-emphasize or keep secret their background. Alternatively, in a situation where ethnic minority status is valued, a person may choose to emphasize or play up his or her ethnic roots. Such manipulation of ethnic identity for economic and social gain is commonplace.

REFERENCES

Allahar, Anton L. 1993. "When Black First Became Worth Less." *International Journal of Comparative Sociology* 34, nos. 1–2:39–55.

Anderson, Benedict. 1983. *Imagined Communities: Reflections on the Origin and Spread of Nationalism.* London: Verso Editions and New Left Books.

Bell, Daniel. 1975. "Ethnicity and Social Change." In *Ethnicity: Theory and Experience*, ed. Nathan Glazer and Daniel P. Moynihan, 141–174. Cambridge, Mass.: Harvard University Press.

Best, Lloyd. 1992. "Ethnic Rivalry and National Unity." *Trinidad and Tobago Review* 14, no. 7.

Bonacich, Edna. 1980. "Class Approaches to Ethnicity and Race." *The Insurgent Sociologist* 10, no. 2:9–23.

Centre for Contemporary Cultural Studies. 1982. *The Empire Strikes Back: Race and Racism in 70s Britain.* London: Hutchinson.

Durkheim, Emile. 1984. *The Division of Labour in Society.* New York: The Free Press.

Eller, Jack David, and Reed M. Coughlan. 1993. "The Poverty of Primordialism: The Demystification of Ethnic Attachments." *Ethnic and Racial Studies* 16, no. 2:183–202.

Geertz, Clifford. 1973. "The Integrative Revolution: Primordial Sentiments and Civil Politics in New States." Chap. 10 in *The Interpretation of Cultures*, 255–310. New York: Basic Books.

Glazer, Nathan, and Daniel P. Moynihan, eds. 1975. Introduction to *Ethnicity: Theory and Experience*, 1–26. Cambridge, Mass.: Harvard University Press.

Gordon, Milton M. 197 "Toward a General Theory of Racial and Ethnic Group Relations." In *Ethnicity: Theory and Experience*, ed. Nathan Glazer and Daniel P. Moynihan, 84–110. Cambridge, Mass.: Harvard University Press.

Grosby, Steven. 1994. "The Verdict of History: The Inexpungeable Tie of Primordiality." *Ethnic and Racial Studies* 17, no. 1:164–171.

Haley, Alex. 1976. *Roots.* New York: Doubleday.

Hall, Stuart. 1980. "Race, Articulation, and Societies Structured in Dominance." In *Sociological Theories: Race and Colonialism*, 305–346. Paris: UNESCO.

Hall, Stuart, C. Critcher, T. Jefferson, J. Clarke, and B. Robert. 1978. *Policing the Crisis: Mugging, the State and Law and Order.* London: Macmillan.

Hoben, Allan, and Robert Hefner. 1990. "The Integrative Revolution Revisited." *World Development* 19, no. 1:17–30.

Hobsbawm, Eric, and Terence Ranger, eds. 1983. *The Invention of Tradition.* Cambridge: Cambridge University Press.

Horowitz, Donald L. 1975. "Ethnic Identity." In *Ethnicity: Theory and Experience*, ed. Nathan Glazer and Daniel P. Moynihan, 111–140. Cambridge, Mass.: Harvard University Press.

Isaacs, Harold R. 1975. "Basic Group Identity: The Idols of the Tribe." In *Ethnicity: Theory and Experience*, ed. Nathan Glazer and Daniel P. Moynihan, 29–52. Cambridge, Mass.: Harvard University Press.

Mason, David. 1986. "Introduction: Controversies and Continuities in Race and Ethnic Relations Theory." In *Theories of Race and Ethnic Relations*, ed. John Rex and David Mason, 1–19. Cambridge: Cambridge University Press.

Miles, Robert. 1982. *Racism and Immigrant Labour*. London: Routledge & Kegan Paul.

———. 1989. *Racism*. London: Routledge & Kegan Paul.

Oxaal, Ivar, Tony Barnett, and David Booth. 1975. *Beyond the Sociology of Development: Economy and Society in Latin America and Africa*. London: Routledge & Kegan Paul.

Parkin, Frank. 1979a. *Marxism and Class Theory: A Bourgeois Critique*. London: Tavistock.

———. 1979b. "Social Stratification." In *A History of Sociological Analysis*, ed. T. Bottomore and R. Nisbet, 599–632. London: Heinemann.

Patterson, H. Orlando. 1975. "Context and Choice in Ethnic Allegiance: A Theoretical Framework and Caribbean Case Study." In *Ethnicity: Theory and Experience*, ed. Nathan Glazer and Daniel P. Moynihan, 305–349. Cambridge, Mass.: Harvard University Press.

———. 1983. "The Nature, Causes, and Implications of Ethnic Identification," In *Minorities: Community and Identity*, ed. C. Fried, 25–50. Berlin: Dahlem Konferenzen.

Rex, John. 1986. *Race and Ethnicity*. Stony Stratford, England: The Open University Press.

Shils, Edward. 1968. "Color, the Universal Intellectual Community, and the Afro-Asian Intellectual." In *Color and Race*, ed. John Hope Franklin, 1–17. Boston: Houghton Mifflin.

Smith, Anthony D. 1984. "National Identity and Myths of Ethnic Descent." *Research in Social Movements, Conflict and Change* 7: 95–130.

Solomos, John. 1986. "Varieties of Marxist Conceptions of 'Race' Class and the State: A Critical Analysis." In *Theories of Race and Ethnic Relations*, ed. John Rex and David Mason, 84–109. Cambridge: Cambridge University Press.

Stack, John F. Jr., ed. 1981. *Ethnic Identities in a Transnational World*. Westport: Greenwood Press.

RACE, ETHNICITY, AND CULTURAL IDENTITY

CHAPTER 3

CARL E. JAMES

Social characteristics such as gender, race, ethnicity, ability, age, and sexual orientation, together with factors such as education, citizenship status, political affiliation, and so on, influence a person's attitudes, perception, personality, and motivation. Socializing agents such as the family, teachers, peers, mentors, coaches, significant others, and the society in which the individual lives play a significant role in the influence of these factors and the way in which they find expression. When combined, these inter-related factors play a role in the socilization process, in the nature of the culture that is transmitted and constructed by the individual, and ultimately in the behaviour of that individual.

RACE AND THE SOCIAL CONSTRUCTION OF IDENTITY

"Race" is an arbitrary and therefore problematic term that is employed in the classification of human beings. Over the years it has been used to refer to (a) lineage (groups of people connected by common descent or origin); (b) subspecies (populations of people with distinct genotypes); (c) ethnic groups (e.g., Anglo-Saxons, Italians); (f) religions (e.g., Jews); (g) nationalities (e.g., Irish, Chinese); (h) minority language groups (e.g., French Canadians); (i) blood groups (e.g., blacks; South East Asians); and (j) people from particular geographic regions (e.g., Mediterranean, European) (Elliot and Fleras 1992, 28; Li 1990, 6). Such varied usage has resulted in race being seen as an objective biological and/or social fact that operates through independent characteristics (Omi and Winant 1993). Further, there is the accompanying belief that there are personalities based on racial characteristics, and that inherited biological or physical characteristics are the most important individual and group traits.

Obviously, the meaning of the term "race" is not "fixed" but is dependent on historical period and context. The problem is this: who really belongs in these categories? Many persons don't fit into any of the five colour-based racial categories (brown, black, red, yellow, white) in use today.[1] Where would we, for example, place Arabs or persons from the Middle East or those with a combined racial background? A list of all such exceptions would be quite long, but one thing is evident—there is no clear, indisputable definition of race. Does this then mean that our reference to different racial groups or identities is merely a means of manipulating and creating division among people? Do racial characteristics play a role in people's lives? Omi and Winant (1993) argue that "the concept of race operates neither as a signifier of comprehensive identity, nor of fundamental difference, both of which are patently absurd, but rather as a marker of the infinity of variations we humans hold as a common heritage and hope for the future" (p. 9).

For the purpose of our discussion, "race" will refer to the socially constructed classification of human beings based on the historical and geographic context of individual experience. An individual's race is determined socially and psychologically, rather than biologically. It is often the basis upon which groups are formed, agency is attained, social roles are assigned, and status is conferred. Consequently, individual and group identities and behaviours are a product of these factors.

It is clear that race affects how individuals identify themselves, interact with others, and understand their place in society. Race is significant as long as groups are determined by their physical traits, and attributes are assigned as a result of these traits. It is significant as long as groups and individuals suffer consequences because of race. The social meaning of race is well understood by all members of society, even though it is racialized Others who often name race as a force within their lives.

Leo Driedger (1986), in writing about ethnic and minority relations, notes that Northern Europeans, the dominant population in Canada, tend to be very conscious of skin colour and often classify people accordingly (p. 284). Yet when asked to describe themselves, members of the dominant population tend to omit race as one of their characteristics, while minority group members, particularly blacks, tend to identify race as a significant characteristic. As the dominant racial group, whites tend to see their colour as the norm while identifying non-whites in terms of colour. In fact, race is a part of everyone's identity.

The assumption that the term "race" refers mainly to racial minorities was revealed in one classroom discussion when students were asked to talk about themselves in racial, ethnic, and cultural terms. One white participant insisted that he was Canadian, and therefore his racial and ethnic identities were irrelevant. When asked how he would feel if a Chinese person and a Black person both insisted that they were Canadian and therefore refused to identify themselves by their ethnicity, the participant responded by saying he would not be satisfied with their answers because, to him, Canadians are people who look like him: "Chinese and blacks are immigrants—they do not look Canadian." Another participant said to me, "I feel when you mention race you're talking about people of different ethnicities and countries."

Another common tendency is to equate talking about or naming race with a display of prejudice or racism. Hence, when asked to talk about race as it relates to their identity and behaviour, white participants tended to become defensive. They responded: "I never see race.... I see the person, not her race.... I don't feel uncomfortable with black people"; or "Every time I've talked about race, it's been about stereotyping or prejudice." Others wrote the following:

Greg: As for my race, I am white, but I never really had to think about it before. I don't feel that it ever affected the people with whom I associated or talked to. My two best friends are black and (Canadian) Indian. I was brought up in a family that didn't believe in prejudice and I'm proud of that. If I don't like a person, it is because of their personality, not their race or heritage.

Henry: Concerning my race, which is Caucasian, I really don't believe that it has contributed enormously to my identity or behaviour. I feel this way because my culture is basically all Canadian.

Laurie: I ... cannot see how my race influences or affects me. I have always been aware of how my ethnicity influences my ideals, morals, values and beliefs, and these personal elements have not changed. For me to say that race affects me would either show that I feel inferior or superior to other races, and this is incorrect.

Why have Greg, Henry, and Laurie given so little or no thought to their race or "whiteness?" How can they claim that their race has not contributed "enormously" to their identity, values, beliefs, and behaviours? Is it really because their culture is, as Henry claims, "basically all Canadian"? And what does it mean to be "Canadian" when one is white? Is their denial of race an attempt, as Laurie hints, not to "show" their feelings of superiority to other races? Is it likely that those who identify themselves racially are people who "feel inferior or superior"? And what about when someone like Greg, who does not think of himself in racial terms, identifies others, such as his "two best friends," by their race or ethnicity? Is he re-inscribing their inferior and his superior status (Kallen 1995)? In a way, Greg is indicating that he is the "norm" (Sleeter 1994; Roman 1993). The norm is understood by all and therefore need not be made explicit. And in identifying the race and ethnicity of his friends, Greg is socially constructing them as racialized Others, as different from his white self. In essence, the comments by Greg, Henry, and Laurie indicate their attempts to avoid naming their whiteness, for to do so would require them to also acknowledge their race privilege (that "invisible package of unearned assets," as Peggy McIntosh [1995] puts it) and surrender the myth of the racial neutrality of Canadian society.

Ruth Frankenberg (1993, 6) argues that speaking of the social construction of whiteness reveals locations, discourse, and material relations to which the term "whiteness" applies. She further points out that whiteness is related to "a set of locations that are historically, socially, politically, and culturally produced." This set of locations is linked to relations of domination (cited in Weis and Fine 1996). This idea of domination and construction of whiteness dates back to early colonial times. European scientists ranked "the 'races' of the world in hierarchical order of innate inferiority and superiority ranging from primitive to highly civilized," and "at the pinnacle of the hierarchy" were the "'white' Euro-Christian 'races'" (Kallen 1995, 24).

It seems likely then that when white participants attempt to deflect discussion about their whiteness or refuse to make their own racial selves or identities explicit (as in the case of Greg, Henry, and Laurie), they are attempting to hide their knowledge of their location and the ways in which they socially, culturally, and politically produce relations of domination.

In the essay excerpt that follows, Carol explores her identity as a black woman who has immigrated from the Caribbean. Her words reveal that her understanding of racial superiority and inferiority and her relationship to white people must be understood within a global context of colonialism. This legacy of colonialism, more specifically, the legacy of colonial discourse, write Lois Weis and Michelle Fine (1996, with reference to Moharty and Zoderfer), operates to construct whiteness as the norm against which all other communities are judged. It helps to produce knowledge that constantly inscribes the marginalization of people of colour. So, in Trinidad as well as Toronto, the colonial discourse operates to influence Carol's sense of self, her values, and behaviour.

Carol: "*I grew up thinking that whites were superior...*"

Sixteen years ago I immigrated to Canada. It was in the early 1970s, when there was an influx of immigrants to Canada, especially from the Caribbean. I was born in the Caribbean island of Trinidad to parents of West Indian nationality. My father's and mother's ethnicity is African.

Racially I am black. I have lived half of my life in Trinidad, where the majority of the population is of African descent and the second major group is of East Indian descent, interspersed with Chinese and whites. Living there, where the majority of people were black, I felt no threat to my self-esteem because of prejudice or racial discrimination. However, from a very early age, I learned that to be white or fair-skinned with long hair was much better than being black. I grew up thinking that whites were superior, prettier, richer, and never did menial jobs because that's what I saw of the whites I came into contact with in Trinidad.

This belief was inculcated in me by my parents, who always spoke highly of whites, showed great respect for them, and made remarks and comparisons that made them appear superior. As I grew older and learned about the history of my race, I realized that the attitude my parents had toward the white race is a legacy that was passed on to my generation, and dates back to slavery and colonialism.

Immigrating to Canada has been an eye-opening experience for me because it has helped to change my beliefs and my concepts of white people. It has also made me more conscious of my race because I am now in the minority, and I am reminded of it daily. For example, when I listen to the news and read the headlines in the newspapers, if there is something negative about a black person, I feel as though I am a part of it. I feel as though everyone is looking at me and thinking about me in the same negative light as that person who committed the crime. I feel as though I am on stage. Similarly, if there is something positive or good, I feel proud.

To an extent my race does influence my values and attitudes because as a member of a visible minority living in Canada, I feel that achieving success in anything means extremely hard work and struggle. As a result, I place a very high value on education, which I feel is one of the main tools to success. I am passing on this value of education to my children because I realize that, without it, their chance of success is almost nil. In addition, I am trying to instill in my children the value of being proud of their black heritage. I am also trying to develop in them a self-esteem that would counteract the darts of racism, prejudice, and discrimination that they will definitely have to face in this society. I am also making them aware of the fact that, even though they are Canadians, their success and achievements can be attained only through working twice as much as their fellow white Canadians.

However, as I reflect on my values, behaviours, morals, and attitudes toward life, I must also note that, whereas culture, ethnicity, and race are significant, I am to a large extent strongly influenced by my religion. As a Christian, I try to apply the principle of love to my fellow men by using the golden rule: "Always treat others as you would have them treat you." Practising this rule sometimes becomes difficult when I am faced with racial discrimination, prejudice, or racial slurs. For example, I remember walking home from the bus stop one day when some young men passing by in a car shouted, "You ... nigger!" A mixed feeling of anger, devastation, and prejudice came over me. I had to quickly console myself by thinking that they were just ignorant strangers who didn't know me, so I should ignore this remark. There were other incidents, like when my husband and I were looking for an apartment. We were told on the phone that an apartment was available. We made an appointment to see it and went there. The superintendent took a white couple to see the apartment and left us waiting in the lobby, then returned and told us it was taken. We were living just across the street, so we walked home, phoned the same building and inquired, and were told by the same superintendent that the apartment was available. We got the message and started to look elsewhere. These and other incidents while job hunting, and even things at school, make it difficult for me sometimes to practise this principle of "love your fellow man" and the golden rule. But over the years, I have learned to cope by practising this rule and ignoring derogatory slangs hurled at me or racial discrimination and prejudice. Now, I do not feel the sting of racial prejudice as much as when I first arrived here.

In my daily life I try not to see people first through their colour or race, but as individual human beings. In spite of cultural differences, ethnicity, race, or religion, we all share a common heritage as members of the human race, and we have the same basic human needs; therefore we should not make ourselves feel superior or inferior to others.

Being a black Canadian who is a part of a minority group, I am aware that my ethnicity and race will always play a role in influencing my values and attitudes in life. However, because my religion is a way of life for me, it determines how much of society's values, behaviours, and attitudes I assimilate. It, therefore, affects my main outlook on life.

ETHNICITY AS PART OF SOCIAL IDENTITY

The terms "ethnic population," "ethnic food," and "ethnic music" are used often in Canada. In some cases, "ethnic" is used to describe Italians, Portuguese, Ukrainians, and others. It is also used as a stereotype. The term "ethnic" is sometimes used interchangeably with "race" and "immigrant" and "culture" to try to socially define or locate people.

Leslie: "*I have thoug.ht of myself only as Canadian...*"
To me, ethnicity was something that belonged to people who differed from the so-called average white Canadian—differing perhaps because of language, accent, or skin colour. Thus, I believed ethnicity was something noticeable or visible. I believe my ignorance regarding my ethnicity is

because I belong to the dominant group in Canada. Because I am white, English speaking and have British ancestry, I have thought of myself only as a Canadian. In essence, I didn't realize I had ethnicity because I did not differ from the stereotypical image of an average Canadian.

The common notion among many Canadians is that ethnicity is based on how people choose to identify themselves and is presumably of no concern to society in general. But ethnicity is not simply a matter of individual choice: members of society play a role in defining ethnicity. For example, class participant Jackie Stewart writes that, when she tells people her name, some respond by saying "Grrrrrrreat day for motorcar racing!"

Jackie: I must hear that line at least once a day. People tend to associate my name with the once-great racing car driver, Jackie Stewart. The last name, Stewart, is a dead giveaway that I am of Scottish origin or ethnicity. People generally don't ask my parents where they are from because they recognize their Scottish accent. However, when I mention that I too was born in Scotland, they look at me questioningly, and ask me why I do not have an accent. Or they ask me why I do not have freckles, or pale skin with rosy cheeks. How am I to know?

Ethnicity gives individuals a sense of identity and belonging based, not only on their perception of being different, but also on the knowledge that they are recognized by others as being different. Isajiw (1977) notes that, in terms of ethnic cultural practices, individuals go through "a process of selecting items, however few, from the cultural past—pieces of ethnic folk art, folk dances, music, a partial use of language, knowledge of some aspects of the group's history—which become symbols of ethnic identity" (p. 36).

Another student participant recalled how he struggled with his identity.

Stefan: "*I saw my ethnicity as an advantage and disadvantage...*"
   My ethnic identity is Polish. My parents were born in Poland and came to Canada in 1967. I was born in Toronto, Ontario, a couple of years later. I saw my ethnicity as an advantage and a disadvantage during my lifetime. When I was younger, I didn't want to admit that I was Polish. Even though I was born here, I felt that admitting my ethnicity would be a barrier to joining the "in-crowd" or the "cool group" at school. I even skipped the Polish language classes my parents sent me to after school. As I became older, I realized I couldn't change my ethnicity. I was who I was. I became more proud of my Polish background. It felt good to be part of a Polish community where I was able to participate in ceremonies and activities based on my Polish background. It gave me a sense of belonging to a group, a sense of identity, a sense of security.

Individuals with several ethnic identities are free to identify with all of them. However, individuals often identify most strongly with the one that forms the basis of their socialization at home or with their peers, the one that seems most acceptable by the dominant group in society or the one by which others identify them.

Some years ago, while facilitating a group discussion with Grade 6 students in Toronto, one blond boy identified himself as Italian (they were all asked to identity their ethnicity). Members of the group doubted that he was Italian: they noted that his last name was "not Italian" and he did not "look" Italian. In fact, his mother was Italian and his father was Irish. He pointed out that he lived in an Italian neighbourhood and spoke Italian. On another occasion, I was chatting with a young man who looked to me to be black and possibly of mixed race. In our conversation, he revealed that he was Italian. He had grown up in an Italian community and spoke Italian fluently. He further said that people often doubted his Italian heritage. However, it was the only one he knew, since he grew up with his Italian mother and did not have much interaction with his father.

In the following essay excerpts, individuals explore their understanding of ethnicity.

Damian: *"My roots are very much embedded in the Slovenian way of life."*

My cultural and ethnic backgrounds are very much Slovenian. More specifically, they originated in a northern province called Slovenia [in the former Yugoslavia]. My parents immigrated from there 22 years ago and I was born here in Canada.

My parents brought with them all of their beliefs, values, and traditions. A big part of their life was, and is, a dedication to hard work and their religious faith. Throughout my life I have been taught to respect those values and accept those religious beliefs.

With regard to ethnicity, its influence ranges from the way I dress to the type of food I eat. For example, my parents hate to see me in torn clothing. When I was a child, and even now, their ethnic values made them feel that I should be well groomed all the time. I feel that now, in my early adult years, I carry a lot of those early impressions with me.

The work ethic is very important to me. I feel that I always make an attempt to do things well and with enthusiasm. This is one of the main cultural differences. Canadian culture dictates a more relaxed attitude toward work. One of the strange things that I tend to do is slack off when in an environment of long-time Canadians, simply because of this attitude. In a predominantly Yugoslavian environment, I tend to work faster and a lot harder. In this way, I am more Slovenian than Canadian.

A central focus in my life is my religious faith. My parents and most who live in the province they come from are Roman Catholic. My faith has always been a basis for my attitudes, actions, and beliefs. With respect to sex and morality, the church dictates a lot in my life. This causes many nagging conflicts. Popular Canadian values and beliefs with which I sympathize come in direct conflict with the teachings of the church. I must, many times, reach some sort of compromise. Abortion is a great example of such a conflict. While the church strictly rejects the idea, I am not sure as to where I stand on the subject. I am, I feel, a little more open-minded than many of the older-generation Slovenians in my community. That is part of their general character, which comes from that deep-rooted faith they grew up with. The fact that I grew up with the many different viewpoints of my friends and their respective backgrounds means that I have a broader outlook. In conclusion, I can say that while I was born here in Canada, my roots are very much embedded in the Slovenian way of life.

It is common to find that religion or religious affiliation is an integral part of a person's ethnic identity, values, and behaviour. In such cases, ethnic culture and religious culture are inseparable. For example, as Damian points out, his Slovenian ethnicity influences his values and behaviour, but his faith is also central to his life. Religion or spirituality is more important to some ethnic groups than others, particularly those of orthodox affiliation.

DOMINANT GROUP MEMBERSHIP

The history of a society provides indicators as to the dominant–minority status of its different ethnic and racial groups. Kinloch (1974) points out that minority groups are characterized by their having experienced oppression at some time in the country's development. Burnet (1981) further points out that minority groups tend to be vulnerable and subject to discrimination. Physical and social attributes, such as race and ethnicity, then determine social interaction and involvement within the society. In Canada, the dominant ethnic group is Anglo-Celtic, and the dominant racial group is white. The remaining racial and ethnic groups can therefore be classed as minorities. Ng (1993) writes about the power of the dominant group and how that power is normalized. She points out that, in Canadian society,

> European men, especially those of British and French descent, are seen to be superior to women and to people from other racial and ethnic origins. Systems of ideas and practices have been developed over time to justify and support their notion of superiority. These ideas become the premise on which societal norms and values are based, and the practices become the "normal" way of doing things. (p. 52)

Insofar as race and ethnicity are a part of identity, so too is dominant–minority group status. Through socialization, "the lifelong learning process through which individuals develop selfhood and acquire the knowledge, skills and motivation required to participate in social life" (Mackie, 1986, 64), individuals acquire a sense of identity as members of the dominant or minority group. Those who belong to a group that strongly identifies with the dominant or minority group will ultimately come to think of themselves as dominant or minority group members respectively. Individuals' cultural identities become linked with their historical experiences, values, ways of life, and the social patterns that are part of their group life.

Acquiring an ethnic and racial identity and a dominant–minority identification, however, is not simple in our contemporary, pluralistic, Canadian society. Individuals are influenced by many factors outside of their home and their immediate ethnic and racial groups. They are influenced by schools, churches, workplaces, media, and other major institutions. Sometimes it is in encounters with these institutions that individuals come to recognize the privileges they have as racial and ethnic group members. Dominant group members may come to realize that they have a privileged and prestigious position in society, and, as a result, access to all the social, political, and economic institutions within that society. They might even come to realize that they can "get ahead" without compromising their identity. Peggy McIntosh (1995) explores this notion of privilege in her essay "White Privilege and Male Privilege: A Personal Account of Coming to See Correspondences through Work in Women Studies." She writes that the phenomenon of white privilege is "denied and protected, but alive and real in its effects."

Minority group members, on the other hand, may come to realize that to get ahead they may have to compromise their ethnic identity. They learn that "if they wish to enjoy the rewards of employment, education or social contact with higher-status groups, it will be necessary to forsake their language and many other cultural attributes of their ethnic [or racial] groups" (Agocs 1987, 170). This could also mean denying their ethnicity or race because these characteristics identify them as "different" or "inferior." They may reject their ethno-racial group experiences or, alternatively, they may embrace what they consider to be the cultural values of their ethnic or racial group and work hard to change the negative perceptions that are held of their group.

In short, the dominant or minority status of an ethnic or racial group mirrors its position within the stratification system of the larger society. Through socialization, individuals learn about their position. This in turn is likely to influence their identity and behaviour. In the following accounts, when writing of themselves as dominant (or majority) group members, participants reveal how they learn about their status, internalize it, and act accordingly. Carol told her story earlier, in the section on race. She showed how her minority status or her status as a racialized Other contributed to the issues with which she is confronted while living in a society where privilege is linked to colour. Here, Lyn and Lorne express that it is not only their white race and Anglo ethnicity that make them the people they are, but also the privilege that comes with being part of the white, dominant group. Interestingly, these Canadians tend not to refer to themselves in hyphenated terms. They are, as Henry claims, "all Canadian," and some go so far as to say that they have no ethnicity, just as they are not raced.

Lyn: "*I am a member of a majority group that has a great deal of power.*"

As a white English Canadian, my values, behaviour, and attitudes are influenced by my origins in direct relation to the fact that 1 am a member of the single largest group, racially, ethnically, and to a large extent, culturally. In this short essay, I would like to focus on how these racial and ethnic cultures reinforce each other and how, when combined together, they can mask a number of assumptions I have about my relationship to the society I live in and my acceptance of that society's norms. In essence, I want to show how the values, attitudes, and behaviours of the cultures I belong to fit into a system of thought and action that perpetuates those cultures and the power they hold.

I would like to take discrimination as an example. My experience of the class system in Britain has made me aware of how differences in origin, in this case most noticeably defined by accent (in speech), have a direct relationship to the position a person may hold in society in terms of economic power, political influence, and control over day-to-day life. What I learned as a teenager in the 1960s in North America, when issues of civil rights and discrimination were in the news, the subject of popular books, and certainly regularly discussed in classrooms, reinforced my awareness of what influences a person's ability to be accepted in society—to succeed in the terms laid down by that society and also in terms of personal freedom.

But I am a member of a majority [i.e., dominant] group that has a great deal of power. So, for example, being racially white, I may have an awareness of these issues, and I may condemn my society for its inherent racism, but it is white culture that I experience day to day, and the very fact that discrimination is rarely an issue for me personally results in my own racial identity becoming an invisible thing. The powerful people within my experience, directly or indirectly—the politician, the employer, the teacher, the social worker—are invariably white. I know that my race will not be an issue with most of the people I must deal with, as I know we will have a commonality from the start. Being in the majority in all three origins, there is also a good chance that either culturally, ethnically, or both, our backgrounds will be similar. Neither will I expect my values or behaviour to be an issue because I fit into the "norm."

It is in the idea of the "norm" that racial and ethnic cultures mesh to form a powerful image of what is accepted or expected. I see myself reflected not only in the powerful people I am in contact with but in the books I read in school, the movies I see, the people I read about in newspapers. My day-to-day experience of life reinforces all that I have learned—the language and behaviour I have been taught; the values I have been told are the most important; the attitudes, inevitably, of which I am or am not conscious. As a result, I begin to see no other, and I then begin to measure other cultures by the standards of my own without being aware that I am doing so.

It is this lack of awareness, this assumption of the norm, that has the strongest ability to perpetuate all the other behaviours, values, and attitudes of my group because it dictates what I do and do not perceive. It blocks my ability, then, to understand and appreciate other values, other cultures, and to question my own. I see what is different, but I don't analyze the difference. And it isn't crucial that I do so because I do not have to adapt myself. My group has the power, and I don't have to attune myself to any other way of living unless I choose to. And choice versus necessity has a strong impact on what I see and learn.

So my group, being dominant, has the power to define what is acceptable, what is most valuable in me and, in doing so, to define the attitudes of which I am and am not conscious. If I cannot see myself, I cannot see others clearly; and if I cannot see others clearly, seeing myself becomes more and more difficult. The mask is never removed. In this way, the power of the majority group is maintained, as their values, behaviours, and attitudes become self-perpetuating.

Lorne: "*I was conscious of belonging to the 'privileged' class...*"

I am a male, born to white Anglo-Saxon parents, and raised in a small town north of Toronto. The European heritage of our family is obscure. We assumed we were British, but there may be some German background as well. My mother has recently done some genealogical research into our origins. She found that both her ancestors and those of my father immigrated to Canada from the United States shortly after the Revolutionary War of 1776 and had lived in the United States for a considerable time before that. We have been in North America for nearly 300 years and in Canada since before it was an independent country, so our connections with Europe can be considered unimportant.

I spent most of my teenage years rebelling against what I perceived as the confines of my cultural heritage. I was conscious of belonging to the (supposedly non-existent) "privileged" class, and was deeply embarrassed about it. I saw smugness and complacency everywhere and was determined never to be a part of it. Like many others my age, I grew my hair long, not simply in an effort to appear different, but to mark myself as being outside of my parents' culture. This was far from rare, but I still consider it an important phenomenon. It was less a case of fashion than a conscious attempt by the youth of the day to define their own culture as visibly different as possible from the one into which they had been born.

I rebelled against both the church (of which my parents were esteemed and active members) and the public school system. I felt that the interest of the church lay more in making its members feel comfortably secure in their own goodness than in spiritual exploration. At school, I refused to be part of what I perceived as training for hypocrisy, and my marks fell as I decided to educate myself as I chose. I was interested in politics and read avidly of the struggles and revolutions of oppressed peoples. Lenin, Castro, and especially Che Guevara were my heroes. I wished that I had a struggle as important as theirs, something solid to fight against, a cause that belonged to me. I realize now that many of the things I thought at that time had a lot to do with my own search for identity. I felt that belonging to the majority was a barrier to my individuality, that I had no real traditions or culture of my own.

I have changed since that time. I am no longer embarrassed about belonging to the majority. I have found enough individuality within myself to assure me that, yes, after all I'm not just like everybody else. Through experimentation in different religions, both Eastern and Western, and associations with people from different backgrounds and cultures, I have come to believe in the power of individuals to define themselves as outside of cultural boundaries and to re-shape their beliefs in the light of experience. This belief has its own drawbacks, however, as I shall discuss shortly.

Since I have ceased to struggle so adamantly against my culture, I have often been surprised to find attitudes and ideas that could not have come from anywhere else. I am speaking primarily of unconscious prejudices and assumptions that surface when I least expect them to.

For example, I take many things for granted as natural rights. I am comfortable in society; I feel that there is nowhere that I am not allowed to go if I wish, and nothing that is not prohibited by law that I cannot do. I don't fear the police. I am not in danger of being the victim of racially inspired violence. The only barriers to work or accommodation are my own qualifications and my financial situation. To illustrate the unconsciousness of this assumption of safety, I will tell a little story.

When I was living in Vancouver, I decided to take a walk at dusk along the beaches near the university. It was early spring and still quite cool, so the beaches were deserted. I walked about five miles, enjoyed a magnificent sunset, and returned home after dark. Some friends were there and naturally I told them all about my stroll. One of my friends, a female, said that she felt very jealous that I was able to do something like that. At first I didn't know exactly what she meant. Surely she was healthy enough to go for a walk if she felt like it. Then I understood that she was speaking about fear. Momentarily I felt defensive, as if she were blowing something out of proportion and making it partially my fault. Then I understood that she was perfectly right. She perceived something as simple as going for a walk alone after dark as a privilege that I enjoyed and that she did not.

Another result of my heritage, and one that stems directly from the feeling of safety that I have spoken of, is the belief that I talked about earlier—that the individual is the author of his or her own destiny, that we make ourselves. This implies another lot of assumptions. Basically, it assumes that the only limits to our choices are of our own making. It does not take into account how individuals may be forced or coerced into situations they would not otherwise have become involved in. It does not take into account how institutionalized racism and violence might hinder the growth of self-esteem. And it does not take into account how living with violence and hatred changes everyone.

Despite this, I still find my little creed valuable to me. For while others may have valid reasons for not being able to overcome the negative influences in their lives, I have no such excuse. It is up to me to make myself the better person I know I can be.

CONCLUSION

We have examined how race and ethnicity contribute to the social, political, and cultural construction of individual cultural identities. We have tried to demonstrate that race, ethnicity, and cultural identity are complex concepts that are historically, socially, and contextually based. These social relations are dynamic; their meanings change over time. Apple (1993) refers to them as "place markers," operating in a complex political and social arena. The social meanings given to racial and ethnic identity are directly related to the dominant and minority variable, and also to many other variables. Social, cultural, and political institutions, as well as individuals, help give meaning to these social factors, which in turn determine how individuals act upon these meanings.

In writing about the relationship between identity and culture in his essay "Beyond Cultural Identity," Adler affirms that

> the psychological, psychosocial, and psycho-philosophical realities of an individual are knit together by the culture which operates through sanctions and rewards, totems and taboos, prohibitions and myths. The unity and integration of society, nature, and the cosmos is reflected in the total image of the self and in the day-to-day awareness and consciousness of the individual. This synthesis is modulated by the larger dynamics of the culture itself. In the concept of cultural identity, then, we see a synthesis of the operant culture reflected by the deepest images held by the individual. (1977, 28)

Indeed, Adler demonstrates the significance of culture in establishing individuals' sense of identity. Their ethnic and racial cultures serve as a means of providing stability and comfort, mediating the ways in which the dominant Canadian culture constructs the group's cultural identity. The degree to which individuals identify with their group culture varies depending on place of birth, social class, abilities, education and occupational expectations and achievements, interaction with members and non-members of their group, and their willingness to adapt to the main cultural norms.

Ethnicity plays an equally important role in the formulation of cultural identity for the members of the dominant cultural group. However, this group's situation contrasts with that of minority groups. Smith (1991) argues that, while the ethnic identity development of the majority group individual is continually being validated and reinforced by both his membership group and by the structure of the society's institutions, such is not the case for members of many ethnic minority groups. Positive reinforcement frees the majority individual to focus on aspects of his or her life other than ethnicity (p. 183).

NOTE

1   It is only in recent times that we have begun to use the term "brown," particularly in Toronto, to refer to people of South Asian origin. In England, South Asians are referred to as black; and in the United States, in Los Angeles, for example, "brown" refers to Latin Americans.

REFERENCES

Adler, Peter S. 1977. "Beyond Cultural Identity: Reflections upon Cultural and Multicultural Man." In *Cultural Learning*, ed. R.W. Brislin. Honolulu: East-West Center.

Agocs, Carol. 1987. "Ethnic Group Relations." In *Basic Sociology*, ed. J.J. Teevan. Scarborough: Prentice-Hall.

Apple, M. 1993. "Constructing the "Other": Rightist Reconstructions of Common Sense." In *Race, Identity and Representation in Education*, ed. Cameron McCarthy and Warren Crichlow. New York: Routledge.

———. 1993. Introduction to *Race, Identity and Representation in Education,* ed. Cameron McCarthy and Warren Crichlow. New York: Routledge.

Burnet, Jean. 1981. "The Social and Historical Context of Ethnic Relations." In *A Canadian Social Psychology of Ethnic Relations,* ed. R.C. Gardener and R. Kalin. Toronto: Methuen.

Driedger, Leo. 1989. *The Ethnic Factor: Identity in Diversity.* Toronto: McGraw-Hill Ryerson Ltd.

Elliott, Jean L., and Augie Fleras. 1992. *Unequal Relations: An Introduction to Race and Ethnic Dynamics In Canada.* Scarborough: Prentice-Hall Canada.

Frankenberg, Ruth. 1993. *White Women, Race Matters: The Social Construction of Whiteness.* Minneapolis: University of Minnesota Press.

Isajiw, Wsevolod W. 1977. "Olga in Wonderland: Ethnicity in a Technological Society." *Canadian Ethnic Studies* 9, no. 1:77–85.

Kallen, Evelyn. 1995. *Ethnicity and Human Rights in Canada,* 2nd ed. Toronto: Oxford University Press.

Kinloch, Graham C. 1974. *The Dynamics of Race Relations: A Sociological Analysis.* Toronto: McGraw-Hill.

Li, Peter S. 1990. *Race and Ethnic Relations in Canada.* Toronto: Oxford University Press.

Mackie, Marlene. 1986. "Socialization." In *Sociology,* ed. R. Hagedorn. Toronto: Holt, Rinehart and Winston.

McIntosh, Peggy. 1995. "White Privilege and Male Privilege: A Personal Account of Coming to See Correspondences through Work in Women's Studies." In *Race, Class and Gender: An Anthology,* ed. M.L. Andersen and P. Hill Collins, 70–81. Belmont: Wadsworth.

Ng, Roxana. 1993. "Racism, Sexism, and Nation Building in Canada." In *Race, Identity and Representation in Education,* ed. M.L. Andersen and P. Hill Collins. New York: Routledge.

Omi, Michael, and Howard Winant. 1993. "On the Theoretical Status of the Concept of Race." In *Race, Identity and Representation in Education,* ed. C. McCarthy and W. Crichlow. New York: Routledge.

Roman, Leslie G. 1993. "White Is a Color! White Defensiveness, Postmodernism, and Anti-Racism Pedagogy." In *Race, Identity and Representation in Education,* ed. C. McCarthy and W. Crichlow. New York: Routledge.

———. 1994. "White Racism." *Multicultural Education* (spring).

Smith, Elsie J. 1991. "Ethnic Identity Development: Toward the Development of a Theory within the Context of Minority/Majority Status." *Journal of Counselling and Development* 70, no. 1:181–188.

Weis, Lois, and Michelle Fine. 1996. "Notes on 'White as Race.'" *Race, Gender & Class: An Interdisciplinary and Multicultural Journal* 3, no. 3:5–9.

POSTMODERN RACE AND GENDER ESSENTIALISM OR A POST-MORTEM OF SCHOLARSHIP

RADHA JHAPPAN

My purpose here is to explore the voice and/or representation debates that have lately dominated feminist discourses, especially the critiques of white feminist theory levelled by women of colour. While I regard those critiques as both timely and substantially correct, I am concerned with the question of what constitutes "scholarship" now that the claims of mainstream male and white feminist scholarship to speak of universal, generic subjects have been debunked, particularly since they have proved remarkably resistant to the critiques of scholars and activists of colour. This chapter offers: a brief overview of the feminist assault on the generic human assumed by the Western male tradition of scholarship and the essentialism engendered by that assault; an outline of the attack by women of colour (and others) on the notion of the "essential woman" assumed by white feminists and the subsequent essentialism engendered by *that* assault; and finally, an accounting of some of the traps of identity politics and race/gender essentialist positions. I am not dealing with essentialisms based on sexuality, class, disability, or other elements of "identity" in this chapter, although I recognize that they are not separate issues but combine with each other in complicated ways. If space permitted, I would in fact apply similar arguments to the essentialist tendencies evident among some of the bearers of those identities.

The present discussion focuses on debates in and around feminism because that is where they have taken place. They have been possible within feminism and feminist theory in a manner and to a degree that has simply not been possible in the older entrenched academic "disciplines," which have proved stubbornly resistant to any sustained analysis of racialization. While some social sciences such as sociology have dealt with race and ethnicity at least as a field of study, if not as a critical component of social theory, my discipline, political "science," is one of the worst offenders in its apparent determination to deny the force of both race and gender (and often even class) in political and social organization.[1] Similarly, while the left and/or political economy streams have come belatedly to include gender as well as class in their analyses, those bodies of scholarship still tend to resist acknowledgement that the world is a fundamentally racialized place where privileges and burdens are dispensed according to the ranking of racial and/or ethnic groups. The Canadian political economy stream, judging by the products of the vast majority of its scholars, has yet to understand that the intersections of race, gender, and class produce far more complex results than can be accounted for by class alone.[2] Therefore, although I am not discussing political economy and the social sciences explicitly in this chapter, it should be read as a critique of them as much as of white feminism.

I must admit from the outset that my European intellectual training has produced within me a deep revulsion to the notions of speaking in the first person, and of having to establish my racial and/or ethnic, gender, class, sexuality, or other credentials as if: firstly, my views of the world are *wholly* shaped, utterly predetermined by those elements of identity (natural or constructed), and are thus entirely predictable; and secondly, the validity of whatever I say will be measured on the basis of those "credentials." There are complex issues here. Everyone has a different set of "standards" — some might disqualify me because I am not dark enough, not immersed enough in West Indian and/or South Asian culture, not oppressed enough (according to Canadian and/or American views of class as distinct from British ones, I have apparently crossed the class divide by virtue of being employed as an academic), while others may expect me to be a representative of some ascribed group of their choice. In view of these problems, the following remarks must be seen as a few preliminary reflections in an ongoing inquiry.

THE FEMINIST ASSAULT ON THE GENERIC HUMAN

Feminism has posed one of the most profound challenges to the standard Cartesian epistemology that traditionally has been employed in political discourse. That approach pursues knowledge, truth, and wisdom almost as if they were external, immutable universals just waiting to be discovered. It assumes that political and social "truths," like laws of physics (cause and effect), can be distilled via reason and logic; if we apply the correct reasoning and the proper methodologies, the answers to all our questions will plop down in front of us like Newton's apples. The Cartesian approach assumes further that we all have the same basic interests, and that the theorist's own position, identity, values, and interests are immaterial. The theorist is regarded as a disembodied, neutral archaeologist of truth who does not need to speak in the first person, but who instead employs supposedly neutral, generic language that transcends the individual—"one" as in "one thinks," refers to everyone or anyone.

This model seems rather silly now. Feminism questioned the voice of traditional political discourse; the voice turned out to be male, the generic pronoun was invariably a masculine one, and nouns like "mankind" really did mean only mankind. Moreover, the "reality" to which the symbolic systems of language referred was a masculinist reality that, far from being neutral toward women, was profoundly hostile, indeed oppressive. The very idea that there can be objective, positionless, genderless knowledge has therefore been soundly reviled.

THE ASSAULT ON THE "ESSENTIAL WOMAN" BY WOMEN OF COLOUR

Over the last couple of decades, many women of colour have pointed out that while the feminist assault on patriarchy and the production of masculinist knowledge is all very well, the entire discourse between the two is fundamentally white and Eurocentric. White feminists have exposed male essentialism, only to replace it with another essentialism based on the notion of an essential woman. However, as it turns out, this generic "woman" is not only white, but middle class, and also able-bodied, heterosexual, and, in Canada, the United States, Britain, Australia, and New Zealand at least, usually anglophone. Over the last couple of decades, people of colour have highlighted the silences of racist Eurocentric history and discourses that render all "others" invisible. Following the seminal work of black feminists,[3] women of colour have debunked the idea that there can be objective knowledge, expertise, and scholarship that is not intimately fashioned by the race, gender, class, sexuality, and (dis)ability identities of the writer or speaker. To put it more pointedly, the "claims to universality and objectivity have been shown to be the alibis of a largely masculinist, heterosexist and white Western subject."[4] Given centuries of cultural and economic imperialism, the ideology of white supremacy, patriarchy, and the concomitant oppression of certain cultures, "races," classes, women, and others, theories that pretend to universalistic application must be discarded in favour of more complex, layered analyses that account for the multi-faceted intersections of race, gender, class, and other variables. Such theories must give space (though not necessarily primacy) to experience, subjectivity, and political agency.

Women of colour, and particularly black feminists, "have reached near unanimity in agreeing that race, rather than gender, has been the primary source of their oppression."[5] They have charged Western women's movements with crusading for causes that are of interest to white women, but which are not necessarily critical or even relevant to women of colour. For example, while white feminists have theorized the male-breadwinner, dependent-female, post–Industrial Revolution family form of the West as a source of women's oppression, different family forms persist in other cultures, even among those living in the diasporas. For many women of colour, in fact, state actions such as immigration and labour policies that have separated and distorted families have oppressed them more than gender relations. Moreover, rather than being confined exclusively to the domestic sphere, women of colour have not only been forced into the slave and indentured labour forces of many countries, but have more recently participated in the paid labour forces of Western countries at much higher rates than have middle-class white women.[6] None of this is to suggest that women of colour do not experience gender oppression, are not subordinated to their male relatives, and do not carry a double day working, for wages as well as maintaining their homes and families.[7] But it is to point out that such oppression takes on significantly different forms and degrees vis-à-vis women of colour.

The question is, how and why are the vast majority of white feminists able to ignore the peculiarity of the race–gender intersection in their theorizing? Increasingly, women of colour are accusing them of racism, whether conscious or unconscious:

> The force that allows white feminist authors ... to make no reference to racial identity in their books about Women that are in actuality about White Women is the same force that would compel any author writing exclusively about Black Women to refer explicitly to their identity. *That force is racism....* There persists a dogged unwillingness to acknowledge and distinguish between varying degrees of discrimination, despite the self-evident reality that *not all women are equally oppressed.*[8]

Similarly, Nkiru Nzegwu argues that, while white women are institutionally disadvantaged, it is only in relation to white males. In the meantime, she charges "all white women for complicity in maintaining a power relation that sustains institutionalized oppression."[9]

bell hooks was saying this a decade ago when she wrote that "much feminist theory emerges from privileged women who live at the centre, whose perspectives on reality rarely include knowledge and awareness of the lives of women and men who live in the margin." As a result, feminist theory "lacks wholeness, lacks the broad analysis that could encompass a variety of human experiences."[10] In view of this, it is not surprising to find women of colour expressing "anger at the white woman's movement for defining for me what my experience is," or Carol Camper's caustic litany of instances when "Your Racism is Showing."[11] It *is* surprising that this anger has had such little positive impact in the sense of inspiring white feminists to come to grips with race and racism in their theorizing (though more has been accomplished in feminist organizations, albeit through intense struggles).

These critiques of white feminist theory have been both timely and necessary. They point out that racism is *not* just an issue for people of colour, because patriarchy and capitalism have been constructed on an international racial hierarchy, and, hence, neither can be understood without facing the fact that we are *all* implicated in oppressive socio-economic and political relations at the global and local levels.

RACE ESSENTIALISM

The assault on the gender essentialism of white feminism, however, seems in some quarters to have resulted in yet another essentialism, now centred on race. As traditionally defined, essentialism is "a belief in true essence—that which is most irreducible, unchanging, and therefore constitutive of a given person or thing."[12] In using this sensitive terminology, I should make it clear that in this chapter, I am *not* referring to race essentialists of the racist or white supremacist variety, whose insistence that the so-called "races" are characterized by fundamental and immutable traits is key to their spurious rankings of supposedly superior and inferior races. On the contrary, I am using the term in quite a different way to refer to the position taken by people of colour who maintain that precisely because of the construction of a racial hierarchy, our knowledges and experiences of the world vary according to our positions within that hierarchy. From various literatures, it would seem that most academics of colour accept the findings of science that "race" does not actually exist per se, there being more genetic variation within than between so-called racial groups, aside from a few visible morphological traits. It is culture, not race, that produces differences, but they cannot be essential differences because culture is not immutable. With few exceptions therefore, writers of colour appear to take a constructionist view of race, and are concerned with revealing and resisting negative racist constructions.

Therefore, as I understand it, in the contemporary context a race essentialist position does not necessarily entail a belief in essential racial differences, but rather assumes, *inter alia*: that there is an international hierarchy of oppression in which race ranks above gender, and hence racism needs to be tackled before sexism; that whites are responsible for racism; that whites are accountable for racism *as individuals;* that by virtue of their positions in the racial hierarchy constructed by white imperialism, all whites, and specifically all white women, oppress all women of colour; that there is a "voice of colour" that has privileged access to race-related "truths," and that whites must not appropriate the voices of people of colour by speaking *for* (or in some cases even *about)* them, or by speaking *in* their voices; and that people of colour must resist white universalism through a politics of "difference" that valorizes ethnic and cultural distinctiveness.[13]

THE TRAPS OF RACE ESSENTIALISM

As noted above, women of colour, particularly those living in white-dominated societies, have generally agreed that they have been more oppressed on the grounds of race than of gender. Even if it were possible, gender equality for racialized women, within an unmodified context of racial inequality, would only mean gender equality with *some* men of colour, who are themselves subjugated to white men and white women. Hence, it is racism rather than sexism that needs to be addressed above all. This is a tricky issue. As noted, women from various cultures have argued that patriarchy was not indigenous to their societies, but was imported via European imperialism. Therefore, racial and/or cultural equality is the primary goal, as exemplified in Turpel's position regarding First Nations in Canada:

> ... before we can consider these debates about gender equality, what about our claims to cultural equality?... Before imposing upon us the logic of gender equality (with white men), what about ensuring for our cultures and political systems equal legitimacy with the Anglo-Canadian cultural perspective which dominates the Canadian state?[14]

In the case of Canada's First Nations, it is hoped that self-government will mean a return to traditional values and ways in which Aboriginal women were regarded as equals with men, even if they were consigned to specific tasks and responsibilities. However, the problem with such arguments is that the origin of patriarchy no longer matters; what matters is the long period of cultural cross-fertilization that means, not only that no culture can claim to be pure in the modern age (with the exception, perhaps, of the few so-called "lost tribes," though they were not lost to themselves), but that no culture can entirely erase the cultural modifications arising from colonization and international communications.

To argue the "racism before sexism" position is to deny two key facts: first, that racism *is* gendered, and it relies profoundly on its ability to subjugate the sexes differentially;[15] second, that even if they were not patriarchal before contact with Europeans, the vast majority of cultures are patriarchal now, especially those in the diasporas under the daily influence of capitalism and white patriarchal systems.

The *generalized* position that racist oppression is more significant in the lives of women of colour from various cultures living in Western industrialized countries is at least questionable, given the very different class positions of women, and the different degrees to which they are exposed to the dominant society. For example, Dua makes the point that South Asian feminist thought (much of it coming from Britain) holds racism as more important than patriarchy, but in so doing obscures the impact of gender oppression in the family, "the site where [women's] paid and unpaid labour is appropriated, where restrictions on their activities are enforced, and where gender relations are reproduced, at times with physical force."[16]

In fact, despite some biting criticisms of black male sexism by authors like hooks, of First Nations male sexism by, for example, the Native Women's Association of Canada, and of Asian male sexism by writers such as Vijay Agnew,[17] the "race before gender" position generally seems to attribute sexism primarily to white men, denying the sexism of men of colour, or maintaining that it is not their fault, that they too are the victims of white patriarchal thinking, and that their sexism will somehow fall away once their cultures are given due respect. As such, the "race before gender" position is akin to the arguments tendered by the male leaders of national liberation movements who promise that "women's issues" will be handled after the revolution. Various examples have shown that women who have succumbed to this assurance have worked vigorously for national liberation only to find themselves subjugated by their men once they have hung up their Uzies and/or cast their ballots, as the current struggles of the women's caucus of South Africa's African National Congress show.[18] The race essentialist can easily fall into the trap, then, of treating as separate two phenomena (racism and sexism) that are intimately dependent, one upon the other.

Whites Are Responsible for Racism

Race essentialist positions almost always set up a white or non-white dichotomy. There is a tendency to simplify the sources of oppression, to take the position, "whites did it to us," as if whites invented racism, imperialism, and slavery. They did not. They have just been more successful over the last few centuries, and they have managed to impress an ideology of white supremacy on the world, thanks in part to their dedication to improving the technologies of travel, communications, and warfare. But to speak as if whites invented racism, imperialism, and slavery is to ignore 5 000 to 10 000 years of human history featuring various empires; interracial, inter-ethnic, and inter-religious wars; and slavery in many areas of the world. It is also to aggregate and romanticize all non-white (indigenous, Asian, African, Australian, and South American) societies prior to contact with Europeans as if they existed in some happy past free of war, imperialism, patriarchy, racism, social stratification, exploitation, and oppression.

The race essentialist position appears to homogenize all whites as "our oppressors," without acknowledging the possibility that "we" may do our own oppressing based on cultural systems and the economic and power interests of certain classes. I am not referring here only to the historical facts that it was African slavers who sold their peoples into slavery to the Europeans, or that the European imperial powers in non-settler colonies such as India depended upon local elites, who were only too happy to support the British rulers who were helping them to maintain their caste and/or ethnic privileges and oppress others. As elsewhere, so complete was their dependence on the collaboration of Indian elites that the British contemplated creating "a class of persons, Indian in blood and colour but English in taste, in opinions, in morals and in intellect."[19] However, as Mohanty notes, "all forms of ruling operate by constructing and consolidating, as well as transforming, already existing social inequalities." As well as constructing "hegemonic masculinities as a form of state rule, the colonial state also transformed *existing* patriarchies and caste and/or class hierarchies.[20]

In arguing that people of colour do our own oppressing, sometimes quite independently of whites, I am also referring to a number of racially xenophobic, patriarchal, and deeply ingrained caste and/or class structures that predate European global dominance, and that are transplanted from continent to continent with the mass migrations that have characterized the last century. My knowledge and direct experience of South Asian culture tells me that, although altered somewhat by European imperialism, that culture was never and is not now characterized by gender, racial, or class equality. Further, Friedman notes that there were 48 ethnic wars or conflicts being fought in Europe, Asia, Africa, South America, and the Middle East during 1993.[21] Many of these conflicts were and/or are based on ethnic animosities wherein each party has racialized an ethnic Other. In many cases such "othering" predated or has survived (in modified forms) European imperialism (for example, the long-standing Hindu–Muslim conflicts in India, manifested today in various insurgencies, including the Kashmiri independence movement; the Buddhist Tamil struggle against the Hindu Sinhalese in Sri Lanka; clan warfare in Somalia; and tribal warfare in Rwanda, Burundi, and Zaire). Indeed, many racisms in different parts of the world (such as Japanese racism against Koreans) seemingly have nothing to do with Europeans at all, while others (such as the generalized racism throughout Asia against the many thousands of exported Filipina domestic workers and nurses, and male Filipino labourers exported for the construction and shipping trades) are indirectly caused by European imperialism by virtue of its stunting of economic development in various regions.

Finally, it is important to remember the ongoing complicity of the elites of Third World countries and cultures in buttressing European and/or American economic imperialism and white supremacy because it serves *their* immediate interests. The specificities of their geopolitical positions, the machinations of international capitalism, and the legacies of co-lonialism may well explain the behaviour of "comprador" elites, but they are not thereby absolved of responsibility for oppressing certain ethnic, cultural, and/or religious groups, classes, or women within their populations. Race essentialist positions that hold only whites accountable for racial oppression are overly simplistic, miss the complexity of the issues involved, and encourage a focus on only one set of villains.

WHITES ARE ACCOUNTABLE FOR RACISM AS INDIVIDUALS

There is a tendency with race essentialist positions to think and act as if oppression by whites is conscious and deliberate. Often it is. But more frequently it is ignorant and habitual, an inevitable consequence of the race hierarchy, social structures, and ideologies within which we all live. When we hold individuals fully accountable for a complex set of social relations into which they are *born,* as we are, we act as if that social structure is of their choosing but not ours. Of course, I am not saying that our subordinate position is of *our* choosing, but simply that the privileged did not create the social structure *as individuals.* They may not perceive their privilege or the nature of the social structure because they are not confronted with negative *racial* experiences in their daily lives, nor are they forced to look at those who are. And even if many white women encounter negative experiences based on their gender, class, disability, sexual, or other identities, it does not automatically follow that such experiences would make them more capable of recognizing, or more sympathetic to, the negative race-based experiences of others.

HOMOGENIZING WHITES—ALL WHITE WOMEN OPPRESS US

As noted above, there has been a tendency in much of the writing by women of colour to assert that all white women oppress all women and/or people of colour. This is worrying because in the first place, white *men* seem to have fallen out of the conversation entirely, an odd turn of events that is no doubt gratifying to some white men. Reading the writings of women of colour on race and racism, it is as if the worst oppression, exclusions, and insults of women of colour have been at the hands of white feminists. This focus is partly explained by the fact that women of colour expect more of white feminists, who are, after all, supposedly bent on social transformation to forward the rights, conditions, status, and opportunities of women. Exclusion by them is particularly grievous, as in Abdo's description of Arab-Palestinian women, who are "silenced, ignored and oppressed, not only by structures and institutions, but also by the very social movement whose legitimation is largely derived from its opposition to oppression, namely feminism."[22] Bannerji goes even further in suggesting that white middle-class women are irredeemably implicated in the subjugation of women of colour:

> Far from being our "sisters," these middle class women are complicit in our domination. Being members of a middle class created on the terrain of imperialism and capitalism—hiding it (even from themselves perhaps) behind ideological methods constructed for ruling—they cannot but be part of our problem, not the solution.[23]

More to the point, the focus on white feminists is best explained by the fact that the whole point of this body of writing is to debunk the mythology of the essential woman.

Its audience is mostly feminist and mostly white, and it aims at correcting the omissions of white feminist theory. However, the charge of oppression is levelled not just at white *feminists,* but at all white *women.* There is a tendency then, particularly in black feminist writing, to homogenize white women as an undifferentiated mass, even as we women of colour are accusing them of obfuscating *our* infinite diversity and complexities. It is true, as Thornhill pointed out, that not all women are equally oppressed, but surely it is also true that not all white women are equally oppressive. Not all white women, not even all white feminists, are middle class. Not all white women are from ethnic groups privileged in specific eras and locations, nor is gender necessarily the only basis of their own subjugation.

HOMOGENIZING WOMEN OF COLOUR

As Mahtani notes, the concept of woman of colour "emphasizes a white versus colour dichotomy in academic debates."[24] This simplification is found in works by both women of colour and white feminists, even anti-racist feminists. Kline, for example, offers "a consideration of the division between the life experiences of women of colour and the life experiences of white women." She argues that "in a white-dominated social order, white women enjoy positions of privilege as part of the dominant culture, and women of colour exist in positions of subordination because of their race."[25] This may be true at a broad level of generality, but again, it tosses gender essentialism over in favour of a form of race essentialism that paints all women of colour uniformly as victims of white racism.

Not only can we not count on homogeneity in background and experience, but Ramazanoglu notes that black women (and women of colour) "are not uniformly oppressed, and they can have contradictory interests in which race, class, ethnicity, and nationality cut across each other."[26] Many variables account for the multiplicity of experiences of racism and levels of oppression among women of colour, including class and context. For example, in the case of first- and second-generation South Asian women living in Western countries, those who are well educated and have university degrees tend to come from the higher castes. Such women, especially those who are twice, thrice, or even quadruple experienced migrants (for example, India to East Africa to Britain to Canada) may experience less oppression than white working-class women, to the extent that class, high standards of living, and various career and other opportunities have been available to them.[27] In fact, it is somewhat disconcerting to me to realize that in many ways my current class and/or occupational position makes me more privileged (materially and socially) than the majority of white working-class women *and men*. Just as it is possible for a white middle- or upper-class woman to exercise privilege by virtue of her race and class even as she is oppressed on account of her lesbianism or disability, women of colour may be privileged and simultaneously oppressed in different contexts as different aspects of their identities shift to foreground or background.

A complex set of issues regarding the role of experience arise in this context. It is almost a truism to observe that material experience shapes knowledge of the world and understanding of social relations in complex and profound ways. The question is, am I oppressed because objectively I am a member of a particular group that has generally been oppressed, even if my actual lived experience has been mediated or buffeted by class and socio-economic privilege? In order to arrive at an affirmative answer to this question, race essentialists are usually forced to fall back upon a "false consciousness" argument: either the individual has been so conditioned by the dominant discourse that she identifies with it and has falsely interpreted her experience, attributing unfavourable treatment to factors other than race; or she is deliberately misinterpreting her experience out of a misplaced desire to deny her racial and/or ethnic identity and reap the benefits of "the system," including oppressing those of lower socio-economic status within her own racial group.

THE VOICE OF COLOUR: AUTHENTICITY AND APPROPRIATION

The "one speaks for all" presumption assumes that there is a "voice of colour." The question of whether race produces a distinctive voice is much like the question of whether gender produces a distinctive voice. In both cases, I would argue that, at a very general level, they do. It seems unnecessary to me to determine whether there is a natural "woman's voice" that differs in some primordial way from a "man's voice." It is possible to argue that there is a "woman's voice" (though not the definitive "woman's voice") when that voice is describing or analyzing experiences that have been *gendered* in specific ways in particular societies. Similarly, I would argue that there is a "voice of colour" (though not the definitive "voice of colour") when that voice is describing or analyzing experiences that have been *racialized* in specific sets of social relations, though Parashar puts it somewhat more strongly:

[There is a voice of colour] only if it articulates objections to [the] so-called "truths" (of liberalism: everyone has equal opportunity; success and failure are dependent on individual merit). If one has no disagreement with these prevailing notions, nor with claims about the justness of the institutions, one can hardly claim to have a distinctive voice or perspective.[28]

Definitions like these do not assume that the race, gender, or class of the speaker or writer automatically guarantee a distinctive voice. However, the tense and sometimes vitriolic debates waged within artistic and academic circles in recent years have focused more on the question of "authentic voice." Many have tried to grapple with the question of what constitutes "authenticity," or as Trinh Minh-ha puts it:

Of all the layers that form the open (never finite) totality of "I," which is to be filtered out as superfluous, fake, corrupt, and which is to be called pure, true, real, genuine, original, authentic? Which, indeed, since all interchange, revolving in an endless process.[29]

On the issue of racial and/or cultural identity, this question has become increasingly complex with physical and cultural cross-fertilization (discussed below), and especially for diasporic communities that have experienced varying degrees of integration or assimilation into European-derived cultures.

The authenticity debates have also centred on the question of whether one's racial ethnic identity determines one's right or authority to speak and write about race, racism, interracial relations and so on. The debates, mostly within artistic circles, have centred on the critical phenomenon of "appropriation of voice," meaning the propensity of white artists (and scholars) to take on the "voice" of people of colour. The voice appropriation debates have been complex and sophisticated, with writers of colour (and in Canada especially Aboriginal writers) presenting careful analyses of material, social, and political positionality and how voices are heard differently. Analyses by people of colour, ignored or dismissed when expressed by them, are heard differently and can suddenly be legitimated when expressed by those of dominant identities.[30] As a result of their experience and analyses, some have come to adopt essentialist positions while others have resisted such positions, usually on the grounds that the result is invisibility and exclusion from discourse, and the forfeiture of opportunities to explore and critique interracial and intercultural relations. As Stasiulis notes, for example, some First Nations writers (including Lee Maracle and Lenore Keeshig-Tobias) have asked non-Native writers to stop writing Native stories, while others, such as Emma LaRocque, take the contrary position that "non-native writers must take responsibility for fighting racism in literature."[31]

THE FETISHIZATION OF "DIFFERENCE"

Several years ago, Edward Said warned of the "ominous trend" of "the fetishization and relentless celebration of 'difference' and 'otherness,'" whereby people of colour become "otherness machines."[32] This trend features seemingly endless personal narratives, the telling of individual stories with all their quirks and particularities; in a sense, the ultimate celebration of individuality. Unfortunately, what is cast out along with homogenization is the possibility of viewing people as integrated wholes rather than as fragmented sub-identities, as the postmodernists would have us believe. As Bannerji points out in her insightful critique:

> If the paradigm of feminist essentialism played up the general/universal at the cost of the socio-cultural and historical particulars, this politics of difference errs on the side of the particulars, often making it impossible to see the forest for the trees. It invents multiple political personalities within one subject and invests expressions of these and other different subject positions with an equal and real value, [but without regard for] the genuinely antagonistic social relations ... that provide the context of and the reason for the "difference."[33]

Far from being radical or progressive, Bannerji argues, "difference" is the ultimate expression of neo-liberalism, since it precludes the use of larger concepts of social organization (such as capital, class, imperialism, and even patriarchy), which are seen as "totalizing" or as falling into "master narratives." So, she observes, "the stories we tell from our immediate life become the end of our political destination," obscuring the fact that "a whole social organization is needed to create each unique experience, and what constitutes someone's power is precisely another's powerlessness."[34]

The fear of generalization that drives the "difference" approach is understandable in view of the previous white male-crafted scholarship and white feminism, each of which in its way claimed to speak in universal terms. The anti-universalistic and perhaps more modest claims that individuals speak from their particular identities and experiences, even as they are members of multiple interconnected social groupings, is certainly an advance on the previous fiction of universality. On the other hand, however, if subjective experience is overplayed, if we do not have or are not allowed to use the tools to understand the world in larger terms, to analyze structures and discourses beyond personal interactions, then instead of social and political analysis, we are condemned to the narcissism of autobiography.

THE PROBLEM OF HYBRIDS

Race essentialist positions face a particularly difficult task in dealing with the increasing phenomenon of "hyphenated identities and hybrid realities,"[35] or those who are the products of two or more races, ethnicities, and/or cultures. Much of the theorizing about racism, especially by black feminists, has conceived of the world in black and white terms. We all know that an international racial hierarchy has been constructed, that whites occupy the summit, blacks are at the bottom (notwithstanding indigenous peoples in Canada and the United States), and in-betweens (such as Asians) are in-between. However, very little of the theorizing of black or white feminists has dealt with the in-betweens. There has been a tendency to theorize in polarities, as hooks does in her statement that "Black women are at the bottom of the societal hierarchy, and bear the brunt of racism, sexism, and classism. They therefore have a more holistic and accurate understanding of social reality than privileged white women."[36] In recent years, however, "in-between" or biracial and/or multiracial women of colour have pointed out that the black–white axis focuses inappropriately on skin colour and confuses the issue of racism:

> Racism is identified with "blackness" and as a result is limited to skin colour.... [S]uch a construction renders many "visible minorities" quite invisible and silences the voices of less-coloured or "differently coloured" groups.[37]

It is not just "differently coloured" groups such as the various Asians, South Americans, and non-black indigenous peoples who are rendered invisible under this schema, however. It is also the increasing number of hybrids, who cannot claim racial or cultural "purity." In my view, no one can claim these things now anyway, given the cross-fertilization of races and cultures as a result of global imperialism. Everything is in flux now, especially in the diasporas. However, racial mixing presents a unique problem for essentialist positions.

NOTES

1   Jill Vickers, *Reinventing Political Science: A Feminist Approach* (Halifax: Fernwood, 1997). Vickers provides an excellent analysis of political science's inability to "see" gender.

2   For a sustained critique of the political economy tradition, see Frances Abele and Daiva Stasiulis, "Canada as a 'White Settler Colony': What About Natives and Immigrants?" in *The New Canadian Political Economy*, ed. W. Clement and G. Williams (Montreal: McGill-Queen's University Press, 1989), 240–277.

3   See, among others, bell hooks, *Talking Back: Thinking Feminist, Thinking Black* (Boston: South End Press, 1989); *idem, Feminist Theory: From Margin to Centre* (Boston: South End Press, 1984); *idem, Ain't I a Woman: Black Women and Feminism* (Boston: South End Press, 1981); Hazel Carby, "White Women Listen! Black Feminism and the Boundaries of Sisterhood," in Centre for Contemporary Cultural Studies, *The Empire Strikes Back* (London: Hutchinson, 1982), 212–235; Angela Davis, *Women, Race and Class* (New York: Vintage Books, 1983); Audre Lorde, *Sister Outsider* (Trumansberg: The Crossing Press, 1984); Patricia Hill Collins, *Black Feminist Thought: Knowledge Consciousness and the Politics of Empowerment* (London: Unwin Hyman Ltd., 1990);

idem, "Learning from the Outsider within: The Sociological Significance of Black Feminist Thought," *Social Problems* 33, no. 6 (1986): 14–32; Patricia Williams, *The Alchemy of Race and Rights: Diary of a Law Professor* (Cambridge, Mass.: Harvard University Press, 1991); Angela P. Harris, "Race and Essentialism in Feminist Legal Theory," in *Feminist Legal Theory: Foundations*, ed. D.K. Weisberg (Philadelphia: Temple University Press, 1990), 348–358; Kimberle Crenshaw, "Demarginalizing the Intersection of Race and Sex," *Stanford Law Review* 42 (1990): 581.

4   Lata Mani, "Multiple Mediations: Feminist Scholarship in the Age of Multinational Reception," *Feminist Review* 35 (1990): 25.

5   Daiva Stasiulis, "Rainbow Feminism: Perspectives on Minority Women in Canada," *Resources for Feminist Research* 16, no. 1 (1987): 5.

6   Ibid.

7   Tania Das Gupta, introduction to and overview of *Race, Class, Gender: Bonds and Barriers*, 2nd ed., ed. Jesse Vorst et al. (Toronto: Society for Socialist Studies/Garamond Press, 1991), 6.

8   Esmeralda Thornhill, "Focus on Black Women!" in *Race, Class, Gender: Bonds and Barriers*, 2nd ed., ed. Jesse Vorst et al. (Toronto: Society for Socialist Studies/Garamond Press, 1991), 28.

9   Nkiru Nzegwu, "Confronting Racism: Towards the Formation of a Female-Identified Alliance," *Canadian Journal of Women and the Law* 7 (1994): 21; see also Linda Carty, introduction to *And Still We Rise: Feminist Political Mobilizing in Contemporary Canada*, ed. L. Carty (Toronto: Women's Press, 1993), 13.

10   hooks, *Feminist Theory*, x.

11   The quote is from Fawzia Ahmad, "How Do You Identify?" *Canadian Woman Studies* 14, no. 2 (1994): 29; Carol Camper, "To White Feminists," *Canadian Woman Studies* 14, no. 2 (1994): 40.

12   Diana Fuss, *Essentially Speaking: Feminism, Nature and Difference* (London: Routledge, 1989), 2.

13   This paper was first presented to the Canadian Learned Societies Conference at the University of Calgary in June 1994. Since then, Susan Stanford Friedman, in "Beyond White and Other: Relationality and Narratives of Race in Feminist Discourse," *Signs* 21, no. 1 (autumn 1995): 1–49, has explored some of the debates about race and racism in what she calls scripts or narratives of denial (by white women, which focus on gender and "covertly refuse the significance of race" [p. 8]), scripts of accusation (largely by women of colour, which accuse white feminists of "ignoring, trivializing, or distorting the lives of women who were 'different'" [p. 9]), and scripts of confession (by white women in response to scripts of accusation, featuring narratives of guilt, "perpetual mea culpas," and sometimes tending "toward a fetishization of women of colour that once again reconstitutes them as other" [p. 11]). In Friedman's view, scripts of accusation can be synopsized as follows: "You are a racist." "I am not like you." "You haven't confronted your racial privilege." "I am both a woman and black (Jewish, Chicana, Native American, etc.), and I can't sort out the oppressions of race and gender." "Gender can't be separated from race and class." "You can never understand my experience or perspective." "You are oppressing me and you don't even know it." "You have left out women of colour and assumed that your own experience is like all other women's." "You shouldn't write (teach, talk, etc.) about women of colour because we women of colour must speak for ourselves." "You must include women of colour in your classes (books, articles, etc.)." "You have to take the responsibility for learning about us on your own; we should not have to take the responsibility (time, energy, etc.) to educate you." "I don't want to waste my time trying to talk with you; I'm going to devote all my energy to my sisters of colour" (p. 10). Friedman does point out that such scripts of accusation have led to "important reconceptualizations of feminist theory in relation to other systems of oppression," so she does not dismiss them as unduly divisive (p. 9).

14   Mary Ellen Turpel, "Patriarchy and Paternalism: The Legacy of the Canadian State for First Nations Women," *Canadian Journal of Women and the Law* 6 (1993): 183.

15   hooks, *Ain't I a Woman*; C.T. Mohanty, A. Russo, and L. Torres, eds., *Third World Women and the Politics of Feminism* (Bloomington: Indiana University Press, 1991).

16 Enakshi Dua, "Racism or Gender? Understanding Oppression of South Asian-Canadian Women," *Canadian Woman Studies* 13, no. 1 (1992): 8–9.

17 Vijay Agnew, *Resisting Discrimination: Women from Asia, Africa, and the Caribbean and the Women's Movement in Canada* (Toronto: University of Toronto Press, 1996).

18 See also the interesting collection of essays assembled in V.M. Moghadam, ed., *Identity Politics and Women; Cultural Reassertions and Feminisms in International Perspective* (Oxford: Westview Press, 1994).

19 Quoted in Himani Bannerji, "But Who Speaks for Us?" in *Unsettling Relations: The University as a Site of Feminist Struggles*, ed. H. Bannerji, L. Carty, K. Delhi, S. Heald, and K. McKenna (Toronto: Women's Press, 1991), 100.

20 Mohanty, Russo, and Torres, eds., *Third World Women*, 18. Emphasis added.

21 Friedman, "Beyond White."

22 Nahla Abdo, "Race, Gender and Politics: the Struggle of Arab Women in Canada," in *And Still We Rise: Feminist Political Mobilizing in Contemporary Canada*, ed. L. Carty (Toronto: Women's Press. 1993), 74.

23 Bannerji, "But Who Speaks for Us?", 12.

24 Minelle K. Mahtani, "Polarity Versus Plurality: Confessions of an Ambivalent Woman of Colour," *Canadian Woman Studies* 14, no. 2 (1994): 15; See also Daiva Stasiulis, "Theorizing Connections: Race, Ethnicity, Gender and Class," in *Race and Ethnic Relations in Canada*, ed. Peter Li (Oxford University Press, 1990), 269–305; and *idem*, "Rainbow Feminism," 5–9.

25 Marlee Kline, "Women's Oppression and Racism: A Critique of the 'Feminist Standpoint,'" in *Race, Class, Gender: Bonds and Barriers*, ed. Vorst et al., 45, 47.

26 Caroline Ramazanoglu, *Feminism and the Contradictions of Oppression* (London: Routledge, 1989), 134.

27 See Parminder Bhachu, "The Multiple Landscapes of Transnational Asian Women in the Diaspora," in *Re-situating Identities: The Politics of Race, Ethnicity and Culture*, ed. V. Amit-Talai and C. Knowles (Peterborough: Broadview, 1996), 283–303.

28 Archana Parashar, "Essentialism or Pluralism: The Future of Legal Feminism," *Canadian Journal of Women and the Law* 6 (1993): 339.

29 Trinh T. Minh-ha, *Woman, Native, Other* (Bloomington: Indiana University Press, 1989), 94.

30 In her supple analysis of the possibilities and traps of speaking for and about others, Alcoff points out that "[w]ho is speaking to whom turns out to be as important for meaning and truth as what is said; in fact, what is said turns out to change according to who is speaking and who is listening ... how what is said gets heard depends on who says it, and who says it will affect the style and language in which it is stated, which will in turn affect its perceived significance (for specific hearers). The discursive style in which some European post-structuralists have made the claim that all writing is political marks it as important and likely to be true for a certain (powerful) milieu; whereas the style in which African-American writers made the same claim marked their speech as dismissable in the eyes of the same milieu." Linda Alcoff, "Cultural Feminism Versus Post-Structuralism: The Identity Crisis in Feminist Theory," *Signs* 13, no. 3 (1998): 291, 292.

31 Daiva Stasiulis, "'Authentic Voice': Anti-Racist Politics in Canadian Feminist Publishing and Literary Production," in *Feminism and the Politics of Difference*, ed. S. Gunew and A. Yeatman (Halifax: Fernwood, 1993), 47. Alcoff mentions the case of Anne Cameron, "a very gifted white Canadian author" who has written several semi-fictional accounts of the lives of Native Canadian women in the first person (thus assuming a Native identity), and who was asked by a group of Native writers to "move over" on the grounds that her works are disempowering for Aboriginal writers. Cameron agreed. Alcoff, "Cultural Feminism Versus Post-structuralism," 285.

32 Edward Said, "Representing the Colonized: Anthropology's Interlocutors," *Critical Inquiry* 15, no. 2 (1989): 213.
33 Bannerji, "But Who Speaks for Us?", 82.
34 Ibid., 84–85.
35 Trinh T. Minh-ha, *When the Moon Waxes Red: Representation, Gender, and Cultural Politics* (New York: Routledge, 1991), ix.
36 hooks, *Feminist Theory,* ix.
37 Abdo, "Race, Gender and Politics," 75.

Questions for Critical Thought

CHAPTER 1 BY ROBERT MILES AND MALCOLM BROWN

1. Why is Miles and Brown's reading passage called "representations of the other"? Why did they not call it "racial representations of the other"?
2. Why can it be argued that race classifications are historically specific ways to represent the human population?
3. What social factors or forces contribute to the ways in which others and, necessarily, selves are represented?

CHAPTER 2 BY ANTON ALLAHAR

1. Differentiate structuralism from primordialism. Are they incompatible theories or approaches?
2. What is the difference between hard and soft primordialism? Which perspective do you think is more appropriate for explaining current-day ethnic or racial identities? Why?
3. What (hard or soft) primordial identities are salient in your daily life? What factors do you think led to the formation of these identities? Do they conflict with each other in certain situations?

CHAPTER 3 BY CARL E. JAMES

1. In what ways do you think that the dialectic of representation involving self and Other, discussed in Miles and Brown's reading passage, applies to the reading passage by James? What dimensions of the dialectic are addressed by James that are not addressed by Miles and Brown?

2. In what ways can soft primordialism be used to explain the experiences and feelings dealt with in James's reading?
3. What role does James assign to power and privilege in the process of racial and ethnic identity formation?

CHAPTER 4 BY RADHA JHAPPAN

1. What is race and gender essentialism?
2. Considering the "traps" of race and gender essentialism identified by Jhappan, think of one way that each trap can be applied to your daily life. How would you avoid these traps (or would you)?
3. Can you think of situations where race essentialism would be a positive and productive force?

FURTHER READING

Foster, Cecil. *A Place Called Heaven: The Meaning of Being Black in Canada.* Toronto: Harper Collins, 1996.
   Foster explores the lived realities of being racialized as black in Canada. These lived realities, argues Foster, take place in the context of a contradictory social system that pits democratic values against racist practices. The book captures some of the complexity in black communities and processes of identity formation.

Ignatiev, Noel. *How the Irish Became White.* New York: Routledge, 1996.
   This book details how millions of Irish immigrants to the USA—many of whom were neither protestant nor Anglo-Saxon—were perceived as not belonging to the white race. Ignatiev shows how the Irish "became white" in the years leading up to and following the American Civil War.

Shipman, Pat. *The Evolution of Racism: Human Differences and the Use and Abuse of Science.* New York: Simon and Schuster, 1994.
   Shipman outlines European efforts to explain race from the 19th century. She examines taxonomy, eugenics, genocide, and contemporary struggles to deal with race.

Snowdon, Frank. *Before Color Prejudice: The Ancient View of Blacks.* Boston: Harvard University Press, 1983.
   In this detailed analysis of the interactions between white explorers, traders, and warriors from the Mediterranean and black Kushites, Nubians, and Ethiopians, Snowdon argues that skin colour was not a basis for evaluation in the ancient world. The book is crucial for the development of a full understanding of human classification.

Wright, Ronald. *A Short History of Progress*. Toronto: Anansi, 2004.

In this recent best-seller, Wright provides a general outline of how civilizations grow, divide, and collapse. From settlement on Easter Island in the 5th century A.D. to the fall of the Roman Empire at Constantinople in 1453, Wright sketches some basic patterns in human conflict and classification.

TWO

IDENTITY, NATION, MEMORY, AND BELONGING

I do not come with timeless truths.

My consciousness is not illuminated with ultimate radiances.... I came into the world imbued with the will to find a meaning in things, my spirit filled with the desire to attain the source of the world, and then I found that I was an object in the midst of other objects.

Sealed in that crushing objecthood, I turned beseechingly to others. (Fanon 1967, 7, 109)

In his only novel, *Not without Laughter,* the American poet Langston Hughes (1969) tells the story of Sandy, a young black boy coming of age in the town of "Stanton," Kansas, between 1911 and 1918. Sandy is the son of Annjee and Jimboy, with whom he enjoys limited but significant interactions early in the book (and prior to their departure from his life), but he is raised almost entirely by his grandmother, Aunt Hager Williams. Hager is burdened by many social disadvantages: she is a black person living in a predominantly white, racist society; she is a woman living in a patriarchal society; and she is a poor person living in a capitalist society. To survive, Hager washes white women's clothes, and, despite her disadvantaged social position, she is able to provide Sandy with stability, encouragement, and feelings of hope for the future.

If there is one thing that is made clear in the first two-thirds of the novel, it is Hager's admiration and respect for Booker T. Washington. Washington (1856–1915) was an ex-slave who became the first president of the Tuskegee Institute in Alabama, where he promoted vocational training for black Americans from 1881 to 1915. He was an influential political figure, consulted regularly by white businessmen, congressmen, and presidents. Washington believed that the path to racial equality in America involved gradual change and the mass incorporation of the black population into the Southern proletariat—a set of arguments he laid out in his 1901 biography, *Up from Slavery*, and, earlier, in the infamous 1895 Atlanta Exposition Address (a.k.a. the Atlanta Compromise). Washington believed that separatism and self-reliance were counterproductive to the collective interests of black Americans in the South, and he argued that the most effective future strategy for the "American Negro" was to accommodate to American capitalism. "No race can prosper till it learns that there is as much dignity in tilling a field as in writing a poem," Washington proclaimed in 1895. "It is at the bottom of life we must begin, and not at the top."[1]

The significance of Hager's admiration for Booker T. Washington, and the significance of the novel to sociological understandings of identity and belonging, is realized most fully in the context of a second set of parallel narratives that run through the book. Whereas Hager washes white women's clothes, lives in a small run-down house, and extols the virtues of Booker T. Washington, Sandy's aunt Tempy, with whom he lives when Hager dies, is an educated, upwardly mobile black woman who has great contempt for black Southerners, for black culture, and for most things non-white. Tempy repeatedly glorifies whiteness, and, at one point, proclaims: "Coloured people certainly need to come up in the world ... up to the level of white people—dress like white people, talk like white people, think like white people—and then, they would no longer be called 'niggers'" (p. 240).

Considering Tempy's views, it is curious that one day Sandy comes across her complete collection of *The Crisis*, the official publication of the National Association for the Advancement of Colored People. As Sandy peruses the magazine, he learns that many of the articles are penned by W.E.B. Du Bois, the magazine's founder. Throughout his life, Du Bois worked as a civil rights activist, and, politically, he encouraged black Americans to collectively resist racism and white Americans to break down systemic racial barriers. He was the first black man to receive a Ph.D. from Harvard University, where he wrote his dissertation on American suppression of the slave trade. Du Bois demonstrated sympathies for Marxism throughout his life, and he is perhaps most recognized for his famous declaration, which opens chapter 2 of *The Souls of Black Folk* (1982): "The problem of the twentieth century is the problem of the colour line—the relation of the darker to the lighter races of men in Asia and Africa, in America and the islands of the sea" (p. 54).

After reading *The Crisis*, Sandy asks his aunt about Du Bois. Tempy responds that he is a great man. Sandy, having heard Hager talk at length about Washington, queries: "Great like Booker T. Washington?" (p. 242). With disdain, Tempy retorts:

> Teaching Negroes to be servants, that's all Washington did! Du Bois wants our rights. He wants us to be real men and women. He believes in social equality.... Don't talk to me about Washington.... Take Du Bois for your model, not some white folks' nigger. (p. 242)

The differences between Hager's and Tempy's political sympathies speak to the wider complexities involved in the formation of racial identities and group belongings. Hager is the archetype of post–Civil War racial oppression; she experiences multiple sources of oppression along race, class, and gender lines, and still she looks forward to a future of racial integration and black accommodation through the political philosophies expounded by Booker T. Washington. Tempy, by contrast, enjoys considerable material successes and comforts: she is educated and she is wealthy. Yet still, Tempy finds strength in the political philosophies of W.E.B. Du Bois, with their emphases on racial conflict, exploitation, and resistance to accommodation.

From the interrelated perspectives of identity, nation, memory, and belonging, the emphases that Langston Hughes places on the political philosophies of Washington and Du Bois in *Not without Laughter* exemplify what Antonio Gramsci (1971) conceptualized as "permanent persuaders": intellectual leaders who emerge "organically" from subordinated class(es) or group(s). Permanent persuaders are a special kind of intellectual leader defined by their ability to influence and inspire large numbers of people on the basis of experience, shared suffering, and charisma, rather than formal characteristics such as education or occupation. They are engaged in everyday activities, and they are able to evoke feeling and passion in oppressed populations based on a shared social and psychological location. While Hager finds feeling and passion in the political philosophy of Washington (accommodation), despite her social position as a poor black woman, Tempy, a wealthy, upwardly mobile black woman, finds feeling and passion in the political philosophy of Du Bois (resistance). The emphasis on each permanent persuader in *Not without Laughter* signifies the massive political influence Washington and Du Bois exerted in the early 20th century, and it also illustrates how one's social location does not determine a priori their political positions or points of view. The complexity involved in processes of identity formation is only enriched in the novel by Tempy's simultaneous endorsement of Du Bois and her encouragement for black people to "act like whites." Irrespective of Tempy's or Hager's political leanings, however, Sandy measures the worth of each man after reading *Up from Slavery*, and he concludes that they are both great men—a realization that speaks to the fluid character and generational dimensions of identity, leadership, and belonging.

SECTION READINGS: NATIONAL CONSCIOUSNESS, MEMORY, STATES, AND DIASPORA

The readings in this section address some of the ways that national identities, memories, and a sense of sameness are created, maintained, and challenged. In popular discourse, collective memories and national, racial, or ethnic identities are rarely explained as historical constructions with specific spatial and temporal dimensions. We tend to assume that identities are characteristics or markers that individuals simply have or possess. The first two readings in this section, however, draw attention to the social, cultural, historical, and political dimensions involved in collective forms of remembering and imagining, and to the role communication media and the state play in the formation of individual and shared identities.

The first reading is drawn from Benedict Anderson's (1991) *Imagined Communities*, a remarkably influential book that examines the processes involved in the origin and spread of global national communities. The general argument presented in *Imagined Communities* is that national identities have not always existed. Prior to the formation of modern nationalisms, religious communities, consolidated through shared, often exclusive, languages (e.g., Latin), were the basis from which individuals derived a shared sense of identity and belonging. Up until the 18th century, religious communities such as Christendom and the Islamic Ummah represented the principal basis of group identification. People did not think of themselves as Chinese or European; instead, they imagined themselves through the medium of sacred texts and written script.

Anderson argues that the declining significance of great religious communities and the dynastic realm (as well as the limited everyday utility of Latin) facilitated the development of European print capitalism, or the development of print-as-commodity, and the popularization of the nation. As he explains, the expansion of book publishing between 1500 and 1600 was tied to an expanding capitalist print market that relied on the availability of cheap editions written in the vernacular (that is, written in native languages and, sometimes, in a straightforward, plain, and comprehensible style). This market was able to attract a "new" reading public, among them women and merchants who did not speak Latin and who were largely poor. The rise of national consciousness, he contends, was also facilitated by the changing character of Latin, by the expansion of Protestantism (the Reformation), and by the birth of administrative vernaculars. These interrelated developments, argues Anderson, influenced the ascendancy of national consciousness by opening channels of communication among otherwise geographically remote and communicatively disconnected persons; by naturalizing or codifying an image of antiquity through the fixity of written language; and by consolidating a print form capable of absorbing regional dialects. The interaction of capitalism, technology, and linguistic diversity, says Anderson, situated in the wider context of religious and cultural transformation, enabled new forms of imagining that took the discursive form of the "nation."

The next reading passage, taken from Ron Eyerman's (2002) *Cultural Trauma: Slavery and the Formation of African-American Identity*, addresses a specific form of imagining in the context of failed reconstruction in the American South. The argument presented in *Cultural Trauma* hinges on the conceptual distinction between "history" and "cultural memory." For Eyerman, history refers to a particular event or set of events, often recorded and institutionalized in books, archives, and film. Examples of historical events include the fall of Constantinople, the Great Depression, the First World War, the Rwandan genocide, and the London bombings of 7 July 2005. Cultural memory, by contrast, refers to the different ways that groups of people remember or interpret history, and the cultural significance they attach to certain historical events. Material artifacts and objects (e.g., monuments, book, documents) are able to evoke a sense of the past, but the symbolic importance attached to those objects changes over time. Examples of the changing nature of cultural memories include the indifferent attitudes young Canadians hold toward Irish labourers in North America, the nuclear arms race, and communist threats in or to the West—each examples of historical events that aroused strong emotions and governmental interventions less than 100 years ago, but no longer attract the attention of younger generations.

In the reading, Eyerman is concerned with a particular form of cultural memory: trauma in the aftermath of American slavery. He argues that the important role of cultural trauma in the formation of post-1865 African-American identity was not so much based on the experience, but rather the mediation, of slavery. In the aftermath of slavery, he argues, reconstruction brought great anticipation for black Americans in the South. Freed slaves were eager to take advantage of new opportunities to educate their children, to seek better occupational opportunities, and to integrate fully into American life. But the failure of reconstruction to deliver on its promises, and the already disintegrating ethnic diversity within the African-American population (e.g., Ibo, Igba), gave rise to the memory of slavery as cultural trauma. In other words, it was not the actual experience of slavery that constituted cultural trauma; rather, it was the mediation of the failure of reconstruction, and the insult that accompanied continued oppression, which gave rise to a collective sense of trauma.

Eyerman argues that, as a form of imagining, the cultural trauma of slavery was articulated most forcefully by a group of educated black intellectuals, writers, and artists following reconstruction. Black-owned newspapers, benefiting from expanding literacy rates among black Americans, began to articulate the representational significance of African-American identity. Black intellectuals were able to take control of the means by which patterns of representation were disseminated, and they were able to articulate the collective interests of black Americans.

In the third reading, Michael Omi and Howard Winant address the trajectory of contemporary racial politics in the USA. The passage is drawn from *Racial Formation in the United States* (1994), where they introduce their popular theory of racial formation. The theory of racial formation, according to Omi and Winant, grants an explanatory primacy to race. Too often, they argue, race is treated as epiphenomenal to ethnicity, class, and nation (pp. 9–47), explaining race as an illusion or mystification; and too often, they argue, sociological explanations that attempt to distance themselves from biological notions of race fail to understand race as an organizing principle of social relationships in the United States. Their perspective conceptualizes racial formation as a process of historically situated "projects" linking individual human beings (e.g., everyday experiences) and social structural arrangements (e.g., courts) along a micro–macro continuum. At each end of the continuum, they contend, the racial state facilitates the trajectory of racial relations and the patterns of conflict and accommodation among racially based social movements and governmental policies and processes.

The reading begins with the argument that, since the early days of colonialism, major institutions and social relationships in America have been structured by the racial order. Despite the monolithic character of racial oppression that has manifested in certain moments of American history, however, repressed groups have engaged in a "war of manoeuvre" to create oppositional cultures and spaces. In recent times, Omi and Winant argue, it has become common for disadvantaged racial groups to supplement a war of manoeuvre with a "war of position." This sequence of relations between the state and movement organizations takes place in the context of an unstable (racial) equilibrium. Racial movements, based on the political interventions of intellectual leaders, seek reform of the racial order, but Omi and Winant warn of recent contemporary trends toward the conservativism of the New Right.

The final reading passage revisits a key theme addressed in Part I: primordialism and the unifying power of a sense of sameness. The passage is taken from Paul Gilroy's (2000) *Against Race: Imagining Political Culture beyond the Colour Line.* Gilroy focuses on contemporary patterns of primordial constructions of origin, territory, and place. He observes that the consciousness of identity, despite its political, economic, and historical foundations, finds particular strength in the articulations of rootedness, place, and location. Past understandings of human belonging were widely understood to emerge from cultural, historical socio-economic forces, he contends, but today identities are increasingly articulated as pre-social, natural, essential, and immutable features of groups of human beings. What this equates to, says Gilroy, is a rejection of understandings of identity formation as socio-historical, contingent relationships, based on interactions and negotiations, in favour of the naturalization of identity through the shared experience of place, location, and language.

From the historic fraternalism demonstrated by Nazism to the many contemporary national, tribal, and ethnic conflicts around the world, Gilroy maintains that what remains constant is the impulse for groups of human beings to turn away from complexity and difference, from uncertainty and insecurity, to covet the familiar and the particular. The socio-ecological referents of territory, place, blood, and nation occupy an important role in primordial discourses, but Gilroy queries to what extent citizenship, identity, and belonging can be understood to depend on movement and placelessness. He argues that diaspora—the geographic dispersion of a once-localized population (e.g., Jews living among Gentiles following Babylonian captivity)—disrupts the simplicity that connects identity with place or location. Through modern mechanisms of communication, he contends, identities are reinforced, refashioned, and reproduced outside territorial homelands. For Gilroy, it is these "placeless identities"—"creolized, syncretized, hybridized, and chronically impure" (p. 129)—that rupture the rationale of racial reason.

NOTE

1   Booker T. Washington. Speech delivered at the Cotton States and International Exposition, Atlanta, Georgia, 8 September 1895. For a copy of the speech, see http://historymatters.gmu.edu/d/39/.

REFERENCES

Du Bois, W.E.B. [1903] 1982. *The Souls of Black Folk*. New York: Signet Publishing.
Fanon, Franz. [1952] 1967. *Black Skin, White Masks*. New York: Grove Press.
Gramsci, Antonio. 1971. *Selections from the Prison Notebooks of Antonio Gramsci*. New York: International Publishers.
Hughes, Langston. [1929] 1969. *Not without Laughter*. New York: Simon and Schuster.
Washington, Booker T. 1901. *Up from Slavery: An Autobiography*. New York: Doubleday.

THE ORIGINS OF NATIONAL CONSCIOUSNESS

BENEDICT ANDERSON

The development of print as commodity is the key to the generation of wholly new ideas of simultaneity. Why, within that type, did the nation become so popular? The factors involved are obviously complex and various. But a strong case can be made for the primacy of capitalism.

At least 20 million books had already been printed by 1500,[1] signalling the onset of Benjamin's "age of mechanical reproduction." If manuscript knowledge was scarce and arcane lore, print knowledge lived by reproducibility and dissemination.[2] If, as Febvre and Martin believe, possibly as many as 200 million volumes had been manufactured by 1600, it is no wonder that Francis Bacon believed that print had changed "the appearance and state of the world."[3]

One of the earlier forms of capitalist enterprise, book publishing felt all of capitalism's restless search for markets. The early printers established branches all over Europe: "in this way a veritable 'international' of publishing houses, which ignored national [sic] frontiers, was created"[4] And since the years 1500–1550 were a period of exceptional European prosperity, publishing shared in the general boom. "More than at any other time" it was "a great industry under the control of wealthy capitalists."[5] Naturally, "booksellers were primarily concerned to make a profit and to sell their products, and consequently they sought out first and foremost those works which were of interest to the largest possible number of their contemporaries."[6]

The initial market was literate Europe, a wide but thin stratum of Latin-readers. Saturation of this market took about 150 years. The determinative fact about Latin—aside from its sacrality—was that it was a language of bilinguals. Relatively few were born to speak it and even fewer, one imagines, dreamed in it. In the 16th century the proportion of bilinguals within the total population of Europe was quite small; very likely no larger than the proportion in the world's population today, and—proletarian internationalism notwithstanding—in the centuries to come. Then and now the bulk of mankind is monoglot. The logic of capitalism thus meant that once the elite Latin market was saturated, the potentially huge markets represented by the monoglot masses would beckon. To be sure, the Counter Reformation encouraged a temporary resurgence of Latin publishing, but by the mid-17th century the movement was in decay, and fervently Catholic libraries replete. Meantime, a Europe-wide shortage of money made printers think more and more of peddling cheap editions in the vernaculars.[7]

The revolutionary vernacularizing thrust of capitalism was given further impetus by three extraneous factors, two of which contributed directly to the rise of national consciousness. The first, and ultimately the least important, was a change in the character of Latin itself. Thanks to the labours of the Humanists in reviving the broad literature of pre-Christian antiquity and spreading it through the print market, a new appreciation of the sophisticated stylistic achievements of the ancients was apparent among the trans-European intelligentsia. The Latin they now aspired to write became more and more Ciceronian and, by the same token, increasingly removed from ecclesiastical and everyday life. In this way it acquired an esoteric quality quite different from that of Church Latin in medieval times. For the older Latin was not arcane because of its subject matter or style, but simply because it was written at all, that is, because of its status as *text*. Now it became arcane because of what was written, because of the language-in-itself.

Second was the impact of the Reformation, which, at the same time, owed much of its success to print capitalism. Before the age of print, Rome easily won every war against heresy in Western Europe because it always had better internal lines of communication than its challengers. But when in 1517 Martin Luther nailed his theses to the chapel door in Wittenberg, they were printed up in German translation, and "within 15 days [had been] seen in every part of the country."[8] In the two decades 1520–1540, three times as many books were published in German as in the period 1500–1520, an astonishing transformation to which Luther was absolutely central. His works represented no less than one-third of *all* German-language books sold between 1518 and 1525. Between 1522 and 1546, a total of 430 editions (whole or partial) of his biblical translations appeared. "We have here for the first time a truly mass readership and a popular literature within everybody's reach."[9] In effect, Luther became the first bestselling author so *known*. Or, to put it another way, the first writer who could "sell" his *new* books on the basis of his name.[10]

Where Luther led, others quickly followed, opening the colossal religious propaganda war that raged across Europe for the next century. In this titanic "battle for men's minds," Protestantism was always fundamentally on the offensive, precisely because it knew how to make use of the expanding vernacular print market being created by capitalism, while the Counter Reformation defended the citadel of Latin. The emblem for this is the Vatican's *Index Librorum Prohibitorum*—to which there was no Protestant counterpart—a novel catalogue made necessary by the sheer volume of printed subversion. Nothing gives a better sense of this siege mentality than Francois I's panicked 1535 ban on the printing of any books in his realm—on pain of death by hanging! The reason for both the ban and its unenforceability was that by then his realm's eastern borders were ringed with Protestant states and cities producing a massive stream of smugglable print. To take

Calvin's *Geneva* alone: between 1533 and 1540 only 42 editions were published there, but the numbers swelled to 527 between 1550 and 1564, by which latter date no less than 40 separate printing presses were working overtime.[11]

The coalition between Protestantism and print capitalism, exploiting cheap popular editions, quickly created large new reading publics—not least among merchants and women, who typically knew little or no Latin—and simultaneously mobilized them for politico-religious purposes. Inevitably, it was not merely the Church that was shaken to its core. The same earthquake produced Europe's first important non-dynastic, non-city-states in the Dutch Republic and the Commonwealth of the Puritans. (Francois I's panic was as much political as religious.)

Third was the slow, geographically uneven, spread of particular vernaculars as instruments of administrative centralization by certain well-positioned would-be absolutist monarchs. Here it is useful to remember that the universality of Latin in medieval Western Europe never corresponded to a universal political system. The contrast with Imperial China, where the reach of the mandarinal bureaucracy and of painted characters largely coincided, is instructive. In effect, the political fragmentation of Western Europe after the collapse of the Western Empire meant that no sovereign could monopolize Latin and make it his-and-only-his language of state, and thus Latin's religious authority never had a true political analogue.

These print languages laid the bases for national consciousnesses in three distinct ways. First and foremost, they created unified fields of exchange and communication below Latin and above the spoken vernaculars. Speakers of the huge variety of Frenches, Englishes, or Spanishes, who might find it difficult or even impossible to understand one another in conversation, became capable of comprehending one another via print and paper. In the process, they gradually became aware of the hundreds of thousands, even millions, of people in their particular language field, and at the same time that *only those* hundreds of thousands, or millions, so belonged. These fellow readers, to whom they were connected through print, formed, in their secular, particular, visible invisibility, the embryo of the nationally imagined community.

Second, print capitalism gave a new fixity to language, which in the long run helped to build that image of antiquity so central to the subjective idea of the nation. As Febvre and Martin remind us, the printed book kept a permanent form, capable of virtually infinite reproduction, temporally and spatially. It was no longer subject to the individualizing and "unconsciously modernizing" habits of monastic scribes. Thus, while 12th-century French differed markedly from that written by Villon in the 15th, the rate of change slowed decisively in the 16th. "By the 17th century languages in Europe had generally assumed their modern forms."[12] To put it another way, for three centuries now these stabilized print languages have been gathering a darkening varnish; the words of our 17th-century forebears are accessible to us in a way that to Villon his 12th-century ancestors were not.

Third, print capitalism created languages of power of a kind different from the older administrative vernaculars. Certain dialects inevitably were "closer" to each print language and dominated their final forms. Their disadvantaged cousins, still assimilable to the emerging print language, lost caste, above all because they were unsuccessful (or only relatively successful) in insisting on their own print form. "Northwestern German" became

Platt Deutsch, a largely spoken, thus substandard, German because it was assimilable to print German in a way that Bohemian spoken Czech was not. High German, the King's English, and, later, Central Thai, were correspondingly elevated to a new politico-cultural eminence. (Hence the struggles in late 20th-century Europe by certain "sub"-nationalities to change their subordinate status by breaking firmly into print—and radio.)

It remains only to emphasize that in their origins, the fixing of print languages and the differentiation of status between them were largely unself-conscious processes resulting from the explosive interaction between capitalism, technology, and human linguistic diversity. But as with so much else in the history of nationalism, once "there," they could become formal models to be imitated and, where expedient, consciously exploited in a Machiavellian spirit. Today, the Thai government actively discourages attempts by foreign missionaries to provide its hill-tribe minorities with their own transcription systems and to develop publications in their own languages: the same government is largely indifferent to what these minorities *speak*. The fate of the Turkic-speaking peoples in the zones incorporated into today's Turkey, Iran, Iraq, and the USSR is especially exemplary. A family of spoken languages, once everywhere assemblable, thus comprehensible, within an Arabic orthography, has lost that unity as a result of conscious manipulations. To heighten Turkish Turkey's national consciousness at the expense of any wider Islamic identification, Atatürk imposed compulsory romanization.[13] The Soviet authorities followed suit, first with an anti-Islamic, anti-Persian compulsory romanization, then, in Stalin's 1930s, with a Russifying compulsory Cyrillicization.[14]

We can summarize the conclusions to be drawn from the argument thus far by saying that the convergence of capitalism and print technology on the fatal diversity of human language created the possibility of a new form of imagined community, which in its basic morphology set the stage for the modern nation. The potential stretch of these communities was inherently limited and, at the same time, bore none but the most fortuitous relationship to existing political boundaries (which were, on the whole, the high water marks of dynastic expansionisms).

Yet it is obvious that while today almost all modern self-conceived nations—and also nation-states—have "national print languages," many of them have these languages in common, and in others only a tiny fraction of the population "uses" the national language in conversation or on paper. The nation-states of Spanish America or those of the "Anglo-Saxon family" are conspicuous examples of the first outcome; many ex-colonial states, particularly in Africa, of the second. In other words, the concrete formation of contemporary nation-states is by no means isomorphic with the determinate reach of particular print languages. To account for the discontinuity in connectedness between print languages, national consciousness, and nation-states, it is necessary to turn to the large cluster of new political entities that sprang up in the Western hemisphere between 1776 and 1838, all of which self-consciously defined themselves as nations and, with the interesting exception of Brazil, as (non-dynastic) republics. For not only were they historically the first such states to emerge on the world stage, and therefore inevitably provided the first real models of what such states should "look like," but their numbers and contemporary births offer fruitful ground for comparative enquiry.

NOTES

1 The population of that Europe where print was then known was about 100 million. Lucien Febvre and Henri-Jean Martin, *The Coming of the Book* (London and New York: Verso, 1976), 248–249.

2 Emblematic is Marco Polo's *Travels,* which remained largely unknown till its first printing in 1559. Polo, *Travels,* xiii.

3 Quoted in Eisenstein, "Some Conjectures," 56.

4 Febvre and Martin, *The Coming of the Book,* 122. (The original text, however, speaks simply of "par-dessus les frontieres." *L'Apparition,* 184.)

5 Ibid., 187. The original text speaks of "puissants" (powerful) rather than "wealthy" capitalists. *L'Apparition,* 281.

6 "Hence the introduction of printing was in this respect a stage on the road to our present society of mass consumption and standardisation." Ibid., 259–260. (The original text has "une civilisation de masse et de standardisation," which may be better rendered "standardised, mass civilization." *L'Apparition,* 394).

7 Ibid., 195.

8 Ibid., 289–290.

9 Ibid., 291–295.

10 From this point it was only a step to the situation in 17th-century France where Corneille, Molière, and La Fontaine could sell their manuscript tragedies and comedies directly to publishers, who bought them as excellent investments in view of their authors' market reputations. Ibid., 161.

11 Ibid., 310–315.

12 *The Coming of the Book,* p. 319. Cf. *L'Apparition,* p. 477: "Au XVIIe siècle, les langues nationales apparaissent un peu partout cristallisées."

13 Hans Kohn, *The Age of Nationalism* (New York, 1944), 108. It is probably only fair to add that Kemal also hoped thereby to align Turkish nationalism with the modern, romanized civilization of Western Europe.

14 H. Seton-Watson, *Nations and States* (Boulder: Westview, 1977), 317.

Re-membering and Forgetting

Ron Eyerman

Four million slaves were liberated at the end of the Civil War. The exact figure was 3,953,696 (1860), which represents about 12.6 percent of the total American population and 32 percent of the Southern population (these figures also are from 1860, but there was no dramatic change during the Civil War). The free black population in the United States in 1860 was 488,070 and in the south, 261,918 (Kolchin 1993, 241–242). In the first comprehensive historical account written by a black man, George Washington Williams offered this description: "Here were four million human beings without clothing, shelter, homes, and alas! most of them without names. The galling harness of slavery had been cut off of their weary bodies, and like a worn out beast of burden they stood in their tracks scarcely able to go anywhere"(1882, 378).[1]

This was written nearly 20 years after the event and is an act of remembrance as much as historical writing. The author was part of a literary mobilization of a new black middle class emerging after the Civil War that aimed at countering the image of blacks being put forward by whites, as the "full and complete" integration promised by radical reconstruction gave way to new forms of racial segregation in the South and elsewhere. In addition to this monumental work, which also appeared in a condensed "popular" version, Williams produced an equally monumental history of black soldiers during the Civil War, and Sarah Bradford published *Harriet, the Moses of Her People* (1886), a dramatization of the life of Harriet Tubman, leading black abolitionist.[2] While constantly growing in number, the black reading public was not the prime audience of these and other literary efforts by educated blacks at the time. The prime contemporary audience remained the sympathetic white reader, in need of bolstering in this reactionary period, and, later, generations of blacks who would require alternative histories than those offered by mainstream white society. For it was just as plausible to argue, as sympathetic white historians later would and contemporary black novelists (who will be discussed below) were about to, that slavery produced hidden social networks that permitted blacks not only to survive, but also to maintain their dignity and traditions. These networks, which some would identify as a distinct cultural form, were an important resource after emancipation and reconstruction. As McMurry (1998, 20–21) writes: "On many plantations and farms, the slave community functioned as an extended family. In freedom those informal support networks became structurally organized as church groups or benevolent organizations and provided aid to families in crisis." Williams painted the former slaves as victims, survivors who would triumph over their condition, proving their worthiness, only to be rejected by a white society busy painting pictures of its own.

Here lie the roots and routes of cultural trauma. For blacks, this rejection after the raised expectations engendered by emancipation and reconstruction forced a rethinking of their relationship to American society. This was traumatic not only because of crushed expectations but also because it necessitated a re-evaluation of the past and its meaning regarding individual and collective identity. Many blacks and a few whites had believed that reconstruction would, if not eliminate entirely race as the basis for identity, at least diminish its significance, as former slaves became citizens like other Americans and the caste system associated with servitude disappeared. This was now clearly not the case, making it necessary to re-evaluate the meaning of the past and the options available in the future. Once again it would be necessary to attempt to transform tragedy into triumph with the uncovering of new strategies in the struggle for collective recognition, in the face of the threat of marginalization.

After long political debate in which many plans were aired and compromises drawn, reconstruction (1865–1877) promised integration and equal rights in the defeated South. The Civil Rights Bill of 1866, passed over the veto of President Andrew Johnson, authorized limited citizenship rights to blacks. The strategy of federal intervention, which included military occupation, had many motivations, some honourable and some less so. Fredrickson (1971) traces the debate concerning possible scenarios to follow emancipation. Most white thinking assumed a fundamental difference in character between blacks and whites, some of which was considered the result of slavery and some of which had more fundamental causes. An early plan had been to move all blacks either to American colonies abroad or to specified areas within the United States. Finally, after permitting blacks to participate on equal footing in the Union Army, making it "difficult to ask a man to fight for a nation without recognizing his right to live in it" (Fredrickson 1971, 167), and rejecting the idea of moving large numbers of blacks to the Midwest or the Georgia Sea Islands, it was accepted that most blacks wanted to remain in the South and that the government must assist in the transition from slave to citizen. Education and limited land redistribution would be the core of this process; one to be energized by paternalistic goodwill. The emphasis on re-education was supported by many middle-class white Southerners, both during and after reconstruction, as long as it was kept within the bounds of "the civilizing process," that is, under their control. For the most part, it was largely the intervention by the federal government, more than the policies themselves, which they found most objectionable and degrading.

The church was a central source of community and identity formation during slavery and continued to be so until its influence waned during the great migration, at least in the Northern cities. In one view, "the Negro church may be regarded as the single institution which has uniquely given a sustained, positive sense of ethnic identity to American Negroes without beating the nationalists' drums" (Essien-Udom 1962, 25). In another, the black church was a "nation within a nation," the core of an emergent black social structure and identity (Frazier 1974).[3] The church was also central in organizing and distributing resources during and after reconstruction, as well as in providing leadership in dealings with the larger society and serving as the centre of social life. Along with semi-secret associations and fellowships like the Masons and Elks, the church was the central "counter-institution" of black American life. With emancipation, blacks left white churches in great numbers and joined already existing black churches or started new ones. This created a new basis for racial self-determination, as well as liberation, as blacks were no longer forced to listen to sermons dictated by the dominant culture. In the decade directly following emancipation, these black churches organized themselves through a convention, "for the purpose of harnessing traditional feelings of mutuality with new assertions of self-respect and self-determination" (Higginbotham 1993, 53).[4]

Even if Essien-Udom is correct in arguing that the church sustained a positive sense of ethnic or racial identity without "beating the nationalist drum," as part of a network of separate black institutions it provided the material basis for sustaining separatism. This is nicely put by Drake and Cayton (1945, 116ff.) in their discussion of how the meaning of the phrase "social equality" differs in the North and South and between blacks and whites. In answering the question "Do Negroes (in Chicago) Want Social Equality?," they write:

> Negroes are generally indifferent to social intermingling with white people, and this indifference is closely related to the existence of a separate, parallel Negro institutional life which makes interracial activities seem unnecessary and almost "unnatural." Since the eighteenth century, a separate Negro institutional structure has existed in America. Through the years it has been developing into an intricate web of families, cliques, churches, and voluntary associations, ordered by a system of social classes. This "Negro World" is, historically, the direct result of social rejection by the white society. For Negroes however, it has long since lost this connotation, and many white people never think of it as such. It is now the familiar milieu in which Negroes live and move from birth till death.

This "world" existed only in embryo in the 1870s and could easily have disappeared had reconstruction functioned as it might have. Because this did not occur, these "counter-institutions" developed into full-scale alternatives and a separate way of life became "natural" and taken for granted by both blacks and whites.

The possibility of higher education and the emergence of a relatively large group of educated blacks occurred just as reconstruction was coming to an end. This group articulated the failure of reconstruction to truly integrate blacks into American society as trauma, and formulated the alternative strategies in response. This points to one of the assumptions and limitations of this theory as applied to American slavery. Trauma is articulated in an intellectual discourse, written or visual, factual or fictional, which limits those who can participate, as well as the forms through which one can participate. This discourse "speaks" for the speechless. In other words, it is itself a form of representation.

The cultural trauma referred to here is that articulated and experienced by intellectuals, writers, and artists, as are the responses debated and proposed.

An improved means of communication helped reinforce a sense of community among emancipated blacks. Anderson (1991) has argued that it is with the assistance of mass media that "imagined" as well as real communities are constituted and sustained. The first black-owned newspaper had appeared in 1827 and "by 1850, black (owned) newspapers were on the streets of most large northern cities" (Banks 1996, 15). In his study of four black newspapers between 1827 and 1965, Charles Simmons (1998, 5) writes, "The basic editorial philosophy of the black press has not changed much since 1827, when *Freedom's Journal* was founded. The goals of all editors were to deliver messages in unity to their readers, deliver them with passion and emotion, and let white editors and citizens know that black citizens were human beings who were being treated unjustly."

With emancipation and expanding literacy black newspapers spread rapidly in the South, their role taking on a new dimension after the end of slavery; 115 black newspapers were started between the Civil War and the end of reconstruction, the first in the South in New Orleans in 1862, an event that "signaled the first change in editorial philosophy—one from freeing the slaves to one of reestablishing the racial identity of Afro-Americans and educating them so that they could survive in society" (Simmons 1998, 14). Southern black newspapers often met strong resistance, making the publishing of a newspaper and the job of editor a very precarious and courageous choice of profession in the South; newspapers had a shorter life span in the South compared to the North for these and other reasons, including the size of the readership (Suggs 1983). Newspapers thus became an important medium through which self-definition could be debated and a new, post-slavery collective identity articulated. After all, slavery had been the root circumstance of black identity, previously a condition and an identity under conditions of extreme alienation, as well as white control. Music and other oral forms of communication had been central to the formation of black collective identity during slavery; they articulated an imagined community, as well as the hope of a better life (Davis 1998, 7). This was now supplemented in a much more extensive way through literary means and media. Newspapers and the press generally were a central medium of public conversation, as well as reflection, that would help constitute the new "imagined" black community, linking the local and national and moderating the formation of a black public opinion. George Fredrickson (1971) concludes his historical study referred to above of "the black image in the white mind" with the following list upon which there was "widespread, almost universal, agreement," among whites, North and South, even after emancipation and reconstruction:

1. Blacks are physically, intellectually, and temperamentally *different* from whites.
2. Blacks are also *inferior to* whites in at least some of the fundamental qualities, wherein races differ, especially in intelligence and in the temperamental basis of enterprise or initiative.
3. Such differences and differentials are either permanent or subject to change only by a very slow process of development or evolution.
4. Because of these permanent or deep-seated differences miscegenation, especially in the form of intermarriage, is to be discouraged ... because the crossing of such diverse types leads either to a short-lived and unprolific breed or to a type that even

if permanent is inferior to the whites in those innate qualities giving Caucasian civilization its progressive and creative characteristics.

5. Racial prejudice or antipathy is a natural and inevitable white response to blacks when the latter are free from legalized subordination and aspiring to equal status. Its power is such that it will not in the foreseeable future permit blacks to attain full equality, unless one believes, like some abolitionists, in the impending triumph of a millenarian Christianity capable of obliterating all sense of divisive human differences.

6. It follows from the above propositions that a biracial equalitarian (or "integrated") society is either completely impossible, now and forever, or can be achieved only in some remote and almost inconceivable future. For all practical purposes the destiny of blacks in America is either continued subordination—slavery or some form of caste discrimination—or their elimination as an element of the population. (Fredrickson 1971, 321)

How should those ascribed this new status respond? If, as Judith Stein (1986, 14) writes, "new world slavery had destroyed the traditional allegiances and loyalties of the past by severing the power and the ways of life that underlay a man's conception of himself as an Ibo, Ashanti, or Igba ... creat[ing] a people who considered themselves black, African or Negro—all synonymous for the same person," on what basis could a new collective identity be constructed? The black "community" was no natural phenomenon, but had to be constructed out of the ruins of the Southern economy and on the basis of an ascribed condition, race, that would replace slavery as its defining condition in relation to American society. If they were now formally integrated as citizens of the new post-war America, they were segregated as a race apart. "We want to understand that we are no longer colored people, but Americans," John Mercer Langston told a black gathering in 1866. "We have been called all manner of names. I have always called our people negroes. Perhaps you don't like it—I do. I want it to become synonymous with character. We are no longer colored people simply, but a part of the great whole of the mighty American nation" (quoted in Litwack 1979, 539).

The term "colored" was associated by many with slavery. Better to move on from that. But what then?

Even as blacks emphasized their American roots, they could not agree on whether they were Negro, colored, black or African Americans. The ongoing debate in the black press and other fora over how they should be addressed revealed at the same time differences over how they conceptualized themselves as a race and a regard for how whites employed the various terms. The objections to "negro" ... rested partly on its association with slavery and the tendency of whites to use it as a term of reproach. "We call each other colored people, black people, but not negro because we used that word in secesh [secessionist] times," a South Carolina freedman testified in 1863. Both "negro" and "black" also suggested unmixed ancestry and hence excluded large numbers of colored people. (Litwack 1979, 540)

In light of such a broad-based and deeply rooted consensus regarding their inherent inferiority, an almost impossible task faced the first generation of blacks after emancipation.

How could one ever hope to overcome such a picture of oneself, created by those with political and economic power, and find dignity in a social order that so firmly denied it? It was not so much the direct experience of slavery that would prove traumatic, but its aftermath as the hope and promise of equality and acceptance were crushed finally and formally in the 1880–1890s by a reconfiguration around the views of blacks and whites that Fredrickson lists. In the attempt to deal with this trauma of rejection, the memory of slavery would prove an important resource.[5]

More generally, the question of the effects and affects of slavery on the black psyche had to be addressed in the face of the dominant culture's racism. Blacks were forced to see themselves through the eyes of whites and to test and prove themselves. Frederick Douglass put the issue this way in 1873:

> The question, which the future has to answer, is: Whether the negro is what he is today because of his mental and moral constitution, or because he has been enslaved and degraded for centuries. If it shall be found, after the lapse of twenty-five years of freedom, that the colored people of this country have made no improvement in their social condition, it will confirm the opinion that the negro is, by his very nature, limited to a servile condition. But if, on the other hand, we supply the world with the proof of our advancement to a plane, even a little above that on which slavery left us, we shall prove that, like all other men, we are capable of civilization.... (1996, 392–393)

This would not be an easy process, for the images of race and the representations of slavery were not simply a matter of intellectual or political discourse; they were reproduced and maintained in popular culture in more seemingly benign ways.

The most famous, if not the most powerful, piece of literature to emerge out of this movement was *Uncle Tom's Cabin* by Harriet Beecher Stowe, which James Baldwin later called "the first protest novel," and which introduced the tragic image of the gentle slave at the mercy of the evil and brutal taskmaster. The names Uncle Tom and Simon Legree remain etched in popular memory to this day, although the connotation of the first has been entirely altered, from a tragic, heroic figure to its opposite. It was the Abolitionist image of slavery as an evil system totally contrary to Christian beliefs, which degraded whites as much as it brutalized blacks, that offered a powerful challenge to the view of slavery as an economic enterprise with benevolent, civilizing, or at least benign, side effects. Stowe's novel was a best-seller when it was published in 1853. So much so that the author published *Key to Uncle Tom's Cabin* the following year. Another literary genre to emerge in this Abolitionist context was the first-hand accounts written by slaves themselves, the so-called slave narratives. As opposed to fictional accounts like Stowe's, these slave narratives are acts of remembering of the first order. Biographical in form, they offered accounts of the experience of slavery from the point of view of those most affected. The Abolitionist context imposed a particular framework on the form and content of these narratives, but still they are the first representations of slavery from the inside, and they form the basis of a counter-memory that is equally important today, as these narratives are seen by some as the founding texts of a distinctive "black aesthetic." From their first appearance, however, they were weapons in an anti-slavery struggle and had essentially two non-literary aims, to recount the dehumanizing effects of slavery and to establish the humanity of the slave. The title of what is perhaps the first such work recounts this: *A*

Narrative of the Uncommon Sufferings and Surprising Deliverance of Briton Hammond, a Negro Man, published anonymously in Boston in 1760 (Bontemps 1969, xii).

The slave narratives have been central to the construction of a counter, collective memory and in the constitution and resolution of cultural trauma. Seen as representations, the images presented are framed by the circumstances of their production, and their reception has varied according to time and place. Even as first-hand and first-person accounts, they are structured according to narrative conventions and by the intended effects on, as well as the expectations of, their presumed audience. They tell a story, a moral tale, which identifies heroes and villains, giving voice to pain and faces to perpetrators but, more importantly, however, they turn victims into agents and tragedy into triumph.

In his analysis of exemplary slave narratives, Robert Stepto (1991) uncovers three distinct types that point to a development in literary terms. In addition to the two mentioned above, a distinct characteristic of the slave narrative according to Stepto is that its authenticity must be established. This "authenticating" strategy can be counter-posed to the "tale" or story itself. The first type he identifies is one in which the authenticating documents, written by well-known whites, append the tale, a practice that was especially common during the Abolitionist movement. In the second type, the two are more integrated, where authenticating documents "formally become voices and/or characters in the tale" (Stepto 1991, 5), and in the third type, the tale itself becomes dominant and the slave narrative slides into autobiography, or the authenticating strategy dominates and the slave narrative authenticates a novel or an historical account.

If the Abolitionist movement provided a context for cultural expression among former slaves, as Stepto's analysis reveals, it also shaped them in a particular way. This was also true in the plastic arts and in other forms of popular culture. As Albert Boime (1990, 171) writes, "images of emancipation, like the actual emancipation rituals and ceremonies, were designed to emphasize the dependence of the emancipated slaves upon their benefactors as well as their ongoing need for the culture and the guidance of their liberators." Thus works of sculpture showed kneeling slaves under the care of standing whites, even as they broke with other stereotypical images of blacks. As the newspaperman and critic Freeman Henry Morris Murray put it in his analysis of sculpture written in 1916, "[s]o Emancipation—even under the circumstances through which it came about in this country—is conceived and expressed nearly always as a bestowal, seldom or never as a restitution. Hence American art—and foreign art, too, it seems—usually puts it: objectively, 'See what's been done for you', or subjectively, 'Look what's been done for me'" (quoted in Boime 1990, 172).[6] In Murray's view, there was another subjectivity here, a black subjectivity, which needed to be represented.[7]

The ambiguous relationship to slavery which shaped this generation, that slavery was at once degrading and civilizing, as revealed in Harper's novel and in Booker T. Washington's memoirs, was shared by Frederick Douglass ([1873] Andrews 1996, 393–394), at least at this late stage of his life: "I have spoken of slavery as our enemy. I have nothing to take back at that point. It has robbed us of education. It has robbed us of the care due us from our mothers. It has written its ugliness in our countenance, deformed our feet, and twisted our limbs out of shape; and yet this same slavery has been, in some sense, our best friend. It has trained us to regular industry, and hardened our muscles to toil, and thus has left in our hands the staff of all accomplishments."

For this generation of black intellectuals and writers, those born after or at the end of slavery, questions of representation were inherently moral concerns of the type, "How should an oppressed minority be represented before and to the dominant society?" Representation was also a political matter, in that considerations of its implications regarding the dominant society were always immanent. Previously, such concerns had been raised and answered to a large extent by sympathetic whites, although not entirely of course, as many free blacks were active Abolitionists. These whites had their own moral and political agendas. Later, blacks gained more control of their own representation as the black public grew in size and self-consciousness. They formulated their own specific agenda. The combining of African and European aesthetic influences, consciously or tacitly recognized and applied, occurred in either circumstance as highly politicized, charged with larger meaning and significance than the purely aesthetic. There was no escaping this, and one wrote and sang always under the watchful eyes of the master, even with one's own voice.

Issues such as these became important for the coming generations of black Americans, when the question "How should blacks be represented?" was posed with increasing intensity and sophistication. This was so because American society had shown black Americans that they were different, a group apart, and would remain so. That this separateness was in part self-willed and the result of unintended historical processes that encouraged group building, did not detract from the obvious and renewed racism of the dominant white society from the 1880s onwards. This meant that blacks would be forced to identify collectively, whether or not they formed a real, rather than an imagined, community and whether they wanted it or not. Their individual actions would always be judged as if they were a community. In this sense, black Americans could never be individuals. An artist or writer who happened to be black would always be judged as a black artist, a reflection on the "race," just as would a black person who committed a crime or an heroic act. Thus, it was argued, each had a responsibility, a duty, to perform well, to present and represent only the good and the worthy before the critical and judgmental eyes of the observing white public. That such a discussion could occur at all points to some significant developments. First, that articulate blacks had acquired both the status and the means to express themselves in more formalized public arenas. Here the emergence of black media, such as newspapers and journals, were a major development. The clergy were central here and would remain so, but other professions emerged as well. Lawyers, journalists, historians, writers, and, most of all, teachers, at first connected to the clergy and religion generally, soon became more autonomous. This created new possibilities, and perspectives, of representation, but also internal social divisions between those who had more access to the means and media of representation, and could claim the right to represent, and those who were represented. This would have consequences for how the past was viewed and collective memory articulated. Again, such developments were not unique to blacks, quite the contrary, but they did take on distinct form because of the new marginalization and reaction to it.

If a distinct "black aesthetic" developed in this period, it had as much to do with the circumstances in which the cultural forms of expression created by black Americans were formed as with a unique blending of African and European influences. While it is certainly true that black music and dance, as well as religious practices and styles of writing, combined African and European aspects, it is also true that this process of cultural creation took shape in a specific social and political context, where forms of representation were intimately interwoven with moral and political concerns. It is certainly possible to argue that this is always the case with any form of representation, but that is neither an issue nor an interesting question. What is more interesting, even if that is the case, is to specify as far as possible how moral and political concerns shape artistic expression. This generation of blacks in the United States faced issues of representation with moral and political concerns forced upon them by the trauma of failed emancipation and in the face of a reactionary cultural and political offensive. As they gained more control over the means of their own representation, they were faced with such opposition that this control was mitigated by the force of circumstance.

In the following generation, blacks would gain more control, and awareness, of their cultural creations and their collective identity, and more opportunities to formulate their own agenda. This was made possible by the distance time allows to select and filter out the past and the power attained through having a larger and more concentrated and self-conscious public. Slavery would look different to this generation, and its collective memory was reconstituted on that basis.

NOTES

1   Even after compensating for the literary style of the time, this reads very much like descriptions of survivors from prison camps after the Second World War. These descriptions after release from the concentration camps make for useful comparison: "During the first years after the war, the energies of the survivors were absorbed in finding their way back to some semblance of conventional life. Most had to learn a new language, search for other occupations, and meet some of the challenges of a society in a foreign land. Many families clung together in their new neighborhoods, creating new ghettos, hoping to create their original communities, surrounded by an alien culture, which, though not usually physically threatening, nevertheless regarded them at best with an ambivalent mixture of awe and mistrust, the very embodiment of a past the survivors wanted to forget. It was rare for an entire family to have survived intact. New partners, more often than not, fellow survivors, had to be found, new families started. While life was safer and certainly more bearable, adaptation was by no means easy" (Bergmann and Jucovy 1982, 5). While one can question whether or not the emancipated slaves considered themselves "survivors" in the same way as those liberated from the camps at the end of the Second World War, descriptions of their social if not their spiritual conditions have much in common. The theory of cultural trauma may well provide a bridge in understanding.

2   On black Abolitionism, see Ripley (1993). G.W. Williams was a controversial figure within the black middle class. On his death in 1891, Ida Wells, editor of the black newspaper *Free Speech*, wrote an article describing his failings as a husband, as well as praising his achievement as a writer, which also created a debate within the black press on the ethics of public discussion of private failings (McMurry 1999, 126). A new biography, by John Hope Franklin, appeared in 1998.

3   Frazier (1974, 13) disagrees with Du Bois over the significance of African heritage regarding the black church and its role under slavery. He writes: "Du Bois evidently thought that social

cohesion among slaves was not totally destroyed.... [H]e makes the assertion that the Negro church was 'the only social institution among the Negroes which started in the African forest and survived slavery' and that 'under the leadership of the priest and the medicine man' the church preserved the remnants of African life." Frazier replies: "From the available evidence ... it is impossible to establish any continuity between African religious practices and the Negro church in the United States."

4   As mentioned earlier, "conventions" were a common means of opening a black public sphere, creating a space for discussion and representation. The Kansas Exodus, for example, created the occasion for a series of "conventions" to discuss its meaning and consequences for the "race." It was here that the conditions of blacks as a group could be discussed and alternative strategies weighed. Painter (1976, 221) calls them a "shadow government," where those who under normal conditions in a democracy would have been elected representatives gave voice to public opinion.

5   It would also prove a detriment. This was especially so in reference to material culture and habitus. Traces of slavery remained in the separate living conditions of whites and blacks, in the obvious differences in the quality and quantity of possessions. It was also embodied in the "arts of survival and accommodation, the posture of demeanor and deference," which black parents taught their children (Litwack 1998: 39).

6   The only piece of sculpture that came close to expressing the true significance of this event according to Murray was that done by the African American artist Meta Vaux Warrick Fuller for the 50th Anniversary Celebration in 1913. Murray wrote of this work: "The portrayal is emptied of the usual accessories as well as of the frequent claptrap—no broken shackles, no obvious parchments, no discarded whips, no crouching slave with uncertain face; no, not even a kindly ... Liberator appears; in short, she essays to set forth and to represent, not a person, not a recipient—not the Emancipator nor one of the Emancipated—not even the Emancipation itself, as a mere formal act, but far higher, the Emancipation as an embracing theme" (in Boime 1990, 181).

7   Powell (1997, 16–18) writes "for Murray, black subjectivity ... presupposed that there was a world in which black peoples and their cultures, rather than always being filtered through white supremacist eyes and mindsets, could be seen and represented differently: either through the non-racist (or at least, multidimensional) lens of whites, or through the knowing and racially self-conscious eyes of blacks themselves."

REFERENCES

Anderson, Benedict. 1991. *Imagined Communities.* London: Verso.

Andrews, William. 1992. Introduction to *The African American Novel in the Age of Reaction.* New York: Mentor Books.

Banks, William. 1996. *Black Intellectuals.* New York: Norton.

Boime, Albert. 1990. *The Art of Exclusion.* Washington: Smithsonian Institution Press.

Bontemps, Arna, and Jack Conroy. 1969. Introduction to *Great Slave Narratives,* ed. A. Bontemps. Boston: Beacon Press.

Davis, David. 1999. "Jew and Blacks in America." *New York Review of Books* (Dec. 2):57–63.

Douglass, Frederick. [1873] 1991. *The Frederick Douglass Papers.* 1st series Vol. 4, *(1964–80),* ed. John Blassingame and John McKivigan. New Haven: Yale University Press.

———. 1969. *My Bondage and My Freedom.* New York: Arno Press.

Drake, St. Clair, and Horace Cayton. 1945. *Black Metropolis.* New York: Harper and Row.

Essien-Udora, E.U. 1962. *Black Nationalism.* Chicago: University of Chicago Press.

Frazier, E. Franklin. 1974. *The Negro Church in America.* New York: Schocken Books.

Fredrickson, George. 1971. *The Black Image in the White Mind: The Debate on Afro-American Character and Destiny, 1817–1914.* New York: Harper and Row.

Higginbotham, Evelyn. 1993. *Righteous Discontent.* Cambridge, Mass.: Harvard University Press.

Kolchin, Peter. 1993. *American Slavery 1619–1877.* New York: Hill and Wang.

Litwack, Leon. 1979. *Been in the Storm So Long.* New York: Vintage.

———. 1998. *Trouble in Mind.* New York: Vintage.

McMurry, Linda. 1998. *To Keep the Waters Troubled.* New York: Oxford University Press.

Painter, Nell. 1976. *Exodusters.* New York: Norton. Reprint 1979.

Powell, Richard. 1997. *Black Art and Culture in the 20th Century.* London: Thames and Hudson.

Ripley, C. Peter, ed. 1993. *Witness for Freedom.* Chapel Hill: University of North Carolina Press.

Simmons, Charles. 1998. *The African American Press.* Jefferson, N.C.: McFarland.

Stein, Judith. 1986. *The World of Marcus Garvey.* Baton Rouge: LSU Press.

———. 1989. "Defining the Race." In *The Invention of Ethnicity,* ed. Werner Sollors, 77–104. New York: Oxford University Press.

Stepto, Robert. 1991. *From behind the Veil.* Urbana: University of Illinois Press.

Suggs, Henry, ed. 1983. *The Black Press in the South 1865–1979.* Westport: Greenwood Press.

Williams, G.W. 1882. *History of the Negro Race in America.* New York: Putnam's Sons.

THE RACIAL STATE

MICHAEL OMI
AND HOWARD WINANT

INTRODUCTION: THE TRAJECTORY OF RACIAL POLITICS

Two recent incidents reveal some of the ironies and incongruities of contemporary racial politics:

- In 1989, the Republican National Committee established a tax-exempt foundation called Fairness for the 90s. The group's mission was to provide money and technical assistance to black and Latino organizations seeking to create minority-dominated legislative and congressional districts. In anticipation of the legislative redistricting that would follow the 1990 census, the Republicans offered black and Latino leaders and organizers the prospect of creating "safe seats" for minority legislators. The Republicans went so far as to ally themselves with black and Latino plaintiffs in redistricting suits brought under the *Voting Rights Act*. What accounted for the strange bedfellows of redistricting politics? The answer was simple: Republicans sought to segregate racial minority voters into separate districts, to divide white from non-white Democrats, and so to increase their opportunities to win legislative seats in adjoining white districts.[1]
- In the late 1980s, Asian-American academic leaders, civil rights organizations, and university students began to suspect that informal quotas for Asian-American admissions had been put in place in the leading U.S. universities in violation of civil rights laws. As they mobilized to confront this situation and initiated negotiations with university administrators on various campuses, they suddenly received support from an unsolicited, and unexpected, quarter. In November 1988, Ronald Reagan's neo-conservative Deputy Attorney General

for Civil Rights, William Bradford Reynolds, not only agreed that such quotas had been established, but blamed these restrictive practices on the existence of affirmative action admissions policies. "The phenomenon of a 'ceiling' on Asian American admissions is the inevitable result of the 'floor' that has been built for a variety of other favored racial groups," Reynolds said. Asian-Americans were alarmed that the issue of "quotas" would be used as part of a broader attack on preferential policies for underrepresented minorities.[2]

As these examples illustrate, advocacy groups and movement organizations that seek to represent racially defined minority interests, mobilize minority group members politically, and articulate minority viewpoints are frequently faced with bitterly ironic political choices. No sooner did egalitarian and anti-discrimination policies emerge from the political tempests of the 1960s than they began to "decay." From the early 1970s of Richard Nixon to the early 1990s of Bill Clinton, the state has sought to absorb, to marginalize, and to transform (or "re-articulate") the meaning of the reforms won in the earlier decade.

How have these transformations occurred? What are the dynamics of the relationships between the state and racial minorities? Why does a pattern of alternating activism and quiescence characterize both state racial activities and movement ebbs and flows? We consider these questions in an effort to understand the *trajectory* that contemporary racial politics—and thus racial formation processes—follow in the contemporary U.S.

By "trajectory" we mean the pattern of conflict and accommodation that takes shape over time between racially based social movements and the policies and programs of the state. We consider the central elements of this trajectory to be the state and social movements, linked in a single historical framework of racial formation.

Social movements and the state are interrelated in a complex way. Racial movements arise, and race becomes a political issue, when state institutions are thought to structure and enforce a racially unjust social order. State institutions acquire their racial orientations from the processes of conflict with and accommodation to racially based movements. Thus "reform," "reaction," "radical change," or "backlash"—indeed every transformation of the racial order—is constructed through a process of clash and compromise between racial movements and the state.

These are the dynamics of present-day racial politics in the U.S. Yet there is nothing permanent or sacred about this pattern. Indeed, the existence of political channels for the expression of racial conflict is a relatively recent phenomenon. The broad sweep of American history is characterized not by racial democracy, but by racial despotism; not by trajectories of reform, but by implacable denial of political rights, dehumanization, extreme exploitation, and policies of minority extirpation. Democracy has never been in abundant supply where race is concerned. The very emergence of political channels through which reform can at times be achieved is an immense political victory for minorities, and for democracy itself.[4]

HISTORICAL CHANGE IN THE U.S. RACIAL ORDER

Since the earliest days of colonialism in North America, an identifiable racial order has linked the system of political rule to the racial classification of individuals and groups.

The major institutions and social relationships of U.S. society—law, political organization, economic relationships, religion, cultural life, residential patterns, and so on—have been structured from the beginning by the racial order.

Clearly the system of racial subjection has been more monolithic, more absolute, at some historical periods than others.[5] Where political opposition was banned or useless, as it was for slaves in the South and for Native Americans during much of the course of U.S. history, transformation of the racial order, or resistance to it, was perforce military (or perhaps took such economic forms as sabotage). An oppositional racial ideology requires some political space, a certain minimal conceptual flexibility about race, upon which to fasten in order to recast racial meanings and constitute alternative racial institutions. During much of U.S. history, this political and ideological space was extremely limited.

But even at its most oppressive, the racial order was unable to arrogate to itself the entire capacity for the production of racial meanings, of racial subjects. Racial minorities were always able to counter-pose their own cultural traditions, their own forms of organization and identity, to the dehumanizing and enforced "invisibility" imposed by the majority society.

As the voluminous literature on black culture under slavery shows, black slaves developed cultures of resistance based on music, religion, African traditions, and family ties through which they sustained their own ideological project: the development of a "free" black identity and a collectivity dedicated to emancipation.[6] The examples of Geronimo, Sitting Bull, and other Native American leaders were passed down from generation to generation as examples of resistance, and the Ghost Dance and Native American Church were employed by particular generations of Indians to maintain a resistance culture.[7] Rodolfo Acuña has pointed out how the same "bandits" against whom Anglo vigilantes mounted expeditions after the Treaty of Guadalupe-Hidalgo—Tiburcio Vasquez, Joaquin Murieta—became heroes in the Mexicano communities of the Southwest, remembered in folktales and celebrated in *corridos*.[8] We do not offer these examples to romanticize brutal repression or to give the air of revolutionary struggle to what were often grim defeats; we simply seek to affirm that even in the most uncontested periods of American racism, oppositional cultures were able, often at very great cost, to maintain themselves.

Without reviewing the vast history of racial conflict, it is still possible to make some general comments about the manner in which the racial order was historically consolidated. Gramsci's distinction between "war of manoeuvre" and "war of position" will prove useful here.

For much of American history, no political legitimacy was conceded to alternative or oppositional racial ideologies, to competing racially defined political projects. The absence of democratic rights, of property, of political and ideological terrain upon which to challenge the monolithic character of the racial order, forced racially defined opposition both *outward,* to the margins of society, and *inward,* to the relative safety of homogeneous minority communities.

Slaves who escaped, forming communities in woods and swamps; Indians who made war on the U.S. in defence of their peoples and lands; Chinese and Filipinos who drew together in Chinatowns and Manilatowns in order to gain some measure of collective control over their existence—these are some examples of the movement of racial opposition *outward,* away from political engagement with the hegemonic racial state.

These same slaves, Indians, and Asians, as well as many others, banned from the political system and relegated to what was supposed to be a permanently inferior socio-cultural status, were forced *inward* upon themselves as individuals, families, and communities. Tremendous cultural resources were nurtured among such communities; enormous labours were required to survive and to develop elements of an autonomy and opposition under such conditions. These circumstances can best be understood as combining with the violent clashes and the necessity of resistance (to white-led race riots, military assaults, etc.) that characterized these periods, to constitute a racial *war of manoeuvre.*

However democratic the U.S. may have been in other respects (and it is clear that democracy has always been in relatively short supply), in its treatment of racial minorities it has been to varying degrees *despotic* for much of its history. "War of manoeuvre" describes a situation in which subordinate groups seek to preserve and extend a definite territory, to ward off violent assault, and to develop an internal society as an alternative to the repressive social system they confront.

More recent history suggests that war of manoeuvre is being replaced by *war of position* as racially defined minorities achieve political gains.[9] A strategy of *war of position* can only be predicated on political struggle—on the existence of diverse institutional and cultural terrains upon which oppositional political projects can be mounted, and upon which the racial state can be confronted. Prepared in large measure by the practices undertaken under conditions of war of manoeuvre, minorities were able to make sustained strategic incursions into the mainstream political process beginning with the Second World War. "Opening up" the state was a process of democratization that had effects both on state structures and on racial meanings. The post-war black movement, later joined by other racially based minority movements, sought to transform dominant racial ideology in the U.S., to locate its elements in a more egalitarian and democratic framework, and thereby to reconstruct the social meaning of race. The state was the logical target for this effort.

HISTORICAL DEVELOPMENT OF THE RACIAL STATE

The state from its very inception has been concerned with the politics of race. For most of U.S. history, the state's main objective in its racial policy was repression and exclusion. Congress's first attempt to define American citizenship, the Naturalization Law of 1790, declared that only free "white" immigrants could qualify. The extension of eligibility to all racial groups has been slow indeed. Japanese, for example, could become naturalized citizens only after the passage of the *McCarran-Walter Act* of 1952.[10]

Historically, a variety of previously racially undefined groups have required categorization to situate them within the prevailing racial order.

Throughout the 19th century, many state and federal legal arrangements recognized only three racial categories: "white," "Negro," and "Indian." In California, the influx of Chinese and the debates surrounding the legal status of Mexicans provoked a brief juridical crisis of racial definition. California attempted to resolve this dilemma by assigning Mexicans and Chinese to categories within the already existing framework of "legally defined" racial groups. In the wake of the Treaty of Guadalupe Hidalgo (1848), Mexicans were defined as a "white" population and accorded the political–legal status of "free white persons." By contrast, the California Supreme Court ruled in *People v. Hall* (1854) that Chinese should be considered "Indian"[!] and denied the political rights accorded to whites.[11]

The state's shifting racial perspective is also revealed by the census. Latinos surfaced as an ethnic category, "Persons of Spanish Mother Tongue," in 1950 and 1960. In 1970 they appeared as "Persons of Both Spanish Surname and Spanish Mother Tongue," and in 1980 the "Hispanic" category was created.[12] Such changes suggest the state's inability to "racialize" a particular group—to institutionalize it in a politically organized racial system. They also reflect the struggles through which racial minorities press their demands for recognition and equality, and dramatize the state's uncertain efforts to manage and manipulate those demands.[13]

The state is the focus of collective demands both for egalitarian and democratic reforms and for the enforcement of existing privileges. The state "intervenes" in racial conflicts, but it does not do so in a coherent or unified manner. Distinct state institutions often act in a contradictory fashion.[14]

Does the state, however clumsily, actually capture, steer, or organize the realities of racial identity and racial conflict? There is some validity to the idea of a racially "interventionist" state. With this theoretical concept, it is possible to investigate certain racial dimensions of state policy. The 1960s civil rights reforms, for example, can be interpreted as federal intervention in the area of racial discrimination.

Yet this approach does not reveal how the state itself is racially structured; it depicts the state as intervening, but not *intervened*, structuring, but not *structured*. Such a state is not basically shaped by race since it intervenes in race relations from *outside* them. The treatment afforded to racial politics is thus confined to "normal" political arenas.

In contrast to this, we suggest that the state *is* inherently racial. Far from *intervening* in racial conflicts, the state is itself increasingly the pre-eminent site of racial conflict. In the following sections of this chapter, we examine this expanding involvement of the state in the racial formation process. We first present a model of the racial state, and then consider contemporary patterns of change in the racial order, focusing on the interaction between state and social movements.

A MODEL OF THE RACIAL STATE

The state is composed of *institutions*, the *policies* they carry out, the *conditions and rules* that support and justify them, and the *social relations* in which they are imbedded.[15]

Every state *institution* is a racial institution, but not every institution operates in the same way. In fact, the various state institutions do not serve one coordinated racial objective; they may work at cross-purposes.[16] Therefore, race must be understood as occupying varying degrees of centrality in different state institutions and at different historical moments.

Through *policies* that are explicitly or implicitly racial, state institutions organize and enforce the racial politics of everyday life. For example, they enforce racial (non)discrimination policies, which they administer, arbitrate, and encode in law. They organize racial identities by means of education, family law, and the procedures for punishment, treatment, and surveillance of the criminal, deviant, and ill.[17]

State institutions and their policies take shape under a series of *conditions and rules*. These "rules of the game" integrate the disparate racial policies of different state agencies, define the scope of state activity, establish "normal" procedures for influencing policy, and set the limits of political legitimacy in general. To speak, for example, of an agency's "mandate," of a policy's "constituency," or of an epochal political "project" (the "Keynesian welfare state," the "conservative opportunity society")[18] is to accept a set of political rules about who is a political actor, what is a political interest, and how the broad state–society relationship is to be organized.[19]

The specific *social relations* through which state activity is structured constitute the materiality of politics. Examples include the complex linkages of agencies and constituencies,[20] the dynamics of coalitions and governing or oppositional blocs, and the varieties of administrative control exercised by state agencies throughout civil society.[21] Racial politics are not exceptional in this respect. For example, civil rights organizations, lobbying groups, and "social programs" with significant constituency bases, legal mandates, and so forth may engage the state in the "normal" politics of interest-group liberalism,[22] adopt movement tactics of direct action and confrontation "from without," or—as is most likely—combine these tactics.

The state is also imbedded in another kind of social relations: the cultural and technical norms that characterize society overall. These affect the organizational capacities of state agencies, their coordination, both with "external" social actors and with each other, and the practices of their own personnel.[23] In racial terms, these relationships are structured by "difference" in certain ways: for example, minority officials may establish caucuses or maintain informal networks with which to combat the isolation frequently encountered in bureaucratic settings.

Despite all the forces working at cross-purposes within the state—disparate demands of constituents, distinct agency mandates and prerogatives, unintended and cross-cutting consequences of policy, and so on—the state still preserves an overall unity. This is maintained in two ways: First, strategic unity is sought at the apex of the apparatus by key policy-makers, and in legislative and judicial agencies by established decision rules.[24] Second, unity is imposed on the state by its thorough interpenetration with society. In advanced capitalist societies *hegemony* is secured by a complex system of compromises, legitimating ideologies (e.g., "the rule of law"), by adherence to established political rules and bureaucratic regularities, and so forth.[25] Under all but the most severe conditions (economic collapse, war), this severely limits the range and legitimacy of both dominant and oppositional political initiatives, no matter how heavy the conflicts among contemporary U.S. political institutions and their constituents may appear to *be*.[26]

THE TRAJECTORY OF RACIAL POLITICS

It is useful to think of the U.S. racial order as an "unstable equilibrium.[27] The idea of politics as "the continuous process of formation and superseding of unstable equilibria" has particular resonance, we think, in describing the operation of the racial state.[28] The racial order is equilibrated by the state—encoded in law, organized through policy-making, and enforced by a repressive apparatus. But the equilibrium thus achieved is unstable, for the great variety of conflicting interests encapsulated in racial meanings and identities can be no more than pacified—at best—by the state. Racial conflict persists at every level of society, varying over time and in respect to different groups, but ubiquitous. Indeed, the state is itself penetrated and structured by the very interests whose conflicts it seeks to stabilize and control.[29]

This unstable equilibrium has at times in U.S. history gone undisturbed for decades and even centuries, but in our epoch its degree of "stability" has lessened. Under "normal" conditions, state institutions have effectively routinized the enforcement and organization of the prevailing racial order. Constituency relationships and established political organizations are at least implicitly and frequently explicitly racial.[30] Challenges to the racial order are limited to legal and political marginality. The system of racial meanings, of racial identities and ideology, seems "natural." Such conditions seemed generally to prevail from the end of reconstruction to the end of the First World War, for example.

Now let us imagine a situation in which this unstable equilibrium is disrupted. There can be many reasons for this, and the disruption may take many shapes, for example, the emergence of a mass-based racial movement such as took place in the 1960s, or of a powerful counter-egalitarian thrust such as appeared in the 1870s (with the beginnings of Asian exclusion and Jim Crow), or in the 1980s (with the institutionalization of New Right and neo-conservative interpretations of race). We shall be concerned with movement phenomena presently. Here we are interested chiefly in the effects on the state of racial disequilibrium.

Under conditions of disrupted equilibrium, inter-institutional competition and conflict within the state is augmented, as some agencies move toward accommodation of challenging forces while others "dig in their heels." Recomposition of constituencies and political alliances takes place. Opposition groups may resort to "direct action," and explicitly seek to politicize racial identities further; challenge will also take the route of "normal politics" (legislation, legal action, electoral activity, etc.), assuming this possibility is open to racially identified minorities. Strategic unity will therefore become more necessary for the governing forces or bloc.

The establishment or restoration of conditions of unstable equilibrium—let us say by means of reform policies—suggests an opposite cyclical phase. Such a situation guarantees the relative unity of the racial state by reducing the stakes of intra-state, or inter-institutional, conflict. It poses formidable obstacles to the fomenting of oppositional political projects. It minimizes the government's need to strategize and promises the automatic reproduction of the prevailing order, obviously an optimum situation from the standpoint of the dominant racial groups.

Disruption and restoration of the racial order suggests the type of cyclical movement or pattern we designate by the term "trajectory." Both racial movements and the racial state experience such transformations, passing through periods of rapid change and virtual stasis, through moments of massive mobilization and others of relative passivity. While the movement and state versions of the overall trajectory are independently observable, they could not exist independently of each other. Racially based political movements as we know them are inconceivable without the racial state, which provides a focus for political demands and structures the racial order. The racial state, in its turn, has been historically constructed by racial movements; it consists of agencies and programs that are the institutionalized responses to racial movements of the past.

The point at which we begin to examine the trajectory of racial politics, then, is arbitrary. Let us assume, therefore, a beginning point of *unstable equilibrium*. At this historical point, the racial order is (relatively) undisturbed by conflict and mobilization. The racial state is able to function (again, relatively) automatically in its organization and enforcement of the racial order. We first address the racial movement version of the trajectory, and then that of the racial state.

Racial movements come into being as the result of political projects, political interventions led by "intellectuals."[31] These projects seek to transform (or re-articulate) the dominant racial ideology. They thereby summarize and explain problems—economic inequality, absence of political rights, cultural repression, and so on—in racial terms. The result of this ideological challenge is a disparity, a conflict, between the pre-existing racial order, organized and enforced by the state, and an oppositional ideology whose subjects are the real and potential adherents of a racially defined movement. When this conflict reaches a certain level of intensity, a phase of *crisis* is initiated.

During a period of crisis, racial movements experiment with different strategies and tactics (electoral politics, "spontaneity," cultural revitalization efforts and alternative institution building, lobbying, direct action, etc.). We assume that at least some of these are successful in mobilizing political pressure, either through "normal" political channels or through disruption of those channels.[32] Indeed the success of a racial movement probably depends on its ability to generate a wide and flexible variety of strategies, ideological themes, and political tactics, as both the minority movements of the 1960s and the New Right and/or neo-conservative movements of the present have demonstrated.

In response to political pressure, state institutions adopt policies of absorption and insulation.[33] *Absorption* reflects the realization that many demands are greater threats to the racial order before they are accepted than after they have been adopted in suitably moderate form. *Insulation* is a related process in which the state confines demands to terrains that are, if not entirely symbolic, at least not crucial to the operation of the racial order. These policies then become ideological elements that are employed both by movements and state institutions. State agencies might argue, for example, that they have already met reasonable movement demands, while movement groups might claim that reforms don't address the problem, don't go far enough, and so on.

Once the general contours of state reformism are clear, movements undergo internal divisions. A certain segment of the movement is absorbed ("co-opted," in 1960s parlance) along with its demands, into the state, and there constitutes the core staff and agenda of the new state programs or agencies with which reform policies are to be implemented. The remaining active segment of the movement is "radicalized," while its more passive membership drops away to take up the roles and practices defined by a re-articulated racial ideology in the newly restabilized racial order *(unstable equilibrium)*.

Considering the trajectory of racial politics from the standpoint of the state, *unstable equilibrium$_1$* at first coexists with a series of effectively marginalized political projects located outside the "normal" terrain of state activity. In racial terms the state's trajectory of reform is initiated when movements challenge the pre-existent racial order. Crisis ensues when this opposition upsets the pre-existing *unstable equilibrium*. The terms of challenge can vary enormously, depending on the movement involved. Opposition can be democratic or authoritarian, primarily based in "normal" politics or in disruption; opposition can even reject explicit political definition, as in the case of cultural movements.

Crisis generates a series of conflicts within and among state agencies as particular demands are confronted and the terms of the state response (repression, concessions, symbolic responses, etc.) are debated. Agency and constituent groups, confronted by racial opposition, explore the range of potential accommodations, the possibilities for reconsolidating the racial order, and their possible roles in a racial ideology "re-articulated" in light of oppositional themes. "Hard-liners" and "moderates" appear, and compromises are sought both with the opposition and within the state itself.

Ultimately a series of reforms is enacted that partially meets oppositional demands. Reform policies are initiated and deemed potentially effective in establishing a new *unstable equilibrium*. These policies are then regularized in the form of agencies and programs whose constituency bases, like those of other state apparatuses, will consist of former adherents and sympathizers of the movement (as well as "free riders," of course). A new racial ideology is articulated, often employing themes initially framed by the oppositional movements.

The concept of the trajectory of racial politics links the two central actors in the drama of contemporary racial politics—the racial state and racially based social movements—and suggests a general pattern of interaction between them. Change in the racial order, in the social meaning and political role played by race, is achieved only when the state has initiated reforms, when it has generated new programs and agencies in response to movement demands. Movements capable of achieving such reforms only arise when there is significant "decay" in the capacities of pre-existing state programs and institutions to organize and enforce racial ideology. Contemporary patterns of change in the racial order illustrate this point clearly.

CONTEMPORARY CHANGE IN THE U.S. RACIAL ORDER

In the period with which we are concerned, the "rules of the game" by which racial politics are organized have become tremendously complex. In the pre–Second World War period change in the racial order was epochal in scope, shaped by the conditions of "war of manoeuvre" in which minorities had very little access to the political system, and understood in a context of assumed racial inequalities (i.e., comprehensive and generally unexamined racism). Today all of this has been swept away.

In the present day, racial change is the product of the interaction of racially based social movements and the racial state. In the post-war period, minority movements, led by the black movement, radically challenged the dominant racial ideology. As a result of this challenge, the racial order anchored by the state was itself de-stabilized, and a comprehensive process of reform was initiated. Later still, the reformed racial state became the target for further challenge, this time from the right. Racial politics now take place under conditions of "war of position," in which minorities have achieved significant (though by no means equal) representation in the political system, and in an ideological climate in which the *meaning* of racial equality can be debated, but the desirability of some form of equality is assumed. The new "rules of the game" thus contain *both* the legacy of movement efforts to re-articulate the meaning of race and to mobilize minorities politically on the basis of the new racial ideologies thus achieved, *and* the heritage of deep-seated racism and inequality.

As we have argued, social movements create collective identity, collective subjectivity, by offering their adherents a different view of themselves and their world; different, that is, from the characteristic world views and self-concepts of the social order that the movements are challenging. Based upon that newly forged collective identity, they address the state politically, demanding change. This is particularly true of contemporary racial movements. In fact these movements largely established the parameters within which popular and radical democratic movements (so-called "new social movements") operate in the U.S.

Racial movement mobilization and "normal" politics (the state, electoral activity, constituency formation, administrative and judicial systems, etc.) are now linked in a reciprocal process. Demands for state reform—for the transformation of racial society as a whole—are the consequences of transformations in collective identity, indeed in the meaning of race itself, "translated" from the cultural and/or ideological terrain of everyday life into the terms of political discourse. Such "translations" may come from movements themselves, or they may originate in "normal" political processes as electoral bases are sought, judicial decisions handed down, administrative procedures contested, and so on. Our conception of the "trajectory" of racial movements and state reform policies suggests that the transformation of the racial order occurs by means of an alternately equilibrated and disrupted relationship between the formation of racial ideology and the elaboration of state policy.

Today racial movements not only pose new demands originating outside state institutions, but may also frame their "common identity" in response to state-based racial initiatives. The concept of "Asian-American," for example, arose as a political label in the- 1960s. This reflected the similarity of treatment that various groups such as Chinese-Americans, Japanese-Americans, Korean-Americans, and so forth (groups that had not previously considered themselves as having a common political agenda) received at the hands of state institutions. The census, the legislatures, the courts, the educational system, the military, the welfare state apparatus—each in its own way a racial institution—are all sources of such racial change.

At the same time racial movements (both radical and conservative) continue to present the state with political demands. We understand this process as the *re-articulation* of racial ideology. Racially based movements begin as political projects that both build upon and break away from their cultural and political predecessors. Movement projects take shape in the interaction of civil society and the racial state. Movements set out to question the meaning of race and the nature of racial identity (e.g., "blackness," "Chicanismo," "minority" status; or for that matter, "majority" status, "whiteness"), while state initiatives seek to reinforce or transform the "unstable equilibrium" of racial politics in response to movement demands. Such "projects" challenge pre-existing racial ideology. They are efforts to *re-articulate* the meaning of race, and responses to such efforts.

The re-articulation of pre-existing racial ideology is a dual process of *disorganization* of the dominant ideology and of *construction* of an alternative, oppositional framework.

The dominant ideology can be disorganized in various ways. An insurgent movement may question whether the dominant racial ideology properly applies to the collective experience of its members. Examples of this interrogation of the pre-existing system of racial categories and beliefs may be found, not only in militant movement rhetoric,[34] but also in popular and intellectual discourse. During the 1960s, for instance, minority economists, political scientists, sociologists, and psychologists rejected dominant social science perspectives on racial grounds:

> For years, traditional (white) social science research—especially on political life and organizations— told us how politically workable and healthy the society was, how all the groups in society were getting pretty much their fair share, or moving certainly in that direction. There was a social scientific myth of consensus and progress developed.[35]

Similarly, during the 1970s, conservative, whites-oriented racial movements, such as those of the "New Right" or the "unmeltable" ethnics, developed counter-egalitarian challenges to the reforms that minority movements had achieved in the previous decade.[36] In this way the overarching racial ideology—in which racial minorities and the white majority alike recognize themselves—is called into question.

Insurgent racial movements also try to redefine the essential aspects of group identity. Demands for "self-determination" (which of course are linked to important democratic traditions in the U.S.) attain currency, while past organizational efforts are criticized. For example, militants of the 1960s attacked the political accommodations and compromises into which pre-existing community organizations and leaderships had entered. The NAACP and Urban League, the G.I. Forum and LULAC were criticized as "Uncle Toms" and "Tio Tacos" who had succumbed to "co-optation."[37] Militants also denounced various cultural practices in minority communities that were judged to reinforce submission and dependence. Malcolm X, for instance, excoriated the black practice of "conking" (i.e., straightening) the hair with lye.[38]

The construction of an oppositional movement employs a wide variety of ideological themes. Racially based movements have as their most fundamental task the creation of new identities, new racial meanings, and a new collective subjectivity. Not only does the articulation of a new racial ideology involve the recombination of pre-existent meanings and identities, but it also draws on quite heterodox and unexpected sources.[39]

The disorganization of the dominant racial ideology, the construction of a new set of racial meanings and identities, the transition from political project to oppositional movement, is a complex, uneven process, marked by considerable instability and tension. Change is being demanded, but any change in the system of racial meanings will affect all groups, all identities. Challenging the dominant racial ideology inherently involves not only reconceptualizing one's own racial identity, but a reformulation of the meaning of race in general. To challenge the position of blacks in society is to challenge the position of whites.[40]

Racial movements, built on the terrain of civil society, necessarily confront the state as they begin to upset the unstable equilibrium of the racial order. Once an oppositional racial ideology has been articulated, once the dominant racial ideology has been confronted, it becomes possible to demand reform of state racial policies and institutions. There has been a change in the "rules of the game." A new political terrain has been opened up.

By the same token, once such challenges have been posed and become part of the established political discourse, they in turn become subject to re-articulation. The state reforms won by minority movements in the 1960s, and the racial definitions and meanings embodied in these reforms, provided a formidable range of targets for "counter reformers" in the 1970s and 1980s. "New Right" and neo-conservative currents, armed with the still-dominant social–scientific paradigm of ethnicity theory, were able to carry on their own political "project." They were able to re-articulate racial ideology and restructure racial politics once again.

NOTES

1　Thomas Byrne Edsall and Mary D. Edsall, *Chain Reaction: The Impact of Race, Rights, and Taxes on American Politics* (New York: W.W. Norton & Co., 1991), 270.

2　Dana Y. Takagi, *The Retreat from Race: Asian American Admissions and Racial Politics* (New Brunswick: Rutgers University Press, 1992), 103–105.

3　Note that such movements can be egalitarian or counter-egalitarian, depending on the concepts of justice, equality, discrimination, and so on, to which they adhere. For a theory of political change focused on this issue (drawing on German reference points), see Barrington Moore, *Injustice: The Social Bases of Obedience and Revolt* (White Plains: Sharpe, 1978).

4　This does not mean that these channels are the sole province of reform-oriented movements or democratizing currents. They are also open to other uses, other interests, including those of reaction.

5　There are important continuities between present-day and past versions of racial ideology. Often in the past, the dominant viewpoint about what race was and what race meant has been believed to represent the culmination of a long struggle to eliminate pre-existing "unenlightened" racial beliefs. Religious and scientific exponents of the dominant racial ideology, for example, have often made such claims. Thus it is all too easy to believe that in the present ("finally") the U.S. has reached a stage at which racial oppression is largely a thing of the past, and that in the future race will play an ever-smaller role in determining the course of U.S. political and social history. We obviously do not share that view.

6　A brief selection of sources: Eugene Genovese, *Roll, Jordan, Roll: The World the Slaves Made* (New York: Pantheon, 1974); Julius Lester, *To Be a Slave* (New York: Dial, 1968); Vincent Harding, "Religion and Resistance among Antebellum Negroes, 1800–1860," in *The Making of Black America*, ed. A. Meier and E. Rudwick, 2 vols. (New York: Atheneum, 1969); George Rawick, *From Sundown to Sunup: The Making of the Black Community* (Westport: Greenwood, 1972); Herbert C. Gutman, *The Black Family in Slavery and Freedom, 1750–1925* (New York: Vintage, 1976); Robert Farris Thompson, *Flash of the Spirit: African and Afro-American Art and Philosophy* (New York: Random House, 1983).

7　Roxanne Dunbar Ortiz, "Land and Nationhood: The American Indian Struggle for Self-Determination and Survival," *Socialist Review* 63–64 (May-August 1982).

8　Rodolfo Acuña, *Occupied America: A History of Chicanos*, 2nd ed. (New York: Harper and Row, 1981); see also Leonard Pitt, *The Decline of the Californios* (Berkeley: University of California Press, 1966).

9　Our treatment here is necessarily very brief. The contemporary configuration of racial politics is a major subject later on in this work.

10 The ideological residue of these restrictions in naturalization and citizenship is the popular equation of the term "American" with "white." Other "Americans" are seen as black, Mexican, Oriental, and so forth.

11 For a comprehensive discussion of racial minorities in 19th-century California, see Tomas Almaguer, *Class, Race, and Capitalist Development: The Social Transformation of a Southern California County, 1848–1903*, (Ph.D. diss., University of California, Berkeley, 1979).

12 Harry P. Pachon and Joan W. Moore, "Mexican Americans," *Annals of the American Academy of Political and Social Science* 454 (March 1981), 111–124.

13 They also set the stage for tragicomic attempts to manipulate this incomprehension. In 1979, for example, an Anglo named Robert E. Lee changed his name to Roberto E. Leon in order to qualify for affirmative action programs available to those with Spanish surnames. See David Hayes-Bautista, "Identifying 'Hispanic' Populations: The Influence of Research Methodology Upon Public Policy," *American Journal of Public Health* 70, no. 4 (April 1980):355.

14 Nobel laureate William Shockley, inventor of the transistor, had advocated a biologistic theory of race, and argues that blacks are genetically inferior to whites in intelligence.

15 State theory is undergoing something of a renaissance, especially in its Marxist (or neo-Marxist) variants. We have been influenced by Bob Jessop, *The Capitalist State* (New York: NYU Press, 1982); Theda Skocpol, "Bringing the State Back in: A Report on Current Comparative Research on the Relationship between States and Social Structures," *Items* 36, nos. 1–2 (New York: Social Science Research Council, 1982)

16 Consider the conflicting 1960s activities of the federal courts and federal urban policies: the courts ordered school desegregation while urban renewal ("Negro removal") programs exacerbated residential segregation. Many similar conflicts in policy could be cited, not only at a given level of the state (i.e., federal, regional, local, etc. agencies), but also between different levels.

17 For a provocative treatment of the evolution of these "micro-political" measures, see Michel Foucault, *Discipline and Punish* (New York: Vintage, 1979), esp. 135–136.

18 On "hegemonic projects," see Bob Jessop, "Accumulation Strategies, State Forms, and Hegemonic Projects," *Kapitalistate*, no. 10–11 (1983): 89–111.

19 On "rules of the game," see Herbert Gintis and Samuel Bowles, "Structure and Practice in the Labor Theory of Value," *Review of Radical Political Economics* 12, no. 4 (winter 1981):4.

20 Thus in agriculture, for example, farm lobbying groups, the Agriculture Department, and the House and Senate agriculture committees together constitute the dominant policy-making mechanism. This concept has its origins in the work of Grant McConnell, and has been further refined by Gordon Adams. See Grant McConnell, *Private Power and American Democracy* (New York: Vintage, 1966); Gordon Adams, *The Politics of Defense Contracting: The Iron Triangle* (New Brunswick: Transaction, 1981).

21 The concept of civil society has a complex intellectual history, which originates in classical political economy, and comes via Hegel and Marx to Gramsci. In Hegel's political philosophy, and still in the work of the early Marx, civil society is seen as the realm of "private" social relationships, and distinguished from that of the state. Economic relationships, understood in the classical sense of the "free market," are also located within civil society. Gramsci's conception is considerably more complicated, though built on these premises. Civil society for him is the terrain upon which hegemony is secured, the complex of social relationships whose existence depends upon the "consent" of their participants. Religion, education, linguistic practices, cultural and artistic life, trade unions, and political organizations are thus included within it. Gramsci is well aware, though, that in the modern epoch there is no clear boundary between "private life" and the "life of the state." In a famous formulation, in fact, he includes civil society with "political society" as part of the state. See Antonio Gramsci, *Selections from the Prison*

Notebooks, ed. Quentin Hoare and Geoffrey Nowell Smith (New York: International, 1971), 263. In our view, the concept of hegemony, through which the dominant social forces acquire the consent of the subordinate ones, in itself presumes an autonomous civil society and a limited capacity for state "intervention" into the realm of "micro-politics," since this "consent" is not given stupidly or blindly but because the needs, interests, and ideas of the subordinate groups are actively incorporated and taken into account in the organization of society.

22 See Theodore J. Lowi, "The New Public Philosophy: Interest-Group Liberalism," in *The Political Economy,* ed. T. Ferguson and J. Rogers (Armonk: Sharpe, 1984).

23 This takes us into the realm of organizational theory, which is beyond the present scope. An interesting discussion of inter-agency relationships and their ability to frustrate innovative racial policy is Roland Warren et al., *The Structure of Urban Reform* (Lexington: D.C. Heath, 1973); on the autonomy of state officials see Fred Block, "Beyond Relative Autonomy: State Managers as Historical Subjects," *New Political Science,* no. 7 (winter 1981).

24 Claus Offe has developed some interesting approaches to these issues in his concepts of "selection mechanisms" by which political demands are rendered salient to state institutions, and of "allocative" vs. "productive" types of state policies, which are brought into play to deal with different rules of state decision making. See, respectively, Offe, "Structural Problems of the Capitalist State," in *German Political Studies,* vol. 1, ed. K. von Beyme (Beverly Hills: Sage, 1974), and *idem,* "The Theory of the Capitalist State and the Problem of Policy Formation," in *Stress and Contradiction in Modern Capitalism,* ed. L. Lindberg et al. (Lexington: D.C. Heath, 1975).

25 See, for example, Gramsci's remarks on parliamentary democracy in *Selections from the Prison Notebooks,* 80n.

26 These are aspects of hegemony that are beyond our present scope, but consider, for example, Roosevelt's failure to "pack" the Supreme Court (which constitutionally may have as many as 15 justices); or the outcry at Nixon's so-called "Saturday Night Massacre" (his firings of Cox, Richardson, and Ruckelshaus were perfectly legal). On the oppositional side, there are enormous difficulties involved in breaking with the supposedly "consensual" aspects of U.S. politics: the logic and justice of the "free enterprise system," anti-communism, the morality and truthfulness of government ("We stand for freedom," etc.). These are examples of a hegemonic domain from which challenges are effectively excluded—and within which basic political unity is therefore preserved.

27 The following discussion assumes the kinds of general racial conditions that have existed in the post-war U.S.: what we have termed racial war of position (e.g., the availability of "normal" political channels for racial politics), and the open existence of racial civil society (e.g., the possibility of minority cultural autonomy, political institutions, observance of traditional customs, linguistic practices, etc.). Obviously these conditions have not existed at all times and all places; indeed the civil rights phase of the black movement was concerned precisely with extending and institutionalizing them in the South. The very success of the Southern struggle shows, though, that at least on a national level, these conditions did already obtain.

28 Gramsci, *Selections from the Prison Notebooks,* 182.

29 The main means available to the state for the equilibration of conflicting interests is precisely their incorporation into the state in the form of policies, programs, patronage, and so on. Gramsci argues that various forms of hegemony flow from this process of incorporation: "expansive" hegemony if state–society relations display sufficient dynamism and are not inordinately plagued by crisis conditions; "reformist" hegemony (what he calls "transformism") if political stability requires continuing concessions to competing forces. See also our discussion of "absorption" and "insulation" below.

30   Racially subordinated groups may not be permitted access to the political system; if they are represented, this will take the form of racially defined political organizations, or by organizations that have racially explicit projects and programs.

31   We use this term in the Gramscian sense of social actors whose position and training permits them to express the world views, ideas, and sense of social identity of various social actors. Priests, teachers, artists, and entertainers fit in this definition, which is not the same as the standard usage of "intelligentsia."

32   Lack of success terminates the crisis. The result may be a restoration of the previous pattern of unstable equilibrium, or the consolidation of a counter-reformist agenda. On cyclical patterns in contemporary movement politics, see Frances Fox Piven and Richard A. Cloward. See their *Poor People's Movements: How They Succeed, Why They Fail* (New York: Vintage, 1979).

33   As seen from a movement standpoint. From the standpoint of the state, these are reform policies.

34   "The Mexican Americans now view the political system as an Anglo system. They feel that only a Mexican American political system can serve their needs...." Jose Angel Gutierrez, "La Raza and Revolution" in *Readings on La Raza*, ed. M.S. Meier and F. Rivera (1968; reprint, New York: Hill and Wang, 1974), 231.

35   Charles V. Hamilton, "Black Social Scientists: Contributions and Problems," in *The Death of White Sociology*, ed. Joyce Ladner (New York: Vintage, 1973), 472–473.

36   Michael Novak, *The Rise of the Unmeltable Ethnics* (New York: Macmillan, 1973); Nathan Glazer, *Affirmative Discrimination* (New York: Basic, 1975).

37   For example, see Gutierrez, "La Raza and Revolution," 232. These organizations had often played a challenging role in a previous phase of the reform trajectory; their leaders had been, in many cases, the militants of their generation. We discuss the concept of "trajectories" of reform movements below.

38   Malcolm X (with Alex Haley), *The Autobiography of Malcolm X* (New York: Grove Press, 1965), 53–56.

39   A good example is the incorporation of the Gandhian concept of non-violence into the civil rights movement.

40   The dislocation of white identity, of the meaning of "whiteness" in contemporary racial conflicts, has received relatively little attention. Some social–psychological studies have been directed at the identity crisis experienced by whites in the face of minority demands for equality, political rights, cultural, and/or organizational autonomy, and so on. The idea that the great Western societies are somehow fundamentally white—which today is espoused by explicitly racist groups like the Ku Klux Klan and the National Front in Britain—seems to us to be an attempt to keep the formerly unquestioned (or barely questioned) subjective coherence of "whiteness" alive. See, for example, Michael Billig, "Patterns of Racism: Interviews with National Front Members," *Race and Class* 20, no. 2 (autumn 1978):161–179.

8
CHAPTER

Identity, Belonging, and the Critique of Pure Sameness

Paul Gilroy

We have seen that the uncertain and divided world we inhabit has made racial identity matter in novel and powerful ways. But we should not take the concept of identity and its multiple associations with "race" and raciology for granted. The term "identity" has recently acquired great resonance, both inside and outside the academic world. It offers far more than an obvious, common-sense way of talking about individuality, community, and solidarity and has provided a means to understand the interplay between subjective experiences of the world and the cultural and historical settings in which those fragile, meaningful subjectivities are formed. Identity has even been taken into the viscera of postmodern commerce, where the goal of planetary marketing promotes not just the targeting of objects and services to the identities of particular consumers but the idea that any product whatsoever can be suffused with identity. Any commodity is open to being "branded" in ways that solicit identification and try to orchestrate identity.[1]

The same troubling qualities are evident where the term has been employed to articulate controversial and potentially illuminating themes in modern social and political theory. It has been a core component in the scholarly vocabulary designed to promote critical reflection upon who we are and what we want. Identity helps us to comprehend the formation of that perilous pronoun "we" and to reckon with the patterns of inclusion and exclusion that it cannot help creating. This situation is made more difficult once identity is recognized as something of a problem in itself, and thereby acquires an additional weighting. Calculating the relationship between identity and difference, sameness and otherness, is an intrinsically political operation. It happens when political collectivities reflect on what makes their binding connections possible. It is a fundamental part of how they comprehend their kinship—which may be an imaginary connection, though nonetheless powerful for that.

The distinctive language of identity appears again when people seek to calculate how tacit belonging to a group or community can be transformed into more active styles of solidarity, when they debate where the boundaries around a group should be constituted and how—if at all—they should be enforced. Identity becomes a question of power and authority when a group seeks to realize itself in political form. This may be a nation, a state, a movement, a class, or some unsteady combination of them all. Writing about the need for political institutions and relationships at the dawn of our era, Rousseau drew attention to the bold and creative elements in the history of how disorganized and internally divided groups had been formed into coherent units capable of unified action and worthy of the special status that defined the nation as a political body. Reflecting on the achievements of heroic individual leaders as builders of political cultures that could "attach citizens to the fatherland and to one another," he noted that the provision of a unifying common identity was a significant part of this political process. Significantly for our purposes, his example was taken from the history of the Children of Israel:

> [Moses] conceived and executed the astonishing project of creating a nation out of a swarm of wretched fugitives, without arts, arms, talents, virtues or courage, who were wandering as a horde of strangers over the face of the earth without a single inch of ground to call their own. Out of this wandering and servile horde Moses had the audacity to create a body politic, a free people.... [H]e gave them that durable set of institutions, proof against time, fortune and conquerors, which five thousand years have not been able to destroy or even alter.... To prevent his people from melting away among foreign peoples, he gave them customs and usages incompatible with those of other nations; he over-burdened them with peculiar rites and ceremonies; he inconvenienced them in a thousand ways in order to keep them constantly on the alert and to make them forever strangers among other men.[2]

In outlining elements of the political technology that would eventually produce the nation as a fortified encampment, Rousseau drew attention to the old association between identity and territory. Moses's achievement is viewed as all the more impressive because it was accomplished without the binding power of shared land. Rousseau underlined that the varieties of connection to which our ideas of identity refer are historical, social, and cultural rather than natural phenomena. Even at that early point in the constitution of modernity, he recognized that work must be done to summon the particularity and feelings of identity that are so often experienced as though they are spontaneous or automatic consequences of some governing culture or tradition that specifies basic and absolute differences between people. Consciousness of identity gains additional power from the idea that it is not the end product of one great man's "audacity" but an outcome of shared and rooted experience tied, in particular, to place, location, language, and mutuality.

When we think about the tense relationship between sameness and difference analytically, the interplay of consciousness, territory, and place becomes a major theme. It afford insights into the core of conflicts over how democratic social and political life should be organized at the start of the 21st century. We should try to remember that the threshold between those two antagonistic conditions can be moved and that identity making has a history even though its historical character is often systematically concealed. Focusing on identity helps us to ask in what sense the recognition of sameness and differentiation is a premise of the modern political culture that Rousseau affirmed and which his writings still help us to analyze.

The dizzying variety of ideas condensed into the concept of identity, and the wide range of issues to which it can be made to refer, foster analytical connections between themes and perspectives that are not conventionally associated. Links can be established between political, cultural, psychological, and psychoanalytic concerns. We need to consider, for example, how the emotional and affective bonds that form the specific basis of raciological and ethnic sameness are composed, and how they become patterned social activities with elaborate cultural features. How are they able to induce conspicuous acts of altruism, violence, and courage? How do they motivate people toward social interconnection in which individuality is renounced or dissolved into the larger whole represented by a nation, a people, a "race," or an ethnic group? These questions are important because, as we have seen, grave moral and political consequences have followed once the magic of identity has been engaged tactically or in manipulative, deliberately over-simple ways. Even in the most civilized circumstances, the signs of sameness have degenerated readily into emblems of supposedly essential or immutable difference. The special appeal of indi-viduality-transcending sameness still provides an antidote to the forms of uncertainty and anxiety that have been associated with economic and political crises. The idea of fundamentally shared identity becomes a platform for the reverie of absolute and eternal division.

The use of uniforms and other symbols to effect the sameness that identity only speaks about has sometimes been symptomatic of the process in which an anxious self can be shed and its concerns conjured away by the emergence of a stronger compound whole. The uniforms worn in the 1930s by fascists (and still worn by some fascist groups today) produced a compelling illusion of sameness both for members of the group and for those who observed their spectacular activities. The British Union of Fascists, one of the less successful black-shirted organizations from that period, argued that their garb was all the more attractive to adherents when contrasted with the conflict and bitterness created by class-based divisions that were tearing the nation apart from within:

> [The "blackshirt"] brings down one of the great barriers of class by removing differences of dress, and one of the objects of Fascism is to break the barriers of class. Already the blackshirt has achieved within our own ranks that classless unity which we will ultimately secure within the nation as a whole.[3]

The ultra-nationalist and fascist movements of the 20th century deployed elaborate technological resources in order to generate spectacles of identity capable of unifying and coordinating inevitable, untidy diversity into an ideal and unnatural human uniformity. Their synthetic versions of fundamental identity looked most seductive where all difference had been banished or erased from the collective. Difference within was repressed in order to maximize the difference between these groups and others. Identity was celebrated extravagantly in military styles: uniforms were combined with synchronized body movement, drill, pageantry, and visible hierarchy to create and feed the comforting belief in sameness as absolute, metaphysical invariance. Men and women could then appear as interchangeable and disposable cogs in the encamped nation's military machine or as indistinguishable cells in the larger organic entity that encompassed and dissolved their individuality. Their actions may even be imagined to express the inner spirit, fate, and historicality of the national community. The citizen was manifested as a soldier, and violence—potential as well as actual—was dedicated to the furtherance of national interests. That vital community was constituted in the dynamic interaction between marchers moving together in austere time and the crowds that watched and savoured the spectacle they created. In disseminating these valuable political effects, identity was mediated by cultural and communicative technologies such as film, lighting, and amplified sound. These 20th-century attributes were only partly concealed by the invocation of ancient ritual and myth.

Today's ubiquitous conflicts between warring constituencies that claim incompatible and exclusive identities suggest that these large-scale theatrical techniques for producing and stabilizing identity and soliciting national, "racial," or ethnic identification have been widely taken up. The reduction of identity to the uncomplicated, militarized, fraternal versions of pure sameness pioneered by fascism and Nazism in the 1930s is now routine, particularly where the forces of nationalism, "tribalism," and ethnic division are at work. Identity is thus revealed as a critical element in the distinctive vocabulary used to voice the geopolitical dilemmas of the late modern age. Where the power of absolute identity is summoned up, it is often to account for situations in which the actions of individuals and groups are being reduced to little more than the functioning of some overarching pre-social mechanism. In the past, this machinery was often understood as an historical or economic process that defined the special, manifest destiny of the group in question. These days, it is more likely to be represented as a pre-political, socio-biological, or bio-cultural feature, something mysterious and genetic that sanctions especially harsh varieties of deterministic thinking.

In this light, identity ceases to be an ongoing process of self-making and social interaction. It becomes instead a thing to be possessed and displayed. It is a silent sign that closes down the possibility of communication across the gulf between one heavily defended island of particularity and its equally well-fortified neighbours, between one national encampment and others. When identity refers to an indelible mark or code somehow written into the bodies of its carriers, "otherness" can only be a threat. Identity is latent destiny. Seen or unseen, on the surface of the body or buried deep in its cells, identity forever sets one group apart from others who lack the particular, chosen traits that become the basis of typology and comparative evaluation. No longer a site for the affirmation of subjectivity and autonomy, identity mutates. Its motion reveals a deep desire for mechanical solidarity, seriality, and hyper-similarity. The scope for individual agency dwindles and then disappears. People become bearers of the differences that the rhetoric of absolute identity invents and then invites them to celebrate. Rather than communicating and making choices, individuals are seen as obedient, silent passengers moving across a flattened moral landscape toward the fixed destinies to which their essential identities, their genes, and the closed cultures they create have consigned them once and for all. And yet, the desire to fix identity in the body is inevitably frustrated by the body's refusal to disclose the required signs of absolute incompatibility people imagine to be located there.

Numerous cross-cultural examples might be used to illustrate this point. Reports from the genocide in Rwanda repeatedly revealed that identity cards issued by the political authorities were a vital source of the information necessary to classify people into the supposedly natural "tribal" types that brought them either death or deliverance. There, as in several other well-documented instances of mass slaughter, the bodies in question did not freely disclose the secrets of identity:

> Many Tutsis have been killed either because their ID cards marked them out as a Tutsi or because they did not have their card with them at the time and were therefore unable to prove they were not a Tutsi.... To escape the relentless discrimination they suffered, over the years many Tutsis bribed local government officials to get their ID card changed to Hutu. Unfortunately, this has not protected them.... The Tutsi give-aways were: one, being tall and two having a straight nose. Such criteria even led hysterical militias to kill a number of Hutus whose crime was "being too tall for a Hutu." Where there was doubt about the person's physical characteristics or because of the complaints that too many Tutsis had changed their card, the Interahamwe called upon villagers to verify the "tutsiship" of the quarry in question.[4]

Similar events were still being reported four years later when the genocidal assault against the Tutsis had been re-articulated into the civil war in Congo—a conflict that had already drawn in several other states and that appeared to provide the key to stability in the region. Under the presidency of Laurent Kabila, people whose physical characteristics made them suspect were still being openly murdered.[5] It is important to remember, however, that the linguistic markers of residual colonial conflict between anglophone and francophone spheres of influence were also implicated in sustaining the killing.

These fragments from a history of unspeakable barbarity underline how the notion of fixed identity operates easily on both sides of the chasm that usually divides scholarly writing from the disorderly world of political conflicts. Recently, identity has also come to constitute something of a bridge between the often discrepant approaches to understanding self and sociality found on the different sides of that widening gulf. As a theme in contemporary scholarship, identity has offered academic thinking an important route back toward the struggles and uncertainties of everyday life, where the idea of identity has become especially resonant. It has also provided the distinctive signatures of an inward, implosive turn that brings the difficult tasks of politics to an end by making them appear irrelevant in the face of deeper, more fundamental powers that regulate human conduct irrespective of governmental superficialities. If identity and difference are fundamental, then they are not amenable to being retooled by crude political methods that cannot possibly get to the heart of primal ontologies, destinies, and fates. When the stakes are this high, nothing can be done to offset the catastrophic consequences that result from tolerating difference and mistaken attempts at practising democracy. Difference corrupts and compromises identity. Encounters with it are just as unwelcome and potentially destructive. They place that most precious commodity, rooted identity, in grave jeopardy.

When national and ethnic identities are represented and projected as pure, exposure to difference threatens them with dilution and compromises their prized purities with the ever-present possibility of contamination. Crossing as mixture and movement must be guarded against. New hatreds and violence arise not, as they did in the past, from supposedly reliable anthropological knowledge of the identity and difference of the

Other, but from the novel problem of not being able to locate the Other's difference in the common-sense lexicon of alterity. Different people are certainly hated and feared, but the timely antipathy against them is nothing compared with the hatreds turned toward the greater menace of the half-different and the partially familiar. To have mixed is to have been party to a great betrayal. Any unsettling traces of hybridity must be excised from the tidy, bleached-out zones of impossibly pure culture. The safety of sameness can then be recovered by either of the two options that have regularly appeared at the meltdown point of this dismal logic: separation and slaughter.

How does the concept of identity provide a means to speak about social and political solidarity? How is the term "identity" invoked in the summoning and binding of individual agents into groups that become social actors? For these purposes, considering identity requires a confrontation with the specific ideas of ethnic, racialized, and national identity and their civic counterparts. This departure introduces a cluster of distinctively modern notions that, in conjunction with discourses of citizenship, have actively produced rather than given a secondary expression to forms of solidarity with unprecedented power to mobilize mass movements and animate large-scale constituencies. The full power of communicative technologies such as radio, sound recording, film, and television has been employed to create forms of solidarity and national consciousness that propelled the idea of belonging far beyond anything that had been achieved in the 19th century by the industrialization of print and the formalization of national languages.[6]

Contemporary conflicts over the status of national identity provide the best examples here. Nelson Mandela's historic inaugural speech as State President illustrated both the malleability of nationalist sentiment and some of the enduring tensions around its radical constitution. Working to produce an alternative content for the new non-racial, post-racial, or perhaps anti-racial political identity that might draw together the citizenry of the reborn country on a new basis beyond the grasp of racializing codes and fantasies of favoured life as a people chosen by God, President Mandela turned to the land—common ground—beneath the feet of his diverse, unified, and mutually suspicious audience. Significantly, he spoke not only of the soil but of the beauty of the country and offered the idea of a common relationship to both the cultivated and the natural beauty of the land as elements of a new beginning. This, for him, was the key to awakening truly democratic consciousness. A transformed relationship between body and environment would transcend the irrelevancies of apartheid South Africa's redundant racial hierarchies:

> To my compatriots, I have no hesitation in saying that each one of us is as intimately attached to the soil of this beautiful country as are the famous jacaranda trees of Pretoria and the mimosa trees of the bushveld.
>
> Each time one of us touches the soil of this land, we feel a sense of personal renewal.... That spiritual and physical oneness we all share with this common homeland explains the depth of pain we all carried in our hearts as we saw our country tear itself apart in a terrible conflict.[7]

Whether these laudable claims were a plausible part of rebuilding South African nationality remains to be seen. What is more significant for our purposes is that territory and indeed nature itself are being engaged as a means to define citizenship and the forms of rootedness that compose national solidarity and cohesion. President Mandela's words were powerful because they work with the organicity that nature has bequeathed to modern ideas of culture. In that blur, Mandela constructed an ecological account of the relationship between shared humanity, common citizenship, place, and identity. The speech subverted traditional assumptions with its implication that apartheid was a brutal violation of nature that could be repaired only if people were prepared to pay heed to the oneness established by their connection to the beautiful environment they share and hold in common stewardship.

The alternative argument set out below recognizes the socio-ecological dynamics of identity formation. However, it asks you to consider what might be gained if the powerful claims of soil, roots, and territory could be set aside. You are invited to view them in the light of other possibilities that have sometimes defined themselves against the forms of solidarity sanctioned by the territorial regimes of the nation-state. We will see that the idea of movement can provide an alternative to the sedentary poetics of either soil or blood. Both communicative technology and older patterns of itinerancy ignored by the human sciences can be used to articulate placeless imaginings of identity as well as new bases for solidarity and synchronized action. With these possibilities in mind, I want to suggest that considering the de-territorialized history of the modern African diaspora into the western hemisphere and the racial slavery through which it was accomplished has something useful to teach us about the workings of identity and identification and, beyond that, something valuable to impart about the claims of nationality and the nation-state upon the writing of history itself.

DIASPORA AS A SOCIAL ECOLOGY OF IDENTIFICATION

The idea of diaspora offers a ready alternative to the stern discipline of primordial kinship and rooted belonging. It rejects the popular image of natural nations spontaneously endowed with self-consciousness, tidily composed of uniform families: those interchangeable collections of ordered bodies that express and reproduce absolutely distinctive cultures as well as perfectly formed heterosexual pairings. As an alternative to the metaphysics of "race," nation, and bounded culture coded into the body, diaspora is a concept that problematizes the cultural and historical mechanics of belonging. It disrupts the fundamental power of territory to determine identity by breaking the simple sequence of explanatory links between place, location, and consciousness. It destroys the naive invocation of common memory as the basis of particularity in a similar fashion by drawing attention to the contingent political dynamics of commemoration.

The ancient word "diaspora" acquired a modern accent as a result of its unanticipated usefulness to the nationalisms and subaltern imperialisms of the late 19th century. It remains an enduring feature of the continuing aftershocks generated by those political projects in Palestine and elsewhere. If it can be stripped of its disciplinarian associations, it might offer seeds capable of bearing fruit in struggles to comprehend the sociality of a new phase in which displacement, flight, exile, and forced migration are likely to be familiar and recurrent phenomena that transform the terms in which identity needs to be understood. Retreating from the totalizing immodesty and ambition of the word "global," diaspora is an outer-national term that contributes to the analysis of intercultural and transcultural processes and forms. It identifies a relational network, characteristically produced by forced dispersal and reluctant scattering. It is not just a word of movement, though purposive, desperate movement is integral to it. Under this sign, push factors are a dominant influence. The urgency they introduce makes diaspora more than a voguish synonym for peregrination or nomadism. Life itself is at stake in the way the word connotes flight following the threat of violence, rather than freely chosen experiences of displacement. Slavery, pogroms, indenture, genocide, and other unnameable terrors have all figured in the constitution of diasporas and the reproduction of diaspora consciousness in which identity is focused, less on the equalizing, pre-democratic force of sovereign territory, and more on the social dynamics of remembrance and commemoration defined by a strong sense of the dangers involved in forgetting the location of origin and the tearful process of dispersal.

Earlier on, in assessing the power of roots and rootedness to ground identity, we encountered invocations of organicity that forged an uncomfortable connection between the warring domains of nature and culture. They made nation and citizenship appear to be natural rather than social phenomena—spontaneous expressions of a distinctiveness that was palpable in deep inner harmony between people and their dwelling places. Diaspora is a useful means to reassess the idea of essential and absolute identity precisely because it is incompatible with that type of nationalist and raciological thinking. The word comes closely associated with the idea of sowing seed. This etymological inheritance is a disputed legacy and a mixed blessing. It demands that we attempt to evaluate the significance of the scattering process against the supposed uniformity of that which has been scattered. Diaspora posits important tensions between here and there, then and now, between seed in the bag, the packet, or the pocket and seed in the ground, the fruit, or the body. By focusing attention equally on the sameness within differentiation and the differentiation within sameness, diaspora disturbs the suggestion that political and cultural identity might be understood via the analogy of indistinguishable peas lodged in the protective pods of closed kinship and subspecies being. Is it possible to imagine how a more complex, ecologically sophisticated sense of interaction between organisms and environments might become an asset in thinking critically about identity?

Imagine a scenario in which similar—though not precisely identical—seeds take root in different places. Plants of the same species are seldom absolutely indistinguishable. Nature does not always produce interchangeable clones. Soils, nutrients, predators, pests, and pollination vary along with unpredictable weather. Seasons change. So do climates, which can be determined on a variety of scales: micro as well as macro and mezzo. Diaspora provides valuable cues and clues for the elaboration of a social ecology of cultural identity and identification that takes us far beyond the stark dualism of genealogy and geography. The pressure to associate, like the desires to remember or forget, may vary with changes in the economic and political atmosphere. Unlike the tides, the weather cannot be predicted accurately. To cap it all, the work involved in discovering origins is more difficult in some places and at some times.

If we can adopt this more difficult analytical stance, the celebrated "butterfly effect" in which tiny, almost insignificant forces can, in defiance of conventional expectations, precipitate unpredictable, larger changes in other locations becomes a commonplace happening. The seamless propagation of cultural habits and styles was rendered radically contingent at the point where geography and genealogy began to trouble each other. We are directed toward the conflictual limits of "race," ethnicity, and culture. When a diaspora talks back to a nation-state, it initiates conflict between those who agree that they are more or less what they were, but cannot agree whether the more or the less should take precedence in contemporary political and historical calculations.

What the African-American writer Leroi Jones once named "the changing same"[8] provides a valuable motif with which to fix this supplement to the diaspora idea. Neither the mechanistic essentialism that is too squeamish to acknowledge the possibility of difference within sameness nor the lazy alternative that animates the supposedly strategic variety of essentialism can supply keys to the untidy workings of diaspora identities. They are creolized, syncretized, hybridized, and chronically impure cultural forms, particularly if they were once rooted in the complicity of rationalized terror and racialized reason. This changing same is not some invariant essence that gets enclosed subsequently in a shape-shifting exterior with which it is casually associated. It is not the sign of an unbroken, integral inside protected by a camouflaged husk. The phrase names the problem of diaspora politics and diaspora poetics. The same is present, but how can we imagine it as something other than an essence generating the merely accidental? Iteration is the key to this process. The same is retained without needing to be reified. It is ceaselessly reprocessed. It is maintained and modified in what becomes a determinedly non-traditional tradition, for this is not tradition as closed or simple repetition. Invariably promiscuous, diaspora, and the politics of commemoration it specifies challenge us to apprehend mutable forms that can redefine the idea of culture through a reconciliation with movement and complex, dynamic variation.

Several generations of blacks have been born in Europe whose identification with the African continent is even more attenuated and remote, particularly since the anti-colonial wars are over. Both the memory of slavery and an orientation toward identity that derives from African origins are hard to maintain when the rupture of migration intervenes and stages its own trials of belonging. However, the notion of a distinctive, African-derived identity has not withered and the moral and political fruits of black life in the western hemisphere have been opened out systematically to larger and larger numbers of people in different areas.

The black musicians, dancers, and performers of the New World have disseminated these insights, styles, and pleasures through the institutional resources of the cultural industries that they have colonized and captured. These media, particularly recorded sound, have been annexed for sometimes subversive purposes of protest and affirmation. The vernacular codes and expressive cultures constituted from the forced new beginning of racial slavery have reappeared at the centre of a global phenomenon that has regularly surpassed innocent notions of mere entertainment. What are wrongly believed to be simple cultural commodities have been used to communicate a powerful ethical and political commentary on rights, justice, and democracy that articulates but also transcends criticism of modern racial typology and the ideologies of white supremacy. The living history of New World blacks has endowed this expressive tradition with flexibility and durability.

Bob Marley, whose recordings are still selling all over the world more than a decade after his death, provides a useful concluding example here. His enduring presence in globalized popular culture is an important reminder of the power of the technologies that ground the culture of simulation. Those same technological resources have subdued the constraints of nature and provided Marley with a virtual life after death in which his popularity can continue to grow unencumbered by any embarrassing political residues that might make him into a threatening or frightening figure. But there is more to this worldwide popularity than clever video-based immortality and the evident reconstruction of Bob Marley's image, stripped of much of its militant Ethiopianism—yet another chosen people and another promised land to set alongside those we have already considered.

Bob's life and work lend themselves to the study of postmodern diaspora identity. They help us to perceive the workings of those complex cultural circuits that have transformed a pattern of simple, one-way dispersal into a webbed network constituted through multiple points of intersection. His historic performance at the Zimbabwe independence ceremony in 1980 symbolized the partial reconnection with African origins that permeates diaspora yearning. Like so many others, he too did not go to Africa to make his home. He chose instead, as many other prominent pan-Africanists had done before and since, a more difficult cosmopolitan commitment and a different form of solidarity and identification that did not require his physical presence in that continent.

His triumph not only marks the beginning of what has come to be known as "world music" or "world beat," an increasingly significant marketing category that helps to locate the transformation and possible demise of music-led youth culture. It was built from the seemingly universal power of a poetic and political language that reached out from its roots to find new audiences hungry for its insights. Bob became, in effect, a plane-tary figure. His music was pirated in Eastern Europe and became intertwined with the longing for freedom and rights across Africa, the Pacific, and Latin America. Captured into commodities, his music travelled and found new audiences and so did his band. Between 1976 and 1980 they criss-crossed the planet, performing in the United States, Canada, the United Kingdom, France, Italy, Germany, Spain, Scandinavia, Ireland, Holland, Belgium, Switzerland, Japan, Australia, New Zealand, the Ivory Coast, and Gabon. Major sales were also recorded in market areas where the band did not perform, particularly Brazil, Senegal, Ghana, Nigeria, Taiwan, and the Philippines.

NOTES

1   Mark Leonard, Briton™ (Demos, 1997).

2   J.-J. Rousseau, "Considerations on the Government of Poland, in *Rousseau Political Writings*, trans. and ed. Frederick Watkins (Nashville: Nelson and Sons, 1953), 163–164.

3   *The Blackshirt* (November 24–30, 1933), 5; quoted in John Harvey, *Men in Black* (Chicago: University of Chicago Press, 1995), 242.

4   African Rights, *Rwanda Death, Despair and Defiance* (London: African Rights, 1994), 347–354. See also Sander L. Gilman, *The Jew's Body* (New York: Routledge, 1991), especially chap. 7, "The Jewish Nose: Are Jews White or The History of the Nose Job."

5   Arthur Malu-Malu and Thierry Oberle, London, *Sunday Times*, 30 August 1998.

6   Benedict Anderson, *Imagined Communities: Reflections on the Origin and Spread of Nationalism* (London: Verso, 1983).

7   President Mandela's inaugural speech was reprinted in *The Independent*, 11 May 1995, p. 12.

8   Leroi Jones, *Black Music* (New York: Quill, 1967), 180–211.

QUESTIONS FOR CRITICAL THOUGHT

CHAPTER 5 BY BENEDICT ANDERSON

1. What is an imagined [national] community? What are some of the main imagined communities in your life?
2. Can you think of some major changes in communication technologies over the last 45 years that influence new and more effective ways of imagining community? How do you think they change the dynamics of imagining?
3. Can you think of a few negative aspects of imagined communities that are facilitated by communication technologies?

CHAPTER 6 BY RON EYERMAN

1. What is cultural trauma? How does it differ from cultural memory?
2. Identify a contemporary example of cultural trauma, and think of ways the memory of that history has changed.
3. Using your example from question 2, identify the major intellectual leaders involved in processes of re-membering, and think about the influences they had on how history was remembered.

CHAPTER 7 BY PAUL GILROY

1. In what ways are racial identities today mediated in diasporic communities?
2. Other than Bob Marley, what figures in popular culture do you think exercise a significant influence on diasporic identities? Explain why.

3. Do you think that developments in instantaneous global communication media facilitate new forms of identity formation? Can you think of ways that communication technologies may erode traditional identities? Use an example to illustrate your arguments.

CHAPTER 8 BY MICHAEL OMI AND HOWARD WINANT

1. What do Omi and Winant mean by the term "racial state"?
2. Identify and explain two strategies utilized by social movement organizations to resist the racial state. Can you think of contemporary Canadian examples?
3. What contemporary changes in the racial order do Omi and Winant see as a threat to American racial politics?

FURTHER READING

Alexander, Jeffrey C., Ron Eyerman, Bernard Giesen, Neil J. Smelser, and Piotr Sztompka. *Cultural Trauma and Collective Identity.* Berkeley: University of California Press, 2004.

This book is a collaborative effort to further social–scientific understanding of cultural trauma. The authors adopt a constructivist approach to trauma and examine the Holocaust, slavery in the United States, and the events of 11 September 2001.

Brunsma, David L., and Kerry Ann Rockuemore. "What Does 'Black' Mean? Exploring the Epistemological Stranglehold of Racial Categorization." *Critical Sociology* 28, nos. 1–2 (2002):101–121.

In this paper, the authors argue that the meaning of "black" in America is multi-dimensional and contextual, yet the category is used to homogenize an otherwise very diverse population. Beginning with an historical overview of the one-drop rule, the authors argue that post-civil rights America must re-evaluate this social designation.

Hughes, Langston. *Not without Laughter.* New York: Simon and Schuster, 1929. Reprint 1969.

This book is a classic in African-American literature. It tells the story of Sandy, a black boy growing up in Kansas. It is very easy to read, and the complexity of identity formation processes addressed in the book is subtle yet profound.

Said, Edward. 1978. *Orientalism.* New York: Vintage Books, 1978.

The late Edward Said offers a set of explanations for how intellectual traditions are transmitted. He argues that Orientalism, "a way of coming to terms with the Orient that is based on the Orient's special place in European Western experience" (p. 1), is situated on an historical dialectic between "Orient" and "Occident." *Orientalism* is recognized as a canon in several interdisciplinary fields.

Satzewich, Victor. *The Ukrainian Diaspora*. New York: Routledge, 2003.

This book details 125 years of Ukrainian migration. Satzewich examines identity in the context of the Ukrainian diaspora, its diversity, and the varied responses to the war crimes trials in the 1980s.

THREE

THE NEGOTIATION OF DIFFERENCE

I remember well when the shadow swept across me. I was a little thing, away up in the hills of New England.... In a wee wooden schoolhouse, something put it into the boys' and girls' heads to buy gorgeous visiting-cards—ten cents a package—and exchange. The exchange was merry, till one girl, a tall newcomer, refused my card—refused it peremptorily with a glance. Then it dawned on me with a certain suddenness that I was different from the others; or like, mayhap, in heart and life longing, but shut out from their world by a vast veil. (Du Bois [1903] 1989, 4)

Sociologists have written about and theorized the relationships among race, ethnicity, and cultural difference for over 100 years. It was not until the 1960s and 1970s, however, that sustained research attention was focused on race, ethnicity, and social integration in Canada. In 1965, the Canadian sociologist John Porter published *The Vertical Mosaic*, for example, the first widely acclaimed post-war Canadian study of ethnicity, class, and social mobility. In *The Vertical Mosaic*, Porter argued that new immigrants from Southern and Eastern Europe experienced barriers to upward social mobility. Porter detailed how immigrants who did not hold membership in one of the "charter groups," the English and the French, were subordinated by these groups and restricted by an "entrance status" that confined them to low-paying and low-status positions in the Canadian occupational hierarchy. Porter theorized that over time, non-traditional European immigrants would shed their ethnic characteristics and blend into Canada's dominant cultural values and norms. Language and ethnic identity retention, in other words, were impediments to social integration and upward social mobility in Porter's assessment.

Porter's study set the pace for sociological research on race, ethnicity, and racism in the 1970s, emphasizing structural factors such as social mobility, education, and labour market opportunities, as well as the elite structure of Canadian society. Neither sociologists nor leaders of immigrant communities were explicitly concerned with issues of identity, individual experience, and equal recognition in, say, Canada's multicultural policy. The main concerns of new immigrants and immigrant communities were, rather, to find adequate housing and jobs, as well as to address racism in Canadian institutions such as the police force (Bannerji 2000). Canadian sociological research, itself in a developmental stage in the 1970s, followed suit. However, the discursive currency of social conflict began to shift in the 1980s with changes in the political and economic structure of Canadian society, in the ethno-racial composition of the country, and in the intellectual context of developments in postmodernism and cultural studies. By the early 1990s, there was widespread sociological interest in the negotiation and experience of ethno-racial difference, and by the mid-1990s, "identity" had become the rubric under which difference and experience was represented in scholarly writing and cultural production.

Contemporary identities, whether racial, ethnic, national, gender, or sexual, are what the late sociologist Pierre Bourdieu (1990) called "categories of practice." What he meant was that, although sociologists use different identity categories to explain the social world, identity categories are simultaneously used in everyday interactions to make sense of and negotiate the world. Using these categories of practice in everyday interaction, people explain the essence of themselves and others in terms of race, class, nationality, and so on, and they come to define who they are in these cultural or structural terms. What troubled Bourdieu is that sociologists have increasingly stopped asking questions such as, "Why and under what circumstances do people identify with a particular category of practice?" or "What is the basis of identification?", favouring instead to examine the actual content of historically specific, experiential identities. Sociological research, in other words, has increasingly abandoned social critique and the hard questions of why social phenomena exist in favour of a more descriptive, documentary form of social comment (MacInnes 2004). This is what we mean by the discursive currency of contemporary social conflict: that social divisions, conflicts, tensions, and struggles are increasingly explained by sociologists in terms of the actual content of identities and differences, rather than on the basis of access to material resources, struggles, and conflicts.

From a sociological point of view, there is a twofold problem with taking identity as a guiding analytical concept, that is, of using categories of practice to explain the nature of social life. First, if sociologists start with categories of practice, then we are forced to assume that by examining categories such as "black" and "white," "heterosexual" and "homosexual," we can know something about the people who occupy or "hold" these identities individually. In other words, by using the general abstract category to infer individual or personal meaning, we homogenize individual experience and generate an over-socialized conception of individual subjectivity. Conversely, if we start with the individual or personal experiences of identity and conduct interviews or hold focus groups to understand what it means to identify as "homosexual" or "white," then we assume that individual experiences can tell us something about the general abstract category of "homosexuality" or "whiteness." By using individual subjective experience as a source of information to infer categorical meaning, we homogenize group experience and lend support to an individualized conception of the social or collective world. Both research scenarios tend to conflate the social or collective meaning of identity categories with individual experience, and in both cases we run the risk of essentializing identity. Of course people have individual thoughts and feelings, and of course there is a categorical or shared reality to the social world that cannot be reduced to any one individual. What this tells us is that sociological research is always partial and incomplete, and that the findings we produce in sociological research are influenced by the assumptions that structure our research and the methods we use to garner data on the activities of human beings. It also tells us that contemporary identities, whether in their categorical or individual form, are a starting point, not an ending point, for sociological investigation.

Among the many social structural factors that influence identity formations (i.e., gender, age, nationality, skin hue, sexual orientation, income), a strong majority of sociologists privileges the category of race in the process of identity formation. They argue that race and skin colour remain significant in social categorization and the involuntary ascription of identities (Walters 1990; Roots 1996; McCarthy and Crichlow 1993; Tuan 1999). All of the readings in this section differentiate between the categories of race and ethnicity, and they all posit that the experiences of blacks and whites are qualitatively different because of this categorical and experiential differentiation. Whereas ethnic categories are conceptualized primarily on the basis of shared cultural traits (e.g., customs, religion, tradition, dress, and language), racial categories are defined in terms of physical appearance. Because of the fact of (racial) visibility, race and ethnicity are said to function differently. The authors in this section consider persons of mixed-race status as individuals who have one parent belonging to a visible minority group, and they contend that racial and ethnic differentiation has a significant impact on individuals' negotiation of difference, identity, and belonging.

SECTION READINGS: OPTIONAL, BIRACIAL, MIXED, AND PAN-ETHNIC IDENTITIES

In the first reading passage, Mary Waters points to the importance of race and ethnicity as distinct social categories in shaping identities in the United States. She argues that white "ethnic" Americans of European ancestry possess "symbolic ethnicity." What she means is that ethnic identity for white Americans is individualistic and optional, without real social costs for individuals, and that it does not influence white Americans' lives in significant and meaningful ways. Symbolic identity options, she contends, are available neither to black Americans nor to other people of colour as something they can "opt" out of.

Waters contrasts the individual symbolic ethnic identity held by many white people with the socially enforced and imposed racial identity (involuntary ascribed identity) of African-Americans. As she argues, because racial categories are defined on the basis of physical appearance, usually skin colour, the intersection of race and ethnicity operates differently for whites and blacks. All ethnicities, she continues, are not equal and involuntary, and she concludes by discussing the implications of symbolic ethnicities for race relations and social change. For white people, she explains, who understand their ethnic identification and its relationship to society and politics as an individual choice, identity may not be recognized as an involuntary ascription associated with the legacy and contemporary reality of racial discrimination. In order to achieve an ideal pluralist society where all people's heritage is treated equally, and where symbolic ethnicities and identities are equally available to all individuals, program and policy development is required—emphasizing programs and policies that are not individual but societal in nature.

The next reading passage, written by Kerry Ann Rockquemore, explores the meaning of biracial identity and the social factors that influence patterns of interpretation, construction, and maintenance of identities by mixed-race respondents. The study is based on a content analysis of extensive interviews with 14 biracial undergraduate Catholic students, ranging in age from 18 to 22 years and coming from middle- to upper-middle-class backgrounds. The purpose of the analysis is to construct a descriptive map of the various ways that respondents understand their own racial identity. The findings suggest that biracial identity does not have a singular meaning, and that there are multiple ways that individuals understand and respond to their biracialness.

Specifically, Rockquemore theorizes four tentative descriptive categories corresponding to the ways respondents understand and interpret their biracialness: border, protean, transcendent, and traditional identity. First, respondents who fall in the category of border identity consider themselves to be neither black nor white. Rather, they stress their in-betweenness as the unique grounding for their identity. As Rockquemore states, they incorporate both blackness and whiteness into a unique category of biracial. Second, those who fall in the category of protean identity report the ability to move among different cultural contexts and to cross boundaries between "black," "white," and "biracial" because they possess or identify with all three categories. Because of their cultural savvy, they claim that they are able to fit into different settings and shift their identities according to the context of their interactions. Third, transcendent identity is available only to those individuals whose physical appearance has a high degree of ambiguity and who do not easily fit into social categories of white or black. These individuals view their biracialness as a unique marginalization, and they discount race as a "master status." This allows them to avoid or reject any type of racial group categorization as the basis of personal identity. And finally, respondents in the traditional identity context acknowledge biracial parents, but their self-definition is categorically definitive: either black or white.

Rockquemore's findings challenge the common-sense assumptions that most people of mixed ancestry identify themselves as biracial and that biracial identity has a singular meaning. There are various understandings of what biracial identity means to individuals, and there are several ways persons in this social context interpret and respond to their socially constituted biracialness. As Rockquemore suggests, these various understandings, interpretations, and responses are grounded in differential experiences, different biographies, and cross-cutting cultural contexts. Social networks provide the terrain on which identities may be negotiated and choices made, and Rockquemore concludes that social status and appearance are mediated by the types of social interactions that set the parameters of meaning, construction, negotiation, and challenge.

The third reading passage presents an investigation of mixed-race women's views of multicultural policy in Canada. Minelle Mahtani examines the relationship between "mixed race" identity and Canadian identity (between ethnic and national belongings), and she points out how some mixed-race women reconstitute their racial, ethnic, and national identities. The reading passage is based on data collected from qualitative, open-ended interviews with 24 self-identified women of mixed race. Women in the study are highly critical of multicultural policy. They do not feel that existing notions of multiculturalism adequately encapsulate their racial and/or ethnic representations, and they report that the way multiculturalism encourages cultural differentiation actually positions them outside the national discourse. This is partly because Canadian multicultural policy privileges ethnicity over other social identities. The ethnic identity of mixed-race women is complex, however, and ethnic identities are comprised of many elements, such as parents' heritage, gender, religion, and racial and cultural affiliation, as well as how others "read their race."

Mahtani argues that Canadian multicultural policy constructs specific social–spatial boundaries between "Canadians" and "non-Canadians." Through narratives, she illuminates the difficulty others had in identifying mixed-race women simply as "Canadian." She argues that to be understood as an "authentic" or "real" Canadian implies being understood as white or European. Thus, those who are designated as "ethnics" or who fall under the "visible minority" status are placed outside the discursive parameters of "Canadianness." They are, consequently, assumed to be "foreigners." Mahtani's arguments are further complicated by the phenomenon of hyphenated identities. Hyphens, she explains, operate to produce spaces of "distance-difference," whereby ethnicity is place outside "Canadianness." It is impossible to position oneself as Canadian without announcing one's ethnic identity. Mahtani concludes her analysis with ruminations on the relationship between "mixed-race" and Canadian identity.

The final reading passage, written by Pyong Gap Min and Rose Kim, examines the ethnic and pan-ethnic attachments and identities among Asian-American professionals through 15 autobiographical essays. Personal narratives by professionals of different generations provide information regarding the process of change in ethnic identity throughout the life course. The reading passage examines three dimensions of Asian-American ethnicity: retention of ethnic culture, participation in ethnic networks, and identity focusing on ethnic and pan-ethnic characteristics. Children of contemporary immigrants are found to have an advantage over children of earlier immigrants in retaining their cultural traditions, primarily because of technological advances in transportation and communication that enable them to maintain transnational ties. They are also able to retain cultural traditions because of changes in policy from Anglo conformity to cultural pluralism. These professionals demonstrate a high level of social assimilation without relinquishing their culture. Many of them even have a strong bicultural orientation.

The professionals in the study experience contradictory pressures in the processes of identity formation and retention. For instance, their residential and occupational assimilation may contribute to the loss of ethnic identity, while other structural factors pressure them to accept their ethnic or pan-Asian and racial identities. Min and Kim also argue that the general perception of Asian-Americans as foreigners figures prominently in their ethnic and racial identities. For "white ethnics," they contend, who are fully accepted as Americans, ethnic identity is a matter of personal choice (symbolic ethnicity), but for Asian-Americans, who are considered as "foreigners," ethnic identity is socially imposed. For this latter group, being "ethnic" is a societal expectation. In Min and Kim's assessment, while ethnic identity, then, is related closely to ethnic subcultures, racial identity stems from consciousness of non-white status in a white-dominated country. Non-white racial identity, in turn, is expressed as either pan-Asian or Developing Nations racial identity.

REFERENCES

Bannerji, Hamani. 2000. *The Dark Side of the Nation*. Toronto: Canadian Scholars' Press Inc.

Basran, G.S., and B. Singh Bolaria. 2003. *The Sikhs in Canada: Migration, Race, Class and Gender*. New Delhi: Oxford University Press.

Bourdieu, Pierre. 1990. *The Logic of Practice*. Palo Alto: Stanford University Press.

Du Bois, W.E.B. [1903] 1982. *The Souls of Black Folk*. New York: Signet Publishing.

McCarthy, C., and W. Crichlow, eds. 1993. *Race, Identity and Representation in Education*. London: Routledge.

MacInnes, John. 2005. "The Sociology of Identity: Social Science or Social Comment?" *British Journal of Sociology* 55, no. 4:531–543.

Porter, John. 1965. *The Vertical Mosaic*. Toronto: University of Toronto Press.

Roots, M. 1996. *The Multiracial Experience*. London: Sage.

Tuan, Mia. 1999. *Forever Foreigners or Honorary Whites? The Asian Ethnic Experience Today*. New Brunswick: Rutgers University Press.

Waters, Mary C. 1990. *Ethnic Options: Choosing Identities in America*. Berkeley: University of California Press.

OPTIONAL ETHNICITIES
FOR WHITES ONLY?

MARY C. WATERS

What does it mean to talk about ethnicity as an option for an individual? To argue that an individual has some degree of choice in their ethnic identity flies in the face of the common-sense notion of ethnicity many of us believe in—that one's ethnic identity is a fixed characteristic, reflective of blood ties and given at birth. However, social scientists who study ethnicity have long concluded that while ethnicity is based on a *belief* in a common ancestry, ethnicity is primarily a *social* phenomenon, not a biological one (Alba 1985, 1990; Barth 1969; Weber [1921] 1968, 389). The belief that members of an ethnic group have that they share a common ancestry may not be a fact. There is a great deal of change in ethnic identities across generations through intermarriage, changing allegiances, and changing social categories. There is also a much larger amount of change in the identities of individuals over their lives than is commonly believed. While most people are aware of the phenomenon known as "passing"—people raised as one race who change at some point and claim a different race as their identity—there are similar life course changes in ethnicity that happen all the time and are not given the same degree of attention as "racial passing."

White Americans of European ancestry can be described as having a great deal of choice in terms of their ethnic identities. The two major types of options white Americans can exercise are (1) the option of whether to claim any specific ancestry, or to just be "white" or American, [Lieberson (1985) called these people "unhyphenated Whites"]; and (2) the choice of which of their European ancestries to choose to include in their description of their own identities. In both cases, the option of choosing how to present yourself on surveys and in everyday social interactions exists for whites because of social changes and societal conditions that have created a great deal of social mobility, immigrant assimilation, and political and economic power for whites in the United States. Specifically, the option of being able to not claim any ethnic identity exists for whites of European background in the United States because they are the majority group—in terms of holding political and social power, as well as being a numerical majority. The option of choosing among different ethnicities in their family backgrounds exists because the degree of discrimination and social distance attached to specific European backgrounds has diminished over time.

SYMBOLIC ETHNICITIES FOR WHITE AMERICANS

What do these ethnic identities mean to people and why do they cling to them rather than just abandoning the tie and calling themselves American? My own field research with suburban whites in California and Pennsylvania found that later-generation descendants of European origin maintain what are called "symbolic ethnicities." Symbolic ethnicity is a term coined by Herbert Gans (1979) to refer to ethnicity that is individualistic in nature and without real social cost for the individual. These symbolic identifications are essentially leisure-time activities, rooted in nuclear family traditions and reinforced by the voluntary enjoyable aspects of being ethnic (Waters 1990). Richard Alba (1990) also found later-generation whites in Albany, New York, who chose to keep a tie with an ethnic identity because of the enjoyable and voluntary aspects to those identities, along with the feelings of specialness they entailed. An example of symbolic ethnicity is individuals who identify as Irish, for example, on occasions such as Saint Patrick's Day, on family holidays, or for vacations. They do not usually belong to Irish-American organizations, live in Irish neighbourhoods, work in Irish jobs, or marry other Irish people. The symbolic meaning of being Irish-American can be constructed by individuals from mass media images, family traditions, or other intermittent social activities. In other words, for later-generation white ethnics, ethnicity is not something that influences their lives unless they want it to. In the world of work and school and neighbourhood, individuals do not have to admit to being ethnic unless they choose to. And for an increasing number of European-origin individuals whose parents and grandparents have intermarried, the ethnicity they claim is largely a matter of personal choice as they sort through all of the possible combinations of groups in their genealogies.

RACE RELATIONS AND SYMBOLIC ETHNICITY

However much symbolic ethnicity is without cost for the individual, there is a cost associated with symbolic ethnicity for the society. That is because symbolic ethnicities of the type described here are confined to white Americans of European origin. Black Americans, Hispanic Americans, Asian-Americans, and American Indians do not have the option of a symbolic ethnicity at present in the United States. For all of the ways in which ethnicity does not matter for white Americans, it does matter for non-whites. Who your ancestors are does affect your choice of spouse, where you live, what job you have, who your friends are, and what your chances are for success in American society, if those ancestors happen not to be from Europe. The reality is that white ethnics have a lot more choice and room for manoeuvre than they themselves think they do. The situation is very different for members of racial minorities, whose lives are strongly influenced by their race or national origin regardless of how much they may choose not to identify themselves in terms of their ancestries.

When white Americans learn the stories of how their grandparents and great-grandparents triumphed in the United States over adversity, they are usually told in terms of their individual efforts and triumphs. The important role of labour unions and other organized political and economic actors in their social and economic successes are left out of the story in favour of a generational story of individual Americans rising up against communitarian, Old World intolerance, and New World resistance. As a result, the "individualized" voluntary, cultural view of ethnicity for whites is what is remembered.

One important implication of these identities is that they tend to be very individualistic. There is a tendency to view valuing diversity in a pluralist environment as equating all groups. The symbolic ethnic tends to think that all groups are equal; everyone has a background that is their right to celebrate and pass on to their children. This leads to the conclusion that all identities are equal and all identities in some sense are interchangeable— "I'm Italian American, you're Polish American. I'm Irish American, you're African American." The important thing is to treat people as individuals and all equally. However, this assumption ignores the very big difference between an individualistic symbolic ethnic identity and a socially enforced and imposed racial identity.

My favourite example of how this type of thinking can lead to some severe misunderstandings between people of different backgrounds is from the *Dear Abby* advice column. A few years back a person wrote in who had asked an acquaintance of Asian background where his family was from. His acquaintance answered that this was a rude question and he would not reply. The bewildered white asked Abby why it was rude, since he thought it was a sign of respect to wonder where people were from, and he certainly would not mind anyone asking *him* about where his family was from. Abby asked her readers to write in to say whether it was rude to ask about a person's ethnic background. She reported that she got a large response, that most non-whites thought it was a sign of disrespect, and whites thought it was flattering:

Dear Abby,

I am 100 percent American and because I am of Asian ancestry I am often asked "What are you?" It's not the personal nature of this question that bothers me, it's the question itself. This query seems to question my very humanity. "What am I? Why I am a person like everyone else!"

Signed, A REAL AMERICAN

Dear Abby,

Why do people resent being asked what they are? The Irish are so proud of being Irish, they tell you before you even ask. Tip O'Neill has never tried to hide his Irish ancestry.

Signed, JIMMY.

Reprinted by permission of Universal Press Syndicate.)

In this exchange Jimmy cannot understand why Asians are not as happy to be asked about their ethnicity as he is because he understands his ethnicity and theirs to be separate but equal. Everyone has to come from somewhere—his family from Ireland, another's family from Asia—each has a history and each should be proud of it. But the reason he cannot understand the perspective of the Asian-American is that all ethnicities are not equal; all are not symbolic, costless, and voluntary. When white Americans equate their own symbolic ethnicities with the socially enforced identities of non-white Americans, they obscure the fact that the experiences of whites and non-whites have been qualitatively different in the United States and that the current identities of individuals partly reflect that unequal history.

In the next section I describe how relations between black and white students on college campuses reflect some of these asymmetries in the understanding of what a racial or ethnic identity means. While I focus on black and white students in the following discussion, you should be aware that the myriad other groups in the United States—Mexican-Americans, American Indians, Japanese-Americans—all have some degree of social and individual influences on their identities, which reflect the group's social and economic history and present circumstance.

RELATIONS ON COLLEGE CAMPUSES

Both black and white students face the task of developing their race and ethnic identities. Sociologists and psychologists note that at the time people leave home and begin to live independently from their parents, often ages 18 to 22, they report a heightened sense of racial and ethnic identity as they sort through how much of their beliefs and behaviours are idiosyncratic to their families and how much are shared with other people. It is not until individuals come in close contact with many people who are different from themselves that they realize the ways in which their backgrounds may influence their individual personality. This involves coming into contact with people who are different in terms of their ethnicity, class, religion, region, and race. For white students, the ethnicity they claim is more often than not a symbolic one—with all of the voluntary, enjoyable, and intermittent characteristics I have described above.

Black students at the university are also developing identities through interactions with others who are different from them. Their identity development is more complicated than that of whites because of the added element of racial discrimination and racism, along with the "ethnic" developments of finding others who share their background. Thus black students have the positive attraction of being around other black students who share some cultural elements, as well as the need to band together with other students in a reactive and oppositional way in the face of racist incidents on campus.

Colleges and universities across the country have seen increasing diversity among their student bodies in the last few decades. This has led in many cases to strained relations among students from different racial and ethnic backgrounds. The 1980s and 1990s produced a great number of racial incidents and high racial tensions on campuses. While there were a number of racial incidents that were due to bigotry, unlawful behaviour, and violent or vicious attacks, much of what happens among students on campuses involves a low level of tension and awkwardness in social interactions.

Many black students experience racism personally for the first time on campus. The upper-middle-class students from white suburbs were often isolated enough that their presence was not threatening to racists in their high schools. Also, their class background was known by their residence, and this may have prevented attacks being directed at them. Often black students at the university who begin talking with other students and recognizing racial slights will remember incidents that happened to them earlier that they might not have thought were related to race.

Black college students across the country experience a sizeable number of incidents that are clearly the result of racism. Many of the most blatant ones that occur between students are the result of drinking. Sometimes late at night, drunken groups of white students coming home from parties will yell slurs at single black students on the street. The other types of incidents that happen include being singled out for special treatment by employees, such as being followed when shopping at the campus bookstore, or going to the art museum with your class and having the guard stop you and ask for your I.D. Others involve impersonal encounters on the street—being called a nigger by a truck driver while crossing the street, or seeing old ladies clutch their pocketbooks and shake in terror as you pass them on the street. For the most part these incidents are not specific to the university environment; they are the types of incidents middle-class blacks face every day throughout American society, and they have been documented by sociologists (Feagin 1991).

In such a climate, however, with students experiencing these types of incidents and talking with each other about them, black students do experience a tension and a feeling of being singled out. It is unfair that this is part of their college experience and not that of white students. Dealing with incidents like this, or the ever-present threat of such incidents, is an ongoing developmental task for black students that takes energy, attention, and strength of character. It should be clearly understood that this is an asymmetry in the "college experience" for black and white students. It is one of the unfair aspects of life that results from living in a society with ongoing racial prejudice and discrimination. It is also very understandable that it makes some students angry at the unfairness of it all, even if there is no one to blame specifically. It is also very troubling, because, while most whites do not create these incidents, some do, and it is never clear until you know someone well whether they are the type of person who could do something like this. So one of the reactions of black students to these incidents is to band together.

In some sense then, as Blauner (1992) has argued, you can see black students coming together on campus as both an "ethnic" pull of wanting to be together to share common experiences and community, and a "racial" push of banding together defensively because of perceived rejection and tension from whites. In this way the ethnic identities of black students are in some sense similar to, say, Korean students wanting to be together to share experiences. And it is an ethnicity that is generally much stronger than, say, Italian-Americans. But for Koreans who come together there is generally a definition of themselves as "different from" whites. For blacks reacting to exclusion, there is a tendency for the coming together to involve both being "different from" but also "opposed to" whites.

The anthropologist John Ogbu (1990) has documented the tendency of minorities in a variety of societies around the world, who have experienced severe blocked mobility for long periods of time, to develop such oppositional identities. An important component of having such an identity is to describe others of your group who do not join in the group solidarity as devaluing and denying their very core identity. This is why it is not common for successful Asians to be accused by others of "acting white" in the United States, but it is quite common for such a term to be used by blacks and Latinos. The oppositional component of a black identity also explains how black people can question whether others are acting "black enough." On campus, it explains some of the intense pressures felt by black students who do not make their racial identity central and who choose to hang out primarily with non-blacks. This pressure from the group, which is partly defining itself by not being white, is exacerbated by the fact that race is a physical marker in American society. No one immediately notices the Jewish students sitting together in the dining hall, or the one Jewish student sitting surrounded by non-Jews, or the Texan sitting with the Californians, but everyone notices the black student who is or is not at the "black table" in the cafeteria.

An example of the kinds of misunderstandings that can arise because of different understandings of the meanings and implications of symbolic versus oppositional identities concerns questions students ask one another in the dorms about personal appearance and customs. A very common type of interaction in the dorm concerns questions whites ask blacks about their hair. Because whites tend to know little about blacks, and blacks know a lot about whites, there is a general asymmetry in the level of curiosity people have about one another. Whites, as the numerical majority, have had little contact with black culture; blacks, especially those who are in college, have had to develop bicultural skills—knowledge about the social worlds of both whites and blacks. Miscommunication and hurt feelings about white students' questions about black students' hair illustrate this point. One of the things that happens freshman year is that white students are around black students as they fix their hair. White students are generally quite curious about black students' hair—they have basic questions such as how often blacks wash their hair, how they get it straightened or curled, what products they use on their hair, how they comb it, and so on. Whites often wonder to themselves whether they should ask these questions. One thought experiment whites perform is to ask themselves whether a particular question would upset them. Adopting the "do unto others" rule, they ask themselves, "If a black person was curious about my hair would I get upset?" The answer usually is "No, I would be happy to tell them." Another example is an Italian-American student wondering to herself, "Would I be upset if someone asked me about calamari?" The answer is no, so she asks her black roommate about collard greens, and the roommate explodes with an angry response such as, "Do you think all black people eat watermelon too?" Note that if this Italian-American knew her friend was Trinidadian-American and asked about peas and rice, the situation would be more similar and would not necessarily ignite underlying tensions.

Like the debate in *Dear Abby*, these innocent questions are likely to lead to resentment. The issue of stereotypes about black Americans and the assumption that all blacks are alike and have the same stereotypical cultural traits has more power to hurt or offend a black person than vice versa. The innocent questions about black hair also bring up a number of asymmetries between the black and white experience. Because blacks tend to have more knowledge about whites than vice versa, there is not an even exchange going on; the black freshman is likely to have fewer basic questions about his white roommate than his white roommate has about him. Because of the differences historically in the group experiences of blacks and whites, there are some connotations to black hair that don't exist for white hair. (For instance, is straightening your hair a form of assimilation? Do some people distinguish between women having "good hair" and "bad hair" in terms of beauty, and how is that related to looking "white"?) Finally, even a black freshman who cheerfully disregards or is unaware that there are these asymmetries will soon slam into another asymmetry if she willingly answers every innocent question asked of her. In a situation where blacks make up only 10 percent of the student body, if every non-black needs to be educated about hair, she will have to explain it to nine other students. As one black student explained to me, after you've been asked a couple of times about something so personal you begin to feel like you are an attraction in a zoo, that you are at the university for the education of the white students.

INSTITUTIONAL RESPONSES

Our society asks a lot of young people. We ask young people to do something that no one else does as successfully on such a wide scale—that is, to live together with people from very different backgrounds, to respect one another, to appreciate one another, and to enjoy and learn from one another. The successes that occur every day in this endeavour are many, and they are too often overlooked. However, the problems and tensions are also real, and they will not vanish on their own. We tend to see pluralism working in the United States in much the same way some people expect capitalism to work. If you put together people with various interests and abilities and resources, the "invisible hand" of capitalism is supposed to make all the parts work together in an economy for the common good.

There is much to be said for such a model—the invisible hand of the market can solve complicated problems of production and distribution better than any "visible hand" of a state plan. However, we have learned that unequal power relations among the actors in the capitalist marketplace, as well as "externalities" that the market cannot account for, such as long-term pollution, or collusion between corporations, or the exploitation of child labour, mean that state regulation is often needed. Pluralism and the relations between groups are very similar. There is a lot to be said for the idea that bringing people who belong to different ethnic or racial groups together in institutions with no interference will have good consequences. Students from different backgrounds will make friends if they share a dorm room or corridor, and there is no need for the institution to do any more than provide the locale. But like capitalism, the invisible hand of pluralism does not do well when power relations and externalities are ignored. When you bring together individuals from groups that are differentially valued in the wider society and provide no guidance, there will be problems. In these cases the "invisible hand" of pluralist relations does not work, and tensions and disagreements can arise without any particular individual or group of individuals being "to blame." On college campuses in the 1990s some of the tensions between students were of this sort. They arose from honest misunderstandings, lack of a common background, and very different experiences of what race and ethnicity mean to the individual.

The implications of symbolic ethnicities for thinking about race relations are subtle but consequential. If your understanding of your own ethnicity and its relationship to society and politics is one of individual choice, it becomes harder to understand the need for programs such as affirmative action, which recognize the ongoing need for group struggle and group recognition in order to bring about social change. It also is hard for a white college student to understand the need that minority students feel to band together against discrimination. It also is easy, on the individual level, to expect everyone else to be able to turn their ethnicity on and off at will, the way you, as white, are able to, without understanding that ongoing discrimination and societal attention to minority status makes that impossible for individuals from minority groups to do. The paradox of symbolic ethnicity is that it depends upon the ultimate goal of a pluralist society yet makes it more difficult to achieve that ultimate goal. It is dependent upon the concept that all ethnicities mean the same thing, that enjoying the traditions of one's heritage is an option available to a group or an individual, but that such a heritage should not have any social costs associated with it.

As the Asian-Americans who wrote to *Dear Abby* make clear, there are many societal issues and involuntary ascriptions associated with non-white identities. The developments necessary for this to change are not individual but societal in nature. Social mobility and declining racial and ethnic sensitivity are closely associated. The legacy and the present reality of discrimination on the basis of race or ethnicity must be overcome before the ideal of a pluralist society, where all heritages are treated equally and are equally available for individuals to choose or discard at will, is realized.

REFERENCES

Alba, Richard D. 1985. *Italian Americans: Into the Twilight of Ethnicity.* Englewood Cliffs: Prentice-Hall.

———. 1990. *Ethnic Identity: The Transformation of White America.* New Haven: Yale University Press.

Barth, Frederick. 1969. *Ethnic Groups and Boundaries.* Boston: Little, Brown.

Blauner, Robert. 1992. "Talking Past Each Other: Black and White Languages of Race." *American Prospect* (summer):55–64.

Feagin, Joe R. 1991. "The Continuing Significance of Race: Anti-Black Discrimination in Public Places." *American Sociological Review* 56:101–117.

Gans, Herbert. 1979. "Symbolic Ethnicity: The Future of Ethnic Groups and Cultures in America." *Ethnic and Racial Studies* 2:1–20.

Lieberson, Stanley. 1985. *Making It Count: The Improvement of Social Research and Theory.* Berkeley: University of California Press.

Ogbu, John. 1990. "Minority Status and Literacy in Comparative Perspective." *Daedalus* 119:141–169.

Waters, Mary C. 1990. *Ethnic Options: Choosing Identities in America.* Berkeley: University of California Press.

Weber, Max. [1921] 1968. *Economy and Society: An Outline of Interpretive Sociology.* Edited by Guenther Roth and Claus Wittich. Translated by Ephraim Fischoff. New York: Bedminister Press.

Between Black and White
Exploring the "Biracial" Experience

Kerry Ann Rockquemore

Public debate concerning proposed modifications to the 2000 census has recently focused on the addition of a "multiracial' category." Proponents argue that the dramatic increase in interracial marriages over the past three decades[1] has caused a biracial baby boom. These rising numbers of biracial and multi-ethnic Americans, advocates argue, should be recognized by the government as "multiracial." They believe a multiracial category is necessary because all people of mixed parentage identify themselves as "biracial" or "mixed" and, if given the opportunity to identify this way on government documents, they would do so.

Despite advocates claims, biracialness[2] is not a newly emergent social phenomenon (Williamson 1980). The census debate is merely the latest manifestation of the ongoing socio-historical problematic of classifying mixed-race people in the United States. Given the historical stratification of racial groups, supported by an ideological belief in genetic differentiation between races, society has continually had to develop norms to classify individuals who straddle the socially constructed boundaries of "black" and "white" (White 1948; Williamson 1980; Davis 1991; Zack 1993). The "one drop rule,"[3] historically articulated in legal statutes, mandated that a mixed-race child be relegated to the racial group of the lower status parent. This norm has survived despite the removal of its various legal codifications. The "one drop rule" dictated that children of black–white unions were considered part of the African-American community. While biracials have had varying statuses within that community,[4] they have always been considered, by both whites and blacks, as part of the "black race" (Davis 1991).

The census issue provides a contemporary variation on the classification dilemma. Advocates demand separate group recognition and membership for mixed-race people and are essentially arguing for a nullification of the cultural norm of hypodescent. In this context, it is not surprising that the movement is led, not by biracial people themselves, but by white mothers on behalf of their children. In this sense, they are arguing for a separate status for their children in the socio-racial hierarchy. The status of "mixed race" would afford their children more privileges than being black, but not quite as many as being white (Spencer 1997). This separate status argument is framed as an attempt toward self-definition on behalf of biracial people who, advocates assume, do not consider themselves black.

The assumption that biracials have a singular understanding of their racial identity (i.e., as biracial) masks the fact that numerous individuals who are biracial identify themselves as African-American and would continue to do so even if presented with the mixed-race category as an option[5] (Jones 1990; McBride 1996; Scales-Trent 1995; Williams 1995). The belief that biracial identity has a singular meaning to members of this population begs numerous questions. What does "biracial identity" mean? Is there a singular way in which people with one black and one white parent understand their racial identity or does "biracial" have multiple meanings? If there are, in fact, multiple ways in which biracial people understand themselves and their group membership, then what types of social factors influence the differences in an individual's choice of racial identity? This chapter explores what mixed-race people say about the meaning of "biracial" identity and how social factors have influenced their identity construction and maintenance.

THEORETICAL FRAMEWORK OF IDENTITY FORMATION

The conceptual framework of this argument rests on the three classic assumptions of symbolic interactionism: (1) that we know things by their meanings, (2) that meanings are created through social interaction, and (3) that meanings change through interaction (Blumer 1969). Given these basic assumptions, it is necessary to clearly delineate the conceptual terminology to be used in the following discussion. First and foremost, what is meant by the term "identity"?

Social actors are situated within societies that designate available categories of identification, how these identities are defined, and their relative importance. The term "identity" refers to a validated self-understanding that situates and defines the individual or, as Stone (1962) suggests, establishes *what* and *where* an actor is in social terms. These are processes by which individuals understand themselves and others, as well as evaluate their self in relation to others. Identity is the direct result of mutual identification through social interaction. It is within this process of validation that identity becomes a meaning of the self. I utilize the term "identity" interchangeably with "self-understanding" throughout the discussion.

By situating identity within an interactionist framework, biracial identity may be understood as an emergent category of identification. If identity is conceptualized as an interactionally validated self-understanding, then identities can function effectively only where the response of the individual to themselves (as a social object) is consistent with the response of others. In contrast, individuals cannot effectively possess an identity, which is not socially typified, or where there exists a disjuncture between the identity an actor appropriates for himself or herself and where others place him or her as a social object. In other words, an individual cannot have a realized identity without others who validate that identity. The challenge of research on biracial identity then is twofold. First, it is necessary to understand how individuals understand their social location as "biracial," and second, to explore what social and interactional factors lead to the development of this identity and how these individuals try to realize their appropriated identities in social context.

WHAT DOES "BIRACIAL IDENTITY" MEAN?

What does "biracial identity" mean to members of this population? If we conceptualize the term "identity" to mean an interactionally validated self-understanding, then the question, more specifically, is how do the individual selves interpret biracialness and respond to it? My data suggest some tentative descriptive categories of the way that individuals with one black and one white parent understand their biracialness. Being biracial can be interpreted as: (1) a border identity, (2) a protean identity, (3) a transcendent identity, or (4) a traditional identity.[6]

A BORDER IDENTITY

Anzaldua (1987) terms biracial identity as a "border identity" or one that lies between predefined social categories. Some individuals viewed the location of their existence between black and white as defining their biracialness. These individuals stressed their in-betweenness, and highlighted that unique status as the grounding for their identity. In other words, they did not consider themselves to be *either* black *or* white, but instead had a self-understanding that incorporated both blackness and whiteness into a unique category of "biracial." It was their location of difference that served as the substantive base of what it meant to be biracial. Kara, a first-year student, explained that it was not only the location of being on the border of socially defined categories, but that the border status itself brought with it an additional dimension:

> It's not that just being biracial is like you're two parts [white and black], you know, you have two parts but then there is also the one part of being biracial where you sit on the fence. There's a third thing, a unique thing.

The extreme border identity was exemplified by individuals who took their border status to a political level. Those who most consistently identified as biracial across all social contexts were likely to parallel their identity as biracial with a perception of shared struggle unique to their social location. They perceived their position as one of both oppression and advantage. For some, it spanned more than the case of black–white biracials, and included all who exist between races and ethnicities. These individuals found it difficult to discuss their self-identification without mentioning the problem of bureaucratic racial categorization and their negative feelings of having to select a singular category of identification (particularly if that category is black or African-American). Jessica, a second-year student, illustrated this difficulty when she stated:

I think there should be a mixed race category, or at least it shouldn't say "choose one."... I just want to put my race down. I don't see what the problem is, acknowledging what you are and I'm mixed! I don't know because I also have this whole problem with the way society says it's okay [if you are biracial] to say that you're black but not to say that you're white because you're both! How can you deny one or the other?

A PROTEAN IDENTITY

For others, biracial identity referred to their protean capacity to move among cultural contexts (Lifton 1993). Their self-understanding of biracialness was directly tied to their ability to cross boundaries between black, white, and biracial, which was possible because they possessed black, white, and biracial identities. These individuals felt endowed with a degree of cultural savvy in several social worlds and understood biracialness as the way in which they were able to fit in, however conditionally, in varied interactional settings. They believed their dual experiences with both whites and blacks had given them the ability to shift their identity according to the context of any particular interaction. This contextual shifting led actors to form a belief that their multiple racial backgrounds were but one piece of a complex self that was composed of assorted identifications that were not culturally integrated.

A student named Mike was able to provide an example in which his dual cultural competencies allowed him to function as an "insider" in differing social groups. He grew up in an all-white neighborhood and attended predominantly white private schools his entire life. He did have, however, frequent contact with his black extended family. Mike felt that his particular circumstances growing up helped him to not only develop both middle-class white and black cultural competencies, but also simultaneous multiple identities. In the following excerpt from our conversation, he uses table manners to illustrate his perception of the subtleties of contextual shifting:

> Because of their [his parents'] status, I always learned, you know start with the outside fork and work your way in, and this one is for dessert, you know. So I know, I know not to eat like this [puts his elbows on the table]. But then again, at the same time, [respondent shifts to black vernacular] when it comes picnic time or some other time and some ribs is on the table, I'm not afraid to get my hands dirty and dig on in and eat with my hands and stuff like that, [respondent shifts back to Standard English] I mean I guess my, the shift is when I'm not afraid to function in either world.

While his depiction may be exaggerated and stereotypical, it reveals his understanding of biracialness as having the ability to contextually shift his self-label between what he perceives as black and white cultural contexts. When the topic of racial identification was initially broached with Mike, he stated: "Well shit, it depends on what day it is and where I'm goin."

A TRANSCENDENT IDENTITY

A third way of understanding biracialness is reminiscent of Robert Parks's "Marginal Man" in its original context (Park 1950). Park discussed the qualities of the cosmopolitan stranger, an individual who was bicultural (as opposed to biracial), and whose marginal status enabled an objective view of social reality. I refer to this as a "transcendent identity" because like Park's "stranger," individuals with this self-understanding view their biracialness as a unique marginalization, one that enables an objective perspective on the social meaning of race. These individuals discount race as a "master status" altogether. This self-understanding is uniquely and exclusively available to individuals whose bodily characteristics have a high degree of ambiguity (i.e., those who look white). This type of self-understanding of biracialness results in an avoidance, or rejection, of any type of racial group categorization as the basis of personal identity. These individuals responded to questions about their identity with answers that were unrelated to their racial status, such as in the following example:

> I'm just Rob, you know. I never thought this was such a big deal to be identified, I just figured I'm a good guy, just like me for that, you know. But, when I came here [to college] it was like I was almost forced to look at people as being white, black, Asian, or Hispanic. And so now, I'm still trying to go 'I'm just Rob' but uh, you gotta be something.

This respondent stated that if required in particular contexts, he would accept the racial categorization thrust upon him. Given the persistence of hypodescent as a cultural norm, the result was his somewhat grudging acceptance of categorization as black. I refrain from saying that he accepted a black identity because it was only the label "black" that was accepted.

This self-understanding was unique in several ways. First, it was available only to those whose appearances fit into the common perception of "white" or "Caucasian." Second, these individuals differed from the protean identity group because they did not have the ability, or the desire, to manipulate their identity before others in various social contexts. Finally, racial group membership did not play any significant role in their self-understanding because they socially experience race in a different way than those with a non-white appearance. Instead, they perceive that their biracialness provides them with a location to view and discard race as a meaningful category of their existence.

A TRADITIONAL IDENTITY

Finally, there are individuals with one black and one white parent whose racial identity falls into the category I term "traditional." In this case, the self-understanding is exclusively as African-American. The meaning of biracialness is merely an acknowledgement of the racial categorization of their birth parents. At the extreme, individuals simply do not deny the existence of their (white) parent. However, it is not salient in defining their self-understanding and may not be offered as identifying information unless specifically requested. Interestingly enough, there were no respondents in the pilot study that identified exclusively as black. However, we can conceptually formulate this category based upon the historical norm of hypodescent.

The voices of biracial people reveal that there are varying understandings of what "biracial identity" means to individuals within this population. Individual selves have not one, but several ways in which they interpret and respond to biracialness. These divergent self-understandings are grounded in differential experiences, varying biographies, and cross-cutting cultural contexts. This multiple meaning perspective breaks from the singular conception of Park's "Marginal Man," the assertions of multiracial advocates, and much recent research on the biracial population that rests on the unquestioned assumption that biracial identity has a singular and widely agreed-upon meaning with which an actor either does or does not understand (Bradshaw 1992; Fields 1996; King and DaCosta 1996). Figure 10.1 provides a schematic representation of this typology.

FIGURE 10.1: THE MULTIPLE MEANINGS OF BIRACIAL IDENTITY

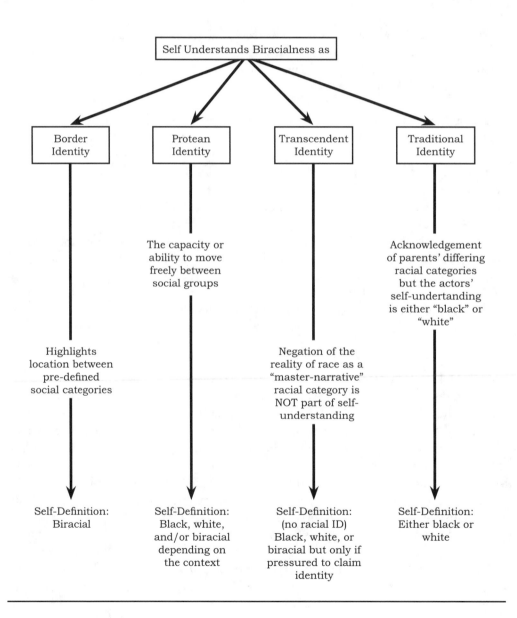

THE EFFECTS OF APPEARANCE AND SOCIAL NETWORKS ON IDENTITY FORMATION

Mary Waters's (1990) work focuses on ethnic options for individuals with multiple white–ethnic heritages. Waters was interested in why individuals with multiple ethnic backgrounds chose to emphasize one of their ethnicities over others. The factors involved in resolving white ethnic options included: (1) knowledge about the ethnicity; (2) surname; (3) appearance; and (4) general popularity of ethnic groups. She concluded that ethnicity was largely "symbolic" in that it had no consequences for an individual's life chances or everyday interactions and that it was characterized by the existence of choice either to assume the ethnic identity or not.

Waters's findings are instructive because they reveal the symbolic basis of white ethnicity and explicitly differentiate it from race. The symbolic ethnicity of whites differs from non-whites because race is not an option from one situation to the next, and race has both immediate and real consequences. In Waters's framework, identity options are either non-existent, or function differently, for members of racial groups compared to whites because racial and ethnic categories are socio-culturally stratified. Her work implies that race and ethnicity function differently due to visibility, the capacity of individual choice, and a history of stratification based on racial group membership.

THE INFLUENCE OF APPEARANCE ON IDENTITY

Appearances provide information about individuals that helps others to define the self as situated. This information enables others to know in advance what they can expect of an actor and what the actor can expect of them (Goffman 1959). Appearances provide the first information (albeit constructed) about an individual to others in the context of face-to-face social interaction. It helps to define the identity of the individual and for him or her to express their self-identification. It is in this process that identities are negotiated and either validated or invalidated.

Appearance is critical in understanding how individuals develop and maintain racial identities (Stone 1962). I limit my use of appearances to the following: physical features, language, and clothing. The physical characteristics of biracial individuals range widely in skin colour, hair texture, and facial features. At one extreme are individuals who physically possess traits that are socially defined as belonging to the black race; at the other are those who are visually unidentifiable as black, or possess no features that are associated with African descent. Because racial categories are defined by appearances, the logic and enactment of racial categorization becomes questionable if individuals cannot be identified on sight. One's skin colour, hair, and facial features are strong membership cues in socially defined racial groups. Figure 10.2 is a schematic representation of the proposed explanatory factors.

In addition to physical features, language and clothing have important functions as supporting interactional cues in establishing the identity of an individual. Language is particularly salient in the case of cueing one's membership in a racial group. Individuals may speak exclusively Standard English, black vernacular, or code switch between

FIGURE 10.2: FACTORS INFLUENCING BIRACIAL IDENTITY

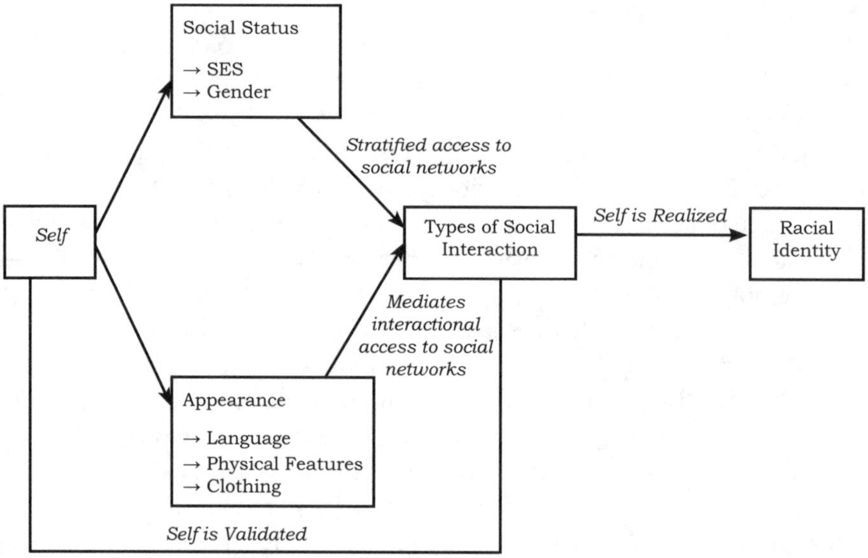

both (Smitherman 1986; Delpit 1988; Fanon 1952). Clothing can work in a similar way as a signifier of racial group membership. Clothing and language differ from physical features, however, in the degree to which they can be manipulated. For example, one of the respondents reported frequenting a tanning salon to make her skin appear darker. In addition, women's hairstyles can decidedly signify group membership and are subject to degrees of manipulation. While certain physical features can be manipulated, some cannot without plastic surgery. Clothing and language, on the other hand, may be strategically used by the individual to gain support from others for a particular identity (Goffman 1959).

Mike told a story that illustrates the link between appearances and identity. He has light brown skin, brown eyes, freckles, and short kinky hair. His physical appearance can be termed as ambiguous in that he doesn't appear to be white, yet his features do not necessarily fit into any easily definable category. Mike talked about negotiating his identity with a (white) girlfriend in the following way:

> I worked at a big national meeting thing here and I spoke on my experience here at Notre Dame, being black. And afterwards, she came up and was like "Hi," really cool, and we started talking and everything. And then she goes, "But you're Irish aren't you?" and I'm like "Yeah." She says, "You got so many freckles!" And from then on we were like, tight, we still are.... She pulled me out, she was like "No, you're not JUST black" like, "you're not special" and I'm like, "Yeah, put me in my place."

This story is interesting because it expresses the tension when others' definition of one's physical appearance fails to be consistent with self-definition (Goffman 1963). In this case, Mike's physical features and use of Standard English were incongruent (for the future girlfriend) with his professed identity as a black student speaking about the black experience on a predominately white college campus. This caused the woman to approach him later and call into question his racial identity. The exchange resulted in the renegotiation of his racial identity, at which time he stated that he was "really" biracial. She accepted the renegotiated identity, and they were able to proceed with the interaction.

This type of experience, when a biracial individual's identity is called into question, or the "What are you?" experience, is a commonly reported phenomenon within the biracial population (Williams 1996). Questioning an individual's identity reflects two types of problematics involving the link between identity and appearance. First, the "What are you?" question can be a result of an ambiguous appearance. Biracial individuals who look neither black nor white may be questioned by random strangers about their racial or ethnic background. Williams interprets this as a failure by the other to place the biracial person into one of their cognitive categorizations for members of particular racial groups. The second type of problematic is that addressed by the above example, which could better be termed the "What are you really?" question. In this case, others may approach the question of the biracial individual's racial background to clarify a discrepancy between the appearance and the professed identity. In this case, there can either be a renegotiation of the identity, or an interactional rupture can take place in which no shared meaning can be agreed upon.[7] Because individuals do not create and maintain an identity in isolation, others in their interactional context must support or validate their self-understanding as black, white, or biracial. Figure 10.3 maps the effect of appearance on identity.

FIGURE 10.3. THE EFFECTS OF APPEARANCE ON IDENTITY

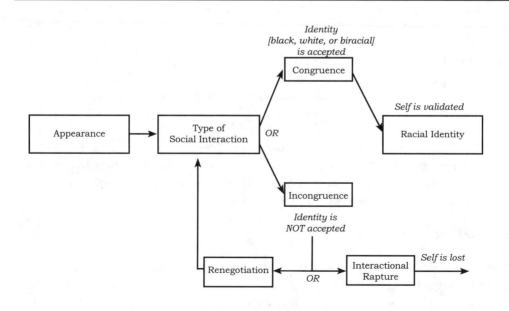

THE INFLUENCE OF SOCIAL STATUS ON IDENTITY

It is too simplistic to say that biracial individuals' appearance alone determines their racial identity. The effect of social networks in which an individual is situated must additionally be considered in order to understand their choice of identity. An individual actor is socially located in a system of networks, or social relationships, which are directly related to their social status. Status brings access to different types of social networks. For biracial individuals, the higher the status of one's parents, the more likely that an individual is to have contact with white peer groups. The more time that individuals spend interacting with white peer groups, the less likely they are to develop an understanding of their biracialness as a singular (black) identity. More specifically, the more time that an individual spends in white peer groups, the more likely they are to cultivate a degree of cultural savvy to fit in with their peers and to see both whiteness and blackness in their self-understanding and interactional presentation of self.

The preceding statement suggests that it is merely the access to different types of networks that influences the directionality of one's biracial identity. It is important to note, however, that it is not merely the amount of contact an individual has with either white or black peers or family members (Hall 1980), nor is it exclusively which group the individual uses as a reference group (Fields 1996; Kerckhoff and McCormick 1995). Instead, it is the type of contact that an individual has with others, or the way in which an individual socially experiences race, that mediates the relationship between one's social status and one's biracial identity.

An additional case may illustrate this argument. Kristy is a biracial woman from New Jersey. She is white in appearance, with fair skin, long, curly light brown hair, freckles, and green eyes. She attended public schools, which were 50 percent black, until Grade 10. She stated the following in reference to her relationships with black students:

> I was always rejected by the black women. I just shied away from the black males because they were a little intimidating and a little too aggressive, I thought. So then when I transferred sophomore year, I went to a Catholic school that only had maybe, about 10 blacks counting the 4 biracial students, so when I got there I was really taken in by these people and it was just a totally different world. It was like, [in public school] I was really never accepted by these black females because well, you probably been told this too, they were jealous because you have good hair and light eyes. I remember thinking what were they jealous of? I didn't choose to be like this, I don't mind it, you know what I mean, so it was really their problem, I think. Then I went to Catholic school.... I didn't really know anybody, and I was just like, hopefully it will be better. Of course it was better because there was less black people for me to contend with.... Maybe because it was a Catholic prep school that was $4,000.00 a year that made people really appreciate education and different cultures and you know, and these people really took me in and it was nice. So we [the black and biracial students], it was a close-knit group, it was kind of like family within that high school....

She said about her college transition:

> When I came here it was like, I'm gonna go to [college] and it's gonna kind of be the same as my high school. Cuz you know, here there's not many black people—it's on a larger scale, but it's the same kind of ratio. So I was asked to do a program [specifically for minority students] the summer before

freshman year, and naturally you're friends with 30 black people right away. So that was great and you know, finally it was like oh, they don't care that I'm so light-skinned or whatever, so that was nice. Especially freshman year, I totally identified with the black population here. And I was telling my parents, this is so opposite of what I've been running away from all my life because finally these people are like, "You're just a person," you know what I mean.

Kristy's experience is interesting specifically because it provides a critical case that defies the simplicity of using the number of black social networks for understanding her biracial identity. In this case, Kristy underwent the greatest degree of rejection by her black peers when she was in an environment with a large number of blacks. Attending a school where one-half of the students are black provided her with numerous opportunities to form friendships with other black students (as compared to a school with lower numbers of black students). It was in this environment, however, that she reports being "rejected" by black women and avoiding interaction with black men. Here, her self-understanding as a black woman was not validated. In fact, the incongruence between her appearance and identity caused numerous interactional ruptures (such as gum being thrown in her "good" hair, and fistfights). This "rejection" by black women was counterbalanced by friendliness from her white peers with whom she had a common economic status. It was in the context of this simultaneous failure to be accepted as black, by blacks, and acceptance by whites as biracial, that Kristy developed her self-understanding of what it means to be biracial.

Once Kristy transferred to a predominately white school, however, with fewer blacks to "contend with," her closest network of friendships shifted from exclusively white to inclusive of black and biracial students. This environment was substantively different than her previous school with different "types" of students. Specifically, the black students at her new school were exclusively middle to upper-middle class and, because they were in an environment that made them a visible minority, they had a strong vested interest in mutual self-acceptance. It was in this group, composed of blacks that accepted her and several other biracial peers, that she found further validation for her biracial identity.

Finally, her movement to college further illustrates the importance of examining the type of social interaction an individual has within any given social network. Again, Kristy was in an environment in which blacks were a small and highly visible minority (less than 2 percent of the student body). Here, the pattern of her high-school relationships was repeated, facilitated by ties made during the summer program. She was accepted by a small cohesive group of black students at a predominately white institution while maintaining her core group of white friends. These experiences solidified her understanding of biracialness as a border identity.

Specific socio-demographic factors may enable an individual to have access to differing types of social networks than would be available to others. Social networks provide the terrain in which identities may be negotiated, particularly where non-existent identities may emerge in order for the participants to understand an individual's presence within a particular network. It is precisely in these networks that the key process of interactional validation occurs and contributes to the differential choices in identification of biracial individuals.

DISCUSSION

This chapter questions the assumption that underlies the push to add a multiracial category to the 2000 census, that most biracial people identify as biracial and that "biracial" identity has a singular meaning. The cases presented reflect a homogeneous and highly skewed group of respondents. All came from middle- to upper-middle-class families, all were raised in predominately white social contexts, none could describe incidents of experiencing discrimination by whites, and yet many talked about feeling "rejected" by blacks. These students had a singular set of experiences that led to their strong identifications as biracial. Possibly it is individuals such as these that multiracial advocates believe an additional census category will represent. We must ask, however, if it is not also exclusively these individuals who would be represented by such a change. Is it possible that biracial identity is largely a middle-class phenomenon? Is this particular self-understanding created and validated by those with a specific and privileged set of social experiences? Would we find a different type of identity among those who have strong ties to black social networks, who live in exclusively black neighbourhoods, and attend predominately black schools?

One final case may help both to support the conceptual model presented and extend our understanding of the diverse meanings of "biracial" identity. Gregory Howard Williams (1995) has written an autobiographical text that explores his social experience of race. Williams grew up in the South believing that both he and his parents were white. At the age of 12, his parents' marriage dissolved and he moved back to their hometown of Muncie, Indiana, with his father. On the bus ride to Muncie, Williams's father revealed that he had been "passing," that he was in fact African-American, and that once they arrived in Muncie, Williams and his younger brother would also be black. This was a shocking realization to Williams and the rest of the book depicts his experiences as a white-appearing black child, his shift into extreme poverty, and his entry and gradual acceptance within Muncie's black community.

In Williams's case, once he moved to Muncie, his social status changed drastically. He went from a relatively comfortable middle-class existence to a life of poverty. His social networks shifted from exclusively white to exclusively black. In fact, his white grandparents also lived in Muncie, but Williams was no longer allowed to visit them (as he had when he was "white"). Despite his white appearance, Williams experienced severe discrimination from whites. It was this experience of discrimination that solidified his self-understanding as black (i.e., not as biracial or white). His social experience of race was characterized by prejudicial treatment by whites and seeing other blacks systematically discriminated against. Once Williams arrived in Muncie, he could no longer have a white identity because it was not validated by any others in his social environment. In contrast, his identity as African-American was cultivated, protected, and nurtured by a significant other who came to be a surrogate mother for Williams and his younger sibling.

This case illustrates how individuals' social status and appearance both affect their access to different types of social networks and influence their interactions within those networks. Identity, as an interactionally validated self-understanding, is by definition a result of these ongoing interactions. It becomes clear how certain types of social contexts, such as those exhibited by the students in this study, may provide the terrain on which an individual is able to develop and cultivate a meaningful identity that is "biracial." It also becomes clear, however, when we consider the case of Gregory Howard Williams, that there exist alternative social contexts in which "biracial" has no significant meaning. Social status and appearance are mediated by the types of social interactions an actor experiences. These interactions set the parameters of meaning from which the biracial individual identity is constructed, negotiated, challenged, reshaped, validated, and ultimately sustained.

NOTES

1   Interracial marriages increased from 150,000 in 1960 to 1.5 million in 1990 (U.S. Bureau of the Census, 1993).

2   No terminology currently exists to accurately describe mixed-race individuals or to reflect the diversity of possible combinations. While recognizing this limitation, throughout this chapter I will utilize the general term "biracial" to describe individuals who have one black self-identifying biological parent and one white self-identifying biological parent.

3   The American answer to the question "Who is black?" has been anyone who has any African ancestry whatsoever (Davis 1991; Myrdal 1944; Williamson 1980). The term "one drop rule" originated in the South where one drop of "black blood" designated an individual as black. This has also been known as the "one black ancestor rule," the "traceable amount rule," and the "hypodescent rule." This definition of blackness that emerged from the South became the rest of the nation's definition and was accepted by both blacks and whites.

4   Williamson (1980) provides a thorough discussion of the shifting statuses of mulattos (within the black community) during various periods of U.S. history.

5   A Current Population Survey Supplement was conducted to assess the effects of adding a multiracial category to the 2000 census. The findings indicated that less than 1.5 percent of all those surveyed identified themselves as multiracial. The addition of the category as an option affected the proportion of those identifying as American Indian/Alaska Native (which dropped) but it had no effect on blacks (Tucker and Kojetin 1996).

6   These categories of self-understanding are not necessarily mutually exclusive; instead they represent ideal types.

7   An illustration of interactional rupture can be drawn from a case presented in Funderberg (1994). The individual is a white-appearing woman, who changed her given name to Zenobia Kujichagulia, and self-identifies for the most part as black, but occasionally as black and Cherokee. She tells the following story: "This was an all-black environment, and as they introduced me to this woman, one friend says to me, "Zenobia, tell her what you are." So I knew what was coming, although I didn't expect this woman to go all the way off.

I said, "I'm black and Cherokee." Like I told you, I always leave the last part off [that she's also white].

The woman looked at me and said, "Like hell you are."

I said, "Yes. Like hell I am."

And she said, "No, I mean"—like I didn't know what she meant—"I mean you are not black. You might be Cherokee but you are not black."

And I said, "I'll be sure to tell my daddy you said so." And she just started cussing, ranting and raving, and I looked at her and I looked at the friend and said, "I think I'll go now," and just went across the room.

REFERENCES

Anzaldua, Gloria. 1987. *Borderlands/La Frontera: The New Mestizo.* San Francisco: Spinsters/Aunt Lute Foundation.

Bertaux, Daniel. 1981. *Biography and Society: The Life History Approach in the Social Sciences.* Beverly Hills: Sage Publications.

Blumer, Herbert. 1969. *Symbolic Interactionism: Perspective and Method.* Englewood Cliffs: Prentice-Hall.

Bogdan, Robert, and Sari Knopp Biklen. 1982. *Qualitative Research for Education: An Introduction to Theory and Methods.* Boston: Allyn and Bacon.

Bradshaw, C.K. 1992. "Beauty and the Beast: On Racial Ambiguity." In *Racially Mixed People in America,* ed. M.P.P. Root. Newbury Park: Sage.

Davis, F.J. 1991. *Who Is Black?* University Park: Pennsylvania State University Press.

Delpit, Lisa. 1988. "The Silenced Dialogue: Power and Pedagogy in Educating Other People's Children." *Harvard Educational Review* 58, no. 3:280–298.

Fanon, Frantz. 1952. *Black Skin, White Masks.* New York: Grove.

Fields, L. 1996. "Piecing Together the Puzzle: Self-Concept and Group Identity in Biracial Black/White Youth." In *Racially Mixed People in America,* ed. M.P.P. Root. Newbury Park: Sage.

Funderburg, Lise. 1994. *Black, White, Other.* New York: Morrow.

Goffman, Erving. 1959. *The Presentation of Self in Everyday Life.* New York: Anchor Press Doubleday.

———. 1963. *Behavior in Public Places: Notes on the Social Organization of Gatherings.* New York: Free Press of Glencoe.

Hall, C.C. 1980. *The Ethnic Identity of Racially Mixed People.* Ph.D. diss., University of California, Los Angeles.

Jones, Lisa. 1994. *Bulletproof Diva: Tales of Race, Sex, and Hair.* New York: Doubleday.

Kerchoff, C., and T. McKormick. 1995. "Marginal Status and Marginal Personality." *Social Forces* 34:48–55.

King, Rebecca, and Kimberly DaCosta. 1996. "Changing Face, Changing Race: The Remaking of Race in the Japanese American and African American Communities." In *Racially Mixed People in America,* ed. M.P.P. Root. Newbury Park: Sage.

Lifton, Robert. 1993. *The Protean Self: Human Resilience in an Age of Fragmentation.* New York: Basic Books.

Marshall, Catherine, and Gretchen B. Rossman. 1989. *Designing Qualitative Research.* Newbury Park: Sage.

McBride, James. 1996. *The Color of Water: A Black Man's Tribute to His White Mother.* New York: Riverhead Books.

Myrdal, G. 1962. *An American Dilemma,* 20th ed. New York: Harper & Row.

Park, R. 1950. *Race and Culture.* Glencoe: Free Press.

Root, Maria P. 1992. "Back to the Drawing Board: Methodological Issues in Research on Multiracial People." In *Racially Mixed People in America,* ed. M. Root. Newbury Park: Sage.

Scales-Trent, J. 1995. *Notes of a White Black Woman.* University Park: Pennsylvania State University Press.

Smitherman, Geneva. 1986. *Talkin and Testifyin: The Language of Black America.* Detroit: Wayne State University Press.

Spencer, J. 1997. *The New Colored People.* New York: New York University Press.

Stone, Gregory. 1962. "Appearance and the Self." In *Human Behavior and Social Processes,* ed. A.M. Rose, 86–118. Boston: Houghton Mifflin.

Taylor, Steven J., and Robert Bogdan. 1984. *Introduction to Qualitative Research Methods: The Search for Meanings.* New York: Wiley.

Tucker, C., and B. Kojetin. 1996. "Testing Racial and Ethnic Origin Questions in the CPS Supplement." *Monthly Labor Review* 119:3–7.

U.S. Bureau of the Census. 1993. *We, The American.* Washington: Government Printing Office.

Waters, Mary. 1990. *Ethnic Options: Choosing Identities in America.* Berkeley: University of California Press.

White, Walter Francis. 1948. *A Man Called White: The Autobiography of Walter White.* New York: Viking Press.

Williams, Gregory. 1995. *Life on the Color Line: The True Story of a White Boy Who Discovered He Was Black.* New York: Dutton.

Williams, T. 1996. "Race as Process." In *Racially Mixed People in America,* ed. M.P.P. Root. Newbury Park: Sage.

Williamson, Joel. 1980. *New People: Miscegenation and Mulattos in the United States.* New York: Free Press.

Zack, Naomi. 1993. *Race and Mixed Race.* Philadelphia: Temple University Press.

INTERROGATING THE HYPHEN-NATION
CANADIAN MULTICULTURAL POLICY AND "MIXED RACE" IDENTITIES

MINELLE MAHTANI

INTRODUCTION

Canada, unhyphenated, held possible in imagination.... (Moss 1996, 136)

Since the inauguration of multicultural policy in Canada in 1971, the notion of the hyphen, employed to articulate the marriage of ethnic and national identity, and witnessed through identifications such as "Italian-Canadian," "Japanese-Canadian," or "Somalian-Canadian," has taken on a particular political, and, at the same time, paradoxical, salience in Canada. For some, the hyphen is seen as a by-product of the implementation of multiculturalism in Canada, a policy that aimed to acknowledge every Canadian's right to identify with the cultural tradition of their choice while retaining Canadian citizenship. For others, however, the hyphen is understood as a "union of contradictions, each word symbolising the inversion of the 'other'" (Hanchard 1990), marking places of both ambiguity and multiplicity. This chapter explores these differences by examining the understanding of the policy of multiculturalism of some Canadian women of "mixed race."

Canadian multicultural policy is important because it has served not only as a guideline for government policy since 1971, but also as a framework for national discourse on the construction of Canadian society. I propose that multiculturalism produces particular discursive and material social spaces within which "mixed race" women negotiate not only their "mixed-race" identities, but also their national affiliations. I deliberately write against the claims that the notion of nation is now a "mere reminder of a vanished body" (Franco 1997, 31). Instead, drawing from the vernacular understandings of nationhood as discussed among participants, I suggest that "mixed-race" women in this study re-appropriate the term "Canadian," imagining new senses of nationalism as places for creating personal meanings of ethnicity, identity, and their relationship to nation among conflicting racial and gendered discourses. Through their voices, I demonstrate the difficulties of speaking of a national or ethnic identity separately in Canada.

The political articulation of citizenship and its relation to nation has been hotly contested among several scholars in Canada (see Bannerji 2000; Hamilton 1996; Kymlicka 1995; Ng 1993; Taylor 1992) in light of constitutional and political debates, often in relation to the Canadian government's troubled relationship with Quebec. Canada has often been billed as a country with a unique political configuration—a bilingual nation with "deux nations"—English Canada and Quebec (see Makropoulos 2000). However, the two nations' conceptualization successfully eclipses the notion of nationhood for those who are not perceived to be members of either of these two groups. The policy and trope of "multiculturalism" has thus been placed (uneasily) within the context of a bilingual Canada as one way of dealing with Canada's ethnic and racial diversity. The chapter begins with a brief overview of the emergence of Canadian multicultural policy. I then explore some "mixed-race" women's readings of the policy. Secondly, I examine the relationship between "mixed-race" identity and Canadian identity by illuminating the ways some "mixed-race" women search out national and ethnic belonging. Thirdly, I point out some of the complexities raised by these narratives, where some women of "mixed race" actively reconstitute racial and ethnic identity by working through their own personal bodies to contemplate the constitution of the Canadian national body politic.

CANADIAN MULTICULTURAL POLICY

Multiculturalism has often been regarded as one of the hallmarks of Canadian identity, given Canada's ethnic and racial diversity (Fleras and Kunz 2001; Elliott and Fleras 1992), but it is crucial not to conflate questions of demographic ethnic and racial diversity with issues of cultural representation. At the most basic level, the term "multicultural" can be used as an adjective to refer to the multiplicity of the world's cultures and the coexistence of these cultures within particular nations. "Multicultural" as a historical adjective, then, is "as banal as it is indisputable" (Stam 1997, 188) because virtually all countries and regions are multicultural in some way. What makes Canada different beyond its status as a multicultural country, however, is that the multicultural project has been enshrined in its constitution and through law, reflecting a salient part of the social and political context of Canada. Canadian multicultural policy has defined the government position on cultural diversity since 1971. Now celebrating its 30th anniversary, multiculturalism is seen as a mechanism through which to engage cultural diversity (Fleras and Kunz 2001). The policy can be read as the official, legislative response in Canada to ethnic plurality, or a multicultural society.

Multiculturalism as policy emerged, in part, because of perceived challenges posed by the influx of ethnically diverse immigrants into Canada (Elliott and Fleras 1992). In light of increased ethnic diversity, and subsequent demands for cultural protection and social equality among ethnic groups, the Canadian government began to rethink its relationship to ethnic minorities. It established the Royal Commission on Bilingualism and Biculturalism in 1962 to examine the issue of identity among Canadians. After travelling from coast to coast, the Commission recommended a major extension of bilingualism to help alleviate the disharmony in English–French relations, conceiving of a bilingual framework within which other ethnic groups could prosper. A contentious policy emerged designed to fit minority cultural differences into a workable national framework. In 1971, the Prime Minister, Pierre Trudeau, gave a speech to Parliament where he outlined the government response to the report. Multiculturalism, within the framework of official bilingualism, accentuated the need to maintain the cultural heritage of all groups within a multicultural population. It also established the right of members of visible minority groups to equality with members of the two charter groups of British and French ancestry. The cornerstone of the 1971 policy was, as Trudeau put it in his speech, multiculturalism within a bilingual framework, essentially what the Royal Commission had advised. The key tenets of multicultural policy were:

1. to assist all Canadian cultural groups that had demonstrated a desire and effort to continue to develop a capacity to grow and contribute to Canada, and a clear need for assistance;
2. to assist members of all cultural groups to overcome cultural barriers to full participation in Canadian society;
3. to promote creative encounters and interchange among all Canadian cultural groups in the interest of national unity;
4. to continue assistance to immigrants to acquire at least one of Canada's official languages in order to become full participants in Canadian society.

(Canada 1980–1993, statement of Pierre Trudeau, 8 October 1971)

In an effort to put these principles into practice, the government established several programs during the 1970s. There were courses to teach English and French to newly arrived immigrants, and programs for Canadian ethnic studies in schools and universities. Multicultural grants were issued to support the development of various cultures and languages. Specific initiatives for language and culture maintenance received substantial government funding—reaching nearly $200 million between 1971 and 1990. A Multicultural Directorate was established within the Department for the Secretary of State in 1972 to promote social, cultural, and racial harmony. To aid in the elimination of discrimination, the Directorate worked to enhance intercultural and interracial understanding and the cultural integration of immigrants. By 1973, almost $10 million had been spent on 500 ethnic groups—on events such as folk festivals—to promote cultural harmony.

In general, multicultural policy encouraged individuals voluntarily to affiliate with the culture and tradition of their choice, supposedly without fear of discrimination or exclusion. Ethnic differences were to be forged into a workable national framework of "unity within diversity." This focus upon "difference through unity" was seen as a remarkable change from the conventional strategies of nation building.

Despite the proliferation of research on particular ethnic groups in Canada, comparatively little research has been conducted on the Canadian public's perception of the multicultural policy (Kalbach and Kalbach 1999). This is a serious deficiency because multiculturalism forms the backdrop against which much of the current research in Canadian ethnic studies becomes meaningful. It is also important to note that although there are many theoretical critical readings of multicultural policy, very few studies have anchored these analyses through empirical work. Although some studies have explored the multiple meanings of multicultural policy among particular ethnic groups (Bienvenue and Goldstein 1985) no one has examined the meanings of multiculturalism among women of "mixed-race" descent. This is a particularly glaring omission, given that the number of "mixed-race" people is growing steadily in Canada (Kilbride et al. 2001). "Mixed-race" women are in a unique position in relation to multicultural policy, as they are both positioned as "ethnic" by the rules of the policy, and often considered to be of European or French origin by virtue of their own "mixed-race" backgrounds (many—but not all—of the women interviewed were partly European and partly Asian, or Quebecois and West Indian, for example). I was curious to unpack their readings of the policy to explore how it has provided a particular social framework within which individuals contemplate their own ethnic and national allegiances. How has multiculturalism affected their lives? What did they think about the policy? What was their relationship to race, place, and nation? Indeed, as many of the women were between the ages of 20 and 30 at the time of the interview, several participants literally grew up alongside the policy that was inaugurated in 1971.

CANADIAN "MIXED-RACE" WOMEN'S READINGS OF MULTICULTURAL POLICY

The fact that existing notions of "multiculturalism" did not adequately encapsulate the racial and/or national self-representations of mixed-race women was manifest in interviews where the policy was rarely raised as a topic for discussion. Conspicuously absent from the women's narratives were positive reflections of multicultural policy. Instead, if the policy was discussed at all, it was critiqued and described as an institutional project that funds and promotes staged ethnic representations, supporting the expression of cultural difference through food, family, personal and religious practices. Many informants indicated that these staged ethnic representations did not communicate much sense of the daily realities of their lives. This perspective resonates with the work of various critical "race" theorists who point out the deficiencies of multiculturalism (see Parekh 2000; Bannerji 2000; Goldberg 1994), insisting that the policy tends to sanction a policed diversity while veiling Eurocentric values.

Any question that I posed about multiculturalism invariably led to extended debate around how participants continually find themselves positioned outside national discourse, despite the project of multiculturalism that insists, "Together, we're better!" (Department of Canadian Heritage 1997). National and racial discourses were inextricably intertwined in interview transcripts. Women in this study voiced exasperation around the difficulty in identifying as Canadian.

ETHNICITY AS THE PRIMARY MARKER OF IDENTITY

Multicultural policy focuses upon ethnicity as a primary identification. The majority of participants in the study grew up alongside the policy and see ethnicity as only one of many aspects defining their sense of self. Ethnic identity, especially among "mixed-race" women, is complex and incorporates many components such as parental heritage, racial and cultural affiliations, and religion, among other factors (Root 1996). In fact, "ethnic identity" itself is intrinsically linked to a politics of location (Bondi 1993), with the women's racialization shifting in different contexts.

Makeda, a 26-year-old graduate student of British and Japanese descent, proposes that the ways she is racialized alters over time and space, pointing out that others tend to rely on particular physical markers that are fluid and flexible, such as clothes and cosmetics, to classify her ethnic and racial makeup.

Gender clearly figures in the ways informants contemplate their own ethno-racial identities, and in turn, how others "read their race." Facial features and hair length, combined with the colour and complexion of participants, all play a role in the ways these women are racialized in various places. These readings influence not only their perceptions of themselves, but also their responses to what others will be. Many "mixed-race" women explained that the places where they live play a role in how they experience their ethnicity in order to point out how their affiliation to culture and ethnicity shifts.

Multicultural policy tends to privilege ethnicity or descent over and above other social identities (like gender and class among other factors), thus obscuring the opportunity to envisage these women's lives on a series of multiple planes. The experience of occupying a doubled space in two ethnic cultures complicates any simplistic reading of ethnicity within multicultural policy, as "mixed-race" women have multiple ethnic allegiances. "Mixed-race" women in this study often shrug off the chain-like restraints of ethnicity as defined by the multicultural policy. Their experiences of ethnicity tell a far more complex story. Multicultural policy's focus on ethnicity emphasizes the past, thus defining Marical's identity by her parents' origins, rather than by her own current set of ethnic allegiances. There are myriad factors that contribute to an individual's sense of ethnic identity, and these factors may change over the course of a lifetime and in different geographical spaces (Parker and Song 2001; Root 1996). These identifications are rarely static—but multicultural policy would have us believe that they are.

CANADIAN VS. NON-CANADIAN: THE "TRUE (WHITE) NORTH STRONG AND FREE"

Multicultural policy states that every ethnic group has the right to preserve and develop its own culture and values within the Canadian context. The phrase "within the Canadian context" is cause for some concern. How do we define "the Canadian context"? I suggest that the policy constructs specific socio-spatial boundaries between the identifications of "Canadian" and "not Canadian." Multicultural policy advocates a strangely paradoxical position. On the one hand, it insists that all Canadians supposedly are handed the right to preserve their ethnic heritage. On the other hand, this optimistic liberal notion tends to veil the assumption among citizens that there is such a thing as a discrete and separate "Canadian" society toward whose development ethnic groups are encouraged to make their multicultural contributions to the nation (Gwyn 1996). This concept was illuminated through many narratives around the theme of who is considered to be a "real" Canadian. If I did ask a question about multiculturalism, it would inevitably lead to discussions about the difficulties others had in identifying the women simply as "Canadian." According to the women interviewed, an "authentic" Canadian is of either British or French blood—those "real" Canadians who are part of a "capital-C Canadian" society. Both these identities are read as white, or European. To be a real Canadian, it is assumed that one must be white (Hill 2001). Subsequently, "mixed-race" women continue to be positioned as outsiders, despite the goals of the multicultural project. Racism and sexism subtly penetrate the national discourse, where those who are positioned as "ethnic" as designated by the policy are consequently placed "outside" Canadianness.

Those with particular phenotypes—or those categorized under the rubric of "visible minority status"—are excluded from the dominant discourse of Canadianness. In other words, you're "not quite if you're not white" (Kondo 1997, 93).

THE PROBLEMATIC NATURE OF THE HYPHEN

Ethnic and national positionings in Canada are entangled further through the hyphen, which effectively produces spaces of distance. This "distance-difference" (Rose 1995) complicates questions of national identity. As I have mentioned, multicultural policy advocates that immigrants in Canada should position their ethnic identity first and foremost, making their individual contribution to the Canadian "mosaic." Gwyn asserts:

> The absurdity here is that no one from Italy, say, or Somalia, comes to Canada to be an Italian or Somali. They come here to be Canadian. As soon as they landed, though, their new state in effect tells them that rather than becoming Canadians they must remain Italian-Canadians, Somali-Canadians, and so on. (Gwyn 1996, 234)

These hyphens of multiculturalism in effect operate to produce spaces of distance, in which ethnicity is positioned outside Canadianness—as an addition to it, but also as an exclusion from it. A 22-year-old student, Zhaleh, who defined herself as "half Japanese, half white," suggests it becomes impossible to position oneself as solely Canadian without announcing one's exoticized ethnic identity:

> I wouldn't just say I'm Canadian and that's it. Because I mean just the fact for me to even say when someone's asked me, what are you, the fact that if I say Canadian, that doesn't satisfy them. That just tells you right there, like you know what I mean? It's not possible to be just Canadian and no race. Like I couldn't realistically live in Canada and think that way.

Zhaleh finds it difficult to claim a national identity without declaring her ethnic allegiances. The policy of multiculturalism is reassuring to those who vigilantly patrol the borders between ethnic and national belonging. The burden of hyphenation, where one is seen as not solely "Canadian" but "Canadian and fill-in-your-ethnic-background" is especially heavy for women of "mixed race," who further trouble the hyphen by employing and intermingling two or more ethnicities in their own definitions of their identities, through the coining of labels like "African-Persian-Cherokee-European-Canadian" for example. The "mixed-race" person resists the occupation of a single ethnic space. These "hyphenated circumlocutions" (Hanchard 1990, 213) also make the process of self-definition lengthy and exhausting, requiring a whole geography and history of explanation. Faith, a 25-year-old tourist agent of Chinese, Polynesian, and British descent, commented:

> I think that's why sometimes I hate discussing it when people ask [where are you from]. Because I can't just say one thing. Like you can't just say you're Canadian and have people understand, oh you're Canadian, or whatever. I always have to go into this lengthy explanation about Chinese, Polynesian, and then British. Then there's the whole thing about, oh well where were your parents born? Which brings me, if I think about it, full space to here. Well, I was born in Canada, so I am Canadian, but what is Canadian? AAARGH! It drives me crazy! And it's just like this whole, long—I'm not just one simple thing.

The hyphen effectively marks a "distance-difference" (Rose 1995) from potential claims to nation, a troubling symbol that refuses to admit the possibility of the co-mingling of ethnicities and national citizenship, compounding difference as a "property marker, a boundary post, a knot, a chain, a bridge, a foreign word, a nomadic, floating magic carpet" (Wah 1996, 60). Participants uncomfortably inhabit that space of the hyphen, where difference is continually expropriated and appropriated within a Eurocentric framework.

Kiirti, herself 26, a waitress, whose mother is Irish and English, and whose father is a combination of French, Caribbean-Indian, and African descent, further demonstrates the frustrations and paradoxes inherent in her desire to identify as Canadian, pointing out the problematic nature of attempts to do so:

> I mean I hate the fact that people ask me where I'm from. And I'll say I'm Canadian. And they say, "No no no no no, but where are you FROM?" "I'm from HERE." "No no no, but where are you FROM?" And I'll say, "Fine, you want to know? I'll tell you." And I'll tell them ALL the different places my parents are from. And then they'll say, "Oh, so you're Canadian." They DO! And it's like, "GO AWAY!"

Kiirti's comment neatly encapsulates the messy contradictions of assuming a Canadian identity. The very constituency of the social fabric of Canada is a reflection of its diverse ethnic population, which has been read as intrinsically "Canadian" outside the country. However, it becomes impossible to identify as Canadian within the country, in spite of the country's diversity, given that when one questions national borders, one also questions the boundary markers of race and ethnicity. As such, it is repeatedly revealed that hegemonic national discourses are not kind to those who live within marginal spaces—especially "mixed-race" women, who might be seen as "the double foreigner, the double stranger ... held up to the phantasmic and found doubly wanting" (Eisenstein 1996, 41; see also Okin 1999).

Participants explored how the widely disparate circumstances of ethnic allegiances are formed and transformed over time, where dominant discourses of racial and national meanings do not reflect their interpretations of their ethnicities. Racist ideologies underlying dominant discourses about the nation further confuse ideas around the nebulous nature of Canadian identity. Indeed, reverberating through many of my interviews are inquiries into who Canadians "really" are. Who is a "real" Canadian? The conception of citizenship suggested by multicultural policy demands a model of homogeneous people that is not representative of the complex and diverse ethnic composition of the country. In the next section, I show how informants challenge and contest socially constructed categories of Canadian identity outside of "the two solitudes" (Taylor 1993, 1) by developing new reconstitutions of cultural citizenship.

RELATIONSHIP BETWEEN "MIXED RACE" AND CANADIAN IDENTITY

Is there a love of the nation which is emancipatory? (Appadurai 1997)

For some "mixed-race" women, a futuristic reading of Canadian identity would move beyond the "deux nations" model as imagined through the grid of multicultural policy. They challenge the ways they are othered by the unitary notions of national identity and assert that being different by no means equates with being un-Canadian. This version of national identity displaces and shifts the terms of a British–French linked nationalism. By opening up the term "Canadian" to scrutiny, participants reformulate the conventional meanings associated with the phrase as Makeda suggests wistfully:

> I think that Canadian, as a term, has a certain reference to a certain kinda person. And I'd LOVE to have that category opened up. So that people can say, Canadian, and imagine all sorts of different people. I'm not making a bid for an amnesiac Canada that can suddenly embrace its own diversity and forget its past transgressions, like the building of the railway by the Chinese, for example. I think they both have to occur. Canada has to come to terms with all those things that comprise Canada, the stories have to be able to address all those people, and those histories. I would like to be part of redefining Canada. I think Canada is a country that can continually open itself up to new people.

As Makeda explains, the act of claiming a Canadian identity would mean the occupation of a distinctly contradictory space, where one can both embrace a sense of country and still unveil the exclusion of specific histories of oppression and resistance. This transformation of the term "Canadian" would include unpacking the embedded racist history of the country. This might include contemplating uncomfortable questions regarding the First Nations peoples' broken and rightful place in the Canadian polity, and acknowledging the work army of Chinese immigrants who painstakingly built the Canadian railroad. Makeda suggests that appropriating the term would include unmasking the hidden histories of the majority, in an attempt to "snatch from the hidden histories another place to stand in, another place to speak from" (Hall 1990, 236). Thus, this tortured past would become part of the present, informing and playing a part in the creation of Makeda's sense of national identity. In reading the present in terms of the past, Makeda proposes the occupation of a space where she can finally be proud to belong. The stories of those who have been continually placed on the outside would become an integral part of this portrait. In doing so, the voices of the marginalized are actively centred as part of a re-imagined citizenship.

Informants read their own "mixed-race" identity as a model for an optimistic Canadian citizenship where their ethnicities are not necessarily compartmentalized, and belonging is forged through difference—but not through the lip service that multicultural policy offers. As I have previously discussed, multiculturalism in Canada confuses issues of ethnicity and nationalism by treating ethnicity as clearly divisible and dichotomous categories outside Canadianness. However, "mixed-race" women continually experience ethnicity as overlapping layers. They are in a unique position to consider the additional challenges of developing a real "multicultural" identity compatible with Canadianness by challenging assumptions about racial and ethnic purity.

For Darius, a 32-year-old actress whose mother is third-generation Japanese-Canadian, and whose father is of French Canadian, Ojibway First Nations, and Irish descent, questions about her "mixed race" were influenced largely by her own sense of nationalism and vice versa, where her own "mixed race" is read as a positive stance to experience the nation:

> I think Canada is really on this frontier of racial miscegenation, so I don't really separate my ethnic and national identity. I see myself as being Canadian and being mixed race. Maybe even more than someone who sees themselves as monoracial, someone who was full-blooded Korean, and their parents were from Korea, and they lived in Canada, but they grew up speaking English all the time, I think it's probably even more of a challenge for them. To me, for me, being Canadian and being mixed race, and the issues around identity there, are not at odds with each other. They are related.

"Mixed-race" women in this study emphasized the impossibility of being divided along the lines of ethnic origins. Maribel, a 25-year-old graduate student with a Swedish mother and a Bangladeshi father, reads her "mixed-race" identity as harmonious with her national ties and insists on calling herself mixed, which encapsulates not only her ethnic identity, but also her sense of citizenship:

> I think mixed is a flexible enough word. That it can catch a lot of people in its net. Mixed background, mixed heritage. I find most useful. I don't know why. But it is my heritage. And it's more than just ethnicity. It's the fact that I'm Canadian too. It's all mixed up. Together.

Women of "mixed race" are used to names, labels, and categories imposed upon them by others. However, as Trinh reminds us, "despite our desperate attempts to mend and maintain, categories always leak" (Trinh 1989, 141). To counteract this compulsion of classification, many "mixed-race" women take on the identification of Canadian as an empowering label. However, it does not necessarily follow that in choosing this identification, they blindly follow the rules advocated by multicultural policy. Instead, their use of "Canadian" reflects their very real experience of growing up in Canada. Some "mixed-race" women I talked to did not feel any particular kinship with either of their ethnicities, and many of their parents were second- or third-generation Canadian, so their parents were born in Canada as well. Participants exercise their right to choose their own ethnic allegiances. Of course, it is important to note that despite this desire to choose, their assertions of ethnic identity are often constrained by the discourses and imagery of racial categorization (Mahtani 2001; Waters 1990). Identifying as Canadian reflects particular social decisions on their part through a clear redefinition of their own allegiances to nationhood.

For Emma, a 33-year-old journalist of Malaysian and British descent, this would mean delineating her own definition of Canadian identity. This sense of national allegiance is rife with paradox. Emma reveals the constant ephemeral and shifting senses of both national and various ethnic selves she experiences on a day-to-day basis, depending upon her location:

> I was born in England and then we moved to Canada, which added a whole new layer of mixed race on it. So I always sort of like to quote a friend, who described herself as a salad of racial genes, you know, because she's just a little bit of everything. And in a way, that's maybe uniquely Canadian. There are so many people here that come from so many different cultures and especially in Toronto, which is where I grew up, that it's just it's kind of typical of who we are. We're an immigrant country with an immigrant culture. [In Canada] you can define yourself however you want in a way that isn't necessarily associated with a certain set of cultural values. So my [national] identity has been just a mixture of all those factors.

Emma compounds questions of race and nation by insisting that moving from England as a "mixed-race" immigrant imposed another layer of "mixed race" upon her identity. Women of "mixed race" are active participants in shaping their own identities by altering others' perception of their place in Canada. Emma writes herself into the national discourse in particular ways, recalling another story where she deliberately chose to identify herself as Canadian in order to defy existing stereotypes related to her phenotype, reflecting a defiant re-appropriation of national identity:

> I remember in Washington a cab driver saying: "So where are you from?" "Oh I'm Canadian," I said, and then it went, "Where are you really from?" "Well, I was born in England," I said, just to stymie him further because what he wanted to hear me say was: "Yeah my father's half Chinese." He wanted to be able to identify me with a racial group. Which I just refuse to be identified with, like either/or, you know. The closest I want to be identified to these kinds of cultural stereotypes is to say I'm Canadian, which defies pretty much all stereotypes because there's nothing really identifiable about it.

Emma employs the term "Canadian" to describe herself in this situation as a foil, forcing another to think about his racist assumptions about what is a real Canadian. By refusing to be identified with a racial group, Emma resists definitions of ethnic identity that re-inscribe conventional notions of traditional culture. Her version of national allegiance re-figures Canada as a more useful "catch-all" phrase because it is nebulous, recognizing that one need not be European to be Canadian. To be Canadian, for many "mixed-race" women in Canada, is to question any notion of a coherent, stable, and autonomous identity—either national or ethnic, as Sara, a 24-year-old student of Filipina and Irish descent, suggests:

> I think [being mixed race] is very typically Canadian. I mean, all I've seen of Canadians are different racial groups. So I think that it's only natural that there would be a very big mixed population. So I think it typifies being Canadian. That's perfectly in tune with that.

The social and ethnic constituency of Canada parallels Sara's own "mixed-race" identity. Identifying with nationalism does not necessarily mean the subsequent adherence to ethnic stereotypes as dictated by the policy of multiculturalism. These women's interpretations of what constitutes difference are constantly shifting, socially constructed, and geographically diverse. They point out the popular misconception that to be Canadian means to be solely of either British or French descent by designating it a site for the recognition of complex national and ethnic allegiances, acknowledging the wide variance within ethnic groups. To claim Canadian status for Faith means to go beyond the legalistic definition of possessing a Canadian passport. It is to experience a sense of home:

> I have a very weird hang-up about [being asked, "Where are you from?"] When they ask, it's like, I'm from Canada. Like, where was I born, where do I fit, what is my country of affiliation? It's Canada. Absolutely. And that's another thing that really irritates me about the whole thing about Canada, when people say where we're from, people respond, "I'm from Czechoslovakia." Well, no you're not! You have a Canadian passport, you're Canadian, with Czechoslovakian heritage. Like I HATE that. Like I'M Canadian. Yes, I have, a variety of roots! But like my experience is Canada. Like I HATE this whole thing, all these people who think they're other things. Especially if you're born here. I'm sorry, but you're Canadian.

Faith has a clear sense of home and belonging in Canada and her identity is closely linked to questions of national identity, marking the connection between geography and culture. This connection between home and identity is not just an attachment to the abstract concept of nation. Choosing to identify as Canadian reflects these women's desires to develop a new vision of Canadian identity, where they continually renegotiate the tropes that assert nationhood as a static entity.

In the narrative below, Kiirti, who was adopted, reveals how she felt when she discovered her parents' individual ethnic identities. Kiirti expresses how that had an impact upon her own sense of country:

> I mean once I knew, once I knew where my parents were from, and there was this massive mix, I was such a mixture that truly I had to ask: Who was I? And the answer came: I am Canadian, this is where I am born, this is the culture that I know, and my mother forever and my father forever telling me how CANADIAN I am, and my accent, and, my Canadian-isms, and God forbid, I say eh?! I mean, they're ON me! (chuckle) I am ... It's like that commercial![1] I-AM-A-CANADIAN. That's what I am. I should be the new symbol for Canada! I am one big melting pot of stuff! (laughter) I'm a stew! (laughter) A big Canadian stew! (laughter).

Kiirti reads her "mixed-race" identity as a model for Canadian citizenship. She explains how her body is marked by her own sense of Canadianness, reflected in her accent and her "Canadian-isms." She refuses to renounce her Canadian identity in the name of a compartmentalized ethnic identity, given the variety of her ethnic mixes, and emphasizes the salience of her own experiences growing up in Canada. Women of "mixed race" challenge not only the social construction of race, but also the social construction of Canadian citizenship by proposing a connection between their own "mixed-race" status and their sense of nationalism. They are articulating for themselves something that exceeds previous categories of race and nation, writing themselves into existence.

CONCLUSION

> [Multicultural policy] entertain[s] and encourage[s] ... cultural diversity, [while correspondingly] containing it. A transparent norm is constituted, a norm given by the host society or dominant culture, which says that "these other cultures are fine, but we must be able to locate them within our own grid." (Bhabha 1990, 208)

The policy of multiculturalism has both impeded and facilitated senses of belonging for "mixed-race" women in this study. While many may still read multicultural policy as an inclusive vision of humanity, the narratives of Canadian "mixed-race" women suggest a more critical reading of the policy's goals and aspirations. Their stories offer new framings of national identity in response to complex processes of social interaction, where they are constantly defining, redefining, playing, and merging with ethnic and national identities. They actively reconstitute and re-present the idea of the nation as represented in Canadian culture by adopting various allegiances.

The voices of these women raise questions about the stark contrast between multiculturalism as a way of life for participants versus its status as a policy for Canadian citizens. Many "mixed-race" women did not look positively upon multicultural policy as an effective strategy to fight racism, suggesting that efforts to combat discrimination need to be further problematized in relation to power. Instead, many women in this study argued that multicultural policy has acted to reinforce stereotypical views of people of colour. I suggest that part of the problem is multicultural policy's steadfast refusal to discuss race as a socially constructed social divide, where seemingly "real" biological differences are used to justify social and economic inequalities and injustice (see Kobayashi 1993). Some women of "mixed race" find it difficult to identify as "Canadian" despite their desire to do so because of systematic racism and dominant definitions of the national narrative as "white" (Hill 2001).

I have also suggested that some participants claimed a Canadian identity as a potentially productive identification linked to their own multiraciality. Conventional definitions of race, gender, and nation are negotiated and contested among participants. Clearly, issues of race are inextricably intertwined with class, age, sexual orientation, gender, and nation, among other salient factors. I suggest further research examine the legislation that configures particular racial and sexist dynamics inherent in the policy of multiculturalism, as well as explore the ways the tensions pulling on these dynamics are spatialized. This would acknowledge how individuals are raced, classed, and gendered in particular spaces. The present debate over multicultural policy should be extended to encompass the vernacular understandings of these women's discursive and material practices with the engagement of national and ethnic alliances in Canada.

Multicultural policy can frame identity through a formalized temporality, placing emphasis upon roots and origins rather than the complicated identity routes of the individual (Gilroy 1993). I propose that "mixed race" women offer new models of citizenship, working out from the individually identified body to the national body politic. Some participants claimed a Canadian identity as a potentially productive identification linked to their own multiraciality, in the process negotiating and contesting conventional definitions of race, gender, and nation.

NOTE

1   Kiirti is referring to a series of Canadian beer commercials, where the viewer is bombarded with numerous Canadian icons, including the maple leaf and prominent Canadian road signs, over a soundtrack of Canadian rock music. At the time of the interview, these commercials were inundating the airwaves continually. I draw the reader's attention to the words of Mukherjee, who insists that "when we non-white Canadians watch beer commercials, we never fail to notice our absence there" (Mukherjee 1994, 72). However, Kiirti draws a comparison between her own sense of nationalism and these commercials, despite the non-white presence in the advertisements.

REFERENCES

Appardurai, A. 1997. "Modernity at Large: the Social Life of Things." Paper presented at the Department of Anthropology, University College, London, 10 June.

Azoulay, K. 1997 *Black, Jewish, and Interracial*. Durham: Duke University Press.

Bannerji, H. 2000. *The Dark Side of the Nation: Essays on Multiculturalism, Nationalism and Gender.* Toronto: Canadian Scholars' Press Inc.

Bienvenue, R. and J. Goldstein. 1985. *Ethnicity and Ethnic Relations in Canada*. Toronto: Butterworths.

Bhabha, H. 1990. "Interview with Homi Bhabha." In *Identity: Community, Culture, Difference*, ed. J. Rutherford. London: Lawrence and Wishart.

———. 1994. *The Location of Culture*. London: Routledge.

Bondi, L. 1993. "Locating Identity Polities." In *Place and the Politics of Identity*, ed. M. Keith and S. Pile. London: Routledge.

Canada. 1980–1983. House of Commons. *Debates*. Ottawa: Queen's Printer.

Caws, P. 1984. "Identities: Cultural, Transcultural, and Multicultural." In *Multiculturalism: A Critical Reader*, ed. D.T. Goldberg. Oxford: Blackwell.

Department of Canadian Heritage. 1997 "Racism. Stop It!" Ottawa: Queen's Printer.

Domosh, M. 1998. "'Those 'Gorgeous Incongruities': Polite Politics and Public Space on the Streets of Nineteenth-Century New York City." *Annals of the Association of American Geographers* 88, no. 2: 209–226.

Dunn, K., and M. Mahtani. 2001. "Adjusting the Colour Bars: Media Representation of Ethnic Minorities under Australian and Canadian Multicultural-isms." *Progress in Planning*.

Eisenstein, Z. 1996. *Hatreds: Racialized and Sexualized Conflicts in the 21st Century*. London: Routledge.

Elliott, J., and A. Fleras. 1992. "Immigration and the Canadian Ethnic Mosaic." In *Multiculturalism in Canada,* ed. A. Fleras and J. Elliott. Scarborough: Nelson Canada.

Fleras, A., and J. Elliott, eds. 1992. *Multiculturalism in Canada* Scarborough: Nelson Canada.

Fleras, A., and J. Kunz. 2001. *Media and Minorities: Representing Diversity in a Multicultural Canada.* Toronto: Thompson Educational Publishing, Inc.

Franco, J. 1997. "The Nation as Imagined Community." In *Dangerous Liaisons: Gender, Nation and Postcolonial Perspectives,* ed. A. McClintock, A. Mufti, and E. Shohat. Minneapolis: University of Minnesota Press.

George, R. 1996. *The Politics of Home.* Cambridge: Cambridge University Press.

Goldberg, D.T. 1994. *Multiculturalism: A Critical Reader.* Oxford: Blackwell.

———. 1995. "Made in the USA." In *American Mixed Race,* ed. N. Zack. Lanham: Rowman and Littlefield.

Gwyn, R. 1996. *Nationalism without Walls.* Toronto: McClelland & Stewart.

Hall, S. 1990. "Cultural Identity and Diaspora." In *Identity: Community, Culture, Difference,* ed. J. Rutherford. London: Lawrence and Wishart.

———. 1993. "Ethnicity, Race and Nation." Paper presented at Senate House, University of London, 12 December.

Hamilton, R. 1998. "The Vertical Mosaic: Canadian Multiculturalism and Feminist Theory." Paper presented at the Canadian High Commission, London, UK, 14 February.

Hanchard, M. 1990. "Identity, Meaning and the African-American." *Social Text* 24, no. 8: 31–42.

Hill, L. 2001. *Black Berry, Sweet Juice: On Being Black and White in Canada.* Toronto: HarperCollins.

Ifekwunigwe, J. 1999. *Scattered Belongings: Cultural Paradoxes of "Race," Nation and Gender.* London: Routledge.

———. 2001. "Re-Membering 'Race': On Gender, 'Mixed Race' and Family in the English-African Diaspora." In *Rethinking "Mixed Race,"* ed. D. Parker and M. Song. London: Pluto Press.

Kalbach, M., and W. Kalbach. 1999. "Becoming Canadian: Problems of an Emerging Identity." *Canadian Ethnic Studies* 31, no. 2:1–16.

Kaplan, C. 1987. "Deterritorializations: The Rewriting of Home and Exile in Western Feminist Discourse." *Cultural Critique,* no. 6:187–198.

Kilbride, K., J. Golden, W. Husbands, and D. Mamatis. 2001. "Identity Formation and Parenting Issues for Biracial Canadians: A Case Study of Black and White Young Canadians in the Greater Toronto Area." Report submitted to Canadian Heritage, Ottawa, Ontario.

King, R., and K. DaCosta. 1996. "Changing Face, Changing Race: The Remaking of Race in the Japanese American and African American Communities." In *The Multiracial Experience,* ed. M. Root. London: Sage.

Kobayashi, A. 1993. "Multiculturalism: Representing a Canadian Institution." In *Place/Culture/Representation,* ed. J. Duncan and D. Ley. London: Routledge.

Kondo, D. 1997. *About Face.* London: Routledge.

Kymlicka, W. 1995. *Multicultural Citizenship: A Liberal Theory of Minority Rights.* Oxford: Clarendon Press.

Mahtani, M. 2001. "I'm a Blonde-Haired, Blue-Eyed Black Girl: Mapping Mobile Paradoxical Spaces among Multiethnic Women." In *Rethinking "Mixed Race,"* ed. D. Parker and M. Song. London: Pluto Press.

———. "What's in a Name: Exploring the Identification of 'Mixed Race' as an Identification." *Ethnicities* 2:4 (2002): 469–490.

———. "Tricking the Border Guards: Performing Race." *Environment and Planning D: Society and Space* 20:425–440.

Mahtani, M., and A. Moreno. 2001. "Same Difference: Towards a More Unified Discourse in 'Mixed Race' Theory." In *Rethinking "Mixed Race,"* ed. D. Parker and M. Song. London: Pluto Press.

Makropoulos, J. 2000. "Racism in Franco-Ontario." Paper presented at the ERA21! Conference, Vancouver, B.C., November.

Mohanty, C. 1991. "Cartographies of Struggle: Third World Women and the Politics of Feminism." In *Third World Women and the Politics of Feminism,* ed. C. Mohanty, A. Russo, and L. Torres. Bloomington: Indiana University Press.

Moss, J. 1996. *Enduring Dreams: An Exploration of Arctic Landscape.* Concord: Anansi Press.

Mukherjee, A. 1994. *Oppositional Aesthetics: Readings from a Hyphenated Space.* Toronto: TSAR Publications.

Ng, R. 1993. "Racism, Sexism and Nation Building in Canada." In *Race, Identity and Representation in Education,* ed. C. McCarthy and W. Crichlow. London: Routledge.

Okin, S. 1999.*"Is Multiculturalism Bad for Women?"* Princeton: Princeton University Press.

Parekh, B. 2000. *Rethinking Multiculturalism: Cultural Diversity and Political Theory.* London: Macmillan.

Parker, D., and M. Song. 2001. "Introduction: Rethinking 'Mixed Race.'" In *Rethinking "Mixed Race,"* ed. D. Parker and M. Song. London: Pluto Press.

Peter, K. 1981. "The Myth of Multiculturalism and Other Political Fables." In *Ethnicity, Power and Politics in Canada,* ed. J. Dahlie and T. Fernando. Toronto: Methuen.

Radcliffe, S. 1999. "Embodying National Identities: *Mestizo* Men and White Women in Ecuadorian Racial-National Imaginaries." *Transactions of the Institute of British Geographers* 24: 213–227.

Root, M. 1996. *The Multiracial Experience.* London: Sage.

Rose, G. 1995. "Distance, Surface, Elsewhere: A Feminist Critique of the Space of Phallocentric Self/ Knowledge." *Environment and Planning D: Society and Space,* no. 13:761–781.

Said, E. 1991. "Special Issue on Patriotism," *The Nation* (15 July):15.

Sibley, D. 1995. *Geographies of Exclusion.* London: Routledge.

Stam, R. 1997. "Multiculturalism and the Neo-Conservatives." In *Dangerous Liaisons: Gender, Nation and Postcolonial Perspectives,* ed. A. McClintock, A. Mufti, and El Shohat. Minneapolis: University of Minnesota Press.

Standen, B. 1996. "Without a Template: the Biracial Korean/White Experience." In *The Multiracial Experience,* ed. M. Root. London: Sage.

Taylor, C. 1992. *Multiculturalism and the "Politics of Recognition."* Princeton: Princeton University Press.

———. 1993. *Reconciling the Solitudes: Essays on Canadian Federalism and Nationalism.* Kingston: McGill-Queen's University Press.

Taylor, L. 2001. "Searching for the 'Exotic': an Exploration of Multiraciality in the Academy." Paper presented at the Canadian Ethnic Studies Association in Halifax, Nova Scotia, 4 November.

Twine, F. 1998. *Racism in a Racial Democracy: The Maintenance of White Supremacy in Brazil.* New Brunswick: Rutgers University Press.

———. 1999. "Bearing Blackness in Britain: The Meaning of Racial Difference for White Birth Mothers of African-Descent Children." *Social Identities* 5, no. 2:185–210.

Wah, F. 1996. "Half-Bred Poetics." *absinthe* 9, no. 2:60–66.

Waters, M. 1990. *Ethnic Options.* Berkeley: University of California Press.

Yuval-Davis, N., and F. Anthias. 1989. *Woman-Nation-State.* London: Macmillan.

FORMATION OF ETHNIC AND RACIAL IDENTITIES
NARRATIVES BY YOUNG ASIAN-AMERICAN PROFESSIONALS

PYONG GAP MIN
AND ROSE KIM

More than 30 years have passed since the influx of immigrants from Third World countries began. The children of those immigrants, who began arriving in the late 1960s, have come of age. As of the late 1990s, many have completed their college education and entered the job market. They are represented in a number of non-science, non-business roles, entering professional fields, such as politics, journalism and the fine arts—arenas that have typically been off-limits to their immigrant parents because of language and cultural barriers.

Social scientists, usually led by immigrant scholars who represented the immigrant groups under investigation, began to conduct research on post-1965 immigrants immediately after the contemporary mass migration started (Gans 1997). Researchers began to examine the "new second generation" in the late 1980s. As a result, a number of articles and several books focusing on the second generation have been published (Gibson 1988; Gans 1992; Portes and Zhou 1993; Rumbaut and Cornelius 1995; Portes 1996; Kibria 1997; Zhou and Bankston III 1998; Hirschman et al. 2000).

An important issue regarding the adaptation patterns of the second generation is the level of their ethnicity or ethnic attachment, as characterized by their retention of ethnic culture, participation in ethnic networks, and ethnic identity. Given this, it is no wonder that most of the studies focusing on second-generation Asian-Americans have examined the issues directly or indirectly related to one or more dimensions of ethnic attachment (Min and Choi 1993; Espiritu 1994; Lee 1996; Kibria 1997, 1999; Zhou and Bankston III 1998; Hong and Min 1999; Thai 1999).

These studies have limitations in understanding Asian-Americans' patterns of ethnic attachment because they are based on survey or ethnographic data, with high-school students usually used as the respondents or informants. High-school samples are not suitable for examining the respondents' or informants' social relations, including their affiliations with ethnic organizations and dating patterns. Moreover, studies based on high-school samples have further limitations in examining ethnic or pan-ethnic identity because the latter is often suppressed in early years but emerges in young adulthood (Kim and Yu 1996; Thai 1999). In addition, the studies cited above have limitations in illuminating information about patterns of pan-Asian ethnicity because, as case studies of one or two Asian ethnic groups, they do not provide comparative perspectives.

To overcome these limitations, we have conducted a study of Asian-Americans' ethnic attachment using personal narratives by 15 young professionals. Personal narratives, rather than personal interviews, may be more effective for analyzing the process of the change in ethnic identity over one's life course.[1] A few books have examined ethnic identity and related issues using personal narratives (Hong 1993; Dublin 1996; Rubin-Dorsly and Fishkin 1996). This chapter intends to examine Asian-Americans' ethnicity through narratives written by 15 young Asian-American professionals. It will examine all three dimensions of Asian-Americans' ethnicity, that is, retention of ethnic culture, participation in ethnic networks, and ethnic identity, focusing on their ethnic and pan-ethnic identities.

RETENTION OF ETHNIC CULTURE

Classical assimilation theorists proposed a zero-sum model of acculturation, in which the acculturation of immigrants and their children involved the gradual replacement of their ethnic culture with American culture (Warner and Srole 1945, 285–286; Cole and Cole 1954; Gordon 1964). From this perspective, the children of immigrants who are from lower-class families and who have grown up in an immigrant enclave are more likely to retain their language and culture than others, while lacking fluency in English. In contrast, children from middle-class and professional families who have grown up in a white middle-class neighbourhoods are expected to be highly assimilated into American culture, with little retention of their cultural traditions. Thus, classical assimilation theory leads us to believe that our highly educated professional essayists will have achieved a high level of acculturation, replacing their ethnic language and culture with English and American culture.

However, research on the "new second generation" during recent years suggests that many of these professional essayists may maintain strong bilingual and bicultural orientations. The children of contemporary immigrants, including Asian immigrants, have advantages over the children of earlier immigrants in retaining their cultural traditions because of several structural factors (Massey 1995; Min 1999). Two structural factors deserve attention here. First, technological advances in communication, air transportation, and the media enable contemporary immigrants and their children to maintain transnational networks with their home country (Basch et al. 1994; Schiller et al. 1994; Foner 1997; Laguerre 1998; Min 1999). Second, since the early 1970s, the federal and local governments and educational institutions have changed policies toward minority groups and minority students from Anglo conformity to cultural pluralism, which has helped the children of contemporary immigrants to maintain their language and culture (Goldberg 1994).

Recent empirical studies indicate that children of contemporary immigrants are highly assimilated to American culture and that they prefer to use English over their mother tongue when communicating with their friends (Min and Choi 1993; Portes and Schauffler 1994; Portes and Rumbaut 1996, chap. 6; Hong and Min 1999). Yet they also show that 1.5-generation high-school students are usually bilingual and that a significant proportion of second-generation students remain bilingual (Rumbaut 1994). As noted above, transnational ties and multicultural policy help immigrant families of all class backgrounds to transmit their language and culture to their children. Yet, middle-class and professional immigrants with more resources are able to take advantage of contemporary technological advances and multicultural policy more effectively to teach their children ethnic language and culture (Portes and Zhou 1993; Portes and Rumbaut 1996, 222–225). Many well-to-do Asian professional and business parents send their children to their home country regularly for an ethnic education. Given their class advantages for preserving their ethnic heritage, many of our essayists may be strongly bicultural.

ETHNIC AND PAN-ETHNIC IDENTITIES

Despite the general public's tendency to lump all Asian groups together, each Asian group has its own language, religion, and unique cultural traditions. Second-generation Asian-American children who live with their immigrant parents in their formative years are exposed to their parental language, religions, and other aspects of their ethnic and sub-ethnic cultures at home. These cultural elements practised at home and in the ethnic community can be an important basis for second-generation Asian-Americans' ethnic identity. Therefore, we expect our essayists to have strong ethnic identities largely based on salient aspects of their ethnic and sub-ethnic cultures.

Second-generation Asian-Americans do not usually live in an ethnic enclave and find their occupations in the general economy rather than in the ethnic economy. Their residential and occupational assimilation may make them feel comfortable and lose their ethnic identity. Yet other structural factors force them to accept their ethnic or pan-Asian identity. Of all structural factors, the general perception of Asian-Americans as foreigners or at least as less than full American citizens probably has the most significant effect on their ethnic and racial identities. For third- and fourth-generation white ethnics, who are accepted as full American citizens, ethnic identity is a matter of personal choice to meet their search for a community (Waters 1990). However, being ethnic is a societal expectation for third- and fourth-generation Japanese- and Chinese-Americans, no matter how far removed they are from their immigrant roots or how different they are from their foreign-born counterparts (Tuan 1999).

Structural factors related to their adjustments to the host society may have stronger effects on second-generation Asian-Americans' pan-Asian racial identity than on ethnic identity. Governments and schools lump together all groups that originate from the Asian continent and the Pacific Islands when compiling data for policy and resource allocation purposes. Most Americans also have difficulty in distinguishing members of various Asian ethnic groups, despite some observable physical differences. Most Americans refer to Koreans and Vietnamese as "Chinese." White and black Americans have physically attacked Asian-Americans on the basis of mistaken ethnic identifications. In 1982, for example, two white men beat to death Vincent Chin, a Chinese-American whom they mistook for a Japanese. Accordingly, all Asian-Americans need to make a broad pan-Asian coalition to protect their interests in social services, education, politics, and other areas (Espiritu 1992; Wei 1993). Some scholars (Omi and Winant 1986; Takagi 1994) have argued that the pan-Asian racial formation will be an important feature of Asian-American experiences in the post-Civil Rights era.

ANALYSES OF THE ESSAYS

STRONG BICULTURAL EXPERIENCES

Our review of the essays indicates that, although as children the contributors resisted learning their ethnic languages and cultures, they showed an increasing interest in them as they grew older. As expected from the literature review, most of the contributors, as young adults, were highly bicultural. According to a majority of accounts, the contributors' parents made great efforts to transmit their native language, customs, and values to their children. William, a native-born Chinese-American, attended Saturday language schools in the 1970s, when such schools were rare. Diana's mother started a Sunday morning language class at home to teach her Bengali. Albert, a native-born Indian-American, visited his parents' homeland when he was 10.

Despite their parents' efforts, the contributors often resisted their ethnic culture, preferring to identify themselves as Americans when they were children. Their resistance stemmed from the pressure to be "normal" and to blend into predominantly white communities that were virtually free of Asians or recent immigrants. Nicole said that she was ashamed of her parents' broken English when they visited her school. Suzuko, a television news producer, said that until her mother reminded her, she had entirely forgotten a childhood episode of locking herself in her bedroom after school as a protest against attending a Japanese language school. Two contributors, however, Michael and Fuji, both native-born Americans of Filipino descent, said that their parents encouraged them to assimilate. When Michael's brother asked his parents to address him only in English in front of his white friends, his parents complied without objection. Fuji said he pursued a variety of different sports in high school to combat the stereotype of a "nerdy" Asian.

Many contributors looked forward to college as an opportunity to escape from the demands of their parents' cultural expectations. For 1.5- and second-generation immigrants, parents are often the strongest link to their ethnicity (Gans 1997). Ironically, many essayists developed an interest and pride in their ethnic subculture at college. Michael said that his arrival at Brown University marked the first time he had seen a significant number of Asian-Americans. He described the evolution of his racial identity: "Growing up, I considered myself to be an 'American' and unconsciously avoided all things 'Asian.' Later I explored and grew proud of my Asian identity." Although Suzuko resisted attending a Japanese language school as a child, she followed her father's advice and went to Japan for college and spent seven years there, obtaining a college degree, and starting a career in television production that she later transplanted to the United States. In high school, Samod often clashed with her father over his efforts to instill in her pride in her Indian heritage. But, upon entering college, she began to develop a great interest in Indian history and culture and spent two years in India to learn more.

The switch from striving to blend into the mainstream culture to adopting their ethnic culture was influenced by several factors. First, Asian-Americans were more visible in the college environment, often composing a significant proportion of the student body. Second, the college environment was much more multicultural and cosmopolitan. Many of the colleges attended by the essayists included Asian language and Asian area study courses that represented their Asian subculture. The availability of such courses was closely related, as previously noted, to the expansion of multicultural studies in the United States ever since the early 1970s. Finally, and most importantly, the interest in their ethnic heritage as they matured had much to do with the psychological process of coming to terms with their own ethnic and racial identities.

HIGH SOCIAL ASSIMILATION

In their pre-college years, the second- and 1.5-generation essayists suffered an inferiority complex about being Asian immigrants or the children of immigrants. Many shunned their ethnic culture and sought to blend into the white mainstream culture, forming friendships with white children, often with Jewish children. Partly this effort was the function of living in predominantly white neighbourhoods and attending predominantly white schools where co-ethnics and other Asian-Americans were rare. The inclination to gravitate toward whites was also the function of the social marginalization of Asian-Americans and Asian culture.

In college, the essayists tended to develop pride in their ethnic and/or pan-Asian identities and to maintain more frequent interactions with co-ethnic and Asian-American friends. Co-ethnics and other Asian-Americans were more common on college campuses. Asian-American student organizations and academic courses that explored Asian culture were also available.

STRUGGLING FOR ETHNIC AND RACIAL IDENTITY

The essayists' struggle to come to terms with their ethnic and racial identities is the most significant aspect of the experiences captured in the 15 personal narratives. The process of claiming their ethnicity often unfolded over years and involved tremendous pain and inner conflict. While two of the three first-generation immigrant essayists discussed how prejudice and discrimination had affected their career mobility in the United States, none referred to the psychological turmoil involved in the formation of their ethnic identities. In contrast, most second- and 1.5-generation essayists devoted much space to this struggle; in fact, this struggle lay at the core of several essays.

The 1.5- and second-generation essayists were raised in homes where their parents spoke their native language, ate their native food, and practised their native customs. Yet, outside the home, their culture was marginal and largely invisible. Those of Filipino, Korean, Indian, Vietnamese, and Bangladesh descent, representing countries with a more recent immigration history, apparently experienced a greater sense of invisibility than those who were Japanese or Chinese. During the 1960s and 1970s, many Americans associated

Asians with China and Japan. As a result, most essayists developed a negative self-image and attempted to reject their ethnic culture and their non-white physical characteristics. They tried to be white and associated with white students.

Yet, as they grew older, they realized that they could not dismiss their differences, particularly their non-white physical differences. Growing up, they became increasingly aware that, regardless of their efforts, they would not be accepted as completely "American." This realization led them to accept their bicultural and non-white ethnic and racial backgrounds. Although the acceptance of their ethnic and racial backgrounds initially was painful, they grew more comfortable and confident with their ethnic identity over time. Recalling the moment she observed in a school hallway mirror how physically different she appeared from her classmates, Michelle describes the painful, but positive transformation of her ethnic identity:

> This incident served as a catalyst for painful soul searching and marked the beginning of an inner journey toward greater self-acceptance. Until that point, my struggle with ethnic identity and the denial of my Koreanness had been largely unconscious, but I began to see that the cost of my denial was too high a price. I accepted the reality of my biculturality, that I was inevitably both Korean and American, and that I had a unique opportunity to learn from both cultures, rather than rejecting one for the other. For the first time since that moment in the second grade when I wished that I was a blond-haired girl with the last name Smith, I began to see my bicultural experience as a blessing and an opportunity rather than a curse.

The formation of ethnic and racial identities greatly influenced the essayists' academic interests and career choices. Though several essayists were pressured by their parents to study medicine or law, they turned to the social sciences, humanities, and the arts in their struggle to define their ethnic identity. Samod abandoned her plans to go to medical school and took courses in Asian studies. Diana spent a year studying painting at a university near Calcutta to learn more about her roots. Michelle, meanwhile, wrote, "My overriding motivation to pursue a career in psychology is directly related to my bicultural experiences." She said that she wanted to help to bridge the gap between first- and second-generation Koreans. Cathy's decision to volunteer for work at a refugee service agency in Denver, and her graduate training in social work were similarly related to the formation of her ethnic and racial identity as a Vietnamese and Asian-American.

While most essayists have strong ethnic identity, they have varying degrees of racial identity. Whereas their ethnic identity is related closely to the ethnic subculture practised in their parents' home and in their parents' home country, their racial identity stems from the consciousness of their non-white status in a white-dominant society. To state it alternatively, their racial identity is related closely to the perception that as non-whites they are not fully accepted in American society. Their non-white racial identity is expressed as either pan-Asian or Third World (people of colour). Throughout his essay, Michael used the terms "Asian-American identity" and "Asian Americans" without ever referring to Filipino-American identity or Filipino-Americans; this suggests a strong Asian-American identity, but a weak ethnic identity. Two Korean-Americans, Michelle and Nicole, and one Chinese-American, William, have a moderate level of pan-Asian identity, but their culturally based ethnic identity is much stronger. Michelle, Nicole, and William also had close friends of other East-Asian backgrounds and are affiliated with pan-Asian organizations.

Samod and Diana, both of South Asian descent, said that they felt little affinity with East Asians, such as Chinese-, Korean-, or Japanese-Americans. Samod seemed to find a more common ground with African-Americans than with East Asians. Giving up her dream of becoming a medical doctor, she chose to work for a predominantly black school district in New Jersey. Her identity as a person of colour developed partly through the realization that South Asians were discriminated against and subject to racial violence because of their skin colour in ways similar to African-Americans. "Even with their economic privilege, Indians remain dark-skinned and vulnerable to the vagaries of cultural and ethnic discrimination," she wrote. Her identification as a person of colour was also influenced by the history of British colonization in India. Remember that the Civil Rights leader Martin Luther King Jr. adopted the technique of non-violence employed by Mahatma Gandhi in the Indian independence movement against the British colonial government. William and Nicole also expressed some kinship with African-Americans and Latinos because of their non-white status. After graduating from college, William created a conflict resolution program for African-American and Latino students in Harlem. Nicole, meanwhile, as a teenager, participated in NAACP-led marches for school desegregation and worked to improve conditions for migrant farm workers through the United Farm Workers organized by Cesar Chavez.

The absence of Asian role models also fostered identification with other minorities. Samod said she was greatly influenced by the writings of Toni Morrison, the Nobel Prize–winning author who has written in rich detail about black experiences in the United States. Nicole and William also mentioned black and Latino role models. William wrote:

> Growing up, I did not have any Asian-American role models aside from my parents. In the ridicule and prejudice that I fought in grade school, I turned instead to African-Americans like Medgar Evers and Martin Luther King Jr. and Latinos like Cesar Chavez for strength and guidance.

Asian immigrants are generally prejudiced against African-Americans and tend to feel they have far more commonalities with white Americans than with African-Americans (Jo 1992; Min 1996; Weitzer 1997; Hochschild 1998). Yet several of the second-generation essayists identify more with African-Americans and Latinos than with whites and adopt a moderate level of racial identification as a person of colour. In terms of their socio-economic status, American-born Asian-Americans are more similar to white Americans than to other minority groups. However, a significant proportion of American-born Asian-American professionals as well as many lower-class Asian-Americans may align with disadvantaged minority groups in political issues. This makes real the possibility of a "rainbow coalition."

Most of the women have varying degrees of gender identity, in addition to their ethnic and racial identities.[2] The combination of these three identities—ethnic, racial, and gender—significantly affects the women's world view, political identity, and overall behaviour and attitudes. The women realize that their parents' home country is far more patriarchal than the United States, and this alone is sufficient reason why they cannot live there permanently. Yet they are also aware that women have disadvantages compared to men in the United States as well. Thus, for women, their gender identity is tied inseparably to their ethnic and racial identities, making them feel doubly handicapped as minority members and women in a white, male-dominated society. Samod clearly expressed this Third-World, feminist political ideology in her essay:

> With this growing awareness of my invisibility, I became much more insistent on being taken on my own terms, as a woman and as an Indian. My friendship with women became much more important to me, and became a space in which to explore my sense of gender identity. This political identity created a lot of conflict with Clay. It became increasingly difficult to understand each other across the enormous differences between how we looked at the world, as man and woman, as Anglo-American and Indian-American, as white and non-white.

Although most essayists born or raised in the United States did not feel fully accepted by American society, they felt more comfortable living in the United States than in their parents' home country or in another foreign country. Interestingly, many essayists grew more conscious of their American identity while travelling abroad. During her visit to India, Samod said that she "became more conscious for the first time of how truly American I am." Diana recollected that "in Japan, I found myself identifying as an American more than I had done before." Cathy, too, came to realize the American side of her identity while teaching English in Japan.

CONCLUSION

The central themes that emerge in the 15 personal narratives cannot be applied to young Asian-Americans as a whole because the number of essays is too small and the authors of the essays are all highly educated Asian-American professionals. Nevertheless, the essays provide important theoretical and practical implications for understanding the ethnicity of newly emerging 1.5- and second-generation Asian-American professionals in general and the formation of their ethnic and racial identities in particular. The major findings from the essays are especially important, because no previous study has examined in detail various aspects of ethnicity on the part of 1.5- and second-generation Asian-American professionals who are children of post-1965 Asian immigrants.

Given available information now, the essayists' experiences with unwelcome remarks and physical harassment in their pre-college school years are not surprising. Yet due to the model minority image, policy-makers, teachers, and even parents seem to be unaware of the harsh experiences that academically successful Asian-American children suffer. By virtue of the phenomenal increase in the Asian-American population and an increasing emphasis on multicultural education, Asian-American school children today may have experiences that are more positive and rewarding than most of our essayists. Yet, as noted in the literature review, many Asian immigrant children and even native-born Asian-American children still encounter rejection and physical harassment from white and black students.

All the essayists born or raised in the United States attended prestigious universities and attained careers in the mainstream economy. According to classical assimilation theory, these younger Asian-American professionals should be acculturated into the mainstream American culture without retaining much of their ethnic subculture. However, many essayists were characterized by strong bicultural experiences. The development of strong bicultural orientations was assisted by the multicultural and cosmopolitan environment of American colleges, as well as the transnational ties maintained with their parents' home countries. This seems to support the view that post-1965 immigrants, whether Asian or not, have advantages over earlier white immigrants in transmitting their cultural traditions to their children (Massey 1995; Min 1999).

The finding that most 1.5- and second-generation essayists experienced psychological conflicts in the process of forming their ethnic identity is interesting, but not unexpected based on available knowledge. More significant findings from the essays are related to their pan-Asian and Third World racial identities. The 1.5- and second-generation essayists holding varying degrees of pan-Asian identity was expected from the bulk of literature on pan-Asian identity and solidarity reviewed at the beginning of this article. However, the essays provide important clues to patterns of pan-Asian ethnicity, not apparent in the existing pan-Asian literature. Focusing on the structural sources of pan-Asian ethnicity, such as racial lumping and anti-Asian violence, researchers have generally emphasized pan-Asian solidarity in general without specifying which particular Asian groups are most likely to band together. The essays indicate that Chinese-, Japanese-, and Korean-Americans, who share similar cultural and physical characteristics, maintain more frequent social contacts. South Asians, however, may feel more kinship with African-Americans and Latinos than with these East-Asian ethnics because of their darker skin colour and their colonial past.[3]

NOTES

1   We can get information about changes in ethnic identity over different life stages through personal interviews by asking retrospective questions. But the informant usually would have difficulty responding quickly to the question of how his or her ethnic identity has changed in the course of his or her life. In a personal narrative, one can describe changes in one's ethnic and racial identities more accurately.

2   Men, too, have a less salient but significant gender identity. However, none of the five male contributors discussed his gender identity. This may have been partly because, unlike the women, we did not ask them to do so.

3   For further information about South Asians being apart from other Asian-Americans, especially from East Asians, see Kibria (1996) and Shankar and Srikanth (1998).

REFERENCES

Basch, Linda, Nina Schiller, and Christina Szanton Blanc, eds. 1994. *Nations Unbound: Transnational Projects, Postcolonial Predicaments, and Deterritorialized Nation States.* New York: Gordon and Breach Science.

Carrera, John Willshire. 1988. *New Voices: Immigrant Students in U.S. Public Schools.* Boston: National Coalition of Advocates for Students.

Cole, S.G., and M. Cole. 1954. *Minorities and American Promise.* New York: Harper and Brothers.

Collins, Patricia Hill. 1990. *Black Feminist Thought: Knowledge, Consciousness, and the Politics of Empowerment.* New York: Routledge and Chapman.

Dublin, Thomas, ed. 1996 *Becoming American Becoming Ethnic: College Students Explore Their Roots.* Philadelphia: Temple University Press.

Dunleep, Harriet Orcutt, and Sheth Sanders, 1992. "Discrimination at the Top: American-Born Asian and White Men." *Industrial Relations* 31:416–432.

Espiritu, Yen. 1992. *Asian American Panethnicity: Bridging Institutions and Identities.* Philadelphia: Temple University Press.

———. 1994. "The Intersection of Race, Ethnicity and Class: The Multiple Identities of Second-Generation Filipinos." *Identities* 1, no. 2:234–251.

———. 1997. *Asian American Women and Men: Labor, Law, and Love.* Newbury Park: Sage Publications.

Foner, Nancy. 1997. "What's New about Transnationalism? New York Immigrants Today and at the Turn of the Century." *Diaspora* 6, no. 3:355–375.

Gans, Herbert. 1992. "Second-Generation Decline: Scenarios for the Economic and Ethnic Futures for the Post-1965 American Immigrants." *Ethnic and Racial Studies* 15, no. 1:179–192.

———. 1997. "Toward a Reconciliation of 'Assimilation' and 'Pluralism': The Interplay of Acculturation and Ethnic Retention." *International Migration Review* 31, no. 4:875–892.

———. 1998. "The Possibility of a New Racial Hierarchy in the Twenty-First-Century United States." In *The Cultural Territories of Race: Black and White Boundaries,* ed. Michele Lamont, 371–396. Chicago: University of Chicago Press.

Gibson, Margaret. 1988. *Accommodation without Assimilation: Sikh Immigrant Children in an American High School.* Ithaca: Cornell University Press.

Goldberg, David Theo. 1994. *Multiculturalism: A Critical Reader.* Cambridge: Basil Blackwell.

Gordon, Milton. 1964. *Assimilation in American Life.* New York: Oxford University Press.

Hirschman, Charles, Philip Kasinitz, and Josh Dewind. 2000. *The Handbook of International Migration: The American Experience.* New York: Russell Sage Foundation.

Hochschild, Jennifer. 1998. "American Racial and Ethnic Politics in the 21st Century: A Cautious Look Ahead." *The Brookings Review* (Winter 1999):43–46.

Hong, Joanne, and Pyong Gap Min. 1999. "Ethnic Attachment among Second-Generation Korean Adolescents." *Amerasia Journal* 25, no. 1:165–180.

Hong, Maria, ed. 1993. *Growing Up Asian American: Stories of Childhood, Adolescence and Coming of Age in America, from the 1800s to the 1990s by 32 Asian American Writers.* New York: Avon Books.

Hurh, Won Moo, and Kwang Chung Kim. 1989. "The 'Success' Image of Asian Americans: Its Validity, and Its Practical and Theoretical Implications." *Ethnic and Racial Studies* 12, no. 3:512–536.

Jo, Moon H. 1992. "Korean Merchants in the Black Community: Prejudice among the Victims of Prejudice." *Ethnic and Racial Studies* 15, no. 3:395–411.

Kibria, Nazli. 1996. "Not Asian, Black or White: Reflections on South Asian Racial Identity." *Amerasia Journal* 22, no. 2:77–88.

———. 1997. "The Construction of 'Asian American': Reflections on Intermarriage and Ethnic Identity among Second-Generation Chinese and Korean Americans." *Ethnic and Racial Studies* 20, no. 3:523–544.

———. 1999. "College and Notions of 'Asian America': Second Generation Chinese and Korean Americans Negotiate Race and Identity." *Amerasia Journal* 25, no. 1:29–52.

Kim, Elaine, and Eui-Young Yu. 1996. *East to America: Korean American Life Stories.* New York: The New Press.

Kim, Sang-Hoon. 1996. "Discovering My Ethnic Roots." In *Becoming American, Becoming Ethnic: College Students Explore Their Roots,* ed. Thomas Dublin, 143–148. Philadelphia: Temple University Press.

Kitano, Harry. 1976. *Japanese Americans: The Evolution of a Subculture.* Englewood Cliffs: Prentice Hall.

Laguerre, Michael S. 1998. *Diasporic Citizenship: Haitian Americans in Transnational America.* New York: St. Martin's Press.

Lee, Sharon, and Marilyn Fernandez. 1998. "Trends in Asian American Racial/Ethnic Intermarriage: A Comparison of 1980 and 1990 Census Data." *Sociological Perspectives* 41, no. 2:323–342.

Lee, Stacy. 1996. *Unravelling the Model Minority Stereotype: Listening to Asian American Youth.* New York: Teachers College Press.

Lieberson, Stanley, and Mary Waters. 1988. *From Many Strands: Ethnic and Racial Groups in Contemporary America.* New York: Russell Sage Foundation.

Lowe, Lisa. 1996. *Immigrant Acts: On Asian American Cultural Politics.* Durham: Duke University Press.

Massey, Douglas. 1995. "The New Immigration and Ethnicity in the United States." *Population and Development Review* 21, no. 4:631–652.

Min, Pyong Gap. 1993. "Korean Immigrants' Marital Patterns and Marital Adjustment." In *Family Ethnicity: Strengths and Diversity,* ed. Hariette McAdoo, 185–204. Newbury Park: Sage Publications.

———. 1996. *Caught in the Middle: Korean Merchants in America's Multiethnic Cities.* Berkeley, CA: University of California Press.

———. 1998. *Changes and Conflicts: Korean Immigrant Families in New York.* Boston: Allen and Bacon.

———. 1999. "A Comparison of Contemporary and Turn-of-the-Century Immigrants in Inter-Generational Mobility and Cultural Transmission." *Journal of American Ethnic History* 19, no. 3:65–94.

Min, Pyong Gap, and Youna Choi. 1993. "Ethnic Attachment among Korean-American High School Students." *Korea Journal of Population and Development* 22, no. 2:167–179.

Omi, Michael, and Howard Winant. 1986. *Racial Formation in the United States: From the 1960s to the 1980s.* New York: Routledge.

Portes, Alejandro, ed. 1996. *The New Second Generation.* New York: Russell Sage Foundation.

Portes, Alejandro, and Ruben Rumbaut. 1996. *Immigrant America: A Portrait,* 2nd ed. Berkeley: University of California Press.

Portes, Alejandro, and Richard Schauffler. 1994. "Language and the Second Generation Bilingualism Yesterday and Today." *International Migration Review* 28, no. 4:640–661.

Portes, Alejandro, and Min Zhou. 1993. "The New Second-Generation: Segmented Assimilation and Its Variants." *The Annals of the American Academy of Political and Social Science* 530:74–96.

Rosenblum, Karen. 1996. *The Meaning of Difference: American Constructions of Race, Sex, Social Class and Sexual Orientation.* New York: McGraw-Hill Company.

Rosenthal, Erich. 1960. "Acculturation without Assimilation." *American Journal of Sociology* 55, no. 2:275–288.

Rumbaut, Ruben. 1991. "The Agony of Exile: A Study of the Migration and Adaptation of Indochinese Refugee Adults and Children." In *Refugee Children: Theory, Research, and Services,* ed. Frederick L. Ahearn Jr. and Jean Athey, 53–91. Baltimore: Johns Hopkins University Press.

———. 1994. "The Crucible Within: Ethnic Identity, Self-Esteem, and Segmented Assimilation among Children of Immigrants." *International Migration Review* 28, no. 4:748–794.

Rumbaut, Ruben, and Kenji Ima. 1988. *The Adaptation of South Asian Refugee Youth: A Comparative Study.* Final Report to the U.S. Department of Health and Human Services. Office of Refugee Resettlement.

Rumbaut, Ruben, and Cornelius Wayne, eds. 1995. *California's Immigrant Children: Theory, Research, and Implications for Educational Policy.* San Diego: University of California at San Diego.

Rubin-Dorsky, J., and Shelly Fisher Fishkin. 1996. *People of the Book: Thirty Scholars Reflect on Their Jewish Identity.* Madison: University of Wisconsin Press.

Schiller, Nina, Linda Basch, and Christina Szanton-Blanc. 1994. *Toward a Transnational Perspective on Migration: Race, Class, Ethnicity, and Nationalism Reconsidered.* New York: New York Academy of Science.

Shankar, Lavina Dhingra, and Rajini Srikanth, eds. 1998. *A Part, Yet Apart: South Asians in Asian America.* Philadelphia: Temple University Press.

Shinagawa, Larry Hajime, and Gin Yong Pang. 1996. "Asian American Panethnicity and Intermarriage." *Amerasia Journal* 22, no. 2:127–152.

Takagi, Dana. 1994. "Post-Civil Rights Politics and Asian-American Identity: Admissions and Higher Education." In *Race,* ed. Steven Gregory and Roger Sanjek, 229–242. New Brunswick: Rutgers University Press.

Tang, Joyce. 1993. "The Career Attainment of Caucasian and Asian Engineers." *Sociological Quarterly* 34:467–496.

———. 1997. "The Model Minority Thesis Revisited: Evidence from the Science and Engineering Field." *Journal of Applied Behavioral Science* 33:291–315.

Thai, Hung. 1999. "Splitting Thins in Half Is White: Conceptions of Family and Friendship, and the Formation of Ethnic Identity among Second Generation Vietnamese Americans." *Amerasia Journal* 25, no. 1:53–88.

Tuan, Mia. 1999. *Forever Foreigners or Honorary Whites?: The Asian Ethnic Experience Today.* New Brunswick: Rutgers University Press.

U.S. Commission of Civil Rights. 1992. *Civil Rights Issue Facing Asian Americans in the 1990s.* Washington: U.S. Government Printing Office.

Warner, W.L., and Leo Srole. 1945. *The Social System of American Groups.* New Haven: Yale University Press.

Waters, Mary. 1990. *Ethnic Options: Choosing Identities in America.* Berkeley: University of California Press.

———. 1994. "Ethnic and Racial Identities of Second-Generation Black Immigrants in New York City." *International Migration Review* 28, no. 4:795–820.

Wei, William. 1993. *The Asian American Movement.* Philadelphia: Temple University Press.

Weitzer, Ronald. 1997. "Racial Prejudice among Korean Merchants in African American Neighborhoods." *The Sociological Quarterly* 38, no. 3:587–606.

Wolfe, Diane. 1997. "Family Secrets: Transnational Struggles among Children of Filipino Immigrants." *Sociological Perspectives* 40, no. 3:457–482.

Wong, Morrison. 1989. "A Look at Intermarriage among Chinese in the United States in 1980." *Sociological Perspectives* 32, no. 1:87–107.

Wong, Sauline Cynthia. 1993. *Reading Asian American Literature: From Necessity to Extravagance.* Princeton: Princeton University Press.

Zhou, Min, and Carl Bankston III. 1998. *Growing Up American: How Vietnamese Children Adapt to Life in the United States.* New York: Russell Sage.

Zhou, Min, and Yoshinori Kamo. 1994. "An Analysis of Earnings Patterns for Chinese, Japanese, and Non-Hispanic Whites in the United States." *The Sociological Quarterly* 35, no. 4:581–602.

QUESTIONS FOR CRITICAL THOUGHT

CHAPTER 9 BY MARY C. WATERS

1. What does Waters mean when she argues that ethnicity is primarily a social phenomenon and not a biological one?
2. Explain what Waters means when she argues that white ethnics can have ethnicity without cost, but people of colour pay the price for their ethnic identity.
3. Do you think that racial minorities have the option of a symbolic ethnicity in Canada? Think of different ways to support your argument.

CHAPTER 10 BY KERRY ANN ROCKQUEMORE

1. What social factors influence the construction and maintenance of biracial identity?
2. Differentiate between "biracial identity" as a border identity, a protean identity, a transcendent identity, and a traditional identity.
3. Think of different ways in which individuals' social status and appearance may both affect their access to different types of social networks and influence their interactions within those networks.

CHAPTER 11 BY MINELLE MAHTANI

1. Discuss how the policy of multiculturalism has both impeded and facilitated senses of belonging for mixed-race women in Canada.

2. Why was multicultural policy not seen by mixed-race women as an effective strategy to fight racism?
3. Discuss the key tenets of multicultural policy, as well as various programs that have been designed to achieve the objectives of the policy.

CHAPTER 12 BY PYONG GAP MIN AND ROSE KIM

1. Discuss the importance of structural factors in facilitating the retention of cultural traditions by contemporary immigrants.
2. Why do children of contemporary immigrants have an advantage over children of earlier immigrants in retaining their cultural traditions?
3. Discuss the structural factors that affect the ethnic and racial identities of second-generation Asian-Americans as compared to white ethnics.

FURTHER READING

Fetcher, Anne-Meike. "The 'Other' Stares Back: Experiencing Whiteness in Jakarta." *Ethnography* 6, no. 1 (2005):87–103.

This recently published study investigates the experiences and significance of being white in a non-white society. Fetcher presents interview data from her study of white Euro-American expatriates working in Jakarta, Indonesia. Fetcher is particularly interesting on how white American business people negotiate whiteness in non-white societies.

Hall, Stuart. "Negotiating Caribbean Identities." *New Left Review* 209 (1995):3–14.

In this lecture, Hall argues that the negotiation of cultural identity is always between the specific roots of identity and the future to be constructed. For Hall, the subject of cultural identity is a matter of representation and the historical play of power/knowledge; it is not the "rediscovery" of an essential past. Indeed, as we discussed in the introduction to this text, Hall seeks an ethical politics of becoming rather than of being.

Kelly, Jennifer. *Under the Gaze: Learning to Be Black in White Society*. Halifax: Fernwood, 1998.

Jennifer Kelly's book examines perceptions and experiences of black high-school students in Canada. She documents the importance of gender relations, peer relations, sources of identity, and popular culture in black students' identity formation.

Said, Edward. *Orientalism*. New York: Vintage, 1978.

Edward Said's classic in post-colonial studies examines Western hegemonic assumptions, perceptions, and beliefs about the Orient. He documents historical and contemporary examples of Orientalism, and critically questions foundational Occidental assumptions about the Orient.

St. Louis, Brett. "Post Race/Post Politics? Activist Intellectualism and the Reification of Race." *Ethnic and Racial Studies* 25, no. 4 (2002):652–675.

This paper is theoretical in nature. St. Louis critically assesses sociological approaches that reject the race concept. He argues that although the dangers of reifying the race concept are significant and real, there are times when race as a situational identity can be used as a source of collective resistance to racism.

MULTICULTURALISM, POLITICS, AND BELONGING

There is a very clear and powerful discourse about cultural identity, especially in the West. Indeed most of us have lived through, and are still living through an exercise in the definition and defence of a particular kind of British cultural identity.... Histories come and go, peoples come and go, situations change, but somewhere down there is throbbing the culture to which we all belong ... something solid, something fixed, something stabilized, around which we can organize our identities and our sense of belongingness. (Hall 1995, 4)

The politics of ethno-racial identification, and the politics of inclusion and national belonging, have stimulated debate among sociologists on a number of salient issues. Sociologists have posed many, often interrelated, questions pertaining to multiculturalism, politics, and belonging. What, for example, are the social and political implications for societies characterized by increasingly diverse populations? What economic, social, and political issues arise from the diversification of the population? What public policies are most appropriate and desirable to "manage" diversity? What social policies are able to facilitate or contribute to the realization of social justice, democratic citizenship, and national unity? Does multiculturalism and the politics of identity contribute to or exacerbate social fragmentation and undermine national identity and unity? What is the impact of globalization on national identity? And what is the future of identity?

To bring greater coherence to these related but multi-faceted questions, it is useful to consider the general analytical assumptions of two opposing perspectives that have been used to explain ethno-racial cleavages and material inequalities in the context of Canadian multiculturalism: the assimilationist perspective and the structuralist perspective. The assimilationist perspective is expressed in various motivational hypotheses such as the "immigrant analogy." This version of the assimilationist perspective posits an alleged similarity between the historical experience of non-traditional European immigrants and the contemporary situation of non-European immigrant groups. A comparison is made between "white ethnics" and "racial minorities," respectively, and it is argued that visible or racial minorities will follow the patterns of white ethnic groups with regards to assimilation and social and economic mobility. It is argued that, given enough time, visible minority groups will integrate into mainstream institutional life in Canada, just as their Southern and Eastern European counterparts did over the past 30 years. Racial groups may have to endure discrimination and prejudice for a somewhat longer period, so the argument goes, but their eventual incorporation into the mainstream is inevitable. The assimilationist perspective, therefore, attributes social and economic inequalities to different degrees of assimilation, and the solution to ethno-racial inequality is found in patterns of cultural assimilation and social integration—the so-called "melting pot."

By maintaining a focus on the inability or incapacity of some groups to assimilate, criticism has been levelled against advocates of the assimilationist perspective on the grounds that they locate the causes of social inequality in racial groups' fundamental or intrinsic makeup. This assumption, critics charge, ignores the structural and ideological dimensions of social inequality in Canadian society. Structuralists challenge assimilationists on ideological, political, and empirical grounds, and they criticize the assimilationists for wrongly assuming that equal opportunities are available for all Canadians in Canadian institutions and structures. The key to understanding and explaining social inequality, structuralists argue, is to address how institutional constraints, labour market segmentation, and the persistence of systems of racial, class, and gender differentiation restrict social mobility for diverse racial groups.

Adherence to divergent theoretical and conceptual perspectives influences what public policy initiatives are endorsed to alleviate patterns of social inequality. Canada's multicultural policy is one major policy area that has received considerable attention. Enunciated in 1971, the policy was, among other things, intended to assist cultural groups to retain and foster identity and to overcome barriers to full participation in Canadian society. The purpose of the policy, according to Prime Minister Pierre Trudeau, was "to break down discriminatory attitudes and cultural jealousies ... [and] form the base of a society which is based on fair play for all" (Canada 1971, 8545). Various programs were established to achieve these goals, including: a federal ministry responsible for multiculturalism, a Multiculturalism Sector in the Department of the Secretary of State, a national strategy on race relations to develop and implement programs to eliminate racial discrimination in Canadian institutions, and a proclamation of an Act in 1988 for the Preservation and Enhancement of Multiculturalism in Canada.

Whether levels of racial discrimination and prejudice are less prevalent today than in the past remains a topic of sociological debate. Despite the intention of multicultural policy to "break down discriminatory attitudes," critics have argued that "the failure of multiculturalism ... is not so much a sound policy mismanaged. Rather it is a failure to solve non-cultural problems with cultural solutions. Issues of ethnic inequality and racial discrimination have political and economic roots in the history and social institutions of Canada, and their solutions lie beyond what multiculturalism can offer" (Li and Bolaria 1983; see also Bolaria and Li 1988). But Canadian multicultural policy is under attack on other grounds as well. The policy is criticized for "ghettoizing" minorities; for its negative impact on the Canadian social fabric, national unity, and national identity; and for further fragmenting identities and belongings (see for example Bibby 1990; Bissoondath 1994). And still others explain multiculturalism as a bold experiment, as one of the hallmarks of Canadian identity, as a model to other countries, and a mechanism through which to engage Canadian diversity (Fleras and Kunz 2001; Fleras and Elliot 2002). The reading passages in this section address these and related controversies, conflicts, and debates.

SECTION READINGS: HUMAN RIGHTS, NEW IDENTITIES, SOCIAL JUSTICE, AND THE FUTURE

The first reading passage, authored by Charles Ungerleider, examines the development of policies and practices pertaining to immigration, citizenship, and multiculturalism in Canada, as well as policy developments related to language and human rights. Underleider argues that human rights policy development has contributed to the establishment of a social justice infrastructure in Canadian society. He begins with a brief description of Canada's discriminatory immigration policies and practices leading into the 1960s, highlighting the discriminatory provisions of the *Immigrant Act* and how they have changed over time. These changes led to an increased number of non-traditional immigrants coming to Canada, he explains, and he provides a brief history of citizenship policies and practices. The main focus of his discussion, however, is the development of the social justice infrastructure, including the development of human rights legislation and the promotion of linguistic equality through proclamation of the *Official Languages Act 1969*.

For Underleider, multiculturalism forms a major part of Canada's social justice infrastructure. Not only does he describe the enunciation of multicultural policy and its objectives in the reading, but he also discusses various programs and initiatives to promote the policy at federal, provincial, and municipal levels. He concludes his analysis by evaluating the impact of Canada's social justice infrastructure on patterns of social inequality. While the evidence of the adequacy of the social justice infrastructure in ensuring equality in schooling, employment, income and, occupational attainment points to mixed successes, Ungerleider nevertheless argues that recent policies that sanction and support social justice at all levels are positive steps. He maintains that human rights politics should, in time, create equality among Canadians, a condition central to democratic citizenship. He nevertheless cautions about obstacles to the future evolution of this infrastructure, the most serious of which is the "new" conservatism.

The second reading passage, authored by Rhoda E. Howard-Hassmann, discusses processes of identity formation among English-speaking, non-Aboriginal Canadians. Howard-Hassmann argues that there is such a thing as an ethnic Canadian identity. While multiculturalism encourages Canadians to retain their ancestral ethnic heritage, she explains, most Canadians—foreign- and Canadian-born—become ethnic Canadians. She argues, however, that multiculturalism, far from promoting fragmentation and divisions among Canada's multiple cultural groups, tends to promote integration and unity.

Howard-Hassmann conceptualizes the debate about the effects of multiculturalism on ethnic and national identity/unity in terms of "liberal" and "illiberal" multiculturalism. She argues that the current policy of liberal multiculturalism fosters or encourages private, individual choices of identity and, paradoxically, also fosters or encourages the formation of Canadian identity. Illiberal multiculturalism, she explains, holds out for stronger identification with ancestral groups at the expense of reduced identification with Canada. Illiberal multiculturalists encourage the state to recognize the fixed, unchanging nature of ethnic identity among Canadians, and they argue that policy must ensure that individuals identify themselves as members of their ancestors' collectivities. Liberal multiculturalists, conversely, conceptualize multiculturalism as a resource that individuals may or may not use. It is not, they contend, a policy to which individuals must conform, because there are no fixed, primordial groups. Official Canadian multicultural policy is liberal in orientation, which makes ethnic and racial identities, religions, ethnic, or cultural affiliation, and identification with ancestral community, a matter of individual choice.

Nancy Fraser is the author of the third reading passage. Fraser, an internationally recognized political philosopher, provides an insightful conceptual analysis, differentiating the material politics of redistribution from the cultural politics of recognition. Fraser distinguishes between two ideal-typical forms of injustice. The first form of injustice is socio-economic injustice, rooted in the political-economic structure of the society. The second form of injustice is cultural or symbolic injustice, rooted in social patterns of representation, interpretation, and communication. Examples of the former include labour exploitation, economic marginalization, and material deprivation. Examples of the latter include cultural domination, non-recognition, and disrespect. Both forms of injustice are, for Fraser, rooted in societal policies and practices that disadvantage certain social groups, and both forms of injustice are intertwined and mutually constitutive.

Despite their entwinements, however, Fraser maintains an analytical distinction between economic and cultural injustices, and distinguishes distinct forms of remedies for each ideal- typical form of injustice. For the ideal-typical mode of collectivity whose existence is rooted in economic structure, she argues that the mode of remedy is political-economic redistribution. For instance, overcoming class exploitation requires restructuring the political economy of the country. At the other end of the spectrum, for the ideal-typical mode of collectivity rooted wholly in culture, she argues that the remedy requires systems of cultural recognition. For instance, in the case of despised sexuality derived from an unjust cultural-valuational structure, the remedy is equal recognition, equal dignity, and respect.

But matters become murkier and more complex when we move away from these idealized extremes—which, however abstracted from their empirical manifestations, help us to conceptualize or think about sources of social injustice—and consider hybrid collectivities that combine features of exploited classes and despised sexualities. Fraser refers to these collectivities as "bivalent." Bivalent collectivities combine both the political-economic structure and the cultural-valuational structure. She uses gender and race as examples of bivalent modes to address the empirical dilemmas of social justice. Redressing gender and racial injustice, she explains, would require both redistribution and recognition remedies. The problem, however, is that they pull in opposite directions. As she explains, the logic of redistribution is to put gender out of business, but the logic of recognition is to valorize gender specificity, that is, to simultaneously abolish gender differentiation and to valorize gender specificity. An analogous dilemma arises in the struggle against racism: the logic of redistribution is to put race out of business and to abolish race as a culturally meaningful signifier, but the logic of recognition is to valorize race specificity and to enhance its power as a cultural marker of identity. As bivalent collectivities, race and gender are implicated simultaneously in both the politics of redistribution and recognition.

Fraser concludes by distinguishing two broad remedies to injustices that cut across the redistribution–recognition divide: affirmation and transformation. Providing illustrative material, she shows how each type of remedy operates in regard to both redistribution and recognition. Based on this distinction, Fraser reformulates the redistribution–recognition dilemma in a form that is more amenable to resolution. She concludes: "For both gender and race, the scenario that best finesses the redistribution–recognition dilemma is socialism in the economy plus deconstruction in the culture. But for this scenario to be psychologically and politically feasible requires that people be weaned from their attachment to current cultural constructions of their interests and identities" (p. 90).

The section closes with a reading passage authored by Stuart Hall. Hall argues that old identities, which previously provided individuals with a stable anchorage in the social world, are in decline. The decline of stable identities, he explains, fragment the modern individual and "decentre the subject." What he means by the subject, or subject positions, is the way in which individuals come to define themselves and to make sense of their own subjectivity through shared identifications or social positions such as "black," "Canadian," or "middle class." For Hall, the decentring of the subject constitutes a "crisis of identity," and he explains the crisis of identity in terms of wider transformations taking place in the cultural landscapes of modern societies—landscapes that once gave individuals a firm, centred sense of self.

To better explain these transformative modern forces, Hall distinguishes different conceptions of identity by positing three subject positions: the Enlightenment, sociological, and postmodern subject. The Enlightenment and sociological subject, Hall explains, correspond to a conception of identity that is formed in the interaction between self and society. Identity bridges the gap between the individual and society—it "stitches" the subject to social structure, stabilizing both subjects and their culture world and making both unified and predictable. Today, however, unified and stable identities are shifting. This shift produces, according to Hall, a new postmodern subject. The postmodern subject has no fixed, essential, or permanent identity. Identity, as Hall puts it, becomes a "moveable feast." The contemporary postmodern subject assumes different identities at different times, and it is entirely possible that a single person's identities may come into conflict.

Finally, Hall addresses the different ways that "fragmented subjects" are placed in terms of cultural identities, and he addresses the question: "How are national cultural identities being affected or displaced by the process of globalization?" He argues that national cultures are one of the principal sources of cultural identity. These identities, however, are not inborn, but rather are formed and transformed in relation to representation. For instance, one only knows what it means to be "English" because of the way "Englishness" has come to be represented as a set of meanings (or a discursive formation) by English national culture. National cultures construct identities by producing meanings about the nation with which one can identify. While national cultures constitute a discursive device that represents difference in terms of unity or identity, the forces of globalization are producing a "pluralization" of national cultures and national identities. Globalization contests and dislocates centred or "closed" national identities, and this decentring process produces a variety of possibilities for identification. The general impact of globalization, however, remains contradictory: some identities gravitate toward "tradition" in the context of globalization, while others gravitate toward "translation." The oscillation between tradition and translation, says Hall, is becoming more evident on a global canvas.

REFERENCES

Bibby, R.W. 1990. *Mosaic Madness: Pluralism without a Cause*. Toronto: Stoddart.

Bissoondath, N. 1994. *Selling Illusions: The Cult of Multiculturalism in Canada*. Toronto: Penguin.

Bolaria, B. Singh. 1983. "Dominant Perspectives and non-White Minorities." In *Racial Minorities in Multicultural Canada*, ed. Peter S. Li and B. Singh Bolaria, 157–169. Toronto: Garamond Press.

Bolaria, B. Singh, and Peter S. Li. 1988. *Racial Oppression in Canada*. Toronto: Garamond Press.

Canada. 1971. House of Commons. *Debates*. Ottawa. (8 October).

Fleras, A., and J. Elliott. 2002. *Engaging Diversity in Canada*. Toronto: Nelson Thompson Learning.

Fleras, A., and J. Kunz. 2001. *Media and Minorities: Representing Diversity in Multicultural Canada*. Toronto: Thompson Educational Publishing.

Hall, Stuart. 1995. "Negotiating Caribbean Identities." *New Left Review* 209:3–14.

Li, Peter S., and B. Singh Bolaria, eds. 1983. *Racial Minorities in Multicultural Canada*. Toronto: Garamond Press.

IMMIGRATION, MULTICULTURALISM, AND CITIZENSHIP
THE DEVELOPMENT OF THE CANADIAN SOCIAL JUSTICE INFRASTRUCTURE

CHARLES S. UNGERLEIDER

INTRODUCTION

For much of Canadian history, there was little concern among policy-makers about the discriminatory treatment of immigrants, minorities, Native peoples, French-Canadians, and women. But, that pattern of discrimination began to reverse when Canada signed the United Nations' Charter in 1948. During the past 40 years Canada has begun constructing an infrastructure that supports the development of the socio-political and socio-economic conditions necessary for democratic citizenship.

In its brief history, Canada has seen many changes in the nature of the policies and practices associated with immigration, citizenship and, most recently, multiculturalism. Although changes in policy or practice in any one of these areas have implications for the others, relatively little attention has been paid to the relations among them. This chapter examines the policies and practices associated with immigration, citizenship, and multiculturalism as well as those concerned with language and human rights, arguing that, in their development, they have contributed to the establishment of a social justice infrastructure for Canadian society. The chapter asserts that social justice will be substantially enhanced by attempts to achieve confluence among the policies.

IMMIGRATION: POLICIES AND PRACTICES

From the time of earliest European settlement to the present, survival has been a dominant theme for Canadians. Canadians have struggled to establish and maintain community in a territory that is vast and on a landscape that is harsh. The creation of Canada itself was difficult. Forging unity among regions with vastly different interests was an act of uncommon political compromise; maintaining it has been no less difficult. Confronted daily by the proximity of its southern neighbour, Canada has walked a fine line between resisting the U.S. way of life and being engulfed by it.

Notwithstanding the opinion of its Native peoples, Canada would not have survived if it were not for immigrants. The Canadian state was forged in 1867 by immigrants from Britain and France and their offspring. Canada's growth and development as a nation is also closely linked with immigration. The Canadian railroads, themselves key features in the country's unification, could not have been built without the labour of immigrant Chinese workers.

Throughout its history, Canada has often used immigrants to fill national needs while ignoring their rights.

Next to Canada's Native peoples, the Chinese may have been the recipients of the most overtly discriminatory treatment in Canadian history. Many Chinese entered Canada during the latter half of the 19th century as workers in canning factories and lumber mills, as domestic labourers, and as railroad workers. Once the railroad was completed and Chinese labour was no longer as necessary as it had been, the Government of Canada began to pass a series of laws restricting the immigration and activities of the Chinese.

The *Chinese Immigration Act* of 1885 placed a $50 head tax on every Chinese immigrant wishing to enter Canada as a means of "restricting and regulating Chinese Immigration into Canada." In 1900 the head tax was raised to $100 and, by 1903, to $500 (*Chinese Immigration Act* 1900, 1903). In 1923, the government passed another *Chinese Immigration Act* barring the entry of all Chinese except students, merchants, and children born in Canada of Chinese ancestry, diplomats, and people travelling to other destinations. As a consequence of this legislation, fewer than 50 Chinese immigrated to Canada between 1923 and 1947 when the Act was repealed.

Similar treatment was accorded people of Indian origin. The 1908 *Act to Amend the Immigration Act* allowed the government to prevent entry to Canada of any immigrant if he or she did not come to Canada by a continuous journey from the country of origin. Though it made no mention of people from India, the Act effectively limited immigration from that point of origin since the only steamship company that provided continuous passage from India was "persuaded" by the Canadian government not to issue tickets to Canada. In the year preceding the passing of the Act, approximately 2 500 Indian immigrants entered Canada. The following year there were only 6.

Discriminatory Canadian immigration policies contributed to the tragic fate of European Jewry in the Holocaust. Between 1933 and 1945 many Jews sought refuge from the persecution of the Nazis. During that period more than 200 000 Jewish refugees entered the United States, 70 000 found refuge in Britain, and 50 000 were accepted in Argentina. During the same period, Canada accepted fewer than 5 000 Jews. Historians Abella and Troper (1982) appraised Canada's performance both during and after the Second World War in their book *None Is Too Many*. Their conclusion was that Canada had arguably the worst record for providing sanctuary to European Jewry of all refugee-receiving nations.

After the Japanese attack on Pearl Harbor, the Canadian government issued orders requiring the relocation, internment, property seizure, and deportation of people of Japanese ancestry. The Order-in-Council (Administrative Orders 40–46, 1942) requiring the relocation was passed under provisions of the *War Measures Act*, which gave the government the power to arrest, detain, exclude, or deport persons when it was "necessary or advisable for the security, defence, peace, order, or welfare of Canada."

Although Canadian immigration policy discriminated against certain groups, immigration of favoured groups was encouraged.

Immigration from European sources diminished in part because economic opportunities had improved at home. As European immigration declined, immigration from Africa, Asia, Central and South America, and the Caribbean increased.

Changes in immigration have been accompanied by changes in the ethnic composition of Canada.

CITIZENSHIP: POLICIES AND PRACTICES

Writers concerned with democratic theory sometimes distinguish between two kinds of citizenship. One is the participatory or *civic* conception of democratic citizenship; the other is the representative or *civil* conception. The former, attributed as flowing from Rousseau, sees democratic citizenship as a "way of life" in which equals define and pursue commonly held goals. The latter, attributed to the more individualistic traditions of English legal and constitutional history, sees democratic citizenship as a legal and social status defined in terms of rights and obligations. Where the civic conception emphasizes participation as an end in itself, the civil conception sees participation primarily as a means to other ends. The civic conception places priority on the public or, at least, places the public on an equal footing with the private. In the civil, the private takes precedence over the public.

As will become increasingly clear, the development of democracy in Canada has followed the path fashioned by the civil conception of democracy. Given Canada's close ties with English legal and constitutional traditions, this is not surprising. Nor is it surprising that the development of citizenship in Canada has been more instrumental than expressive—a means to an end rather than an end in itself.

Although it can trace its origins to the political thought of the Enlightenment, the concept of Canadian citizenship has been ambiguous if not obscure. In fact, until 1947 there were no Canadian citizens. Until that time, Canadian citizens were simply British subjects residing in Canada. And, until 1976, a person regarded as a Canadian citizen was also a British subject owing allegiance to the English Crown.

The concept of Canadian citizenship has also been inextricably connected to Canadian immigration policies, the relations between the French and English, and the status of treaty Indians and Inuit. As Carty and Ward (1986) put it, "Canadian citizenship, at least in so far as the immigration and naturalization processes reveal, has been a concept rooted more in electoral need than in any highly developed principles" (p. 70). They assert that "[i]f native birth, migration, immigration policy, and naturalization law have provided the raw materials of the Canadian political citizenry, the franchise was the tool used in its making" (p. 71). Cognizant of the variations in the definition of the franchise over time, Carty and Ward assert that all laws pertaining to the franchise have had two fundamental consequences. The first is that they have defined the basic political units in Canada. The second is that they have identified "the segment of the population which was to be propitiated, solicited, organized and manipulated by practising politicians in their competition for office" (ibid.).

Throughout history, in "the slow evolution of a single national franchise, the egalitarian political ideals commonly associated with suffrage reform in a liberal democracy were always qualified in Canada" (Carty and Ward 1986, 73). It was in 1917 that some women were granted the right to vote by the federal government; the wives, sisters, and daughters of the military were permitted as part of electoral interests linked to the passage of conscription legislation for the First World War. Only in 1919 was enfranchisement extended to all women in Canada. Until the latter part of the 1940s, most Canadians who were of Chinese, Japanese, and Indian ancestry could not vote (Roy 1981). Treaty Indians and Inuit who were not veterans could not vote before 1960. Only after 1960 could Canada be said to have a universal franchise. It would take still another 22 years before the concept of citizenship represented by the political thinking of the Enlightenment would be entrenched in law in the *Canadian Charter of Rights and Freedoms*.

In reviewing the history of the extension of the franchise in Canada, Carty and Ward (1986) assert that "these activities have not been informed by any consistent notion of a Canadian citizenship nor any regular patterns institutionalizing political rights" (p. 76). One consequence of the politically expedient approach to the issue of citizenship is that consensus is lacking about the essential elements of a national political community. This is a signal to the electorate, according to Carty and Ward, that the basis of Canadian citizenship itself remains at issue.

THE DEVELOPMENT OF THE SOCIAL JUSTICE INFRASTRUCTURE

Sensitivity to discriminatory treatment of immigrants and minorities has not always been a priority of Canadian policy-makers. The mistreatment of Canada's indigenous peoples, the impositions placed upon Asian and South Asian immigrants, the anglophone domination of francophone Canadians, the denial of entry into Canada of Jewish refugees, and the internment of Japanese-Canadians are more than minor departures from fair and equitable treatment of people. However, since the Second World War and especially during the past 20 years, policies have changed to make the discriminatory treatment of minorities less permissible.

HUMAN RIGHTS

It may seem ironic that in 1944, at approximately the same time as Canadians of Japanese ancestry were interned, the Province of Ontario passed what is regarded as the first Canadian human rights statute. The Act, designed to counter the discriminatory treatment that lay behind signs proclaiming "Whites Only" or "No Jews or Dogs Allowed," prohibited the publication, display, or broadcast of material proclaiming an intention to discriminate on the basis of race or belief. Three years later, the Province of Saskatchewan enacted a Bill of Rights that, in addition to establishing freedom of speech, religion, and association, prohibited discrimination on the basis of race, creed, colour, or national or ethnic origin.

During the 1950s, several of Canada's provinces adopted legislation that permitted the launching of complaints about unfair employment practices and discrimination in the provision of accommodation. However, it was not until 1962, with the passage of the *Ontario Human Rights Code,* that the concern for human rights began to increase. The Ontario legislation prohibited discrimination based on race, religion, colour, nationality, ancestry, and place of origin. It also provided for a full-time commission responsible for handling complaints, investigation, and remediation. Today, all the Canadian provinces and territories have human rights legislation, though the strength of the legislation and the vigour with which it is applied vary greatly from province to province.

FRENCH–ENGLISH RELATIONS

As a consequence of political compromise between the French and English, the Canadian notion of nationhood was relatively open-ended and imprecisely defined. It has been argued (Smith 1981) that the basic duality of two founding nations "prevented the framing of a national idea in terms of a single creed or type" (p. 232). However, Canadian nationhood was, for most of Canadian history, distinctly more British than French.

The inequalities between French and English Canadians became a preoccupation for Canadians during the post-Second World War period. Beginning with the Royal Commission on National Development in the Arts, Letters and Sciences in 1949, the Canadian government found it necessary to recognize that there were at least two Canadas that were unequal and almost completely separate. During the same period French Canada underwent a transformation from identification based primarily upon religion to one based primarily upon language. In response to growing Quebec nationalism, the Government of Canada made modest concessions, including simultaneous translation in parliamentary proceedings (1958) and the issuance of cheques in French (1962). But these primarily symbolic gestures did not quell the increasing demands for more substantive changes.

Thus, when the Liberal government of Lester Pearson took power in 1963, it called for a Royal Commission on Bilingualism and Biculturalism "to recommend what steps would be taken to develop the Canadian Confederation on the basis of an equal partnership between the two founding races" (Waddell 1986, 88–89).

Among the many consequences of the Commission's work was recognition of the linguistic inequality between Canadians of French and English origins. In response, the government developed and proclaimed the *Official Languages Act* (1969), granting equal, official status to both English and French for all governmental purposes in the proceedings of Parliament, the judiciary, and Crown corporations. Within a brief period, the government had established a wide range of programs to promote bilingualism, including the promotion of second language instruction in each of Canada's official languages (Waddell 1986).

According to some observers, official bilingualism was instrumental in improving the climate of respect not only between the British and French in Canada, but among Canadians of other ethnic origins.

If the British had to tolerate and respect the French, and the French the British, then there was no basis for treating other ethnic or religious communities differently.... This fact, so remote in the past and so apparently unrelated to the subsequent multiculturalism policy, established the fundamental relationship that defines Canada ... namely toleration and respect for other cultural and linguistic communities. (Thorburn, quoted in Samuel 1988)

IMMIGRATION REFORM

Throughout its history, Canada has maintained tight control over the immigrants that it accepted. In contrast to Britain, where the goal of its immigration policy was to meet its obligation to Commonwealth subjects, Canada's immigration goals were related to its social and economic development. While Britain practised an "open-door" policy for all British subjects, Canada employed rigorous selection criteria.

Nevertheless, during the same period that the government was wrestling with the reformation of French-Canadian identity and the issue of equality it presented, the government began the process of removing the overtly discriminatory provisions in the *Immigration Act* of 1910. The Act permitted the government of Canada to "prohibit for a stated period or permanently, the landing in Canada ... of immigrants belonging to any race unsuited to the climate or requirements of Canada." In 1967, the government introduced a point system to tie immigrant selection more closely to the needs of the Canadian labour market. But it was not until the *Immigration Act* of 1976 was implemented in 1978 that the aforementioned discriminatory provision was removed from Canadian law.

MULTICULTURALISM

On 8 October 1971, Prime Minister Pierre Elliott Trudeau steered Canada along a controversial course by proclaiming a policy of "multiculturalism within a bilingual framework" (Canada 1971). The policy enunciated by Trudeau had four broad objectives:

1. to assist cultural groups to retain and foster their identity;
2. to assist cultural groups to overcome barriers to their full participation in Canadian society;
3. to promote creative exchanges and interchanges among all Canadian cultural groups; and
4. to assist immigrants in acquiring at least one of the official languages.

During the next year, the government created a federal ministry responsible for multiculturalism and, in 1973, the Canadian Consultative Council on Multiculturalism was formed. The multicultural policy was subjected to numerous criticisms. Among them were the ideas that the policy was:

1. a politically expedient attempt to maintain a broad base of support for the Liberal Party among European immigrants of previous generations;
2. an attempt to blunt anti-French sentiment among non-francophones angry about Canada's policy of bilingualism; and

3. a paean to pluralism in a climate that was increasingly supportive of assimilation because the welfare state and the improved legal position of immigrants had diminished the importance of ethnic solidarity and associational life (c.f. Moodley 1983).

By 1979, the Multiculturalism Sector of the Department of the Secretary of State had begun a process of consultation with major institutions in Canadian society to improve the "awareness of key groups in public life to promote a better understanding of the multicultural nature of Canadian society" (Multiculturalism Canada 1983). The Sector established a unit devoted to race relations in 1981. This unit commissioned situational reports on the state of race relations in Canada's major cities. A year later, a symposium on Race Relations and the Law was held in Vancouver to commemorate the 10th anniversary of the Canadian multiculturalism policy.

By December 1983, the Sector had established a National Strategy on Race Relations to develop and implement programs aimed at eliminating racial discrimination in Canadian institutions. The Strategy was organized around five objectives:

1. enhance the role of the federal government in setting examples and playing a continuing role in promoting institutional change to eliminate discrimination based on race;
2. develop within visible minority groups and organizations programs that will enhance their capacity to further their roles as full and equal citizens and to participate in efforts to eradicate racism;
3. develop coalitions involving visible minority groups and other parties committed to promoting institutional change in order to improve the state of race relations;
4. develop within the institutions governing education, justice, employment and culture, programs that will counteract discriminatory practices; and
5. commission action-oriented research to enable a better understanding of the Canadian dimension of this problem and to develop policies and programs to improve race relations (Multiculturalism Canada 1983, 4–5).

Beginning in the late 1970s and early 1980s, Canadian municipalities began to establish civic committees to address what seemed to be growing racial tension. The committees had a broad mandate to "foster and improve race relations" by: proposing to the bodies that created them short- and long-term strategies and actions to promote social harmony and reduce racial tension; reviewing proposed and current legislation, policies, and practices designed to combat racism and promote multiculturalism; and maintaining close contact with departments, boards, commissions, and agencies inside and outside of civic government concerning race relations (Ungerleider 1985b). In 1986, with the assistance of the Multiculturalism Directorate of the Department of the Secretary of State, the Federation of Canadian Municipalities adopted a policy statement committing it to establishing a Municipal Race Relations Program.

Civic governments such as Toronto (City of Toronto n.d.), recognizing the need for measures to ensure equity in employment, established programs to reach out to prospective minority employees, to track their access to jobs and promotional opportunities, and to set out fair employment conditions for those wishing to do business with civic governments. Recognizing that approximately 4.7 percent of the Canadian population was made up of visible minorities but only 1.7 percent of the employees in the federal public service were members of these groups, the Government of Canada in 1986 implemented an employment equity program for visible minorities to augment its earlier efforts on behalf of women, Natives, and the disabled.

School boards throughout Canada began to adopt race relations and multicultural education policies at roughly the same time that municipalities were developing their policies and procedures. In addition to adopting policies, local school boards established guidelines for employee and student behaviour, procedures for handling race-related incidents, committees to review curricula and materials for their suitability, and employment equity policies procedures to govern hiring (c.f.. Metropolitan Separate School Board 1984; Zinman 1988; Echols and Fisher 1989).

Relations between Canadian police and minorities have from time to time been fragile, if not hostile. As a consequence, the improvement of those relations has been a priority of the Multiculturalism Sector of the Department of the Secretary of State, which, in collaboration with the Canadian Association of Chiefs of Police, has funded a variety of initiatives. The initiatives have included a symposium on Race Relations and the Law in 1982; a police–minority symposium in 1984; three research projects pertaining to recruitment and selection, intercultural training and police–community liaison; intercultural training pilot projects in Vancouver and Ottawa (Ungerleider 1985a); the establishment of the National Police Multicultural Liaison Committee of the Canadian Association of Chiefs of Police; pilot projects in the Quebec and Atlantic regions to recruit and train visible minority candidates for careers in policing; intercultural training programs at police academies in Charlottetown and Nicolet, and in other cities across Canada; and provincial conferences on police–minority relations in British Columbia, Alberta, Quebec, and Ontario (c.f. Winterton 1984).

In 1988, Canada proclaimed *An Act for the Preservation and Enhancement of Multiculturalism in Canada,* making it the first nation to "recognize and promote" as a matter of policy "the understanding that multiculturalism reflects the cultural and racial diversity of ... society" and to acknowledge "the freedom of all members of ... society to preserve, enhance and share their cultural heritage." Among the specific requirements of the Act is the declaration as policy that all federal institutions shall:

(a) ensure that Canadians of all origins have an equal opportunity to obtain employment and advancement in those institutions;

(b) promote policies, programs, and practices that enhance the ability of individuals and communities of all origins to contribute to the continuing evolution of Canada;

(c) promote policies, programs, and practices that enhance the understanding of and respect for the diversity of the members of Canadian society;

(d) collect statistical data in order to enable the development of policies, programs, and practices that are sensitive and responsive to the multicultural reality of Canada;

(e) make use, as appropriate, of the language skills and cultural understanding of individuals of all origins; and

(f) generally, carry on their activities in a manner that is sensitive and responsive to the multicultural reality of Canada.

Following the redress settlement for Japanese-Americans, on 22 September 1988, the Canadian government announced the terms of an agreement between the Government of Canada and the National Association of Japanese Canadians. In the agreement, the Government of Canada acknowledged "that the treatment of Japanese Canadians during and after World War II was unjust and violated principles of human rights as they are understood today" (Agreement 1988). In addition to officially acknowledging the injustices suffered by the Japanese, the government indicated that it would make "symbolic" redress payments of $21,000 to each person affected who is still living, provide $24 million to create a Canadian Race Relations Foundation "to foster racial harmony and cross-cultural understanding, and to contribute to the elimination of racism and racial discrimination in Canada."

CONSTITUTIONAL REFORM

Although a written constitution with a declaration of rights placing limits on the sphere of government is among those features of government regarded as fundamental by democratic theorists, the inclusion of rights in a written constitution is a relatively recent phenomenon. The colony of Virginia is generally credited with providing the model for both North America and Europe when it adopted its Declaration of Rights on 12 June 1776 (Finer 1949). In a relatively brief period, rights were enunciated in the Constitution of the United States (1787) and in the French Declaration of the Rights of Man and Citizens (1789). The entrenchment of individual rights in a written constitution did not occur in Canada for another 200 years (*Constitution Act, 1982*).

Whereas the U.S. Constitution contained a Bill of Rights, Canada's Constitution, the *British North America Act,* made no mention of human rights. From Confederation until the late 1940s, Canada's courts tended to uphold commercial and propertied interests rather than human rights. Thus the infrastructure supporting democratic citizenship was significantly strengthened when, in 1982, the *Canadian Charter of Rights and Freedoms* was added to Canada's Constitution. Section 27 of the Charter specifies what are commonly referred to as the multicultural rights of Canadians. The section says that the Charter "shall be interpreted in a manner consistent with the preservation and enhancement of the multicultural heritage of Canadians."

In a free and democratic society, it is important that citizens know exactly what their rights and freedoms are, and where to turn for help and advice in the event that those freedoms are denied or rights infringed upon. In a country like Canada — vast and diverse, with 11 governments, two official languages and a variety of ethnic origins — the only way to provide equal protection to everyone is to enshrine those basic rights and freedoms in the Constitution. (Jean Chrétien, Minister of Justice, 1982)

DEMOCRATIC CITIZENSHIP: AN APPRAISAL OF THE INFRASTRUCTURE

People cannot exercise their rights of democratic citizenship fully unless the opportunities and constraints on their citizenship are distributed without regard to status attributes such as ethnicity, religion, or colour. This section evaluates the impact of the emerging Canadian infrastructure on the distribution of social justice. The main question to be addressed is: How successful has the development of the Canadian infrastructure been in eliminating ethnicity and colour as barriers to full and equal participation in Canadian society?

Using historical evidence and social survey techniques, Reitz (1980) explored the significance and meaning of ethnic group survival in the Canadian context. Reitz observed that, "over the long run, there is a progressive trend toward the abandonment of ethnic group ties for all groups in which long-term experience can be measured." This progressive loss of group cohesion should not be taken as evidence of assimilation into mainstream society, says Reitz, since cohesion and assimilation, though related, are not conceptually different points on the same continuum. Furthermore, his data show that (a) ethnic solidarity (contrary to Porter 1965) does not lead to economic inequality, and that (b) levels of political participation were unaffected by ethnicity except in the case of southern Europeans.

In the same year, Breton, Reitz, and Valentine (1980) appraised cultural boundaries and cultural cohesion of Canada. In an essay devoted to national unity and ethnic community cohesion, Reitz makes observations similar to the ones he has made before. He observes that:

> The evidence may be seen as suggesting that (a) members of the other groups do develop Canadian identity and commitment over time; (b) the degree of their commitment to Canada is muted and restrained, though perhaps no more so than among Canadians generally; and (c) the degree of their commitment to Canada is related to a weakening of ethnic attachments and identity, but these two processes occurring together over lime may not actually affect one another either positively or negatively. In other words, there is no evidence that societal cohesion is seriously undermined by the presence of a large number of persons of diverse ethnic origins or by their varying levels of attachment to an ethnic subculture. The evidence, however, is scanty and inconclusive. The situation may be different in some of the smaller and recently arrived non-white groups. (pp. 406–407)

Evidence of the adequacy of the Canadian infrastructure in ensuring equality in schooling, employment, income, and occupational attainment was obtained from tables prepared by the Technical Services Directorate, Employment Equity Branch, Employment and Immigration Canada in March 1986. The data were obtained from special tabulations of unpublished data from the 1981 Census of Canada using the ethnic origin question and, in some cases, supplemented by questions regarding birthplace, religion, and mother tongue (Kralt and D'Costa 1987). The following are among the patterns evident in the data:

1. Although there are some notable discrepancies among groups and between males and females, Canada's visible minority group members are overrepresented among the most educated members of society.

2. With notable variations between groups and between men and women, Canada's visible minority group members participate in the workforce in greater proportion than their non-visible counterparts and are under-represented among the unemployed.
3. In spite of their educational attainments and their participation in the labour force, visible minority group members earn less than their non-visible counterparts.
4. Where the opportunities for employment are more directly under the control of the individual (professional workers), members of visible minority groups fare reasonably well. Where, however, they are dependent upon being hired by others (management or skilled craft or trades work), they fare less well than Canadians who are not visible minorities.

Evidence of racial discrimination in employment practices is often difficult to obtain. Nevertheless, recent research (Billingsley 1985; Henry 1985; Henry 1989) sheds light on the extent of such discrimination and the ways in which it occurs. In 1985, Henry showed that, all other things being equal, being a member of a visible minority group or speaking accented English was an impediment to getting a job interview. Billingsley (1985) showed that employers in Toronto were willing to disclose overtly racist attitudes even when attitudes were not solicited by the investigators. Fifty-one percent of the respondents expressed some negative attitudes toward non-whites as a group; only 9 percent expressed a firm belief in and commitment to racial equality.

In 1989, Henry replicated her 1985 study with somewhat ambiguous results. She found that, in contrast to her earlier study, blacks received more offers of employment, but they also received more negative treatment when they applied for jobs over the telephone. Commenting upon her replication of the 1985 study, Henry noted that "in the employment arena, some players are still playing by the old rules whereas others have already accommodated to the new social realities" (p. 48).

A CONCLUDING REFLECTION ON INFRASTRUCTURE

When Canada became a signatory to the United Nations' Universal Declaration of Human Rights in 1948, it embarked upon a series of social changes that, though unintended at the time, has helped to create an infrastructure that facilitates democratic citizenship. It is this emergent infrastructure that defines the limits and possibilities of democratic citizenship for immigrants.

Unlike its neighbour to the south, Canada had neither a tradition of social justice born out of the persecution of its founders nor well-established groups of citizens advocating an expansion of that tradition. And, where the United States has had independent groups speaking out on behalf of disfranchised minorities, Canada's advocacy groups depend to a great extent upon the support of the state in order to change social policy and programs.

Long overdue, the recent changes in Canadian government policies at the federal, provincial, and municipal levels that sanction and support social justice are positive steps in this process. The gradual development of an infrastructure that promotes social justice for all Canadians should, in time, create the one condition most central to democratic citizenship—equality among all Canadians.

There are nevertheless several obstacles to the future evolution of this infrastructure. Among the most serious are the "new" conservatism. The evolution of the social justice infrastructure has resulted in Canadians coming to recognize that their similarities outweigh their differences. From this perspective, the declaration of any regional, cultural, or linguistic group as distinctive poses problems for advancing claims of social justice based upon the premise that all people should be treated equally unless there is good reason to do otherwise. Objections to establishing primacy for the French language in Quebec are, in part, based upon the view that such legislation runs counter to the notion of equality of treatment and that notions of equality of outcome and of social equity do not apply.

The view of people implicit in the "new" conservatism is a major obstacle to the achievement of social justice. According to the new conservatism, individuals are autonomous—albeit unequal—moral agents who are responsible for the consequences that befall them. The new conservatism accepts inequality and emphasizes the individual's own resources and resourcefulness. According to this ideology, inequality is a natural condition affecting all human relations, which should be preserved to ensure social and economic progress. Equality then is considered to be incompatible with progress because it is through competition among individuals, each seeking to increase his share of scarce resources, that progress is achieved. Personal denial and self-control are necessary for one to progress economically and socially. Those who possess resources and use them wisely win competitive advantages over those who are profligate and ill-disciplined. The competitive forces that produce progress are naturally occurring conditions that affect all human beings. As such, it is futile for the state to attempt to alter them and immoral for the individual to resist them (Ungerleider 1987).

In the same way that some would argue that all issues of social justice in Quebec should be subordinated to the issue of language, there are those who advocate that matters of social policy and social justice should be subordinated to the market. This new and more virulent form of conservatism poses problems for groups that depend upon government to fund their advocacy and service programs. The recent reductions in support for Native communications and temporary reductions in support for women's programs, as well as the 10-year lapse of legislative activity in most provinces with respect to the implementation of section 23 of the Charter, dealing with minority language education, are but three instances in which issues of social justice were subordinated to economic and political considerations.

REFERENCES

Abella, I., and H. Troper. 1983. *None Is Too Many: Canada and the Jews of Europe 1933–1945*. Toronto: Lester and Orphen Dennys, Publisher.

Administrative Orders 40–46. (1942). Passed under the *War Measures Act*, R.S.C. 1927, c. 206.

Agreement (1988, September 22). "Historic Agreement Reached on Japanese Canadian Redress." Government of Canada News Release, M-09/88-69.

An Act for the Preservation and Enhancement of Multiculturalism in Canada. Bill C-93, 33rd Parliament, 35-36-37, Elizabeth II, 1986-87-88.

Act to Amend the Immigration Act. 1908. S.C. Edw. VII. c. 33, s. 1.

Basavarajappa, K.G., and R.B.P. Verma. 1985. "Asian Immigrants in Canada: Some Findings from 1981 Census." *International Migration* 23, no. 1:97–121.

Beaujot, R., K.G. Basavarajappa, and R. Verma. (1986. "The Relative Income of Immigrants: Are the New Immigrant Groups at a Disadvantage?" Paper presented at the meetings of the Canadian Population Society, Winnipeg, Manitoba, March.

Berry, J.W. 1984. "Multicultural Policy in Canada: A Social Psychological Analysis." *Canadian Journal of Behavioural Science* 16, no. 4: 353–370.

Billingslcy, B., and L. Muszynski. 1985. *No Discrimination Here? Toronto Employers and the Multi-racial Workforce.* Toronto: Social Planning Council of Metropolitan Toronto and the Urban Alliance for Race Relations.

Black, J. 1982. "Immigrant Political Adaptation in Canada: Some Tentative Findings." *Canadian Journal of Political Science* 15, no. 1 (March):3–27.

———. 1987. "The Practice of Politics in Two Settings: Political Transferability among Recent Immigrants to Canada." *Canadian Journal of Political Science* 20, no. 4 (December):731–752.

Breton, R., J.G. Reitz, and V. Valentine. 1980. *Cultural Boundaries and the Cohesion of Canada.* Montreal: The Institute for Public Policy.

Canada. 1971. House of Commons. *Debates* (8 October): 8545–8546.

Canada. 1987. House of Commons. *Multiculturalism: Building the Canadian Mosaic.* Report of the Standing Committee on Multiculturalism. Canada: Minister of Supply and Services.

Canada, Secretary of State. 1982. *Race Relations and the Law.* Report of a symposium held in Vancouver, British Columbia, 22–24 April. Ottawa: Minister of Supply and Services, 1983.

Canadian Charter of Rights and Freedoms. 1982.

Canadian Multiculturalism Act. 1988. 35-36-37 Elizabeth II, 1986-87-88.

Carty, R.W., and W.P. Ward. 1986. "The Making of a Canadian Political Citizenship." In *National Politics and Community in Canada*, ed. R.W. Cany and W.P. Ward, 65–79. Vancouver: University of British Columbia Press.

Chinese Immigration Act. 1885. S.C. 48-49 Viet., c. 71. s. 4.

Chinese Immigration Act, 1900. S.C. 63-64 Viet., c. 32, s. 6.

Chinese Immigration Act. 1903. S.C. 3 Edw., c. 8. s. 6.

Chinese Immigration Act. 1923. S.C. 13-14 Geo. V., c. 38, ss. 5-8.

City of Toronto. n.d. *Employment Equity: An Employer's Handbook.*

Cohen, T. 1988. *Race Relations and the Law.* The Canadian Jewish Congress.

Constitution Act, 1982.

Echols, F.H., C.S. Ungerleider, L.B. Daniels, and C. La Bar. 1991. "Student's Knowledge of the Charter of Rights and Freedoms and their Agreement with Its Provisions." *Alberta Journal of Educational Research* 36, no. 1:1–15.

Employment and Immigration Canada. 1987. *Profiles of Canadian Immigration.* Ottawa: Minister of Supply and Services Canada.

Employment Equity Act. 1985. Bill C-62. 33rd Parliament.

Federation of Canadian Municipalities. n.d. *Getting Started: Local Government and Community/Race Relations.* Race Relations Series #1.

Finer, H. 1949. *The Theory and Practice of Modern Government.* New York: Henry Holt and Company.

Harney, R.F. 1988. "So Great a Heritage as Ours: Immigration and the Survival of the Canadian Polity." *Daedalus: Journal of the American Academy of Arts and Sciences* 117, no. 4:51–97.

Henry, F. 1989. *Who Gets the Work in 1989?* Manuscript submitted to Economic Council of Canada, October.

Henry, F., and F. Ginsberg. 1985. *Who Gets the Work?: A Test of Racial Discrimination in Toronto.* Toronto: Social Planning Council of Metropolitan Toronto and the Urban Alliance for Race Relations.

Immigration Act. 1910. S.C. 9-10 Edw. VII, c. 27, s. 38.

Immigration Act. S.C. 1976–1977, C. 52. s. 3(b).

Kralt, J., and R. D'Costa. 1987. "Statistical Profile of Visible Minorities in Canada (1981)." Tabular material prepared for Conference on Canada 2000, Race Relations and Public Policy, Carleton University, Ottawa, 30 October–1 November.

Metropolitan Separate School Board. 1984. *Race and Ethnic Relations and Multicultural Policy: Guidelines and Procedures.* Willowdale: Metropolitan Separate School Board.

Moodley, K. 1983. "Canadian Multiculturalism as Ideology." *Ethnic and Racial Studies* 6 no. 3 (July):320–331.

Multiculturalism Canada. 1983. *National Strategy on Race Relations.*

Multiculturalism Canada. n.d. *Visible Minorities and the Media Conference Report.*

Newman, W. 1975. *American Pluralism.* Toronto: Prentice Hall.

Ontario Human Rights Code. 1981. Statutes of Ontario, C. 53.

Porter, J. 1965. *The Vertical Mosaic: An Analysis of Social Class and Power in Canada.* Toronto: University of Toronto Press.

Province of British Columbia. 1986. Proceedings of the provincial symposium on Multicultural and Multiracial Policing, Vancouver, British Columbia, 26–27 March. Victoria: Queen's Printer for British Columbia.

Reitz, J. 1987 "The Institutional Structure of Immigration as a Determinant of Inter-racial Competition: A Comparison of Britain and Canada." *International Migration Review* 22, no. 1:117–146.

Reitz, J.G. 1980. *The Survival of Ethnic Groups.* Toronto: McGraw-Hill Ryerson Limited.

Roy, P.E. 1981. "Citizens without Votes: East Asians in British Columbia, 1872–1947." In *National Politics and Community in Canada*, ed. R.W. Cary and W.P. Ward, 151–171. Vancouver: University of British Columbia Press.

Samuel, T.J. 1988. "Third World Immigration: Multiculturalism and Ethnicity in Canada." Paper presented at the National Symposium on Demography and Immigrant Racial and Ethnic Groups in Canada, Winnipeg, Manitoba, August.

Smith, A. 1981. "National Images and National Maintenance: The Ascendancy of the Ethnic Idea in North America." *Canadian Journal of Political Science* 14, no. 2:227–257.

Ungerleider, C.S. 1985a. "Police Intercultural Education: Promoting Understanding and Empathy between Police and Ethnic Communities." *Canadian Ethnic Studies* 17, no. 1:51–66.

Ungerleider, C.S. 1985b. "A Tale of One City: Advancing Human Rights through Civic Committee Action." *Currents: Readings in Race Relations* 3, no. 1:5–10.

Ungerleider, C.S. 1987. "Inequality and Education: The Ideological Context of Educational Change in British Columbia." *Journal of Educational Administration and Foundations* 1, no. 2:17–27.

Ungerleider, C.S., F.H. Echols, L.B. Daniels, and C. La Bar. 1990. "Constitutional Rights and Citizenship." In *Ends in View: Analysis of the Goals of Law Related Education*, ed. J. Coombs, S. Parkinson, and R. Case, 71–81.Vancouver: Centre for the Study of Curriculum and Instruction.

Ungerleider. C.S., and L. Sherlock. 1988. *Multicultural and Race Relations Training Database.* Report submitted to the Multiculturalism Directorate of the Department of the Secretary of State.

Verma, R.B.P., K.G. Basavarajappa, and R. Beujot. 1986. "The Economic Adaptation of Immigrants: Income of Immigrants in Canada, 1980." Paper presented to XIth World Congress of Sociology, New Delhi, India, August.

Waddell, E. 1986. "The Vicissitudes of French in Quebec and Canada." In *The Politics of Gender, Ethnicity and Language in Canada,* ed. A. Cairns and C. Williams, 67–100. Toronto: University of Toronto Press.

Winterton, D. et. al. 1984. Proceedings of the symposium on Policing in Multicultural/Multiracial Urban Communities, Vancouver, British Columbia, 14–16 October.

Zinman, R. 1988. *A Multicultural/Multiracial Approach to Education in the Schools of the Protestant School Board of Greater Montreal: Report of the Task Force on Multicultural/Multiracial Education.* The Protestant School Board of Greater Montreal.

14

"CANADIAN" AS AN ETHNIC CATEGORY
IMPLICATIONS FOR MULTICULTURALISM AND NATIONAL UNITY

RHODA E. HOWARD-HASSMANN

In a world of increasing ethnic fragmentation and nationalism, Canada is a social experiment that other countries view with some astonishment. Canada is populated by persons who come themselves, or whose ancestors come, from hundreds of different ethnic groups. Yet they coexist in what seems in many other countries to be remarkable harmony. Even more extraordinary from the point of view of outsiders, Canada has a paradoxical policy of multiculturalism, which, far from promoting divisions among Canadians, seems to promote their integration.

To explain this paradox, this chapter addresses the question of identity among English-speaking, non-Aboriginal Canadians. It argues that there is such a thing as an ethnic Canadian identity. Frequently, biological ancestry is confused with social ethnicity, so that everyone's "true" identity is presumed to be rooted somewhere else. Yet most people who are born in Canada, or who immigrate to Canada at young ages, become ethnic Canadians. The application to English Canadians of standard sociological theory about the characteristics and creation of ethnicity is rarely done, yet it reveals Canadian ethnicity. The government policy of multiculturalism permits—even encourages—Canadians to retain aspects of their ancestral ethnic heritage, yet it does not undo the tendency of most people living in Canada to become ethnic Canadians.

Part of the debate about multiculturalism pits illiberal against liberal multiculturalists. Illiberal multiculturalists argue for stronger identification of Canadians with ancestral ethnic groups. By contrast, Canada's present public policy of liberal multiculturalism encourages private, individual choices of identity. Paradoxically, this liberal policy also encourages identification with a Canadian nation. The more members of minorities are encouraged to retain their ancestral identities, the more welcome they feel in Canada, and the more they identify with Canada and with Canadian citizenship, both vital to Canadian unity. But if, as some illiberal critics argue should occur, multiculturalism were diverted to promote identification with ancestral ethnicities at the expense of social assimilation into Canadian ethnicity, the net result would be to reduce identification with Canada.

SOCIAL ETHNICITY, BIOLOGICAL ANCESTRY

In early 1996, Lucien Bouchard shocked many people in the "rest of Canada" by stating that unlike Quebec, Canada was not a real country (Seguin 1996, A4). Canada, it seemed, had no sense of coherence and unity, and Canadians (other than Quebecois) were just a mishmash of individuals from all over the place. Bouchard was wrong. English Canadians, like Quebecois, are an ethnic group; like Quebecois, they form a nation as well as living within a state. By English Canadian is meant Canadians, other than indigenous peoples, who normally speak English, rather than French, in the public realm. (Indigenous peoples are not included as English Canadians because they are the original inhabitants of the country with their own original languages, and they are covered in law by their own sets of rights, separate from the policy of multiculturalism.)

As this paper will argue, there is such a thing as an ethnic Canadian. But both public policy and much academic analysis conspire to prevent Canadians from recognizing this by insisting that their "ethnic" identity must be that of their ancestors. This occurs in public policy via the failure, until very recently, to recognize "Canadian" as an ethnic category. At the same time, among some academics, as discussed below, Canadianness is viewed as a covert means of promoting immigrants' assimilation, at the expense of their cultural heritage.

Social scientists frequently confuse ethnicity with ancestry. Then, wishing to promote the multiculturalism that is so much a part of prevailing Canadian ideology, they propose public policies based on people's ancestries. Evelyn Kallen asserts that Canada should become a multilingual as well as a multicultural society; all children should be taught in their "ethnic languages" (1990, 178). Kallen believes that all privileging of French and English as the founding (non-Aboriginal) languages of Canada should end. No assimilative policies should exist: the Canadian government should do as much as it possibly can to ensure that immigrants to Canada retain their ancestral language and culture. Yet in 1996, 84 percent of people living in Canada listed English or French as their sole mother tongue or one of their mother tongues (calculated from Statistics Canada 1998b), and only 1.7 percent of the population claimed to speak neither English nor French (calculated from Statistics Canada 1998a).

In Kallen's reading, the policy of multiculturalism means that the government must encourage citizens to define their ethnicity as that of their ancestors. The government must preserve the ancestral languages, customs, and religions of immigrants. No matter how long an individual or her family has lived in Canada, her ethnicity is still that of her ancestors who never left the "old country." Moreover, such ancestry always can be identified and is always unitary; there is no room in Kallen's analysis for the products of mixed marriages with multiple ethnic ancestries. Yet in 1996, 10 224 500 Canadians, or

36 percent of the population, reported that they had mixed ethnic ancestries (calculated from Statistics Canada 1998c).

The 1991 Citizens' Forum on Canada's Future revealed a strong sense of Canadianness. Overall, the commissioners of the forum wrote, "participants told us that reminding us of our different origins is less useful in building a united country than emphasizing the things we have in common." As one group from Richmond, B.C., stated: "We are generally in favour of celebrating our cultural heritage.... However, we must remain Canadian first.... We must have a strong core"(Spicer 1991, 85). Yet Abu-Laban and Stasiulis, writing in *Canadian Public Policy*, were strongly critical of the Citizens' Forum, claiming that "what is being favoured in this report is for multiculturalism to serve as a device for immigrant integration" (1992, 370).

There is, among these academics, a notion of ethnicity as a fixed, concrete entity. Ethnicity cannot be changed; you are what your ancestors were. Yet many students of ethnicity argue that it is a social creation. Ethnicity is not a "thing" outside and immune from human action and perception; it is "a process by which individuals either identify themselves as being different from others or belonging to a different group or are identified as different by others" (Isajiw 1985, 9). Max Weber defined ethnic groups as "human groups that entertain a subjective belief in their common descent"; ethnic membership, according to Weber, was a "presumed identity" (1978, 389). There is no such thing as a fixed primordial group: there are only socially constructed groups, sometimes so constructed by ethnic entrepreneurs for reasons of self-promotion rather than preservation of a romanticized ethnic heritage (Amit-Talai 1996; Burnet 1987, 74).

To posit ethnicity as a static entity derived from one's ancestors is to ignore socialization. Socialization is the process by which individual members of the human species learn to be human beings, to be members of society. Socialization occurs in the home, but it also occurs in peer relationships, in the schoolyard, via the media, and via the larger world. Yet in the Canadian discussion of multiculturalism, socialization frequently has become forced assimilation, seemingly a racist practice denying to immigrants the right to maintain their own culture. The changes in identity that happen to any immigrant to Canada, and the Canadian identity that any immigrant's child born in Canada absorbs, are viewed as enemies of the immutable, "natural" ancestral ethnicity that immigrants and their children ought to exemplify (on this, see also DiSanto 1989, 147).

There are many advantages to the Canadian policy of multiculturalism: most important is that non-European and/or non-Christian immigrants receive a strong message that they are welcome in this predominantly white, predominantly Christian country. But these advantages should not be allowed to obscure that, as this chapter argues, there are also ethnic Canadians in Canada. The complexity of social roles and identities in modern Canadian life creates a new type of individual, not closely tied to his ancestral origins.

By encouraging individuals to think of themselves, and identify themselves, in terms of their ancestral ethnicity, public policy may render it difficult to instill a sense of Canadian identity in the population at large. As Weinfeld stated, "support for the image of Canada as an ethnic mosaic is facilitated when census data reify arbitrarily assigned census categories" (1981, 91). If, on the other hand, people living in Canada are permitted to be Canadians in public policy and official ideology, the result is likely to be a thickening of the sense of citizenship, and a consequent strengthening of the sense of nationhood.

LIBERAL VERSUS ILLIBERAL MULTICULTURALISM

In a discussion of educational policies in the U.S., K. Anthony Appiah distinguishes between liberal and illiberal multiculturalism. Liberal multicultural education allows each child "to negotiate the creation of his or her own individual identity, using ... collective [racial, ethnic, etc.] identities as one (but only one) of the resources" available to him or her; illiberal multicultural education "wants to force children to live within separate spheres defined by the common culture of their race, religion or ethnicity" (1997, 34). Liberal multiculturalism, that is, makes racial or ethnic identity a choice; illiberal multiculturalism categorizes people and obliges them to live within those categories. The individual takes precedence over the group in liberal multiculturalism; in illiberal multiculturalism, the group takes precedence.

Academics such as Kallen and Abu-Laban and Stasiulis are illiberal multiculturalists. Kallen wants all children to remain within their ancestral collectivities, with state-supported multilingual education dedicated to this goal; Abu-Laban and Stasiulis also want the state to recognize the fixed, unchanging ethnic identity of all Canadians. For these scholars, multiculturalism as a policy must ensure that individuals identify themselves as members of their ancestors' ethnicities. They believe in the idea of fixed primordial groups.

But for liberal multiculturalists, multiculturalism is a resource of which citizens may or may not avail themselves as they see fit. It is not a policy to which citizens must conform, in part because there are no fixed primordial groups. Official Canadian multiculturalism is liberal, reflecting Canada's overall liberal political democracy. Section 27 of Canada's *Charter of Rights and Freedoms* (1982) states explicitly that "[t]his Charter shall be interpreted in a manner consistent with the preservation and enhancement of the multicultural heritage of Canadians." Following this, the Canadian *Multiculturalism Act* (Bill C-23, 1988) notes in its preamble "the importance of preserving and enhancing the multicultural heritage of Canadians." It also proclaims (in s. 3, b) that "multiculturalism is a fundamental characteristic of the Canadian heritage and identity." The Act makes clear the government's intention not merely to recognize the multicultural origins of Canadians, but to maintain and foster their various cultural heritages by engaging in policies that enhance the diversity of Canada's culture, such as disbursement of funds to groups promoting their ancestral languages and arts. This includes policies to "facilitate the acquisition, retention and use of all languages that contribute to the multicultural heritage of Canada" (s. 5, 1, f). Thus the government encourages Canadians not only to retain languages they may speak already, but also to repossess or adopt languages that they and several generations of ancestors may never have spoken. Canadians do so, however, on an entirely voluntary basis: the groups they "belong" to cannot oblige them to preserve or repossess their ancestral languages.

This official commitment to a culture of racial and ethnic diversity is less than 30 years old. For it to become absorbed as part of the underlying cultural belief system of most Canadians requires constant promotion by the state and by educational institutions. This effort seems to have had some effect—public opinion polls indicate less racism and fear of strangers in Canada in the late 20th century than 30 years ago. For example, in 1968, 53 percent of Canadians polled answered "disagree" to the question: "Do you agree/disagree with a marriage between whites and non-whites?" (Gallup Report 1968). But in 1991 only 15 percent of Canadians agreed that "[i]t is a bad idea for people of different races to marry" (Angus Reid Group 1991). Yet even if racism has declined substantially in Canada, memories of past discrimination fester and demand recognition. Here, too, the federal government has taken action, for example, by agreeing in 1988 to pay compensation to the entire community of Canadians of Japanese ancestry who had been stripped of their property and interned as enemy aliens (some despite Canadian citizenship) during the Second World War (Griffin 1992).

By compensating groups for discrimination that they themselves or their ancestors suffered, the Canadian government makes a symbolic gesture that reaffirms Canadian values. The liberal values enshrined in Canada's *Charter of Rights and Freedoms* symbolize a change from religio-ethnic exclusivity to religio-ethnic openness. Racist expressions and assertions of religious superiority are excluded from the realm of acceptable public discourse, as the application of hate speech laws demonstrates (Jones 1998, 205–211). The prescribed political culture at the end of the 20th century assumes that all ethnic affiliations are equally valuable.

But this political culture rests on the assumption that in the final analysis, religion and ethnicity are private matters. Life in Canada is characterized by choice. Regardless of race (used here in the sense of phenotypical variety), ethnicity, or religion, one is supposed to be able to choose one's occupation, to be fully mobile, to work and live wherever one can afford. One is supposed to be free to choose friends and a spouse from any background, religion, or race. Religion, ethnic or cultural affiliation, indeed choice of language used in private, are matters of official public indifference; the groups that practise different religions, promote cultural or ethnic memberships, or speak unofficial languages are private groups. It is not the business of the government to ensure the preservation or influence of such private groups. The government can only encourage their preservation when their individual members indicate their desire for its assistance.

Nevertheless, in the interests of acknowledging the diverse origins of Canadians, the state supports some aspects of multiculturalism. "Heritage" language programs provide public funds for children to learn the language of their immediate or even more remote ancestors. But again, no child is obliged to attend such a program, and children who are not members of the ethnic group identified with the language are free to enrol in the class if their parents wish. Language usage is part of the private sphere. Anyone in Canada is permitted to speak whatever language she wishes in private conversation. Each individual Canadian can choose to identify herself as a member of her ancestral community or to withdraw from that community and stress other aspects of identity, such as occupation. Public multiculturalism is thus a liberal multiculturalism, posited on the preservation of private identity. And indeed, despite the academic and social movements of identity politics that have dominated much discussion of multiculturalism in the 1980s and 1990s, early evidence suggests that members of minorities in Canada preferred that the multiculturalism policy take this approach; "members of ethnic groups do not want to be 'locked in' by ethnic boundaries" (Breton 1986, 54).

ETHNICITY: ENGLISH CANADIAN

The current buzzword for multiculturalism, tolerance, and racial harmony is "diversity." Diversity must be not only protected but also promoted, many multiculturalist activists believe. Yet while diversity does shower a host of blessings onto Canada, nevertheless national unity requires a Canadian community with a common, shared understanding of identity in all citizens. Such a community is based on common experiences in Canada and a common set of fundamental principles. Citizenship in Canada, as in any other country, must have more meaning than merely legal rights; it must imply shared ways of living, shared values, and loyalty to the country. Without a deep sense of shared citizenship, an emotional attachment of Canadians to the country and to each other, little except common material goals will hold Canada's inhabitants together.

A country will be more closely knit if it shares a special sense of common life; if it is indeed a national community, not merely a collection of individuals sharing the common legal status of citizen. Communities are often thought to require common ethnic (actually ancestral) origins. But in Canada, there are fewer and fewer commonalities of historic ancestral origin. Immigration patterns and intermarriage create a melange of citizens, many with four or more ethnic ancestries. At the same time, official policy requires that a community be created voluntarily by people from myriad different ancestral groups. Community in Canada is not supposed to, and cannot, require ethnic, religious, or other types of ascriptive conformity.

To many citizens, community is also an ideal that can remedy the individualism that seems to afflict modern Western society. There is a general concern that modernity has produced aggregates of individuals plagued by angst, anomie, and malaise who are incapable of exercising responsibility to their families and the wider society (see e.g., Bibby 1990). One recent result of urban angst has been a social movement toward preoccupation with one's ancestral identity. Tightly knit communities of recent immigrants, often centred around a temple, mosque, or church, seem to have retained the sense of community that native-born Canadians have foolishly lost in the pursuit of material prosperity (Frideres 1993, 65). Thus, many individuals are returning to their religious, national, and ancestral "roots," frequently several generations removed. As in the United States, these ancestral roots endow their fictive Canadian descendants with a symbolic sense of difference from the North American mainstream. (Gans 1979; Breton 1986).

In part, this preoccupation with roots enhances equality, as it signifies the passing of the social domination of the Anglo-Protestant elite. For example, Canadians of Eastern European origin who 50 years ago might have changed their names to something sounding more English now feel little or no pressure to do so. In part, however, this new preoccupation with ethnic identity is a manifestation of a social fiction. Yearning to be different, to somehow escape the social malaise of urban life, Canadians seek identity in symbolic adoptions of ancestral ethnicity. "Small differences" of dress, food, or ritual behaviour are cultivated as symbolic indicators of uniqueness, in a pattern identified decades ago by Weber (1978, 388). But this social movement toward recognition of ancestral difference obscures the reality, argued in this chapter, that there is such a thing as an English-Canadian ethnicity.

Community is possible in heterogeneous societies. It is not a community of ascriptive assignment to particular ethnic, religious, or ancestral groups; it is a community of diversity, heterodoxy, and individual choice. To a significant extent, Canadians have in the last three decades accommodated themselves to the increasing diversity of their society. They have, in fact, created a new ethnic group, the ethnic English Canadian. The ethnic English Canadian is not necessarily a possessor of English or even British ancestry. Mainstream Canadian culture has long since ceased to be "English": even the language bears differences in Canada and the United Kingdom, and English immigrants to Canada frequently find the country, its customs, and linguistic usages strange (Greenhill 1994, 33). The ethnic English Canadian is a new social creation.

Ethnicity is not a static entity; it is not a marker of what one intractably *is*. Ethnicity is a form of cultural practice. It is created and recreated by the perceptions and actions of individuals in society. In part, a sense of ethnicity is located in obvious social markers such as territory, language, religion, and ancestry. But ethnicity is also a complex of cultural behaviours that people have in common. Ethnicity is located in shared customs, beliefs, rituals, norms, and social conventions.

Two important characteristics of English Canadians are their territory, Canada, and their language, English. Territory gives individuals a mental map of the world and a sense of how space, time, and topography interact. Even if one has never travelled, as a Canadian one has a sense of expanse, of the flatness of the prairies and the enormity of the Arctic; this sense is inculcated in school geography lessons and national news and weather reports. Canada, for Canadians, is the centre of the world.

Likewise, English is the public language of social intercourse. English is the vibrant, dynamic language of technical change, modern slang, and the arts. In the public world, language evolves; together, groups of English-speakers create a language that reflects the changing world around them. By contrast, the private non-English maternal language of the home that some Canadians speak may well be dated and outmoded, not having a living public world with which to keep up.

While territory and language are usually accepted as markers of ethnicity elsewhere in the world, they are often ignored in the discussion of what makes a Canadian. Only characteristics brought to Canada by immigrants, not characteristics acquired by virtue of immigration, are deemed relevant to the discussion of Canadian ethnicity. If one speaks English and one's ancestors did not, that is an indication that one has had to give up one's ethnic identity to live in Canada, even if one's nearer ancestors have been speaking English in Canada for several generations. One is similarly expected to have a fictive sense of place, an attachment to a homeland one has never seen, rather than to view Canada as one's homeland.

Another common shared characteristic of Canadians is religion. In the 1991 census 83.4 percent of Canadians identified themselves as Christians (calculated from Statistics Canada 1993). Given the weakness of Christian practice in Canada, the divisions among Christians, and the tendency of some Christian churches to be identified with different ancestral groups, this commonality is little more than an overarching belief system (on actual religious practice, see Bibby 1993). It does, however, provide most Canadians with common festive days, and a common belief in Sunday as an appropriate day of rest.

Again, religion is seen as a standard mark of ethnicity in the rest of the world, yet in Canada it is often thought that to point out that there is a common religious heritage, experienced by the vast majority of the population, is to undermine the multiculturalist premise of diversity. Yet many Canadians whose ancestors lived in parts of the world outside Europe are also Christian: there are Christians in Canada of Indian, Korean, Chinese, and African ancestry. This is because in a liberal country such as Canada, religion—like culture in general—is not merely a matter of ancestral identity, it is a matter of choice.

Another overarching commonality of Canadian life is that in 1996 about 87 percent of Canadians were of European ancestry (calculated from Statistics Canada 1998c, 1998d). Again, many analysts hesitate to point out this obvious fact, assuming that an observation of statistical frequency might be taken to be an observation about the ideal Canadian. But when we observe other parts of the world, "racial" homogeneity, whether African, Indian, or Chinese, immediately strikes us as a marker of ethnicity. Nevertheless, common European ancestry is neither sufficient nor necessary to create a Canadian community. In Europe itself, divisions such as language and type of Christianity sharply distinguish one group from another. And as the proportion of Canadians not of European ancestry—or of mixed European and other ancestries—increases, the "racial" identification of Canadians changes to an identification with broader Canadian culture. In Canada, the sharpness of diverse ancestral origins is blurred easily among those who are either born in the country or immigrate at an early age. This is because ethnicity is active and malleable.

Ethnicity evolves, shifts, and changes partly as a consequence of structural factors. An important structural factor in Canada has been the generational upward mobility that characterized almost all European immigrant groups during Canada's long period of settlement. Immigrants wishing to rise in the social scale knew that adoption of dominant Canadian customs would advance their opportunities. Some changed religions, or adopted more "Canadian" forms of Christianity such as membership in the Anglican or United Churches (Bibby 1993, 25–27). Most encouraged their children to learn and speak English, many going so far as to abandon their original language even within the home. Immigrant children attended Canadian schools, where they learned not only the English language but also Canadian rules, customs, and values. They met people not "of their own kind" whom they later frequently married (Reitz and Breton 1994, 52).

Among those favouring illiberal multiculturalism, immigrants' adoption of the English language or Christian religion indicates the "racist" (perhaps better "ethnicist") biases of the Anglo-Canadian elite. Certainly such biases existed. But choice also impelled immigrants. Life in Europe, like life in many parts of Asia, Africa, and Central and South America now, was hard and dangerous. Political democracy was unknown in most of the countries, producing Canada's early waves of non-British immigrants. Parents who migrated often wished to shed their pasts, literally to change their children into the new breed of free, educated Canadians. Parents did suffer as their children abandoned their customs and churches and brought home previously unthinkable marriage partners. But this does not mean that immigrants abjured all change, that had it been possible they would have transported their entire cultures lock, stock, and barrel to the new world. A new Canadian ethnicity was adopted and created by immigrants, whose ancestral identifications were but one aspect of their sense of self in the new society.

Although Canada's economy is no longer as expansionist as it was during the decades of high European immigration, more recent immigrants from Asia, Africa, and Central and South America do find much economic opportunity, both for themselves and their children. Many also enjoy political democracy for the first time in their lives. In Canada, an orderly, hard-working, law-abiding life can bring security and comfort; this is a luxury in many other parts of the world where property can be arbitrarily confiscated, unemployment rates reach 30 or 40 percent, and political police can incarcerate and torture citizens at will. Canadian multicultural norms of religious tolerance are also attractive to many immigrants, who can equally take advantage of that tolerance by rejecting or by re-embracing their ancestral religions. If the price of this freedom and security is loss of language and strange sons- and daughters-in-law, it is a price that for many is well worth paying.

This does not mean that becoming Canadian is a smooth, painless process for immigrants. Particular actions, such as religious worship, participation in ceremonial occasions, courtship rituals, and types of food preferred, are often taken in Canada as the most important markers of one's ethnic identity. These actions—Weber's small differences—do differentiate groups of Canadians from each other. How and on what occasions a family serves food to outsiders, how one welcomes a new child into the world, and how one mourns one's dead are all important aspects of one's life. Feeling uncomfortable with "Canadian" social norms, recent immigrants may well prefer to socialize with one another, to ignore the public world of Canadianness in favour of the private world of familiarity (see, e.g., Hoffman 1989). Nevertheless, as Howard Brotz pointed out, most of these customs are merely "private or social differences in ethnic tastes" (1980, 41). As he explained, with the exception of Aboriginal Canadians, "there are no ethnic differences in Canada about the desirability of the bourgeois-democratic way of life" (ibid.) Moodley makes the same point: "few immigrants choose to exchange attractive individualism, North American style, for the sake of cultural sentimentalities" (1983, 322).

To be English Canadian, then, is to have an ethnic identity. Someone speaking English as a first language, or as the public language outside the home, is an English Canadian. An English Canadian may be of any ethnic or racial background; he may have Ukrainian or Ghanaian rather than British Protestant ancestry. While the parents' sense of place may be Ukraine or Ghana, the English Canadian's sense of place will be his immediate environment, the town or city that he knows well enough to get around—the personal map of schools, shops, offices, relatives, and friends (Fischer 1982). His personal life history will have taken place in Canada, not abroad. Though he may eat foods different from other Canadians and worship at a mosque or a temple rather than a church, he will have attended the same schools, learned the same Canadian history and geography, and been present at the same lessons in family studies and sex education.

An English Canadian is likely to share many of her customs, desires, and ambitions with people of dissimilar ethnic or even racial ancestry. Her class position will be an important marker of cultural behaviour. In the occupational sphere, everyone in Canada behaves in much the same way; choice depends significantly on education. Consumer choices are also much the same among groups with different ancestors. Canadians of all ancestral backgrounds favour one-family houses, and purchase cars and labour-saving household appliances.

Ethnicity is also characterized by common norms and values. Among the most important of these norms and values in Canada are the very principles of multiculturalism that the ideological elite now strives to implant in all Canadians via the educational system and state publicity, and which are absorbed (at least in part) by anyone whose education is primarily in Canada. To be Canadian, increasingly, is in state ideology and public practice to be a multiculturalist: multiculturalism is a key Canadian value.

This is not to deny that racial, religious, and ethnic prejudices still exist in Canada. They do, and they affect how Canadians think of themselves. To be of Ghanaian ancestry, for example, is to be vulnerable to racism, whereas to be of Ukrainian is not. To bear non-European phenotypical features or speak with a heavy non-Canadian accent is always to be vulnerable to inquiries regarding where one is "from." Those perceived to be part of the "multicultural (minority) communities" may find that some of their fellow citizens do not accord them the status of being a "real" Canadian, although this implicit hierarchy of Canadianness long precedes the establishment of the policy of multiculturalism. And discrimination does affect the employment opportunities of some ethnic and racial groups (Henry and Ginzberg 1993; Reitz 1993; but for differences among non-European groups, showing that some earn above the average for British-Canadians, see Winn 1985). Yet incidents of racism are not sufficient in and of themselves to convince citizens of non-European descent that they are not Canadians. For example, of 19 civic leaders in Hamilton, Ontario, of non-Aboriginal, non-European descent interviewed from 1996 to 1997, only one said racism made her feel an outsider in Canada: all the others expressed a strong sentiment that they were Canadian (Howard 1998).

That Canadians themselves recognize their ethnicity is evident in their willingness to identify themselves as "Canadian" when given the chance. In a national survey conducted in 1991, 89 percent of respondents "identified with being a Canadian," while only 6 percent did not. When told that they could choose only one answer to indicate their identity, 63 percent chose Canadian. Most tellingly, only 13 percent of those born in Canada identified themselves primarily by their "ethnic origin" (i.e., their ancestry), while among those born outside Canada, only 33 percent so identified themselves (Angus Reid Group 1991, 3–4).

On the 1991 national census, only 2.8 percent of respondents wrote in that they were Canadian (in the box marked "other"). Yet prior to that census, Statistics Canada had conducted a series of mini-polls and focus groups that suggested that large numbers of people chose "Canadian" as their full or partial ethnic identification when that option was presented to them. In one experiment the total of those choosing full or partial Canadian identification was 53 percent, although in others it was 30 or 35 percent. Wanting information about ancestral, not social, ethnicity, Statistics Canada did not include Canadian as a specific ethnic option on the 1991 census, leaving individuals to figure out for themselves that it was an ethnic category (Pryor et al. 1992; for other studies showing the tendency of respondents to identify as ethnic Canadians, see Mackie and Brinkerhoff 1984; Roberts and Clifton 1982).

By 1996 Statistics Canada had decided to include "Canadian" as an example of an ethnic group in its census form. As a result, 18.7 percent of the population reported Canadian as their sole ethnic origin. Another 12.2 percent reported mixed origins that included Canadian, for a total of 30.9 percent reporting to be fully or partially Canadian in an ethnic sense (calculated from Statistics Canada 1998c). In recognizing Canadian as an ethnic category, Statistics Canada has opened the possibility of a stronger sense of Canadian identity. It remains for the government to follow suit, to encourage citizens' ethnic identification with Canada at the same time as it continues to pursue its policy of liberal multiculturalism.

LIBERAL MULTICULTURALISM AND CANADIAN UNITY

In 1994 Montreal novelist Neil Bissoondath created a stir by publishing a book criticizing multiculturalism.

> I would venture that a Canadian of Italian descent and a Canadian of Pakistani descent are likely to have more in common with one another than with Italians or Pakistanis.... Such commonality is not possible, however, if a racial vision leads the way.... [M]ulticulturalism has failed us. In eradicating the centre, in evoking uncertainty as to what and who is a Canadian, it has diminished all sense of Canadian values, of what is a Canadian. (Bissoondath 1994, 71)

Originally from Trinidad, and possessing extremely remote Indian/Hindu ancestral background, Bissoondath may be read as an immigrant pleading to be recognized as an ethnic Canadian. His behaviour, he says, is Canadian, like the behaviour of many other immigrants, no matter what their ethnic or racial background. He lives in Canada, not Trinidad; he lives in the present, not the mythical Hindu past of his distant Indian ancestors. It is one thing to recognize the interesting and valued cultural backgrounds of the many immigrants to Canada: it is another to force those backgrounds on them as their sole ethnic identity.

Bissoondath seems to be afraid of the illiberal multiculturalism—forcing individuals to stay in their ancestral boxes—that he thinks is the dominant ideological trend in Canadian discussion. This is a fear also expressed by Reginald W. Bibby in his provocatively titled *Mosaic Madness*: "Since the 1960s ... [Canada] has been leading the world in advocating freedom through pluralism and relativism ... trying to be a multinational society, enshrining coexistence and tolerance. The preliminary results are beginning to appear. The news is not that good" (1990, 3).

Bibby confuses multiculturalism with multinationalism, a policy that, if it did exist, might indeed fracture the Canadian nation, as Bibby believes is happening (ibid., 96). For critics such as Bibby and Bissoondath, multiculturalism is an illiberal policy that promotes individuals' and families' preoccupations with ancestral identity to such an extent that it undermines the sense of community necessary to shared citizenship in Canada. But this is a false fear. The official multiculturalism policy in Canada to date is liberal, and as such, it promotes the integration of immigrants into the dominant society. It does not promote multinationalism; rather, by incorporating immigrants and non-whites into the Canadian mainstream as equals whose ancestral cultures are symbolically valued, it promotes Canadianness.

This democratic and egalitarian approach to all religions, languages, and customs promotes Canadian inclusivity. Multiculturalism "normalizes" a wide range of customs and makes the enjoyment of such customs part of what it means to be a Canadian. It paradoxically universalizes specificity; all Canadians are expected to have and to enjoy a specific ethno-cultural ancestral identity as well as their universal Canadian identity. To be Canadian now, in the dominant ideology, is to revel in the exciting international flavour of the society. Far from threatening it, as they might have been perceived to do in the past, recent immigrants vivify Canadian culture.

For the state to symbolically recognize the varied cultural origins of Canadians, as Canada's multiculturalism policy does, is to acknowledge that individuals have identities other than mere citizen. Liberal multiculturalism acknowledges the social need for difference, for smaller, more close-knit communities separated from the Canadian mainstream. But it does not mandate such difference. In contrast, to stretch multiculturalism to the point at which it becomes an illiberal principle, as academics such as Kallen and Abu-Laban and Stasiulis suggest, would force Canadians into ethnic groups and ignore the fundamental individualism of Canadians' cultural choices.

Abu-Laban and Stasiulis want group identities to take precedence over individual ones: "At best," they state of Canada's policy of multiculturalism, "what is left is a discourse emphasizing individual as opposed to group rights through the subsumption of the pluralist notion of multiculturalism under the individualist notion of citizenship" (1992, 372). In an earlier article Peter made a similar comment, criticizing multiculturalism for promoting ethnicity as a sort of cultural festival, while actually advocating "societal mobility of the ethnic individual while retarding the advancement of ethnic groups" (1981, 65).

But the Canadian multicultural policy is indeed predicated on individual citizenship, not on group rights. Citizenship requires a "thick" sense of belonging: individual citizens of a country must feel that they have ties to other members. As Fierlback notes, "Too strong an emphasis upon cultural identity discourages identification with those who are clearly different from oneself (1996, 20). An illiberal multiculturalism policy that forgets or ignores the many commonalities of citizenship—such as regionalism, professional affiliation, personal interests, or intermarriage—that emerge from identities other than religion, culture, and ethnicity would undermine individual citizens' connectedness with other Canadians and their sense of belonging to Canada. Canada's multiculturalism policy does not protect the rights of groups. It protects individuals' rights to enact or preserve ancestral cultures, as they see fit, without any obligation whatsoever to the groups to which they may be perceived to belong.

The danger of moving from a liberal policy of individual rights to an illiberal one of group rights underlies much of the recent concern with multiculturalism in both the U.S. and Canada; Schlesinger, for example, worries about a cult of ethnicity whose "underlying philosophy is that America is not a nation of individuals at all but a nation of groups ... and that division into ethnic communities establishes the basic structure of American society" (1992, 16). This is the attitude reflected in Bannerji's (1997) argument that race and ethnicity are such salient aspects of the identity of all Canadians that there is in effect no difference in the way minorities were treated in 1920 and the way they were treated in the mid-1990s. Relying in part on her own experience as an adult immigrant, Bannerji implies that it is impossible for an individual not of European descent to feel Canadian.

Such a feeling is common, though certainly not universal among first-generation adult immigrants (Howard 1998). But as much empirical evidence shows (Reitz and Breton 1994), the salience of ethnicity declines drastically among second- and third-generation immigrants (that is, Canadians with immigrant parents or grandparents), who normally feel a sense of connection to others in the country who have ethnically different ancestors. Even many first-generation immigrants feel such a connection, especially those who are already professionals prior to coming to Canada, who speak English before arrival, and who have a generally cosmopolitan outlook (Moodley 1983). A public policy that encourages liberal multiculturalism can simultaneously encourage identification with ancestral culture and a sense of connection with other Canadians.

The danger of a policy of illiberal multiculturalism, as Appiah suggests and as Bibby and Bissoondath fear, is that ethnic and racial essentialism could replace the complex, diverse identities of individual Canadians that enable them routinely to form ties with those who do not share their religious, ethnic, or racial background. In the short term, a policy of illiberal multiculturalism might result in more social recognition of, and more pride in, a minority religion such as Islam, or a non-white race. But in the long run, the result might well be a fragmentation of society and a closing in of the different groups. Differentiated ethnic and national groups would coexist uneasily in a shared public space. This would be the result of the type of multiculturalism that Kallen and Abu-Laban and Stasiulis advocate.

But in fact, this warning about illiberal multiculturalism is presently a warning about a false danger. The Canadian public policy of multiculturalism remains—and ought to remain—liberal, rooted in individual citizens' choices; academic and activist advocacy of illiberal group-oriented policies has had no effect on government in this regard. And social behaviour reflects the appropriateness of government policy. Immigrants and their children do become ethnic Canadians.

Paradoxically, liberal protection of cultural "uniqueness" promotes a universal sense of citizenship. Immigrants' "strong affiliation with their new country seems to be based in large part on its willingness not just to tolerate but to welcome cultural difference" (Kymlicka and Norman 1995, 307). Members of minorities and new Canadians feel more valued than previously; as such, they find it easier, and more to their liking, to become Canadians. Canadians exist: there is a Canadian identity in which all Canadians, regardless of ethnic ancestry, can share. Identity is a state of mind; to think of oneself as Canadian is to be Canadian. Public policy needs to promote this Canadianness, which increases citizens' loyalty to each other and the nation as a whole. A loyal Canadian will not question the nation "as a project" (MacIntyre 1995, 221): the entity Canada is something of which a person feels part and to which he or she is bound.

At its best, nationhood is based on a sense of commonality among all legal citizens; at its worst, on an exclusivist sense that only people of certain ethnic, racial, or religious background can be citizens. In part via its policy of multiculturalism, Canada has progressed beyond a notion of citizenship based on exclusion of the Other. But it has not yet created a strong sense of citizenship based on common experience in, and loyalty to, the country of Canada. Yet Canada is increasingly composed not of strangers from different parts of the world and different cultural backgrounds, but of people who share not only the flat, thin legal state of citizenship, but also the complex, thickening state of fictive kinship that underlies the sense of nationhood.

The policy of illiberal multiculturalism suggested by Kallen and Abu-Laban and Stasiulis (and more broadly by those who adhere to the social movement of the politics of identity) would reduce Canadians' sense of citizenship and nationhood. National unity, a sense of identification with the country at large and with fellow citizens, would be undermined by a public policy that fears to acknowledge that people who live in Canada for any length of time become ethnic Canadians. The trick is in the balance. Ethnic ancestry and actual personal culture are both valued forms of identity. But they are not the only forms. Personal life experience, personal connection with others in the land of one's birth or adoption, is also a form of identity. Individual immigrants frequently insist that they are Canadians. They value their citizenship papers and their new sense of belonging: their sense of Canadianness thickens as they and their descendants stay in Canada (Howard 1998). Canadian public policy can easily acknowledge and strengthen that thickened identity without undermining liberal multiculturalism.

The more important issue, though, is not the sense of identity adopted by recent immigrants: it is the sense of identity of all Canadians. Whether Quebec separates or not, Canadians in the rest of Canada will need a stronger identity in the 21st century than they presently have. A public policy that stresses difference and diversity, but forgets also to stress sameness and similarity, will make it more difficult for such an identity to coalesce. *Pace* Bouchard, English Canada is a nation, but it is a hidden nation, not yet revealed to itself. One step in preserving and strengthening the nation of English Canada is to recognize that there is such a thing as Canadian ethnicity. The other step is to preserve the policy of multiculturalism as it now exists; that is, to preserve liberal multiculturalism and not adopt its illiberal variant.

REFERENCES

Abu-Laban, Y., and D. Stasiulis. 1992. "Ethnic Pluralism under Siege: Popular and Partisan Opposition to Multiculturalism." *Canadian Public Policy/Analyse de Politiques* 18, no. 4:365–386.

Amit-Talai, V. 1996. "The Minority Circuit: Identity Politics and the Professionalization of Ethnic Activism." in *Re-situating Identities: The Politics of Race, Ethnicity and Culture,* ed. V. Amit-Talai and C. Knowles, 89–114. Peterborough: Broadview Press.

Angus Reid Group. 1991. *Multiculturalism and Canadians.*

Appiah, K.A. 1997. "The Multiculturalist Misunderstanding." *New York Review of Books* 44, no. 15:30–36.

Attitude Study 1991. National Survey Report submitted to Multiculturalism and Citizenship Canada.

Bannerji, H. 1997. "Geography Lessons: On Being an Insider/Outsider to the Canadian Nation." In *Dangerous Territories: Struggles for Difference and Equality in Education,* ed. L.G. Roman and L. Eyre, 23–41. New York: Routledge.

Bibby, R.W. 1990. *Mosaic Madness: Pluralism without a Cause.* Toronto: Stoddart.

———. 1993. *Unknown Gods: The Ongoing Story of Religion in Canada.* Toronto: Stoddart.

Bissoondath, N. 1994. *Selling Illusions: The Cult of Multiculturalism in Canada.* Toronto: Penguin.

Breton, R. 1986. "Multiculturalism and Canadian Nation-Building." In *The Politics of Gender, Ethnicity and Language in Canada,* ed. A. Cairns and C. Williams, 27–66. Toronto: University of Toronto Press.

Brotz, H. 1980. "Multiculturalism in Canada: A Muddle." *Canadian Public Policy/Analyse de Politiques* 6, no. 1:41–46.

Burnet, J. 1987. "Multiculturalism in Canada." In *Ethnic Canada: Identities and Inequalities*, ed. L. Driedger, 65–79. Toronto: Copp Clark Pitman.

DiSanto, J.E. 1989. "Nonhyphenated Canadians—Where are You?" In *Multiculturalism and Intergroup Relations*, ed. J.S. Frideres, 141–148. Westport: Greenwood Press.

Fierlbeck, K. 1996. "The Ambivalent Potential of Cultural Identity." *Canadian Journal of Political Science* 29, no. 1:3–22.

Fischer, C.S. 1982. *To Dwell among Friends: Personal Networks in Town and City.* Chicago: University of Chicago Press.

Frideres, J.S. 1993. "Changing Dimensions of Ethnicity in Canada." In *Deconstructing a Nation: Immigration, Multiculturalism and Racism in '90s Canada*, ed. V. Satzewich, 47–67. Halifax: Fernwood Publishing.

Gallup Report. 1968. "Canadians Express Disapproval of Marriages between White and Non-white" (11 September).

Gans, H.J. 1979. "Symbolic Ethnicity: The Future of Ethnic Groups and Cultures in America." *Ethnic and Racial Studies* 2, no. 1:1–20.

Greenhill, P. 1994. *Ethnicity in the Mainstream: Three Studies of English Canadian Culture in Ontario.* Montreal and Kingston: McGill-Queen's University Press.

Griffin, K. 1992. "Ottawa Redress Total Climbs to $365 Million." *Vancouver Sun* (24 February): B4.

Henry, F., and E. Ginzberg. 1993. "Racial Discrimination in Employment." In *Social Inequality in Canada: Patterns, Problems, Policies*, 2nd ed., ed. J. Curtis, E. Grabb, and N. Guppy, 353–360. Scarborough: Prentice-Hall Canada.

Hoffman, E. 1989. *Lost in Translation: A Life in a New Language.* New York: Penguin.

Howard, R.E. 1998. "Being Canadian: Citizenship in Canada." *Citizenship Studies* 2, no. 1:133–152.

Isajiw, W.W. 1985. "Definitions of Ethnicity." In *Ethnicity and Ethnic Relations in Canada*, ed. R.M. Bienvenue and J.E. Goldstein, 5–17. Toronto: Butterworth.

Jones, T.D. 1998. *Human Rights: Group Defamation, Freedom of Expression and the Law of Nations.* Boston: Martinus Nijhoff.

Kallen, E. 1990. "Multiculturalism: The Not-So-Impossible Dream." In *Human Rights in Canada: Into the 1990s and Beyond*, ed. R.I. Cholewinski, 165–181. Ottawa: Human Rights Research and Education Centre, University of Ottawa.

Kymlicka, W., and W. Norman. 1995. "Return of the Citizen: A Survey of Recent Work on Citizenship Theory." In *Theorizing Citizenship*, ed. R. Beiner, 283–322. Albany: State University of New York Press.

Mackie, M., and M.B. Brinkerhoff. 1984. "Measuring Ethnic Salience." *Canadian Ethnic Studies* 16, no. 1:114–131.

MacIntyre, A. 1995. "Is Patriotism a Virtue?" In *Theorizing Citizenship*, ed. R. Beiner, 209–228. Albany: State University of New York Press.

Moodley, K. 1983. "Canadian Multiculturalism as Ideology." *Ethnic and Racial Studies* 6, no. 3:320–331.

Peter, K. 1981. "The Myth of Multiculturalism and Other Political Fables." In *Ethnicity, Power and Politics in Canada.* Vol. 13, ed. J. Dahlie and T. Fernando, 56–67. Toronto: Methuen.

Pryor, E.T., G.J. Goldmann, M.J. Sheridan, and P.M. White. 1992. "Measuring Ethnicity: Is 'Canadian' an Evolving Ethnic Category?" *Ethnic and Racial Studies* 15, no. 2:214–235.

Reitz, J.G. 1993. "Statistics on Racial Discrimination in Canada." *Policy Options* (March):32–36.

Reitz, J.G., and R. Breton. 1994. *The Illusion of Difference: Realities of Ethnicity in Canada and the United States.* Toronto: C.D. Howe Institute.

Roberts, L.W., and R.A. Clifton. 1982. "Exploring the Ideology of Canadian Multiculturalism." *Canadian Public Policy/Analyse de Politiques* 8, no. 2:88–94.

Schlesinger, A.M., Jr. 1992. *The Disuniting of America: Reflections on a Multicultural Society.* New York: W.W. Norton.

Seguin, R. 1996. "Cabinet Edgy as Bouchard Takes Over." *The Globe and Mail* (29 January): A4.

Spicer, K. (Chairman). 1991. *Citizens' Forum on Canada's Future: Report to the People and Government of Canada.* Ottawa: Supply and Services Canada.

Statistics Canada. 1991. *Census of Canada 1991: The Nation-Knowledge of Languages.* Ottawa: Statistics Canada.

———. 1993. *Census of Canada: Religions in Canada.* Ottawa: Industry, Science and Technology Canada.

———. 1998a. *1996 Census: Population by Knowledge of Official Languages, Showing Age Groups, for Canada, Provinces and Territories.* http:// www.statcan.ca/english/census96/dec2/off.htm.

———. 1998b. *1996 Census: Population by Mother Tongue, Showing Age Groups, for Canada, Provinces and Territories.* http://www.statcan.ca/english/cen-sus96/dec2/mother.htm.

———. 1998c. *1996 Census: Total Population by Ethnic Origin.* http://www.statcan.ca/english/census96/feb 17/ eo2can.htm.

———. 1998d. *Total Population by Visible Minority Population for Canada, 1996 Census.* http:// www.statcan.ca/english/census96/feb 17/vmcan.htm.

Weber, M. 1978. *Economy and Society,* ed. G. Roth and C. Wittich. Los Angeles: University of California Press.

Weinfeld, M. 1981. "Myth and Reality in the Canadian Mosaic: 'Affective Ethnicity.'" *Canadian Ethnic Studies* 13, no. 3:80–100.

Winn, C. 1985. "Affirmative Action and Visible Minorities: Eight Premises in Quest of Evidence." *Canadian Public Policy/Analyse de Politiques* 11, no. 4:684–700.

From Redistribution to Recognition?
Dilemmas of Justice in a "Post-Socialist" Age

Nancy Fraser

The "struggle for recognition" is fast becoming the paradigmatic form of political conflict in the late 20th century. Demands for "recognition of difference" fuel struggles of groups mobilized under the banners of nationality, ethnicity, "race," gender, and sexuality. In these "post-socialist" conflicts, group identity supplants class interest as the chief medium of political mobilization. Cultural domination supplants exploitation as the fundamental injustice. And cultural recognition displaces socio-economic redistribution as the remedy for injustice and the goal of political struggle.

That, of course, is not the whole story. Struggles for recognition occur in a world of exacerbated material inequality—in income and property ownership; in access to paid work, education, health care, and leisure time; but also more starkly in caloric intake and exposure to environmental toxicity, hence in life expectancy and rates of morbidity and mortality. Material inequality is on the rise in most of the world's countries. It is also increasing globally, most dramatically across the line that divides North from South. How, then, should we view the eclipse of a socialist imaginary centred on terms such as "interest," "exploitation," and "redistribution"? And what should we make of the rise of a new political imaginary centred on notions of "identity," "difference," "cultural domination," and "recognition"? Does this shift represent a lapse into "false consciousness"? Or does it, rather, redress the culture-blindness of a materialist paradigm rightfully discredited by the collapse of Soviet Communism?

Neither of those two stances is adequate, in my view. Both are too wholesale and un-nuanced. Instead of simply endorsing or rejecting all of identity politics *simpliciter,* we should see ourselves as presented with a new intellectual and practical task: that of developing a *critical* theory of recognition, one that identifies and defends only those versions of the cultural politics of difference that can be coherently combined with the social politics of equality.

In formulating this project, I assume that justice today requires *both* redistribution *and* recognition. And I propose to examine the relation between them.

THE REDISTRIBUTION–RECOGNITION DILEMMA

Let me begin by noting some complexities of contemporary "post-socialist" political life. With the decentring of class, diverse social movements are mobilized around cross-cutting axes of difference. Contesting a range of injustices, their claims overlap and at times conflict. Demands for cultural change intermingle with demands for economic change, both within and among social movements. Increasingly, however, identity-based claims tend to predominate, as prospects for redistribution appear to recede. The result is a complex political field with little programmatic coherence.

To help clarify this situation and the political prospects it presents, I propose to distinguish two broadly conceived, analytically distinct understandings of injustice. The first is socio-economic injustice, which is rooted in the political-economic structure of society. Examples include exploitation (having the fruits of one's labour appropriated for the benefit of others); economic marginalization (being confined to undesirable or poorly paid work or being denied access to income-generating labour altogether); and deprivation (being denied an adequate material standard of living).

Egalitarian theorists have long sought to conceptualize the nature of these socio-economic injustices. Their accounts include Marx's theory of capitalist exploitation, John Rawls's account of justice as fairness in the distribution of "primary goods," Amartya Sen's view that justice requires ensuring that people have equal "capabilities to function," and Ronald Dworkin's view that it requires "equality of resources."[1] For my purposes here, however, we need not commit ourselves to any one particular theoretical account. We need only subscribe to a rough and general understanding of socio-economic injustice informed by a commitment to egalitarianism.

The second kind of injustice is cultural or symbolic. It is rooted in social patterns of representation, interpretation, and communication. Examples include cultural domination (being subjected to patterns of interpretation and communication that are associated with another culture and are alien and/or hostile to one's own); non-recognition (being rendered invisible via the authoritative representational, communicative, and interpretative practices of one's culture); and disrespect (being routinely maligned or disparaged in stereotypic public cultural representations and/or in everyday life interactions).

Despite the differences between them, both socio-economic injustice and cultural injustice are pervasive in contemporary societies. Both are rooted in processes and practices that systematically disadvantage some groups of people vis-à-vis others. Both, consequently, should be remedied.

Of course, this distinction between economic injustice and cultural injustice is analytical. In practice, the two are intertwined. Even the most material economic institutions have a constitutive, irreducible cultural dimension; they are shot through with significations and norms. Conversely, even the most discursive cultural practices have a constitutive, irreducible political-economic dimension; they are underpinned by material supports. Thus, far from occupying two airtight separate spheres, economic injustice and cultural injustice are usually inter-imbricated so as to reinforce one another dialectically. Cultural norms that are unfairly biased against some are institutionalized in the state and the economy; meanwhile, economic disadvantage impedes equal participation in the making of culture, in public spheres, and in everyday life. The result is often a vicious circle of cultural and economic subordination.[2]

Despite these mutual entwinements, I shall continue to distinguish economic injustice and cultural injustice analytically. And I shall also distinguish two correspondingly distinct kinds of remedy. The remedy for economic injustice is political-economic restructuring of some sort. This might involve redistributing income, reorganizing the division of labour, subjecting investment to democratic decision making, or transforming other basic economic structures. Although these various remedies differ importantly from one another, I shall henceforth refer to the whole group of them by the generic term "redistribution."[3] The remedy for cultural injustice, in contrast, is some sort of cultural or symbolic change. This could involve upwardly revaluing disrespected identities and the cultural products of maligned groups. It could also involve recognizing and positively valorizing cultural diversity. More radically still, it could involve the wholesale transformation of societal patterns of representation, interpretation, and communication in ways that would change *everybody's* sense of self.[4] Although these remedies differ importantly from one another, I shall henceforth refer to the whole group of them by the generic term "recognition."

Once again, this distinction between redistributive remedies and recognition remedies is analytical. Redistributive remedies generally presuppose an underlying conception of recognition. For example, some proponents of egalitarian socio-economic redistribution ground their claims on the "equal moral worth of persons"; thus, they treat economic redistribution as an expression of recognition.[5] Conversely, recognition remedies sometimes presuppose an underlying conception of redistribution. For example, some proponents of multicultural recognition ground their claims on the imperative of a just distribution of the "primary good" of an "intact cultural structure"; they therefore treat cultural recognition as a species of redistribution.[6]

EXPLOITED CLASSES, DESPISED SEXUALITIES, AND BIVALENT COLLECTIVES

Consider, first, the redistribution end of the spectrum. At this end let us posit an ideal, typical mode of collectivity whose existence is rooted wholly in the political economy. It will be differentiated as a collectivity, in other words, by virtue of the economic structure, as opposed to the cultural order, of society. Thus any structural injustices its members suffer will be traceable ultimately to the political economy. The root of the injustice, as well as its core, will be socio-economic maldistribution, while any attendant cultural injustices will derive ultimately from that economic root. At bottom, therefore, the remedy required to redress the injustice will be political-economic redistribution, as opposed to cultural recognition.

In the real world, to be sure, political economy and culture are mutually intertwined, as are injustices of distribution and recognition. Thus we may doubt whether there exist any pure collectivities of this sort. For heuristic purposes, however, it is useful to examine their properties. To do so, let us consider a familiar example that can be interpreted as approximating the ideal type: the Marxian conception of the exploited class, understood in an orthodox and theoretical way.[7]

In the conception assumed here, class is a mode of social differentiation that is rooted in the political-economic structure of society. A class only exists as a collectivity by virtue of its position in that structure and of its relation to other classes. Thus, the Marxian working class is the body of persons in a capitalist society who must sell their labour power under arrangements that authorize the capitalist class to appropriate surplus productivity for its private benefit. The injustice of these arrangements, moreover, is quintessentially a matter of distribution. In the capitalist scheme of social reproduction, the proletariat receives an unjustly large share of the burdens and an unjustly small share of the rewards. To be sure, its members also suffer serious cultural injustices, the "hidden (and not so hidden) injuries of class." But far from being rooted directly in an autonomously unjust cultural structure, these derive from the political economy, as ideologies of class inferiority proliferate to justify exploitation. The remedy for the injustice, consequently, is redistribution, not recognition. Overcoming class exploitation requires restructuring the political economy so as to alter the class distribution of social burdens and social benefits. In the Marxian conception, such restructuring takes the radical form of abolishing the class structure as such. The task of the proletariat, therefore, is not simply to cut itself a better deal, but "to abolish itself as a class." The last thing it needs is recognition of its difference. On the contrary, the only way to remedy the injustice is to put the proletariat out of business as a group.

Now consider the other end of the conceptual spectrum. At this end we may posit an ideal, typical mode of collectivity that fits the recognition model of justice. A collectivity of this type is rooted wholly in culture, as opposed to in political economy. It only exists as a collectivity by virtue of the reigning social patterns of interpretation and evaluation, not by virtue of the division of labour. Thus, any structural injustices its members suffer will be traceable ultimately to the cultural-valuational structure. The root of the injustice, as well as its core, will be cultural misrecognition, while any attendant economic injustices will derive ultimately from that cultural root. At bottom, therefore, the remedy required to redress the injustice will be cultural recognition, as opposed to political-economic redistribution.

Once again, we may doubt whether there exist any pure collectivities of this sort, but it is useful to examine their properties for heuristic purposes. An example that can be interpreted as approximating the ideal type is the conception of a despised sexuality, understood in a specific stylized and theoretical way. Let us consider this conception, while leaving aside the question of whether this view of sexuality fits the actual historical homosexual collectivities that are struggling for justice in the real world.

Sexuality in this conception is a mode of social differentiation whose roots do not lie in the political economy, as homosexuals are distributed throughout the entire class structure of capitalist society, occupy no distinctive position in the division of labour, and do not constitute an exploited class. Rather, their mode of collectivity is that of a despised sexuality, rooted in the cultural-valuational structure of society. From this perspective, the injustice they suffer is quintessentially a matter of recognition. Gays and lesbians suffer from heterosexism: the authoritative construction of norms that privilege heterosexuality. Along with this goes homophobia: the cultural devaluation of homosexuality. Their sexuality thus disparaged, homosexuals are subject to shaming, harassment, discrimination, and violence, while being denied legal rights and equal protections—all fundamentally denials of recognition. To be sure, gays and lesbians also suffer serious economic injustices; they can be summarily dismissed from work and are denied family-based social welfare benefits. But far from being rooted directly in the economic structure, these derive instead from an unjust cultural-valuational structure. The remedy for the injustice, consequently, is recognition, not redistribution. Overcoming homophobia and heterosexism requires changing the cultural valuations (as well as their legal and practical expressions) that privilege heterosexuality, deny equal respect to gays and lesbians, and refuse to recognize homosexuality as a legitimate way of being sexual. It is to revalue a despised sexuality, to accord positive recognition to gay and lesbian sexual specificity.

Matters are thus fairly straightforward at the two extremes of our conceptual spectrum.

Matters become murkier, however, once we move away from these extremes. When we consider collectivities located in the middle of the conceptual spectrum, we encounter hybrid modes that combine features of the exploited class with features of the despised sexuality. These collectivities are "bivalent." They are differentiated as collectivities by virtue of both the political-economic structure *and* the cultural-valuational structure of society.

Both gender and "'race" are paradigmatic bivalent collectivities. Although each has peculiarities not shared by the other, both encompass political-economic dimensions and cultural-valuational dimensions. Gender and "race," therefore, implicate both redistribution and recognition.

Gender, for example, has political-economic dimensions. It is a basic structuring principle of the political economy. On the one hand, gender structures the fundamental division between paid "productive" labour and unpaid "reproductive" and domestic labour, assigning women primary responsibility for the latter. On the other hand, gender also structures the division within paid labour between higher-paid, male-dominated manufacturing and professional occupations and lower-paid, female-dominated "pink-collar" and domestic-service occupations. The result is a political-economic structure that generates gender-specific modes of exploitation, marginalization, and deprivation. This structure constitutes gender as a political-economic differentiation endowed with certain class-like characteristics. When viewed under this aspect, gender injustice appears as a species of distributive injustice that cries out for redistributive redress. Much like class, gender justice requires transforming the political economy so as to eliminate its gender structuring. Eliminating gender-specific exploitation, marginalization, and deprivation requires abolishing the gender division of labour—both the gendered division between paid and unpaid labour and the gender division within paid labour. The logic of the remedy is akin to the logic with respect to class: it is to put gender out of business as such. If gender were nothing but a political-economic differentiation, in sum, justice would require its abolition.

That, however, is only half the story. In fact, gender is not only a political-economic differentiation, but a cultural-valuational differentiation as well. As such, it also encompasses elements that are more like sexuality than class and bring it squarely within the problematic of recognition. Certainly, a major feature of gender injustice is androcentrism: the authoritative construction of norms that privilege traits associated with masculinity.

Gender, in sum, is a bivalent mode of collectivity. It contains a political-economic face that brings it within the ambit of redistribution. Yet it also contains a cultural-valuational face that brings it simultaneously within the ambit of recognition. Of course, the two faces are not neatly separated from one another. Rather, they intertwine to reinforce one another dialectically, as sexist and androcentric cultural norms are institutionalized in the state and the economy, while women's economic disadvantage restricts women's "voice," impeding equal participation in the making of culture, in public spheres, and in everyday life. The result is a vicious circle of cultural and economic subordination. Redressing gender injustice, therefore, requires changing both political economy and culture.

But the bivalent character of gender is the source of a dilemma. Insofar as women suffer at least two analytically distinct kinds of injustice, they necessarily require at least two analytically distinct kinds of remedy—both redistribution and recognition. The two remedies pull in opposite directions, however. They are not easily pursued simultaneously. Whereas the logic of redistribution is to put gender out of business as such, the logic of recognition is to valorize gender specificity.[8] Here, then, is the feminist version of the redistribution–recognition dilemma: how can feminists fight simultaneously to abolish gender differentiation and to valorize gender specificity?

An analogous dilemma arises in the struggle against racism. "Race," like gender, is a bivalent mode of collectivity. On the one hand, it resembles class in being a structural principle of political economy. In this aspect, "race" structures the capitalist division of labour. It structures the division within paid work between low-paid, low-status, menial, dirty, and domestic occupations, held disproportionately by people of colour, and higher-paid, higher-status, white-collar, professional, technical and managerial occupations, held disproportionately by "whites."[9] Today's racial division of paid labour is part of the historic legacy of colonialism and slavery, which elaborated racial categorization to justify brutal new forms of appropriation and exploitation, effectively constituting "blacks" as a political-economic caste. Currently, moreover, "race" also structures access to official labour markets, constituting large segments of the population of colour as a "superfluous," degraded sub-proletariat or underclass, unworthy even of exploitation and excluded from the productive system altogether. The result is a political-economic structure that generates "race"-specific modes of exploitation, marginalization, and deprivation. This structure constitutes "race" as a political-economic differentiation endowed with certain class-like characteristics. When viewed under this aspect, racial injustice appears as a species of distributive injustice that cries out for redistributive redress. Much like class, racial justice requires transforming the political economy so as to eliminate its racialization. Eliminating "race"-specific exploitation, marginalization, and deprivation requires abolishing the racial division of labour—both the racial division between exploitable and superfluous labour and the racial division within paid labour. The logic of the remedy is like the logic with respect to class: it is to put "race" out of business as such. If "race" were nothing but a political-economic differentiation, in sum, justice would require its abolition.

However, "race," like gender, is not only political-economic. It also has cultural-valuational dimensions, which bring it into the universe of recognition. Thus, "race" too encompasses elements that are more like sexuality than class. A major aspect of racism is Eurocentrism: the authoritative construction of norms that privilege traits associated with "whiteness." Along with this goes cultural racism: the pervasive devaluation and disparagement of things coded as "black," "brown," and "yellow," paradigmatically—but not only—people of colour. This depreciation is expressed in a range of harms suffered by people of colour, including demeaning stereotypical depictions in the media as criminal, bestial, primitive, stupid, and so on.

As in the case of gender, these harms are injustices of recognition. Thus the logic of their remedy, too, is to accord positive recognition to devalued group specificity.

"Race," too, therefore, is a bivalent mode of collectivity with both a political-economic and a cultural-valuational face. Its two faces intertwine to reinforce one another dialectically, as racist and Eurocentric cultural norms are institutionalized in the state and the economy, while the economic disadvantage suffered by people of colour restricts their "voice." Redressing racial injustice, therefore, requires changing both political economy and culture. And as with gender, the bivalent character of "race" is the source of a dilemma. Insofar as people of colour suffer at least two analytically distinct kinds of injustice, they necessarily require at least two analytically distinct kinds of remedy, which are not easily pursued simultaneously. Whereas the logic of redistribution is to put "race" out of business as such, the logic of recognition is to valorize group specificity.[10] Here, then, is the anti-racist version of the redistribution–recognition dilemma: How can anti-racists fight simultaneously to abolish "race" and to valorize racialized group specificity?

Both gender and "race," in sum, are dilemmatic modes of collectivity. Unlike class, which occupies one end of the conceptual spectrum, and unlike sexuality, which occupies the other, gender and "race" are bivalent, implicated simultaneously in both the politics of redistribution and the politics of recognition. Both, consequently, face the redistribution–recognition dilemma. Feminists must pursue political-economic remedies that would undermine gender differentiation, while also pursuing cultural-valuational remedies that valorize the specificity of a despised collectivity. Anti-racists, likewise, must pursue political-economic remedies that would undermine "racial" differentiation, while also pursuing cultural-valuational remedies that valorize the specificity of despised collectivities. How can they do both things at once?

AFFIRMATION OR TRANSFORMATION? REVISITING THE QUESTION OF REMEDY

Let me begin by briefly distinguishing affirmation and transformation. By affirmative remedies for injustice I mean remedies aimed at correcting inequitable outcomes of social arrangements without disturbing the underlying framework that generates them. By transformative remedies, in contrast, I mean remedies aimed at correcting inequitable outcomes precisely by restructuring the underlying generative framework. The nub of the contrast is end-state outcomes versus the processes that produce them. It is *not* gradual versus apocalyptic change.

This distinction can be applied, first of all, to remedies for cultural injustice. Affirmative remedies for such injustices are currently associated with mainstream multiculturalism. This proposes to redress disrespect by revaluing unjustly devalued group identities, while leaving intact both the contents of those identities and the group differentiations that underlie them. Transformative remedies, by contrast, are currently associated with deconstruction. They would redress disrespect by transforming the underlying cultural-valuational structure. By destabilizing existing group identities and differentiations, these remedies would not only raise the self-esteem of members of currently disrespected groups. They would change *everyone's* sense of belonging, affiliation, and self.

To illustrate the distinction, let us consider, once again, the case of the despised sexuality. Affirmative remedies for homophobia and heterosexism are currently associated with gay-identity politics, which aims to revalue gay and lesbian identity. Transformative remedies, in contrast, include the approach of "queer theory," which would deconstruct the homo–hetero dichotomy. Gay-identity politics treats homosexuality as a substantive, cultural, identificatory positivity, much like an ethnicity. This positivity is assumed to subsist in and of itself and to need only additional recognition. "Queer theory," in contrast, treats homosexuality as the constructed and devalued correlate of heterosexuality; both are reifications of sexual ambiguity and are co-defined only in virtue of one another. The transformative aim is not to solidify a gay identity, but to deconstruct the homo–hetero dichotomy so as to destabilize all fixed sexual identities. The point is not to dissolve all sexual difference in a single, universal human identity; it is rather to sustain a sexual field of multiple, debinarized, fluid, ever-shifting differences.

Both these approaches have considerable interest as remedies for misrecognition. But there is one crucial difference between them. Whereas gay-identity politics tends to enhance existing sexual group differentiation, queer-theory politics tends to destabilize it—at least ostensibly and in the long run. The point holds for recognition remedies more generally. Whereas affirmative recognition remedies tend to promote existing group differentiations, transformative recognition remedies tend, in the long run, to destabilize them so as to make room for future regroupments. I shall return to this point shortly.

Analogous distinctions hold for the remedies for economic injustice. Affirmative remedies for such injustices have been associated historically with the liberal welfare state. They seek to redress end-state maldistribution, while leaving intact much of the underlying political-economic structure. Thus they would increase the consumption share of economically disadvantaged groups, without otherwise restructuring the system of production. Transformative remedies, in contrast, have been historically associated with socialism. They would redress unjust distribution by transforming the underlying political-economic structure. By restructuring the relations of production, these remedies would not only alter the end-state distribution of consumption shares; they would also change the social division of labour and thus the conditions of existence for everyone.

Let us consider, once again, the case of the exploited class. Affirmative redistributive remedies for class injustices typically include income transfers of two distinct kinds: social insurance programs share some of the costs of social reproduction for the stably employed, the so-called "primary" sectors of the working class; public assistance programs provide means-tested, "targeted" aid to the "reserve army" of the unemployed and underemployed. Far from abolishing class differentiation per se, these affirmative remedies support it and shape it. Their general effect is to shift attention from the class division between workers and capitalists to the division between employed and non-employed fractions of the working class. Public assistance programs "target" the poor, not only for aid but for hostility. Such remedies, to be sure, provide needed material aid. But they also create strongly cathected, antagonistic group differentiations.

The logic here applies to affirmative redistribution in general. Although this approach aims to redress economic injustice, it leaves intact the deep structures that generate class disadvantage. Thus it must make surface reallocations time and again. The result is to mark the most disadvantaged class as inherently deficient and insatiable, as always needing more and more. In time such a class can even come to appear privileged, the recipient of special treatment and undeserved largesse. An approach aimed at redressing injustices of distribution can thus end up creating injustices of recognition.

In a sense, this approach is self-contradictory. Affirmative redistribution generally presupposes a universalist conception of recognition, the equal moral worth of persons. Let us call this its "official recognition commitment." Yet the practice of affirmative redistribution, as iterated over time, tends to set in motion a second—stigmatizing—recognition dynamic, which contradicts universalism. This second dynamic can be understood as the "practical recognition effect" of affirmative redistribution. It conflicts with its official recognition commitment.

Now contrast this logic with transformative remedies for distributive injustices of class. Transformative remedies typically combine universalist social welfare programs, steeply progressive taxation, macro-economic policies aimed at creating full employment, a large non-market public sector, significant public and/or collective ownership, and democratic decision making about basic socio-economic priorities. They try to assure access to employment for all, while also tending to de-link basic consumption shares from employment. Hence their tendency is to undermine class differentiation. Transformative remedies reduce social inequality without, however, creating stigmatized classes of vulnerable people perceived as beneficiaries of special largesse. They tend therefore to promote reciprocity and solidarity in the relations of recognition. Thus an approach aimed at redressing injustices of distribution can help redress (some) injustices of recognition as well.

This approach is self-consistent. Like affirmative redistribution, transformative redistribution generally presupposes a universalist conception of recognition, the equal moral worth of persons. Unlike affirmative redistribution, however, its practice tends not to undermine this conception. Thus, the two approaches generate different logics of group differentiation. Whereas affirmative remedies can have the perverse effect of promoting class differentiation, transformative remedies tend to blur it. In addition, the two approaches generate different subliminal dynamics of recognition. Affirmative redistribution can stigmatize the disadvantaged, adding the insult of misrecognition to the injury of deprivation. Transformative redistribution, in contrast, can promote solidarity, helping to redress some forms of misrecognition.

All this suggests a way of reformulating the redistribution–recognition dilemma. We might ask: for groups who are subject to injustices of both types, what combinations of remedies work best to minimize, if not altogether to eliminate, the mutual interferences that can arise when both redistribution and recognition are pursued simultaneously?

FINESSING THE DILEMMA: REVISITING GENDER AND "RACE"

Imagine a four-celled matrix. The horizontal axis comprises the two general kinds of remedy we have just examined, namely, affirmation and transformation. The vertical axis comprises the two aspects of justice we have been considering, namely, redistribution and recognition. On this matrix we can locate the four political orientations just discussed. In the first cell, where redistribution and affirmation intersect, is the project of the liberal welfare state; centred on surface reallocations of distributive shares among existing groups, it tends to support group differentiation; it can also generate backlash misrecognition. In the second cell, where redistribution and transformation intersect, is the project of socialism; aimed at deep restructuring of the relations of production, it tends to blur group differentiation; it can also help redress some forms of misrecognition. In the third cell, where recognition and affirmation intersect, is the project of mainstream multiculturalism; focused on surface reallocations of respect among existing groups, it tends to support group differentiation. In the fourth cell, where recognition and transformation intersect, is the project of deconstruction; aimed at deep restructuring of the relations of recognition, it tends to destabilize group differentiations.

TABLE 15.1

	Affirmation	**Transformation**
Redistribution	*the liberal welfare state* surface reallocations of existing goods to existing groups; supports group differentiation; can generate misrecognition	*socialism* deep restructuring of relations of production; blurs group differentiation; can help remedy some forms of misrecognition
Recognition	*mainstream multiculturalism* surface reallocations of respect to existing identities of existing groups; supports group differentiation	*deconstruction* deep restructuring of relations of recognition; blurs group differentiation

This matrix casts mainstream multiculturalism as the cultural analogue of the liberal welfare state, while casting deconstruction as the cultural analogue of socialism. It thereby allows us to make some preliminary assessments of the mutual compatibility of various remedial strategies. We can gauge the extent to which pairs of remedies would work at cross purposes with one another if they were pursued simultaneously. We can identify pairs that seem to land us squarely on the horns of the redistribution–recognition dilemma. We can also identify pairs that hold out the promise of enabling us to finesse it.

Prima facie at least, two pairs of remedies seem especially unpromising. The affirmative redistribution politics of the liberal welfare state seems at odds with the transformative recognition politics of deconstruction; whereas the first tends to promote group differentiation, the second tends rather to destabilize it. Similarly, the transformative redistribution politics of socialism seems at odds with the affirmative recognition politics of mainstream multiculturalism; whereas the first tends to undermine group differentiation, the second tends rather to promote it.

Conversely, two pairs of remedies seem comparatively promising. The affirmative redistribution politics of the liberal welfare state seems compatible with the affirmative recognition politics of mainstream multiculturalism; both tend to promote group differentiation. Similarly, the transformative redistribution politics of socialism seems compatible with the transformative recognition politics of deconstruction; both tend to undermine existing group differentiations.

To test these hypotheses, let us revisit gender and "race." Recall that these are bivalent differentiations, axes of both economic and cultural injustice. Thus people subordinated by gender and/or "race" need both redistribution and recognition. They are the paradigmatic subjects of the redistribution–recognition dilemma. What happens in their cases, then, when various pairs of injustice remedies are pursued simultaneously? Are there pairs of remedies that permit feminists and anti-racists to finesse, if not wholly to dispel, the redistribution–recognition dilemma?

Consider, first, the case of gender. Recall that redressing gender injustice requires changing both political economy and culture, so as to undo the vicious circle of economic and cultural subordination. As we saw, the changes in question can take either of two forms, affirmation or transformation. Let us consider, first, the prima facie promising case in which affirmative redistribution is combined with affirmative recognition. As the name suggests, affirmative redistribution to redress gender injustice in the economy includes affirmative action, the effort to assure women their fair share of existing jobs and educational places, while leaving unchanged the nature and number of those jobs and places. Affirmative recognition to redress gender injustice in the culture includes cultural feminism, the effort to assure women respect by revaluing femininity, while leaving unchanged the binary gender code that gives the latter its sense. Thus, the scenario in question combines the socio-economic politics of liberal feminism with the cultural politics of cultural feminism. Does this combination really finesse the redistribution–recognition dilemma?

Despite its initial appearance of promise, this scenario is problematic. Affirmative redistribution fails to engage the deep level at which the political economy is gendered. Aimed primarily at combatting attitudinal discrimination, it does not attack the gendered division of paid and unpaid labour, nor the gendered division of masculine and feminine occupations within paid labour. Leaving intact the deep structures that generate gender disadvantage, it must make surface reallocations again and again. The result is not only to underline gender differentiation. It is also to mark women as deficient and insatiable, as always needing more and more. In time women can even come to appear privileged, recipients of special treatment and undeserved largesse. Thus an approach aimed at redressing injustices of distribution can end up fuelling backlash injustices of recognition.

This problem is exacerbated when we add the affirmative recognition strategy of cultural feminism. That approach insistently calls attention to, if it does not performatively create, women's putative cultural specificity or difference. In some contexts, such an approach can make progress toward decentring androcentric norms. In this context, however, it is more likely to have the effect of pouring oil onto the flames of resentment against affirmative action. Read through that lens, the cultural politics of affirming women's difference appears as an affront to the liberal welfare state's official commitment to the equal moral worth of persons.

The other route with a prima facie promise is that which combines transformative redistribution with transformative recognition. Transformative redistribution to redress gender injustice in the economy consists in some form of socialist feminism or feminist social democracy. And transformative recognition to redress gender injustice in the culture consists in feminist deconstruction aimed at dismantling androcentrism by destabilizing gender dichotomies. Thus the scenario in question combines the socio-economic politics of socialist feminism with the cultural politics of deconstructive feminism. Does this combination really finesse the redistribution–recognition dilemma?

This scenario is far less problematic. The long-term goal of deconstructive feminism is a culture in which hierarchical gender dichotomies are replaced by networks of multiple intersecting differences that are de-massified and shifting. This goal is consistent with transformative socialist-feminist redistribution. Deconstruction opposes the sort of sedimentation or congealing of gender difference that occurs in an unjustly gendered political economy. Its Utopian image of a culture in which ever new constructions of identity and difference are freely elaborated and then swiftly deconstructed is only possible, after all, on the basis of rough social equality.

As a transitional strategy, moreover, this combination avoids fanning the flames of resentment. If it has a drawback, it is rather that both deconstructive-feminist cultural politics and socialist-feminist economic politics are far removed from the immediate interests and identities of most women, as these are currently culturally constructed.

Analogous results arise for "race," where the changes can again take either of two forms, affirmation or transformation. In the first prima facie promising case, affirmative action is paired with affirmative recognition. Affirmative redistribution to redress racial injustice in the economy includes affirmative action, the effort to assure people of colour their fair share of existing jobs and educational places, while leaving unchanged the nature and number of those jobs and places. And affirmative recognition to redress racial injustice in the culture includes cultural nationalism, the effort to assure people of colour respect by revaluing "blackness," while leaving unchanged the binary black–white code that gives the latter its sense. The scenario in question thus combines the socio-economic politics of liberal anti-racism with the cultural politics of black nationalism or black power. Does this combination really finesse the redistribution–recognition dilemma?

Such a scenario is again problematic. As in the case of gender, here affirmative redistribution fails to engage the deep level at which the political economy is racialized. It does not attack the racialized division of exploitable and surplus labour, nor the racialized division of menial and non-menial occupations within paid labour. Leaving intact the deep structures that generate racial disadvantage, it must make surface reallocations again and again. The result is not only to underline racial differentiation. It is also to mark people of colour as deficient and insatiable, as always needing more and more. Thus they too can be cast as privileged recipients of special treatment. The problem is exacerbated when we add the affirmative recognition strategy of cultural nationalism. In some contexts, such an approach can make progress toward decentring Eurocentric norms, but in this context the cultural politics of affirming black difference equally appears as an affront to the liberal welfare state. Fuelling the resentment against affirmative action, it can elicit intense backlash misrecognition.

In the alternative route, transformative redistribution is combined with transformative recognition. Transformative redistribution to redress racial injustice in the economy consists in some form of anti-racist democratic socialism or anti-racist social democracy. And transformative recognition to redress racial injustice in the culture consists in anti-racist deconstruction aimed at dismantling Eurocentrism by destabilizing racial dichotomies. Thus, the scenario in question combines the socio-economic politics of socialist anti-racism with the cultural politics of deconstructive anti-racism or critical "race" theory. As with the analogous approach to gender, this scenario is far less problematic. The long-term goal of deconstructive anti-racism is a culture in which hierarchical racial dichotomies are replaced by de-massified and shifting networks of multiple intersecting differences. This goal, once again, is consistent with transformative socialist redistribution. Even as a transitional strategy, this combination avoids fanning the flames of resentment. Its principal drawback, again, is that both deconstructive anti-racist cultural politics and socialist anti-racist economic politics are far removed from the immediate interests and identities of most people of colour, as these are currently culturally constructed.[10]

What, then, should we conclude from this discussion? For both gender and "race," the scenario that best finesses the redistribution–recognition dilemma is socialism in the economy plus deconstruction in the culture. But for this scenario to be psychologically and politically feasible requires that people be weaned from their attachment to current cultural constructions of their interests and identities.

The redistribution–recognition dilemma is real. There is no neat theoretical move by which it can be wholly dissolved or resolved. The best we can do is try to soften the dilemma by finding approaches that minimize conflicts between redistribution and recognition in cases where both must be pursued simultaneously.

I have argued here that socialist economics combined with deconstructive cultural politics works best to finesse the dilemma for the bivalent collectivities of gender and "race"—at least when they are considered separately. The next step would be to show that this combination also works for our larger socio-cultural configuration. After all, gender and "race" are not neatly cordoned off from one another. Nor are they neatly cordoned off from sexuality and class. Rather, all these axes of injustice intersect one another in ways that affect everyone's interests and identities. No one is a member of only one such collectivity. And people who are subordinated along one axis of social division may well be dominant along another.

The task then is to figure out how to finesse the redistribution–recognition dilemma when we situate the problem in this larger field of multiple, intersecting struggles against multiple, intersecting injustices. Although I cannot make the full argument task here, I will venture three reasons for expecting that the combination of socialism and deconstruction will again prove superior to the other alternatives.

First, the arguments pursued here for gender and "race" hold for all bivalent collectivities. Thus, insofar as real-world collectivities mobilized under the banners of sexuality and class turn out to be more bivalent than the ideal, typical constructs posited above, they too should prefer socialism plus deconstruction. And that doubly transformative approach should become the orientation of choice for a broad range of disadvantaged groups.

Second, the redistribution–recognition dilemma does not only arise endogenously, as it were, within a single bivalent collectivity. It also arises exogenously, so to speak, across intersecting collectivities. Thus, anyone who is both gay and working class will face a version of the dilemma, regardless of whether or not we interpret sexuality and class as bivalent. And anyone who is also female and black will encounter it in a multi-layered and acute form. In general, then, as soon as we acknowledge that axes of injustice cut across one another, we must acknowledge cross-cutting forms of the redistribution–recognition dilemma. And these forms are, if anything, even more resistant to resolution by combinations of affirmative remedies than the forms we considered above. For affirmative remedies work additively and are often at cross purposes with one another. Thus, the intersection of class, "race," gender, and sexuality intensifies the need for transformative solutions, making the combination of socialism and deconstruction more attractive still.

Third, that combination best promotes the task of coalition building. This task is especially pressing today, given the multiplication of social antagonisms, the fissuring of social movements, and the growing appeal of the Right in the United States. In this context, the project of transforming the deep structures of both political economy and culture appears to be the one overarching programmatic orientation capable of doing justice to *all* current struggles against injustice. It alone does not assume a zero-sum game.

If that is right, then, we can begin to see how badly off track is the current U.S. political scene. We are currently stuck in the vicious circles of mutually reinforcing cultural and economic subordination. Our best efforts to redress these injustices via the combination of the liberal welfare state plus mainstream multiculturalism are generating perverse effects. Only by looking to alternative conceptions of redistribution and recognition can we meet the requirements of justice for all.

NOTES

1   Karl Marx, *Capital,* Vol. 1; John Rawls, *A Theory of Justice* (Cambridge: Harvard University Press, 1971) and subsequent papers; Amartya Sen, *Commodities and Capabilities* (Amsterdam: North-Holland, 1985); and Ronald Dworkin, "What is Equality? Part 2: Equality of Resources," *Philosophy and Public Affairs* no. 4 (fall 1981):283–345. Although I here classify all these writers as theorists of distributive economic justice, it is also true that most of them have some resources for dealing with issues of cultural justice as well. Rawls, for example, treats "the social bases of self-respect" as a primary good to be fairly distributed, while Sen treats a "sense of self" as relevant to the capability to function. (I am indebted to Mika Manty for this point.) Nevertheless, as Iris Marion Young has suggested, the primary thrust of their thought leads in the direction of distributive economic justice. See her *Justice and the Politics of Difference,*(Princeton: Princeton University Press, 1990).

2   For the inter-imbrication of culture and political economy, see my "What's Critical About Critical Theory? The Case of Habermas and Gender," in Nancy Fraser, *Unruly Practices: Power,*

Discourse and Gender in Contemporary Social Theory, ed. Nancy Fraser (Oxford: Polity Press, 1989; "Rethinking the Public Sphere," in *Justice Interruptus,* ed. Nancy Fraser (New York: Routledge, 1997); and Nancy Fraser, "Pragmatism, Feminism, and the Linguistic Turn," in *Feminist Contentions: A Philosophical Exchange,* ed. S. Benhabib, J. Butler, D. Cornell, and Fraser, (New York: Routledge, 1995). See also Pierre Bourdieu, *Outline of a Theory of Practice* (Cambridge: Cambridge University Press, 1977. For critiques of the cultural meanings implicit in the current U.S. political economy of work and social welfare, see the last two chapters of *Unruly Practices* and the essays in Part 3 of *Justice Interruptus.*

3   In fact, these remedies stand in some tension with one another, a problem I shall explore in a subsequent section of this paper.

4   These various cultural remedies stand in some tension with one another. It is one thing to accord recognition to existing identities that are currently undervalued; it is another to transform symbolic structures and thereby alter people's identities. I shall explore the tensions among the various remedies in a subsequent section of the paper.

5   For a good example of this approach, see Ronald Dworkin, "Liberalism," in *A Matter of Principle* (Cambridge: Harvard University Press, 1985).

6   For a good example of this approach, see Will Kymlicka, *Liberalism, Community and Culture* (Oxford: Oxford University Press, 1989). The case of Kymlicka suggests that the distinction between socio-economic justice need not always map onto the distinction between distributive justice and relational or communicative justice.

7   In what follows, I conceive class in a highly stylized, orthodox, and theoretical way in order to sharpen the contrast to the other ideal, typical kinds of collectivity discussed below. Of course, this is hardly the only interpretation of the Marxian conception of class. In other contexts and for other purposes, I myself would prefer a less economistic interpretation, one that gives more weight to the cultural, historical, and discursive dimensions of class emphasized by such writers as E. P. Thompson and Joan Wallach Scott. See E.P. Thompson, *The Making of the English Working Class* (London: Victor Gollancz, 1963; and J.W. Scott, *Gender and the Politics of History* (New York: Columbia University Press, 1988).

8   This helps explain why the history of women's movements records a pattern of oscillation between integrationist, equal rights feminisms and "difference"-oriented "social" and "cultural" feminisms. It would be useful to specify the precise temporal logic that leads bivalent collectivities to shift their principal focus back and forth between redistribution and recognition. For a first attempt, see my "Rethinking Difference" *in Justice Interruptus.*

9   In addition, "race" is implicitly implicated in the gender division between paid and unpaid labour. That division relies on a normative contrast between a domestic sphere and a sphere of paid work, associated with women and men respectively. Yet the division in the United States (and elsewhere) has always also been racialized in that domesticity has been implicitly a "white" prerogative. African-Americans especially were never permitted the privilege of domesticity either as a (male) private "haven" or a (female) primary or exclusive focus on nurturing one's own kin. See Jacqueline Jones, *Labor of Love, Labor of Sorrow: Black Women, Work, and the Family from Slavery to the Present* (New York: Vintage Books, 1985; and Evelyn Nakano Glenn, "From Servitude to Service Work: Historical Continuities in the Racial Division of Reproductive Labor," *Signs: Journal of Women in Culture and Society* 18, no. 1 (autumn 1992): 1–43.

10   This helps explain why the history of black liberation struggle in the United States records a pattern of oscillation between integration and separatism (or black nationalism). As with gender, it would be useful to specify the dynamics of these alternations.

CHAPTER 16

THE FUTURE OF IDENTITY

STUART HALL

INTRODUCTION: IDENTITY IN QUESTION

The question of "identity" is being vigorously debated in social theory. In essence, the argument is that the old identities that stabilized the social world for so long are in decline, giving rise to new identities and fragmenting the modern individual as a unified subject. This so-called "crisis of identity" is seen as part of a wider process of change that is dislocating the central structures and processes of modern societies and undermining the frameworks that gave individuals stable anchorage in the social world.

For those theorists who believe that modern identities are breaking up, the argument runs something like this. A distinctive type of structural change is transforming modern societies in the late 20th century.

This is fragmenting the cultural landscapes of class, gender, sexuality, ethnicity, race, and nationality, which gave us firm locations as social individuals. These transformations are also shifting our personal identities, undermining our sense of ourselves as integrated subjects. This loss of a stable "sense of self" is sometimes called the dislocation or decentring of the subject. This set of double displacements—decentring individuals both from their place in the social and cultural world, and from themselves—constitutes a "crisis of identity' for the individual. As the cultural critic Kobena Mercer observes, "identity only becomes an issue when it is in crisis, when something assumed to be fixed, coherent and stable is displaced by the experience of doubt and uncertainty" (Mercer 1990, 43).

THREE CONCEPTS OF IDENTITY

For the purposes of exposition, I shall distinguish three very different conceptions of identity: those of the (a) Enlightenment subject, (b) sociological subject, and (c) postmodern subject. The Enlightenment subject was based on a conception of the human person as a fully centred, unified individual, endowed with the capacities of reason, consciousness, and action, whose "centre" consisted of an inner core that first emerged when the subject was born, and unfolded with it, while remaining essentially the same—continuous or "identical" with itself—throughout the individual's existence. The essential centre of the self was a person's identity. I shall say more about this in a moment, but you can see that this was a very "individualist" conception of the subject and "his" (for Enlightenment subjects were usually described as male) identity.

The notion of the sociological subject reflected the growing complexity of the modern world and the awareness that this inner core of the subject was not autonomous and self-sufficient, but was formed in relation to "significant others," who mediated to the subject the values, meanings, and symbols—the culture—of the worlds he or she inhabited. G.H. Mead, C.H. Cooley, and the symbolic interactionists are the key figures in sociology who elaborated this "interactive" conception of identity and the self (see *Penguin Dictionary of Sociology*: Mead, George H.; Symbolic Interactionism). According to this view, which has become the classic sociological conception of the issue, identity is formed in the "interaction" between self and society. The subject still has an inner core or essence that is "the real me," but this is formed and modified in a continuous dialogue with the cultural worlds "outside" and the identities which they offer.

Identity, in this sociological conception, bridges the gap between the "inside" and the "outside"—between the personal and the public worlds. The fact that we project "ourselves" into these cultural identities, at the same time internalizing their meanings and values, making them "part of us," helps to align our subjective feelings with the objective places we occupy in the social and cultural world. Identity thus stitches (or, to use a current medical metaphor, "sutures") the subject into the structure. It stabilizes both subjects and the cultural worlds they inhabit, making both reciprocally more unified and predictable.

Yet these are exactly what are now said to be "shifting." The subject, previously experienced as having a unified and stable identity, is becoming fragmented; composed, not of a single, but of several, sometimes contradictory or unresolved, identities. Correspondingly, the identities that composed the social landscapes "out there," and that ensured our subjective conformity with the objective "needs" of the culture, are breaking up as a result of structural and institutional change. The very process of identification, through which we project ourselves into our cultural identities, has become more open-ended, variable, and problematic.

This produces the postmodern subject, conceptualized as having no fixed, essential, or permanent identity. Identity becomes a "moveable feast": formed and transformed continuously in relation to the ways we are represented or addressed in the cultural systems that surround us (Hall 1987). It is historically, not biologically, defined. The subject assumes different identities at different times, identities that are not unified around a coherent "self." Within us are contradictory identities, pulling in different directions, so that our identifications are continuously being shifted about. If we feel we have a unified identity from birth to death, it is only because we construct a comforting story or "narrative of the self" about ourselves (see Hall 1990). The fully unified, completed, secure, and coherent identity is a fantasy. Instead, as the systems of meaning and cultural representation multiply, we are confronted by a bewildering, fleeting multiplicity of possible identities, any one of which we could identify with—at least temporarily.

You should bear in mind that the above three conceptions of the subject are, to some extent, simplifications. As the argument develops, they will become more complex and qualified. Nevertheless, they are worth holding on to as crude pegs around which to develop the argument of this chapter.

THE CHARACTER OF CHANGE IN LATE MODERNITY

A further aspect of the issue of identity relates to the character of change in late modernity; in particular, to that process of change known as "globalization" and its impact on cultural identity.

In essence, the argument here is that change in late modernity has a very specific character. As Marx said about modernity, "[it is a] constant revolutionizing of production, uninterrupted disturbance of all social relations, everlasting uncertainty and agitation.... All fixed, fast-frozen relationships, with their train of venerable ideas and opinions, are swept away, all new-formed ones become obsolete before they can ossify. All that is solid melts into air...." (Marx and Engels 1973, 70).

Modern societies are therefore by definition societies of constant, rapid, and permanent change. This is the principal distinction between "traditional" and "modern" societies. Anthony Giddens argues that, "[i]n traditional societies, the past is honoured and symbols are valued "because they contain and perpetuate the experience of generations. Tradition is a means of handling time and space, which inserts any particular activity or experience within the continuity of past, present and future, these in turn being structured by recurrent social practices" (Giddens 1990, 37–38). Modernity, by contrast, is not only defined as the experience of living with rapid, extensive, and continuous change, but is a highly reflexive form of life in which "social practices are constantly examined and reformed in the light of incoming information about those very practices, thus constitutively altering their character" (ibid.).

Giddens cites in particular the *pace of change* and the *scope of change*—"as different areas of the globe are drawn into interconnection with one another, waves of social transformation crash across virtually the whole of the earth's surface"—and the *nature of modern institutions* (Giddens 1990, 6).

David Harvey speaks of modernity as not only entailing "a ruthless break with any or all preceding conditions," but as "characterized by a never-ending process of internal ruptures and fragmentations within itself" (1989, 12). Ernesto Laclau (1990) uses the concept of "dislocation." A dislocated structure is one whose centre is displaced and not replaced by another, but by "a plurality of power centres." Modern societies, Laclau argues, have no centre, no single articulating or organizing principle, and do not develop according to the unfolding of a single "cause" or "law." Society is not, as sociologists often thought, a unified and well-bounded whole, a totality, producing itself through evolutionary change from within itself, like the unfolding of a daffodil from its bulb. It is constantly being "decentred" or dislocated by forces outside itself.

Late modern societies, he argues, are characterized by "difference"; they are cut through by different social divisions and social antagonisms that produce a variety of different "subject positions"—i.e., identities—for individuals. If such societies hold together at all, it is not because they are unified, but because their different elements and identities can, under certain circumstances, be articulated together. But this articulation is always partial: the structure of identity remains open. Without this, Laclau argues, there would be no history.

Laclau argues that dislocation has positive features. It unhinges the stable identities of the past, but it also opens up the possibility of new articulations—the forging of new identities, the production of new subjects, and what he calls the "recomposition of the structure around particular nodal points of articulation" (Laclau 1990, 40).

Giddens, Harvey, and Laclau offer somewhat different readings of the nature of change in the postmodern world, but their emphasis on discontinuity, fragmentation, rupture, and dislocation contains a common thread.

WHAT IS AT STAKE IN THE QUESTION OF IDENTITIES?

So far the arguments may seem rather abstract. To give you some sense of how they apply to a concrete situation, and what is "at stake" in these contested definitions of identity and change, let us take an example that highlights the *political* consequences of the fragmentation or "pluralization" of identities.

In 1991, President Bush, anxious to restore a conservative majority to the U.S. Supreme Court, nominated Clarence Thomas, a black judge of conservative political views. In Bush's judgment, white voters (who may have been prejudiced about a black judge) were likely to support Thomas because he was conservative on equal rights legislation, and black voters (who support liberal policies on race) would support Thomas because he was black. In short, the president was "playing the identities game."

During the Senate "hearings" on the appointment, Judge Thomas was accused of sexual harassment by a black woman, Anita Hill, a former junior colleague of Thomas's. The hearings caused a public scandal and polarized American society. Some blacks supported Thomas on racial grounds; others opposed him on sexual grounds. Black women were divided, depending on whether their "identities" as blacks or as women prevailed. Black men were also divided, depending on whether their sexism overrode their liberalism. White men were divided, depending, not only on their politics, but on how they identified themselves with respect to racism and sexism. White conservative women supported Thomas, not only on political grounds, but because of their opposition to feminism. White feminists, often liberal on race, opposed Thomas on sexual grounds. And because Judge Thomas is a member of the judicial elite and Anita Hall, at the time of the alleged incident, a junior employee, there were issues of social class position at work in these arguments too.

The question of Judge Thomas's guilt or innocence is not at issue here; what is, is the "play of identities" and its political consequences. Consider:

- The identities were contradictory. They cross-cut or "dislocated" each other.
- The contradictions operated both "outside," in society, cutting across settled constituencies, *and* "inside" the heads of each individual.
- No single identity—e.g., that of social class—could align all the different identities into one, overarching "master identity" on which a politics could be securely grounded.
- People no longer identify their social interests exclusively in class terms; class cannot serve as a discursive device or mobilizing category through which all the diverse social interests and identities of people can be reconciled and represented.
- Increasingly, the political landscapes of the modern world are fractured in this way by competing and dislocating identifications—arising, especially, from the erosion of the "master identity" of class and the emerging identities belonging to the new political ground defined by the new social movements: feminism, black struggles, national liberation, anti-nuclear and ecological movements (Mercer 1990).
- Since identity shifts according to how the subject is addressed or represented, identification is not automatic, but can be won or lost. It has become politicized. This is sometimes described as a shift from a politics of (class) identity to a politics of *difference*.

NATIONAL CULTURES AS "IMAGINED COMMUNITIES"

What is happening to cultural identity in late modernity? Specifically, how are national cultural identities being affected or displaced by the process of globalization?

In the modern world, the national cultures into which we are born are one of the principal sources of cultural identity. In defining ourselves we sometimes say we are English or Welsh or Indian or Jamaican. Of course, this is to speak metaphorically. These identities are not literally imprinted in our genes. However, we do think of them as if they are part of our essential natures. The conservative philosopher, Roger Scruton, argues that

> [t]he condition of man (*sic*) requires that the individual, while he exists and acts as an autonomous being, does so only because he can first identify himself as something greater—as a member of a society, group, class, state or nation, of some arrangement to which he may not attach a name, but which he recognizes instinctively as home. (Scruton 1986, 156)

Ernest Gellner, from a more liberal position, also believes that without a sense of national identification the modern subject would experience a deep sense of subjective loss:

> The idea of a man (*sic*) without a nation seems to impose a [great] strain on the modern imagination. A man must have a nationality as he must have a nose and two ears. All this seems obvious, though, alas, it is not true. But that it should have come to seem so very obviously true is indeed an aspect, perhaps the very core, of the problem of nationalism. Having a nation is not an inherent attribute of humanity, but it has now come to appear as such. (Gellner 1983, 6)

The argument we will be considering here is that, in fact, national identities are not things we are born with, but are formed and transformed within and in relation to *representation*.

We only know what it is to be "English" because of the way "Englishness" has come to be represented, as a set of meanings, by English national culture. It follows that a nation is not only a political entity but something which produces meanings—*a system of cultural representation.* People are not only legal citizens of a nation; they participate in the *idea* of the nation as represented in its national culture. A nation is a symbolic community and it is this which accounts for its "power to generate a sense of identity and allegiance" (Schwarz 1986, 106).

National cultures are a distinctly modern form. The allegiance and identification that, in a pre-modern age or in more traditional societies, were given to tribe, people, religion, and region, came gradually in Western societies to be transferred to the *national* culture. Regional and ethnic differences were gradually subsumed beneath what Gellner calls the "political roof" of the nation-state, which thus became a powerful source of meanings for modern cultural identities.

The formation of a national culture helped to create standards of universal literacy, generalized a single vernacular language as the dominant medium of communication throughout the nation, created a homogeneous culture, and maintained national cultural institutions, such as a national education system. In these and other ways, national culturebecame a key feature of industrialization and an engine of modernity. Nevertheless, there are other aspects to a national culture that pull it in a different direction, bringing to the fore what Homi Bhabha calls "the particular ambivalence that haunts the idea of the nation" (Bhabha 1990, l). Some of these ambiguities are explored later. First,we will consider how a national culture functions as a system of representation, and then whether national identities are really as unified and homogeneous as they represent themselves to be. It is only when these two questions have been answered that we can properly consider the claim that national identities were once centred, coherent, and whole, but are now being dislocated by the processes of globalization.

NARRATING THE NATION: AN IMAGINED COMMUNITY

National cultures are composed not only of cultural institutions, but of symbols and representations. A national culture is a *discourse*—a way of constructing meanings that influences and organizes both our actions and our conception of ourselves (see *Penguin Dictionary of Sociology:* Discourse; also Hall and Gieben 1992. National cultures construct identities by producing meanings about "the nation" with which we can *identify*; these are contained in the stories that are told about it, memories that connect its present with its past, and images that are constructed of it. As Benedict Anderson (1983) has argued, national identify is an "imagined community."

Anderson argues that the differences between nations lie in the different ways in which they are imagined. But how is the modern nation imagined? What representational strategies are deployed to construct our common-sense views of national belonging or identity? What are the representations of, say, "England," which win the identifications and define the identities of "English" people? "Nations," Homi Bhabha has remarked, "like narratives, lose their origins in the myths of time and only fully realize their horizons in the mind's eye" (Bhabha 1990, 1). How is the narrative of the national culture told?

Of the many aspects that a comprehensive answer to that question would include, I have selected *five* main elements.

1. First, there is the *narrative of the nation*, as it is told and retold in national histories, literatures, the media, and popular culture. These provide a set of stories, images, landscapes, scenarios, historical events, national symbols, and rituals that stand for, or *represent*, the shared experiences, sorrows, and triumphs and disasters that give meaning to the nation. As members of such an "imagined community," we see ourselves in our mind's eye sharing in this narrative. It lends significance and importance to our humdrum existence, connecting our everyday lives with a national destiny that pre-existed us and will outlive us.

2. Secondly, there is the emphasis on *origins, continuity, tradition, and timelessness*. National identity is represented as primordial—"there, in the very nature of things," sometimes slumbering, but ever ready to be "awoken" from its "long, persistent, and mysterious somnolence" to resume its unbroken existence (Gellner 1983, 48). The essentials of the national character remain unchanged through all the vicissitudes of history. It is there from birth, unified and continuous, "changeless" throughout all the changes, eternal.

3. A third discursive strategy is what Hobsbawm and Ranger call *the invention of tradition*: "Traditions which appear or claim to be old are often quite recent in origin and sometimes invented.... 'Invented tradition' [means] a set of practices, ... of a ritual or symbolic nature which seek to inculcate certain values and norms of behaviours by repetition which automatically implies continuity with a suitable historical past." For example, "Nothing appears more ancient, and linked to an immemorial past, than the pageantry which surrounds British monarchy and its public ceremonial manifestations. Yet ... in its modern form it is the product of the late nineteenth and twentieth centuries" (Hobsbawm and Ranger 1983, 1).

4. A fourth example of the narrative of national culture is that of a *foundational myth*: a story that locates the origin of the nation, the people, and their national character so early that they are lost in the mists of, not "real," but "mythic" time—like basing the definition of the English as "free-born" on the Anglo-Saxon parliament. Invented traditions make the confusions and disasters of history intelligible, converting disarray into "community" disasters into triumphs. Myths of origin also help disenfranchised peoples to "conceive and express their resentment and its contents in intelligible terms" (Hobsbawm and Ranger 1983, 1). They provide a narrative in terms of which an alternative history or counter-narrative, which predates the ruptures of colonization, can be constructed.

5. National identity is also often symbolically grounded on the idea of a *pure, original people or "folk."* But, in the realities of national development, it is rarely this primordial folk who persist or exercise power.

The discourse of national culture is thus not as modern as it appears to be. It constructs identities that are ambiguously placed between past and future. It straddles the temptation to return to former glories and the drive to go forwards ever deeper into modernity. Sometimes national cultures are tempted to turn the clock back, to retreat defensively to that "lost time" when the nation was "great," and to restore past identities. This is the regressive, the anachronistic, element in the national cultural story. But often this very return to the past conceals a struggle to mobilize "the people" to purify their ranks, to expel the "others" who threaten their identity, and to gird their loins for a new march forwards. During the 1980s, the rhetoric of Thatcherism sometimes inhabited both these aspects of what Tom Nairn calls the "Janus-face" of nationalism (Nairn 1977): looking back to past imperial glories and "Victorian values" while simultaneously undertaking a kind of modernization in preparation for a new stage of global capitalist competition.

DECONSTRUCTING THE "NATIONAL CULTURE": IDENTITY AND DIFFERENCE

We have considered how a national culture functions as a source of cultural meanings, a focus of identification, and a system of representation. This section now turns to the question of whether national cultures and the national identities they construct are actually *unified*. In his famous essay on the topic, Ernest Renan said that three things constitute the spiritual principle of the unity of a nation: "the possession in common of a rich legacy of memories, ... the desire to live together, [and] the will to perpetuate the heritage that one has received in an undivided form" (Renan 1990, 19). You should bear in mind these three resonant concepts of what constitutes a national culture as an "imagined community": *memories* from the past; the *desire* to live together; the perpetuation of the *heritage*.

Timothy Brennan reminds us that the word *nation* refers "both to the modern nation-state and to something more ancient and nebulous—the *natio*—a local community, domicile, family, condition of belonging" (Brennan 1990, 45). National identities represented precisely the result of bringing these two halves of the national equation together—offering both membership of the political nation-state and identification with the national culture: "to make culture and polity congruent" and to endow "reasonably homogeneous cultures, each with its own political roof" (Gellner 1983, 43). Gellner clearly establishes this impulse to *unify* in national cultures:

> ... culture is now the necessary shared medium, the life-blood, or perhaps rather the minimal shared atmosphere, within which alone the members of the society can breathe and survive and produce. For a given society it must be one in which they can all breathe and speak and produce; so it must be the *same* culture. (Gellner 1983, 37–38)

To put it crudely, however different its members may be in terms of class, gender, or race, a national culture seeks to unify them into one cultural identity, to represent them all as belonging to the same great national family. But is national identity a unifying identity of this kind, which cancels or subsumes cultural difference?

Such an idea is open to doubt, for several reasons. A national culture has never been simply a point of allegiance, bonding and symbolic identification. It is also a structure of cultural power. Consider the following points:

1. Most modern nations consist of disparate cultures that were only unified by a lengthy process of violent conquest—that is, by the forcible suppression of cultural

difference. "The British people" are the product of a series of such conquests—Celtic, Roman, Saxon, Viking, and Norman. Throughout Europe the story is repeated *ad nauseam.* Each conquest subjugated conquered peoples and their cultures, customs, languages, and traditions and tried to impose a more unified cultural hegemony. As Ernest Kenan has remarked, these violent beginnings that stand at the origins of modern nations have first to be "forgotten" before allegiance to a more unified, homogeneous national identity could begin to be forged. Thus "British" culture still does not consist of an equal partnership between the component cultures of the U.K., but of the effective hegemony of "English," a southern-based culture that represents itself as the essential British culture, over Scottish, Welsh, and Irish and, indeed, other regional cultures. Matthew Arnold, who tried to fix the essential character of the English people from their literature, claimed when considering the Celts that such "provincial nationalisms had to be swallowed up at the level of the political and licensed as cultural contributors to English culture" (Dodd 1986, 12).

2. Secondly, nations are always composed of different social classes, and gender and ethnic groups. Modern British nationalism was the product of a very concerted effort, in the late Victorian and high imperial period, to unify the classes across social divisions by providing them with an alternative point of identification—common membership of "the family of the nation." The same point can be made about gender. National identities are strongly gendered. The meanings and values of "Englishness" have powerful masculine associations. Women play a secondary role as guardians of hearth, kith and kin, and as "mothers" of the nation's "sons."

3. Thirdly, modern Western nations were also the centres of empires or of neo-imperial spheres of influence, exercising cultural hegemony over the cultures of the colonized. Some historians now argue that it was in this process of comparison between the "virtues" of "Englishness" and the negative features of other cultures that many of the distinctive characteristics of English identities were first defined (see C. Hall 1992).

Instead of thinking of national cultures as unified, we should think of them as constituting a *discursive device* that represents difference as unity or identity. They are cross-cut by deep internal divisions and differences, and "unified" only through the exercise of different forms of cultural power. Yet—as in the fantasies of the "whole" self of which Lacanian psychoanalysis speaks—national identities continue to be represented as *unified.*

One way of unifying them has been to represent them as the expression of the underlying culture of "one people." Ethnicity is the term we give to cultural features—language, religion, custom, traditions, feeling for "place"—which are shared by a people. It is therefore tempting to try to use ethnicity in this "foundational" way. But this belief turns out, in the modern world, to be a myth. Western Europe has no nations that are composed of only one people, one culture or ethnicity. *Modern nations are all cultural hybrids.*

It is even more difficult to try to unify national identity around race. First, because— contrary to widespread belief—race is not a biological or genetic category with any scientific validity. There are different genetic strains and "pools," but they are as widely dispersed *within* what are called "races" as they are *between* one "race" and another. Genetic difference—the last refuge of racist ideologies—cannot be used to distinguish one people from another. Race is a *discursive* not a biological category. That is to say, it is the organizing category of those ways of speaking, systems of representation, and social practices (discourses) that utilize a loose, often unspecified set of differences in physical characteristics—skin colour, hair texture, physical and bodily features, and so forth—as *symbolic markers* in order to differentiate one group socially from another.

Of course the unscientific character of the term "race" does not undermine "how racial logics and racial frames of reference are articulated and deployed, and with what consequences" (Donald and Rattansi 1992, l). In recent years, biological notions of races as a distinct species (notions that underpinned extreme forms of nationalist ideology and discourse in earlier periods: Victorian eugenics, European race theories, fascism) have been replaced by *cultural* definitions of race, which allow race to play a significant role in discourses about the nation and national identity. Paul Gilroy has commented on the links between "cultural racism" and "the idea of race and the ideas of nation, nationality, and national belonging":

> We increasingly face a racism which avoids being recognized as such because it is able to line up "race" with nationhood, patriotism and nationalism. A racism which has taken a necessary distance from crude ideas of biological inferiority and superiority now seeks to present an imaginary definition of the nation as a unified *cultural* community. It constructs and defends an image of national culture—homogeneous in its whiteness yet precarious and perpetually vulnerable to attack from enemies within and without.... This is a racism that answers the social and political turbulence of crisis and crisis management by the recovery of national greatness in the imagination. Its dream-like construction of our sceptered isle as an ethnically purified one provides special comfort against the ravages of [national] decline. (Gilroy 1992, 87)

But even when "race" is used in this broader discursive way, modern nations stubbornly refuse to be resolved into it. As Renan observed, "the leading nations of Europe are nations of essentially mixed blood": "France is [at once] Celtic, Iberic and Germanic. Germany is Germanic, Celtic and Slav. Italy is the country where ... Gauls, Etruscans, Pelagians and Greeks, not to mention many other elements, intersect in an indecipherable mixture. The British Isles, considered as a whole, present a mixture of Celtic and Germanic blood, the proportions of which are singularly difficult to define" (Renan 1990, 14–15). And these are relatively simple "mixtures" as compared with those to be found in Central and Eastern Europe.

This brief examination undermines the idea of the nation as a unified cultural identity. National identities do not subsume all other forms of difference into themselves and are not free of the play of power, internal divisions, and contradictions, cross-cutting allegiances and difference. So when we come to consider whether national identities are being dislocated, we must bear in mind the way national cultures help to "stitch up" differences into one identity.

GLOBALIZATION

The previous section qualified the idea that national identities have ever been as unified or homogeneous as they are represented to be. Nevertheless, in modern history, national cultures have dominated "modernity" and national identities have tended to win out over other, more particularistic sources of cultural identification.

What, then, is so powerfully dislocating national cultural identities now, at the end of the 20th century? The answer is, a complex of processes and forces of change, which for convenience can be summed up under the term "globalization." Globalization implies a movement away from the classical sociological idea of a "society—as a well-bounded system, and its replacement by a perspective that concentrates on "how social life is ordered across time and space" (Giddens 1990, 64). These new temporal and spatial features, resulting in the compression of distances and time-scales, are among the most significant aspects of globalization affecting cultural identities, and they are discussed in greater detail below.

Remember that globalization is not a recent phenomenon: "Modernity is inherently globalizing" (Giddens 1990, 63). And as Wallerstein reminds us, capitalism "was from the beginning an affair of the world economy and not of nation states. Capital has never allowed its aspirations to be determined by national boundaries" (Wallerstein 1979, 19). So *both* the trend toward national autonomy and the trend toward globalization are deeply rooted in modernity (see Wallerstein 1991, 98).

You should bear in mind these two contradictory tendencies within globalization. Nevertheless, it is generally agreed that, since the 1970s, both the scope and pace of global integration have greatly increased, accelerating the flows and linkages between nations. In this and the next section, I shall attempt to track the consequences of these aspects of globalization on cultural identities, examining *three* possible consequences:

1. National identities are being *eroded* as a result of the growth of cultural homogenization and "the global postmodern."
2. National and other "local" or particularistic identities are being *strengthened* by the resistance to globalization.
3. National identities are declining but new identities of hybridity are taking their place.

TIME-SPACE COMPRESSION AND IDENTITY

What impact has the latest phase of globalization had on national identities? One of its main features is "time-space compression"—the speeding up of global processes, so that the world feels smaller and distances shorter, so that events in one place impact immediately on people and places a very long distance away. David Harvey argues:

> As space appears to shrink to a "global" village of telecommunications and a "spaceship earth" of economic and ecological inter-dependencies—to use just two familiar and everyday images—and as time horizons shorten to the point where the present is all there is, so we have to learn to cope with an overwhelming sense of compression of our spatial and temporal worlds. (Harvey 1989, 240)

What is important for our argument about the impact of globalization on identity is that time and space are also the basic coordinates of all systems of *representation*. Every medium of representation—writing, drawing, painting, photography, figuring through art, or the telecommunications systems—must translate its subject into spatial and temporal dimensions. Thus, narrative translates events into a beginning-middle-end time sequence; and visual systems of representation translate three-dimensional objects into two dimensions. Different cultural epochs have different ways of combining these time–space coordinates.

I have argued that identity is deeply implicated in representation. Thus, the shaping and reshaping of time–space relationships within different systems of representation have profound effects on how identities are located and represented.

Another way of thinking about this is in terms of what Giddens (1990) calls the separation of space from place. "Place" is specific, concrete, known, familiar, bounded: the site of specific social practices that have shaped and formed us, and with which our identities are closely bound up.

> In premodern societies, space and place largely coincided, since the spatial dimensions of social life are, for most of the population ... dominated by "presence"—by localised activity.... Modernity increasingly tears space away from place by fostering relations between "absent" others, locationally distant from any given situation of face-to-face interaction. In conditions of modernity ... locales are thoroughly penetrated by and shaped in terms of social influences quite distant from them. What structures the locale is not simply that which is present on the scene; the "visible form" of the locale conceals the distanced relations which determine its nature. (Giddens 1990, 18)

Places remain fixed; they are where we have "roots." Yet space can be "crossed" in the twinkling of an eye—by jet, fax, or satellite. Harvey calls this "the annihilation of space through time" (1989, 205).

TOWARD THE GLOBAL POSTMODERN?

Some theorists argue that the general effect of these globalizing processes has been to weaken or undermine national forms of cultural identity. They argue that there is evidence of a loosening of strong identifications with the national culture, and a strengthening of other cultural ties and allegiances, "above" and "below" the level of the nation-state. National identities remain strong, especially with respect to such things as legal and citizenship rights, but local, regional, and community identities have become more significant. Above the level of the national culture, "global" identifications begin to displace, and sometimes override, national ones.

Some cultural theorists argue that the trend toward greater global interdependence is leading to the breakdown of *all* strong cultural identities and is producing that fragmentation of cultural codes, that multiplicity of styles, emphasis on the ephemeral, the fleeting, the impermanent, and on difference and cultural pluralism on a global scale—what we might call *the global postmodern*. Cultural flows and global consumerism between nations create the possibilities of "shared identities"—as "customers" for the same goods, "clients" for the same services, "audiences" for the same messages and images—between people who are far removed from one another in time and space. As national cultures become more exposed to outside influences it is difficult to preserve cultural identities intact, or to prevent them from becoming weakened through cultural bombardment and infiltration.

People in small, apparently remote villages in poor "Third World" countries can receive in the privacy of their homes the messages and images of the rich, consumer cultures of the West, purveyed through television sets or the transistor radio, which bind them into the "global village" of the new communications networks. Jeans and trainers—the "uniform" of the young in Western youth culture—are as ubiquitous in Southeast Asia as in Europe or the U.S., not only because of the growth of the worldwide marketing of the youth consumer image, but because they are often actually produced in Taiwan or Hong Kong or South Korea for the New York, Los Angeles, London, or Rome high-street shop. It is hard to think of "Indian cooking" as something distinctive of the ethnic traditions of the Asian subcontinent when there is an Indian restaurant in the centre of every city and town in Britain.

The more social life becomes mediated by the global marketing of styles, places, and images, by international travel, and by globally networked media images and communications systems, the more *identities* become detached—disembedded—from specific times, places, histories, and traditions, and appear "free-floating." We are confronted by a range of different identities, each appealing to us, or rather to different parts of ourselves, from which it seems possible to choose. It is the spread of consumerism, whether as reality or dream, which has contributed to this "cultural supermarket" effect. Within the discourse of global consumerism, differences and cultural distinctions that hitherto defined *identity* become reducible to a sort of international *lingua franca* or global currency into which all specific traditions and distinct identities can be translated. This phenomenon is known as "cultural homogenization."

To some extent, what is being debated is the tension between the "global'" and the "local" in the transformation of identities. National identities, as we have seen, represent attachment to particular places, events, symbols, histories. They represent what is sometimes called a *particularistic* form of attachment or belonging. There has always been a tension between these and more *universalistic* identifications—for example, to "humanity" rather than to "Englishness." This tension has persisted throughout modernity: the growth of nation-states, national economies, and national cultures continuing to provide a focus for the first; the expansion of the world market and modernity as a global system providing the focus for the second. With the next section, which examines how globalization in its most recent forms impacts on identities, you may find it helpful to think of such impact in terms of new ways of articulating the particularistic and the universalistic aspects of identity, or new ways of negotiating the tension between the two.

THE GLOBAL, THE LOCAL, AND THE RETURN OF ETHNICITY

Are national identities being "homogenized"? Cultural homogenization is the anguished cry of those who are convinced that globalization threatens to undermine national identities and the "unity" of national cultures. However, as a view of the future of identities in a postmodern world this picture is too simplistic, exaggerated, and one-sided as it stands.

We can pick up at least *three* major qualifications or counter-tendencies. The first arises from Kevin Robins's argument and the observation that, alongside the tendency toward global homogenization, there is also a fascination with *difference* and the marketing of ethnicity and "otherness." There is a new interest in "the local" together with the impact of "the global." Globalization (in the form of flexible specialization and "niche" marketing) actually exploits local differentiation. Thus, instead of thinking of the global *replacing* the local, it would be more accurate to think of a new articulation between "the global" and "the local." This "local" is not, of course, to be confused with older identities, firmly rooted in well-bounded localities. Rather, it operates within the logic of globalization. However, it seems unlikely that globalization will simply destroy national identities. It is more likely to produce, simultaneously, *new* "global" and *new* "local" identifications.

The second qualification to the argument about the global homogenization of identities is that globalization is very unevenly distributed around the globe, between regions and between different strata of the population *within* regions. This is what Doreen Massey calls globalization's "power geometry."

The third point in the critique of cultural homogenization is the question of who is most affected by it. Since there is an uneven direction to the flow, and since unequal relations of cultural power between "the West" and "the Rest" persist, globalization—though by definition something that affects the whole globe—may appear to be essentially a Western phenomenon.

Kevin Robins reminds us:

> For all that it has projected itself as transhistorical and transnational, as the transcendent and universalizing force of modernization and modernity, global capitalism has in reality been about westernization—the export of western commodities, values, priorities, ways of life. In a process of unequal cultural encounter, "foreign" populations have been compelled to be the subjects and subalterns of western empire, while, no less significantly, the west has come face to face with the "alien" and "exotic" culture of its "Other". Globalization, as it dissolves the barriers of distance, makes the encounter of colonial centre and colonized periphery immediate and intense. (Robins 1991, 25)

In the latest form of globalization, it is still the images, artifacts, and identities of Western modernity, produced by the cultural industries of "Western" societies (including Japan), that dominate the global networks. The proliferation of identity choices is more extensive at the "centre" of the global system than at its peripheries. The patterns of unequal cultural exchange, familiar from earlier phases of globalization, persist into late modernity. If you want to sample the exotic cuisines of other cultures in one place, it would be better to eat in Manhattan, Paris, or London than in Calcutta or Delhi.

On the other hand, societies of the periphery have *always* been open to Western cultural influences and are now more so. The idea that these are "closed" places—ethnically pure, culturally traditional, undisturbed until yesterday by the ruptures of modernity—is a Western fantasy about "otherness": a "colonial fantasy" maintained *about* the periphery *by* the West, which tends to like its natives "pure" and its exotic places "untouched." Nevertheless, the evidence suggests that globalization is impacting everywhere, including the West, and the "periphery" is experiencing its pluralizing impact too, though at a slower, more uneven pace.

"THE REST" IN "THE WEST"

The preceding pages have presented three qualifications to the first of the three possible consequences of globalization: i.e., the homogenization of global identities. These are:

(a) Globalization can go hand in hand with a strengthening of local identities, though this is still within the logic of time–space compression;
(b) Globalization is an uneven process and has its own "power geometry";
(c) Globalization retains some aspects of Western global domination, but cultural identities everywhere are being relativized by the impact of time–space compression.

Perhaps the most striking example of this third point is the phenomenon of migration. After the Second World War, the de-colonizing European powers thought they could pull out of their colonial spheres of influence, leaving the consequences of imperialism behind them. But global interdependence now works both ways. The movements of Western styles, images, commodities, and consumer identities outwards has been matched by a momentous movement of peoples from the peripheries to the centre in one of the largest and most sustained periods of "unplanned" migration in recent history. Driven by poverty, drought, famine, economic undevelopment and crop failure, civil war and political unrest, regional conflict and arbitrary changes of political regime, the accumulating foreign indebtedness of their governments to Western banks, very large numbers of the poorer peoples of the globe have taken the "message" of global consumerism at face value, and moved toward the places where "the goodies" come from and where the chances of survival are higher. In the era of global communications, the West is only a one-way airline charter ticket away.

There have been continuous, large-scale, legal, and "illegal" migrations into the U.S. from many poor countries of Latin America, and the Caribbean basin (Cuba, Haiti, Puerto Rico, the Dominican Republic, the islands of the British Caribbean), as well as substantial numbers of "economic migrants" and political refugees from Southeast Asia and the Far East—Chinese, Koreans, Vietnamese, Cambodians, Indians, Pakistanis, Japanese. Canada has a substantial minority Caribbean population. One consequence is a dramatic shift in the "ethnic mix" of the U.S. population.

Over the same period, there has been a parallel "migration" into Europe of Arabs from the Maghreb (Morocco, Algeria, Tunisia), and Africans from Senegal and Zaire into France and Belgium; of Turks and North Africans into Germany; of Asians from the ex-Dutch East and West Indies and Surinam into the Netherlands; of North Africans into Italy; and, of course, of people from the Caribbean and from India, Pakistan, Bangladesh, Kenya, Uganda and Sri Lanka into the U.K. There are political refugees from Somalia, Ethiopia, the Sudan and Sri Lanka and other places in small numbers everywhere.

This formation of ethnic minority "enclaves" within the nation-states of the West has led to a "pluralization" of national cultures and national identities.

THE DIALECTIC OF IDENTITIES

How has this situation played itself out in Britain in terms of identity? The first effect has been to contest the settled contours of national identity, and to expose its closures to the pressures of difference, "otherness" and cultural diversity. This is happening, to different degrees, in all the Western national cultures and as a consequence it has brought the whole issue of national identity and the cultural "centredness" of the West into the open.

> Older certainties and hierarchies of British identity have been called into question in a world of dissolving boundaries and disrupted continuities. In a country that it is now a container of African and Asian cultures, the sense of what it is to be British can never again have the old confidence and surety. Other sources of identity are no less fragile. What does it mean to be European in a continent coloured not only by the cultures of its former colonies, but also by American and now Japanese cultures? Is not the very category of identity itself problematical? Is it at all possible, in global times, to regain a coherent and integral sense of identity? Continuity and historicity of identity are challenged by the immediacy and intensity of global cultural confrontations. The comforts of Tradition are fundamentally challenged by the imperative to forge a new self-interpretation based upon the responsibilities of cultural Translation. (Robins 1991, 41)

Another effect has been to trigger a widening of the field of identities, and a proliferation of new identity positions together with a degree of polarization among and between them. These developments constitute the second and third possible consequences of globalization—the possibility that globalization might lead to a *strengthening* of local identities, or to the production of *new identities.*

The strengthening of local identities can be seen in the strong defensive reaction of those members of dominant ethnic groups who feel threatened by the presence of other cultures. In the U.K., for example, such defensiveness has produced a revamped Englishness, an aggressive little Englandism, and a retreat to ethnic absolutism in an attempt to shore up the nation and rebuild "an identity that coheres, is unified and filters out threats in social experience" (Sennett 1971, 15). This is often grounded in what I have earlier called "cultural racism," and is evident now in legitimate political parties of both Left and Right, and in more extremist political movements throughout Western Europe.

It is sometimes matched by a strategic retreat to more defensive identities among the minority communities themselves in response to the experience of cultural racism and exclusion. Such strategies include re-identification with cultures of origin (in the Caribbean, India, Bangladesh, Pakistan); the construction of strong counter-ethnicities—as in the symbolic identification of second-generation Afro-Caribbean youth, through the symbols and motifs of Rastafarianism, with their African origin and heritage; or the revival of cultural traditionalism, religious orthodoxy, and political separatism, for example, amongst *some* sections of the Muslim community.

There is also some evidence of the third possible consequences of globalization—the production of new identities. A good example is those new identities that have emerged in the 1970s, grouped around the signifier "black," which in the British context provides a new focus of identification for *both* Afro-Caribbean and Asian communities. What these communities have in common, which they represent through taking on the "black" identity, is not that they are culturally, ethnically, linguistically, or even physically the same, but that they are seen and treated as "the same" (i.e., non-white, "other") by the dominant culture. It is their exclusion that provides what Laclau and Mouffe call the common "axis of equivalence" of this new identity. However, despite the fact that efforts are made to give this "black" identity a single or unified content, it continues to exist *as* an identity *alongside a wide range of other differences.* Afro-Caribbean and Indian people continue to maintain different cultural traditions. "Black" is thus an example, not only of the *political* character of new identities—i.e., their *positional* and conjunctural character (their formation in and for specific times and places)—but also of the way identity and difference are inextricably articulated or knitted together in different identities, the one never wholly obliterating the other.

As a tentative conclusion it would appear then that globalization *does* have the effect of contesting and dislocating the centred and "closed" identities of a national culture. It does have a pluralizing impact on identities, producing a variety of possibilities and new positions of identification, and making identities more positional, more political, more plural and diverse; less fixed, unified, or trans-historical. However, its general impact remains contradictory. Some identities gravitate toward what Robins calls "Tradition," attempting to restore their former purity and recover the unities and certainties that are felt as being lost. Others accept that identity is subject to the play of history, politics, representation, and difference, so that they are unlikely ever again to be unitary or "pure"; and these consequently gravitate toward what Robins (following Homi Bhabha) calls "Translation."

The next section will briefly sketch this contradictory movement between Tradition and Translation on a wider, global canvas and ask what it tells us about the way identities need to be conceptualized in relation to modernity's futures.

FUNDAMENTALISM, DIASPORA, AND HYBRIDITY

Where identities are concerned, this oscillation between Tradition and Translation is becoming more evident on a global canvas. Everywhere, cultural identities are emerging that are not fixed, but poised, *in transition,* between different positions; that draw on different cultural traditions at the same time; and that are the product of those complicated crossovers and cultural mixes that are increasingly common in a globalized world. It may be tempting to think of identity in the age of globalization as destined to end up in one place or another: either returning to its "roots" or disappearing through assimilation and homogenization. But this may be a false dilemma.

For there is another possibility: that of "Translation." This describes those identity formations that cut across and intersect natural frontiers, and that are composed of people who have been *dispersed* forever from their homelands. Such people retain strong links with their places of origin and their traditions, but they are without the illusion of a return to the past. They are obliged to come to terms with the new cultures they inhabit, without simply assimilating to them and losing their identities completely. They bear upon them the traces of the particular cultures, traditions, languages, and histories by which they were shaped. The difference is that they are not and will never be *unified* in the old sense because they are irrevocably the product of several interlocking histories and cultures, belong at one and the same time to several "homes" (and to no one particular "home"). People belonging to such *cultures of hybridity* have had to renounce the dream or ambition of rediscovering any kind of "lost" cultural purity, or ethnic absolutism. They are irrevocably *translated*. The word "translation," Salman Rushdie notes, "comes etymologically from the Latin for 'bearing across,'" Migrant writers like him, who belong to two worlds at once, "having been borne across the world ... are translated men" (Rushdie 1991). They are the products of the new *diasporas* created by the post-colonial migrations. They must learn to inhabit at least two identities, to speak two cultural languages, to translate and negotiate between them. Cultures of hybridity are one of the distinctly novel types of identity produced in the era of late modernity, and there are more and more examples of them to be discovered.

Some people argue that "hybridity" and syncretism—the fusion between cultural traditions—is a powerful creative source, creating new forms that are more appropriate to late modernity than the old, embattled national identities of the past. Others, however, argue that hybridity, with the indeterminacy, "double consciousness," and relativism it implies, also has its costs and dangers. Salman Rushdie's novel about migration, Islam, and the prophet Mohammed, *The Satanic Verses,* with its deep immersion in Islamic culture *and* its secular consciousness of the exiled "translated man," so offended the Iranian fundamentalists that they passed sentence of death on him for blasphemy. It also outraged many British Muslims.

On the other hand, there are equally powerful attempts to reconstruct purified identities, to restore coherence, "closure," and Tradition, in the face of hybridity and diversity. Two examples are the resurgence of nationalism in Eastern Europe and the rise of fundamentalism.

In an era when regional integration in the economic and political fields, and the breaking down of national sovereignty, are moving very rapidly in Western Europe, the collapse of the communist regimes in Eastern Europe and the breakup of the old Soviet Union have been followed by a powerful revival of ethnic nationalism, fuelled by ideas of both racial purity and religious orthodoxy. The ambition to create new, culturally and ethnically unified nation-states was the driving force behind the breakaway movements in the Baltic states of Estonia, Latvia, and Lithuania, the disintegration of Yugoslavia, and the move to independence of many former Soviet Republics, from Georgia, the Ukraine, Russia, and Armenia to Kurdistan, Uzbekistan, and the "Muslim" Asian republics of the old Soviet state. Much the same process has been taking place in the "nations" of Central Europe, which were carved out of the disintegration of the Austro-Hungarian and Ottoman Empires at the end of the First World War.

These new would-be "nations" try to construct states that are unified in both ethnic and religious terms, and to create political entities around homogeneous cultural identities. The problem is that they contain within their "borders" minorities who identify themselves with different cultures. Thus, for example, there are "ethnic" Russian minorities in the Baltic Republics and the Ukraine, ethnic Poles in Lithuania, an Armenian enclave (Nagorno-Karabakh) in Azerbaijan, Turkic-Christian minorities among the Russian majorities of Moldavia, and large numbers of Muslims in the southern republics of the old Soviet Union who share more, in cultural and religious terms, with their Middle-Eastern Islamic neighbours than with many of their "countrymen."

The other significant form of the revival of particularistic nationalism and ethnic and religious absolutism is, of course, the phenomenon of "fundamentalism." This is evident everywhere, though its most striking example is to be found in some Islamic states in the Middle East. Beginning with the Iranian Revolution, fundamentalist Islamic movements, which seek to create religious states in which the political principles of organization are aligned with the religious doctrines and laws of the *Koran,* have arisen in many, hitherto secular Islamic societies. In fact, this trend is difficult to interpret. Some analysts see it as a reaction to the "forced" character of Western modernization; certainly, Iranian fundamentalism was a direct response to the efforts of the Shah in the 1970s to adopt Western models and cultural values wholesale. Some interpret it as a response to being left out of "globalization." The reaffirmation of cultural "roots" and the return to orthodoxy has long been one of the most powerful sources of counter-identification among many Third World and post-colonial societies and regions (one thinks here of the roles of nationalism and national culture in the Indian, African, and Asian independence movements). Others see the roots of Islamic fundamentalism in the failure of Islamic states to throw up successful and effective "modernizing" leaderships or secular, modern parties. In conditions of extensive poverty and relative economic underdevelopment (fundamentalism is stronger in the poorer Islamic states of the region), a restoration of the Islamic faith is a powerful mobilizing and binding political and ideological force, especially where democratic traditions are weak.

The trend toward "global homogenization," then, is matched by a powerful revival of "ethnicity," sometimes of the more hybrid or symbolic varieties, but also frequently of the exclusive or "essentialist" varieties cited above.

The resurgence of nationalism and other forms of particularism at the end of the 20th century, alongside and intimately linked to globalization, is of course a remarkable reversal, a most unexpected turn of events. Nothing in the modernizing Enlightenment perspectives or ideologies of the West—neither liberalism nor indeed Marxism, which for all its opposition to liberalism also saw capitalism as the unwitting agent of "modernity"—foresaw such an outcome.

Both liberalism and Marxism, in their different ways, implied that the attachment to the local and the particular would gradually give way to more universalistic and cosmopolitan or international values and identities; that nationalism and ethnicity were archaic forms of attachment—the sorts of thing that would be "melted away" by the revolutionizing force of modernity. According to these "metanarratives" of modernity, the irrational attachments to the local and the particular, to tradition and roots, to national myths and "imagined communities," would gradually be replaced by more rational and universalistic identities. Yet globalization seems to be producing neither simply the triumph of "the global" nor the persistence, in its old nationalistic form, of "the local." The displacements or distractions of globalization turn out to be more varied and more contradictory than either its protagonists or opponents suggest. However, this also suggests that, though powered in many ways by the West, globalization may turn out to be part of that slow and uneven but continuing story of the decentring of the West.

REFERENCES

Abercrombie, N., S. Hill, and B. Turner. 1986. *Sovereign Individuals of Capitalism.* London: Allen and Unwin.

———. eds. 1988. *The Penguin Dictionary of Sociology,* 2nd ed. Harmondsworth: Penguin.

Althusser, L. 1966. *For Marx.* London: Verso.

Anderson, B. 1983. *Imagined Communities.* London: Verso.

Barnett, A. 1982. *Iron Britannia.* London: Allison and Busby.

Bauman, Z. 1990. "Modernity and Ambivalence." In *Global Culture,* ed. M. Featherstone, 143–170. London: Sage.

Bhabha, H., ed. 1990. *Narrating the Nation.* London: Routledge.

Bocock, R., and K. Thompson, eds. 1992. *Social and Cultural Forms of Modernity.* Cambridge: Polity Press.

Brennan, T. 1990. "The National Longing for Form." In *Nation and Narration,* ed. H. Bhabha, 44–70. London: Routledge.

Derrida, J. 1981. *Writing and Difference.* London: Routledge.

Dodd, P. 1986. "Englishness and the National Culture." In *Englishness: Politics and Culture, 1880–1920,* ed. R. Colls and P. Dodd, 1–28. London: Croom Helm.

Donald, J., and A. Rattansi, eds. 1992. *'Race', Culture and Difference.* London: Sage.

Dreyfus, H., and P. Rabinow. 1982. *Michel Foucault: Beyond Structuralism and Hermeneutics.* Brighton: Harvester.

Forester, J. 1987. "A Brief History of the Subject." In *Identity: The Real Me.* ICA Document 6. London: Institute for Contemporary Arts.

Foucault, M. 1967. *Madness and Civilization.* London: Tavistock.

———. 1973. *Birth of the Clinic.* London: Tavistock.

———. 1975. *Discipline and Punish.* London: Allen Lane.

———. 1986. "The Subject and Power." In *Michel Foucault: Beyond Structuralism and Hermeneutics,* ed. J. Dreyfus and P. Rabinow, 208–226. Brighton: Harvester.

Frisby, D. 1985. *Fragments of Modernity.* Cambridge: Polity Press.

Gellner, E. 1983. *Nations and Nationalism.* Oxford: Blackwell.

Giddens, A. 1990. *The Consequences of Modernity.* Cambridge: Polity Press.

Gilroy, P. 1992. "The End of Anti-Racism." In *"Race," Culture and Difference,* ed. J. Donald and A. Rattansi, 49–61. London: Sage.

———. 1987. *There Ain't No Black in the Union Jack.* London: Hutchinson.

Hall, C. 1992. *White, Male and Middle Class: Explorations in Feminism and History.* Cambridge: Polity Press.

Hall, S. 1985. "Religious Cults and Social Movements in Jamaica." In *Religion and Ideology,* ed. R. Bocock and K. Thompson, 269–296. Manchester: Manchester University Press.

———. 1987. "Minimal Selves." In *Identity: The Real Me.* ICA Document 6. London: Institute for Contemporary Arts.

———. 1990. "Cultural Identity and Diaspora." In *Identity,* ed. J. Rutherford. London: Lawrence and Wishart.

Hall, S., and B. Gieben, eds. 1992. *Formations of Modernity.* Cambridge: Polity Press.

Harvey, D. 1989. *The Condition of Post-Modernity.* Oxford: Oxford University Press.

Hobsbawm, E., and T. Ranger, eds. 1983. *The Invention of Tradition.* Cambridge, Cambridge University Press.

Lacan, J. 1977. "The Mirror Stage as Formative of the Function of the I." In *Ecrits.* London: Tavistock.

Laclau, E. 1990. *New Reflections on the Revolution of Our Time.* London: Verso.

Locke, J. 1967. *An Essay Concerning Human Understanding.* London: Fontana.

Marx, K., and F. Engels. 1973. *The Communist Manifesto.* In *Revolutions of 1848.* Harmondsworth: Penguin Books.

Massey, D. 1991. "A Global Sense of Place." *Marxism Today* (June): 24–29.

Mercer, K. 1990. "Welcome to the Jungle." In *Identity,* ed. H. Rutherford. London: Lawrence and Wishart.

Nairn, T. 1977. *The Break-up of Britain.* London: Verso.

Parekh, B. 1989. "Between Holy Text and Moral Void." *New Statesman and Society* (23 March): 29–33.

Penguin Dictionary of Sociology: see Abercrombie et al. 1988.

Platt, A. 1991. *Defending the Canon.* Fernand Braudel Centre and Institute of Global Studies, Binghamton, State University of New York.

Renan, E. 1990. "What Is a Nation?" In *Narrating the Nation,* ed. H. Bhabha. London: Routledge.

Robins, K. 1991. "Tradition and Translation: National Culture in Its Global Context." In *Enterprise and Heritage: Crosscurrents of National Culture,* ed. J. Corner and S. Harvey, 21–44. London: Routledge.

Rushdie, S. 1991. *Imaginary Homelands.* London: Granta Books.

Said, E. 1990. "Narrative and Geography." *New Left Review,* no. 180 (March/April):81–100.

Schwarz, B. 1986. "Conservatism, Nationalism and Imperialism." In *Politics and Ideology,* ed. J. Donald and S. Hall, 154–186. Milton Keynes: Open University Press.

Scruton, R. 1986. "Authority and Allegiance." In *Politics and Ideology,* ed. J. Donald and S. Hall. Milton Keynes: Open University Press.

Sennett, R. 1971. *The Ideas of Disorder.* Harmondsworth: Penguin.

Urry, J. 1990. *The Tourist Gaze.* London: Sage.

Wallerstein, I. 1979. *The Capitalist Economy.* Cambridge: Cambridge University Press.

———. 1984. *The Politics of the World Economy.* Cambridge: Cambridge University Press.

———. 1991. "The National and the Universal." In *Culture, Globalization and the World System,* ed. A. King, 184–199. London: Macmillan.

Williams, R. 1976 *Keywords.* London: Fontana.

QUESTIONS FOR CRITICAL THOUGHT

CHAPTER 13 BY CHARLES S. UNGERLEIDER

1. Do you agree or disagree with the assertion that social justice will be substantially enhanced by confluence among the policies associated with immigration reforms, citizenship, and multiculturalism? Why?
2. Discuss various dimensions of Canada's social justice infrastructure that support the development of socio-political and socio-economic conditions necessary for democratic citizenship.
3. How successful has the development of the Canadian social justice infrastructure been in eliminating race, colour, and ethnicity as barriers to full and equal participation in Canadian society? What, if any, limitations persist?

CHAPTER 14 BY RHODA E. HOWARD-HASSMANN

1. Compare and contrast liberal multiculturalism and illiberal multiculturalism.
2. What is Canadian ethnic identity? What factors are involved in constituting Canadian ethnicity?
3. Discuss the notion of ethnicity as a fixed concrete entity derived from one's ancestors and compare it with the notion that ethnicity is a social creation.

CHAPTER 15 BY NANCY FRASER

1. Differentiate recognition and redistribution politics. How are these two forms of politics intertwined?

2. What is meant by bivalent collectivities? Why are the categories of gender and race characterized as bivalent mode of collectivities?
3. Distinguish between affirmative remedies and transformative remedies. Use examples of identity (e.g., racial identity) to illustrate the distinction in terms of contemporary politics.

CHAPTER 16 BY STUART HALL

1. What does Hall mean by "crises of identity"? What structural forces account for these crises?
2. Discuss representational strategies used to construct common-sense views of national belonging or identity?
3. Discuss the impact of globalization on particularistic and universalistic aspects of identities.

FURTHER READING

Bissoondath, Neil. *Selling Illusions: The Cult of Multiculturalism*. Toronto: Penguin, 1994.
   Bissoondath's controversial book presents the argument that Canadian multiculturalism produces ethnic ghettoization. He forcefully contends that, instead of fostering harmony and integration, multicultural policy produces marginalization and separation. Bissoondath uses his own identity to muster support for his arguments.

Bonnett, Alastair. *Anti-Racism*. New York: Routledge, 2000.
   This book situates multiculturalism in wider philosophical and empirical debates. Students will be intrigued by Bonnett's argument that much of mainstream anti-racism actually reinforces racism.

Fraser, Nancy. "Reframing Justice in a Globalizing World." *New Left Review* 36 (2005): 69–88.
   In this recent publication, Fraser develops the political implications of her dualistic framework of social justice. Published 10 years after her article in this section originally appeared, the implications of her framework are still highly significant.

Fraser, Nancy, and Axel Honneth. *Redistribution or Recognition? A Political-Philosophical Exchange*. New York: Verso, 2003.
   The first chapter of this book will be of particular interest to students interested in paradigms of social justice. Fraser outlines in great detail the implications of cultural and social politics, and she offers insight into the political dimensions of "participatory parity."

Torpey, John. *Politics and the Past.* New York: Rowman and Littlefield, 2000.

This collection of essays has been largely ignored in mainstream Canadian sociology. This is truly unfortunate. The essays address the significance of cultural politics through highly stimulating discussions of struggles for reparations. Given recent struggles for Chinese and Ukrainian Canadian redress, Aboriginal residential school reparations, and general cultural healing, the book's significance is great.

Appendix:
Relevant Websites

About Canada: Multiculturalism in Canada

This site offers information on the history of immigration to Canada, Canadian nation building, and Canadian multiculturalism.

http://www.mta.ca/faculty/arts/canadian_studies/english/about/multi/

Canadian Ethnic Studies Association

The Canadian Ethnic Studies Association (CESA) offers a number of resources pertaining to research on race and ethnicity in Canada. The CESA also publishes *Canadian Ethnic Studies*, a peer-reviewed academic journal.

http://www.ss.ucalgary.ca/ces/

Canadian Race Relations Foundation

The mission statement of the CRRF states: "The Foundation is committed to building a national framework for the fight against racism in Canadian society. We will shed light on the causes and manifestations of racism; provide independent, outspoken national leadership; and act as a resource and facilitator in the pursuit of equity, fairness, and social justice." This site offers a number of interesting resources.

http://crr.ca

Crossing Cultures

Students may be interested in the links on cultural identity and in the contents of the magazine.

http://www.digitrends.com/crossingcultures/

Diaspora: The Journal of Transnational Studies

http://www.utpjournals.com/jour.ihtml?lp=diaspora/diaspora.html

Histor!ca

Histor!ca is a website devoted to Canadian education generally. There are many links to immigration, nationalism, identity, and history.

http://www.histori.ca/default.do?page=.index

The Metropolis Project

The purpose of the Metropolis Project is to improve policies for managing migration and cultural diversity in major cities through the collaborative efforts of academic researchers and policy-makers. The site offers links to a variety of resources.

http://Canada.metropolis.net/

The Nationalism Project

This site offers extensive collection of materials related to the study of nationalism.

http://www.nationalismproject.org/index.htm

Postcolonial Theories

Students interested in advanced studies of identity, memory, nation, and belonging may wish to consult references to postcolonial theory.

http://www.eng.fju.edu.tw/Literary_Criticism/postcolonism/postcolonial_link.htm or http://orion.it.luc.edu/~mparks1/Postcolonial/Bibliography/bib.html

Race and Ethnicity

A comprehensive website concerned with race, ethnicity, and identity in America.

http://www.trinity.edu/~mkearl/race.html

COPYRIGHT ACKNOWLEDGEMENTS